GODOLPHIN

GODOLPHIN
From the sculpture by John Michael Rysbrack at Althorp

GODOLPHIN

His Life and Times

by

SIR TRESHAM LEVER, Bt.

LONDON
JOHN MURRAY, ALBEMARLE STREET, W.

First Edition . . 1952

Printed in Great Britain by
Wyman & Sons, Limited, London, Fakenham and Reading
and published by John Murray (Publishers) Ltd.

CONTENTS

BOOK I

APPRENTICESHIP

BOOK II

ACHIEVEMENT

v

LIST OF ILLUSTRATIONS

FOREWORD

MORE than sixty years have elapsed since the publication in 1888 of Hugh Elliot's brief sketch on Godolphin. In those days very little material was available for such a life, and Elliot was forced to admit in his preface that "no biography of Lord Godolphin can be really complete till much material which is at present entombed in family archives is rendered accessible to the author", and of the material which was available to him he stated frankly that "some is new, most of it is old, and all of it is dispersed". In the last half-century, a great mass of letters unknown to Elliot have come to light, some in private and public archives, many in the various publications of the Historical Manuscripts Commission. But even now a good deal is lacking that could shed light on certain aspects of Godolphin's career. How satisfying it would be to have been able to give a fuller demonstration of Godolphin's financial genius and to discuss in detail his relations with Montagu! I would also like to have been in a position to reveal more about his management of the Treasury and his attitude to such questions as party patronage in administrative appointments. Unfortunately, absence of material makes impossible at present any detailed exposition of these aspects of Lord Godolphin's life and work. Nevertheless, in spite of some gaps, the abundance of manuscripts now available renders long overdue a full-length biography of Queen Anne's great Lord Treasurer.

Of those who have made the writing of this biography possible, I must first thank the Duke of Marlborough who gave me free access to his muniment room at Blenheim Palace. This put me in the advantageous position of being able to study the Godolphin–Marlborough correspondence between the years 1702 and 1710 in the originals, instead of relying on the not too accurate Coxe transcripts in the British Museum. To the Marquess of Bath I am indebted for the access he so generously afforded me to his muniments at Longleat; and at the same time I would like to thank Lord Bath's librarian, Miss Dorothy Coates, for her welcome assistance whilst I was working amid the congenial surroundings of Bishop Ken's Library. The Countess of Seafield was so courteous as to send me on loan from the charter room at Cullen House a number of Lord Godolphin's letters to her ancestor, Lord Seafield, the Scottish Chancellor at the time of the Union; Mr. John Evelyn kindly allowed me to examine the Evelyn Papers from Wotton; and the Earl of Mount Edgcumbe was good enough to institute a search for some Godolphin family papers preserved in the Royal Institution of Cornwall, Truro. To Lady Seafield, Mr. Evelyn and Lord Mount Edgcumbe my thanks are due.

Of the historians who assisted me, I must first acknowledge the great debt that I owe to Mr. Esmond S. de Beer, who read my typescript, made many suggestions to correct and improve it, answered my many questions and showed me innumerable kindnesses: furthermore, he very obligingly made available to me the page-proofs of his forthcoming new edition of Evelyn's *Diary*. I must also thank Mr. David Ogg and Mrs. Marjorie Cox, both of whom read my proofs and gave me the benefit of their wide knowledge of the period, and Mr. W. G. Hiscock for his guidance through the Evelyn Papers, formerly at Wotton and now under his care at Christ Church, Oxford, and for having read and advised me on the opening chapters of my book.

For guidance on the illustrations generally I am indebted to Mr. Kingsley Adams, Director of the National Portrait Gallery, and for permission to reproduce paintings or manuscripts as illustrations to the work, I am grateful to the Duke of Marlborough, the Duke of Portland, K.G., the Duke of Leeds, Earl Spencer, the executors of the Will of the late Earl of Berkeley, Mr. John Evelyn, the Clerk of the Records, the Record Office, House of Lords, the trustees of the National Museum, Stockholm, and the trustees of the National Portrait Gallery, London. I must also thank Mr. Geoffrey Cumberlege and the Oxford University Press for the loan of their block of the Dixon portrait of Margaret Blagge, and Mr. William Longman and Messrs. Longmans, Green & Company for permission to reproduce from Dr. G. M. Trevelyan's *England under Queen Anne* the table of ministers forming the Godolphin Administration.

I would like to acknowledge my debt to the Council and Senate of University College, Leicester, for so kindly permitting me the use of their library and for agreeing to accept responsibility for documents sent to Leicester for my inspection: I also wish to thank Miss Rhoda Bennett, the Librarian, for her unfailing courtesy and kindness. Others who have assisted me in various ways and to whom I am grateful are Dr. C. E. Wright, Department of Manuscripts, British Museum; Mr. R. S. Atkinson, Director of the Public Record Office; Sir Edmund Craster, Librarian of All Souls, for help in the Codrington Library and for permission to quote from the All Souls MSS.; Mrs. Osyth Leeston, literary adviser to John Murray; Miss Margaret Franklin, for her research work on my behalf at the British Museum, the Public Record Office, and at Blenheim; and, as always, my old friend, Mr. V. Cameron Turnbull.

Finally, I must thank Dr. Robert D. Horn of the University of Oregon and Professor Bonamy Dobrée for their advice and assistance in the writing of the second appendix.

April, 1952.   T. L.

BOOK I

Apprenticeship

CHAPTER I

AT THE COURT OF CHARLES II

THE reign of Charles II is, as it were, a shaft of sunlight between the storms of the Great Rebellion and the Glorious Revolution. But it is an autumnal sun, its pale rays lacking the glow of warmth and friendliness. Frivolity and selfishness were the order of the day. The nation as a whole was reacting sharply from the Puritan experiment,[1] the nobles and those about the throne from the days of misery in poverty and exile. The men and women of the Court, made familiar to us in the pages of the engaging Frenchman who came to this country to win an English bride, thought only of self-indulgence; and the restored King, at once a wise ambitious politician and a charming, cynical, easy-going voluptuary, had returned from his exile resolutely determined on two things: first, that he would never again set out on his travels, and secondly, that the England that had restored him must pay for his pleasures. And pay she certainly did! Small wonder that Mr. Pepys was to record the duties of Sir Alexander Fraizer, the King's physician, in language more frank than tasteful:[2] small wonder that pious Mr. Evelyn shortly after King Charles's death should express his disapproval in no uncertain terms. "I can never forget the inexpressible luxury and profaneness, gaming and all dissoluteness, and as it were total forgetfulnesse of God (it being Sunday evening), which this day se'n-night I was witnesse of the King sitting and toying etc. his concubines, Portsmouth, Cleaveland, and Mazarine, with a French boy singing love songs, in that glorious gallery, whilst about 20 of the greate courtiers and other dissolute persons were at basset round a large table, a bank of at least 2000 in gold before them upon which two gentlemen who were with me made reflections with astonishment. Six days after was all in the dust."[3]

It was to this vicious Court that a young Cornishman came in September, 1662: short, ungainly, taciturn, and of somewhat melancholy countenance,* he was aged seventeen, and he had just been appointed Page of Honour to the King.[4] Some four years later, a tall, handsome fourteen-year-old girl of good Suffolk stock, the daughter of a Royalist colonel who with his family

---

* "... every man with a face as long as a Godolphin's." Prior to Harley, "Westminster, 2, afternoon Sept 22 (Oct. 3) 1720." H.M.C. *Bath*, III, 490.

3

had returned to England at the Restoration, was appointed Maid of Honour to Anne Hyde, the Duchess of York. The name of the page was Sidney Godolphin; the name of the maid was Margaret Blagge.*

The ancient family of Godolphin of Godolphin takes its name from the manor first possessed by the line at the time of the Norman conquest. In early days the name was spelt "Godalgahn", Cornish for "White Eagle", and that device was borne on the family shield. The first known lord of the manor was John de Godolphin, born about 1050 and—save for one break in the male line in the fourteenth century—the manor passed from father to son from Norman to Tudor times.

Early in the sixteenth century, John Godolphin was made High Sheriff for the Duchy, and, jointly with Lord Brooke, steward of the mines in Cornwall and Devon. He was succeeded by his eldest son, William, who was made Comptroller of the Coinage of Tin. Later he was knighted, and not long afterwards we find him writing to Cromwell on the knighthood that has just been conferred on his son.[5] This son, also Sir William, was a mighty warrior and he covered himself with glory in the short war waged by Henry VIII against Francis I which ended with the total defeat of the French at the Battle of the Spurs. Upon his return from the wars, Sir William was made warden of the Stannaries, was on several occasions elected Knight of the Shire, and was High Sheriff for Cornwall no less than five times. Upon his death in 1575, the family estates devolved upon his nephew, Sir Francis Godolphin, to whom had been granted three years previously the first lease of the Scilly Isles for a period of thirty-eight years.

Sir Francis busied himself with politics, and in 1589 was elected Member for his native county. But he was also a soldier, and in the summer of 1595, soon after Elizabeth's favourite, Essex, had completed his memorial to the Queen on the subject of protecting England from foreign invasion, Sir Francis wrote anxiously to him about the need for a stronger garrison to defend the new fortifications in Scilly, ". . . for the gathering of these Spaniards seemeth as a cloud that is like to fall shortly in some part of her Majesty's dominions."[6] A fortnight later, he was in contact with the enemy. Early in the morning of July 23rd, 1595, as the rising sun dispersed the fog, four hostile galleys were seen close in to shore. Soon they landed about two hundred men armed with pikes and shot, who quickly set the villages aflame and drove the meanly-armed inhabitants from their dwellings. The natives, fleeing from the marauders, chanced to fall in with Sir Francis Godolphin, near Penzance; and he at once took charge of the proceedings.

* Spelt variously Blagge or Blague. Except when quoting from documents, when I shall follow the original, I shall adopt the spelling Blagge.

He summoned aid from the surrounding military, and sent messengers post haste to Sir Francis Drake and Sir John Hawkins, who were with the fleet at Plymouth. Then he led the townsfolk into Penzance in order to defend the place and await reinforcements. "Had the people stood with Sir Fr. Godolphin, who engaged himself very worthily", reported Sir Nicholas Clifford, "it had been saved, but the common sort utterly forsook him, saving some four or five gentlemen."[7] Nevertheless, Sir Francis remained undaunted, even though the Spaniards broke into the town and fired many of the houses; and soon the invaders were retreating, so that by the time help arrived from Plymouth, they were sailing from our shores.[8]

This skirmish taught Sir Francis Godolphin a lesson, and henceforth he constantly advocated the fortifying of our seaboard against invasion. "For the better defence of the Western ports, especially Cornwall, from the enemy's invasions . . ." he told the great Cecil some two years later, "there is great need of powder and pikes, for the country's provisions will not suffice two days encounter with the enemy, and supply is not to be had other than from London."[9] In November of the following year he was in correspondence with Sir Walter Raleigh on the strategic importance of Pendennis Castle and the weakness of its defences.[10] "If the Spaniard should attempt to hold it with 2,000 men, furnished with sufficient store of victuals and munitions . . ." he does not see how he can be driven out, "by a force ten-fold greater than his, or what other place is so seated for the advantage both to keep his ship and galleys and to annoy and spoil us in most of our trades."[11] Early in August, 1599, he reported to Cecil a rumour that the Spanish Fleet was ready to invade us;[12] and a week later he wrote anxiously about the lack of defence at Milford Haven, "one of the Fairest and capablest harbours of this realm." That being so, "If he covert that place, he will be like to land and make it good for fortifying, which fort and fleet together may prove a very hard encounter for her Majesty's navy, being also a very dangerous coast, void of any other harbour wherein they may be succoured. And the enemy being in Milford, you see their nigher neighbourhood to Ireland . . ."[13] Some time later, he reported the landing of a Spanish force at Kinsale in Ireland.[14] According to his deputy in Scilly thirty-five sail of Spaniards had summoned the town to yield.

The occupying force was reported to be only some 4,000 men with money but no food: so prices soon rose and in no time people were giving £5 for a cow, "two pieces of eight for a mutton," and "four seals for a hen." But salvation was at hand. Lord Mountjoy was in Cork with 8,000 men, who ". . . are all on fire to have them by the ears." Furthermore, an enthusiast named Keyser of Plymouth, then at Cork, volunteered to take three small ships into Kinsale Harbour, and fire the Spanish galleons.[15]

A year later there was good news, "God, I hear, by the pursuit of her Majesty's ships and others, hath foundered four of the six Spanish galleys in the seas near Dunkirk and Nieuport . . . Therefore . . . it may prove serviceable for some of her Majesty's ships that draw least water, with some other warlike ships of the states, being directed by any marks to the places where those galleys perished, may be there well employed . . . to find where these sunken commodities do lie; and by double grapples of iron to be depressed with poles fastened one to another, and so continued in length until it may seize on and bring up that which they are applied into."[16]

But Francis Godolphin was not only a gallant soldier, he was also a respected country gentleman; and by his marriage with the daughter of Sir John Killigrew of Arwenack, he much increased his influence in Cornwall. Moreover, his scientific development of his estates, enriched as they were with tin mines, rendered him the true founder of the family fortunes. Godolphin did not hesitate to seek help from any quarter where it could be found; and it is believed that he employed both a German and a Dutchman to advise him. Thus under his guidance, the Godolphin mines grew rapidly in value and added, we are told, no less than £10,000 to the national revenue.

Sir Francis, who died in 1606, was succeeded by his eldest son, William, to whom in 1608 a second lease of the Scilly Isles was granted for sixty years. A soldier like his father, he fought under Essex in Ireland and was knighted for his gallantry at Arklaw. He died in 1613, leaving four children. The youngest, William, died young. The second, Sidney, attained some distinction as a minor poet. Admired by Hobbes, the intimate of Falkland, we learn that he was a small man, shy, sensitive, melancholy, though univerally admired—the "Little Sid" of Suckling's *Session of the Poet*. First elected to Parliament as member of Helston in 1628, he was re-elected to both the Short and Long Parliaments in the spring and autumn of 1640. He was soon recognised as one of the staunchest of the adherents of Strafford and one of the most devoted supporters of the King. At the outbreak of the Civil War he made a notable speech in which he solemnly warned the House of the hidden dangers of a conflict, ". . . for when the cards are shuffled, no man knows what the game will be."[17] Then he joined the forces under the command of Sir Ralph Hopton, which had just routed the Parliamentarians at Bradock Down, and were advancing into Devonshire. Here he was well received, and, though wanting in military training and experience, his advice was, so Clarendon tells us, eagerly sought by the commanders.[18] But they were soon denied the advantage of his counsel, for at the skirmish at Chagford he was mortally wounded. His friend and admirer, Thomas Hobbes, has written his noble epitaph:

"Thou'rt dead, Godolphin, who lov'dst reason true
Justice and peace, soldier belov'd, adieu."[19]

And beneath the chancel of the ancient church at Okehampton, he sleeps, not far from the spot where he fell.

Sir William's daughter, Penelope, married Sir Charles Berkeley, who had the unique distinction of succeeding his own son as Viscount Fitz-hardinge. Penelope's brother, Sir Francis Godolphin, wed Dorothy Berkeley, a daughter of Sir Henry Berkeley of Yarlington, her husband's uncle.[20] These alliances with the noble house of Berkeley were to prove very advantageous to the Godolphins in the days ahead.

Of this Sir Francis Godolphin, Sir William's eldest son, little is recorded. Indeed, his chief title to fame seems to be that he was the father of the future Lord Treasurer, the subject of this memoir. He did, however, at his majority in 1626 continue the family connections by becoming governor of Scilly, and ten years later he was granted the third lease of the islands for a term of fifty years. Subsequently he was Member of Parliament for St. Ives. At the outbreak of the Civil War, he settled on his Cornish estates, where he raised a regiment of foot which his brother William commanded for the King. He also had the distinction of harbouring at Godolphin Hall the future King Charles II, who took refuge there on his flight to the Scilly Isles on the total collapse of the royal cause.* Nevertheless, before the death of Charles I he certainly compounded with the Parliament.[21] At the Restoration Francis Godolphin was knighted and made Governor of the Scilly Isles. Furthermore, the new King showed the reliance he placed upon the loyalty of his servant by entrusting to him the custody of the important prisoner of State, the younger Sir Harry Vane.[22]

But if Sir Francis Godolphin was no very prominent public figure, he was certainly a good family man. By his wife, Dorothy Berkeley, he had no less than sixteen children,[23] but of these only a very few need concern us. The eldest, William, created a baronet in 1661, never married and lived in retirement, mostly with his spinster sisters, Anne and Penelope: he will occasionally appear in these pages. The third son was Sidney, the future Lord Treasurer, and the fourth, Henry, took Holy Orders, and was destined to become Provost of Eton and Dean of St. Paul's. The second daughter, Jael, married Edward Boscawen, a well-known House of Commons man, and by him became the mother of the first Viscount Falmouth, and of two daughters, the younger of whom, Anne, married Sir John Evelyn, grandson of the diarist. As early as about 1663, Sir Francis began to look

* The room at Godolphin Hall or Manor, where Charles is supposed to have hidden at this time, may still be seen.

round for suitable mates for his first-born and at some uncertain date in that year we find him writing to a lady whom he regarded as an eligible daughter-in-law.[24] Unfortunately his application came to nothing, and his son, Sir William, died a bachelor nearly fifty years later. But if his efforts for his first-born were vain, those exerted on behalf of a younger son had already borne fruit. In the autumn of 1662, as will be recalled, Sir Francis's third son, Sidney, had appeared at Court as a Page of Honour to King Charles II.

During the Civil War, there was a certain colonel of a regiment of foot much respected in royalist circles. His name was Thomas Blagge, and he came of an old family, long settled at Horningsheath in Suffolk. His great-great-grandfather was a Baron of the Exchequer in 1511, his great-grandfather was that Sir George Blagge, the witty friend of Wyat and of Surrey, who in 1543 distinguished himself at the Siege of Landreci. Three years later Blagge was cast into the Tower and condemned to be burnt at Smithfield, escaping that fate, so it is said, solely through the intervention of King Henry VIII, who loved the man whom he affectionately dubbed "his pig". Knighted by Somerset on the field of Musselburgh in 1547, Blagge lived to appear as a witness against the Lord Admiral Seymour a year later. Sir George's descendant, Colonel Thomas Blagge was, prior to the outbreak of hostilities, one of the grooms of the bedchamber to Charles I. Early on in the war, his Sovereign had demonstrated the confidence he felt in his fidelity by appointing him Governor of Wallingford,[25] a post he held for more than three years.[26] At length, however, he was forced to surrender, though on honourable terms,[27] when he left for France bearing a letter from the harassed Charles to his anxious Queen.[28] Subsequently Blagge fought gallantly for his Sovereign at the battle of Worcester, and he aided the Duke of Buckingham in his escape from the field. It was after this disastrous battle that the fugitive King entrusted his George into his faithful servant's keeping. Blagge for a time escaped the attentions of his enemies by lodging in the house of a certain George Barlow, to whose wife he entrusted the precious Garter. A week later Mrs. Barlow succeeded in smuggling the emblem out of the house and conveying it to one Robert Milward, who, when taken prisoner at Stafford, delivered it to Izaak Walton, one day to be famous, who had for some weeks been lodging in that town, anxiously awaiting news of the recent battle.[29] Meanwhile, misfortune had overtaken Colonel Blagge. "Blagge is indeed a prisoner, and was soe almost a month agoe, but is it any great loss?" asked Thomas Todd unkindly of Colonel Gervase Holles. "Certainly hee had noe interest where he pretended it, and he has the misfortune to be taken soe foolishly, that some believe it willingly."[30] Nevertheless, he was considered a prisoner

MARGARET BLAGGE
AFTERWARDS MRS. GODOLPHIN
From the portrait by Matthew Dixcn.   Formerly at Wotton House

of consequence and lodged in the Tower.[31] Walton brought the King's
Garter to London and managed to restore it to Blagge, who on his escape
later in the year hastened to cross the Channel and attach himself to the
Court of the exiled King. Then at last was he able to restore the lost George
to King Charles's hands.[32]

By his wife, a daughter of Sir Roger North of Mildenhall in his native
county of Suffolk, Thomas Blagge was already the father of three girls—
Henrietta Maria and Dorothy a few years old at this time, and a third, Mary,
born about 1651, perhaps during her father's imprisonment. It was whilst
Blagge was an exile that his last child, Margaret, was born. * After various
adventures and a further lodgement in the Tower,[33] Colonel Blagge joined
Hyde at Rotterham, and at the Restoration was re-united with his family in
England. As a reward for his services, the gallant officer was promptly
re-appointed to the Governorship of Languard and at the same time was
made Governor of Yarmouth.[34] But though only forty-seven, he was a
tired man, and on November 14th, only a few months after his return to
England, he died. They buried him in Westminster Abbey.†

To the poor widow, the loss was a crushing blow. In times of stress
and anxiety she suddenly found herself alone in the world with a family
of young daughters on her hands, and with the heavy burden of the Colonel's
debts, largely incurred in the royal service.‡ She was soon petitioning Sir
Joseph Williamson to use his influence to procure her a pension.[35] Fortunately her pleadings and those of her family[36] did not go unheeded, and
she was granted a pension of £500 a year and other favours:[37] furthermore, she was saved from the responsibility of looking after her younger
daughter, for Margaret had in July 1658[38] been taken to France by the
Duchess of Richmond, sister of the Duke of Buckingham whom Colonel
Blagge had aided after the battle of Worcester. But the Duchess, having
to return to England after some two years abroad, handed over her young
charge to her kinswoman, Lady Guilford, first woman of the bedchamber
to the Dowager Queen. This lady, we are told, a recent convert to Catholicism, was harsh and bigoted, and was soon striving to persuade Margaret

* Miss Sampson suggests that Margaret was probably born in London (Evelyn,
Mrs. Godolphin, 182), but this seems unlikely. Blagge was sent to the Tower in
September 1651, and on October 23rd, Mrs. Blagge received permission to visit him
and "goe & come out as she shall have occasion." (P.R.O. *S.P. Dom. Interregnum,
Council of State's Pro.* i., 23, f.55). Blagge escaped from imprisonment about the end of
1651 and fled to the exiled Court. Margaret was born on August 2nd, 1652.

† In the Register of Burials in the Abbey he is incorrectly recorded as "Thomas
Blake, Esq., one of the Grooms of His Majesty's Bed-chamber: in the north side of
the Church." Chester, *Registers of Westminster Abbey*, 152.

‡ They amounted to £1,500 at his death. *S.P. Dom. Car. II*, 62, f. 116.

Blagge to become a Papist. But all was in vain; the child withstood the blandishments of her tormentor. It was observed that already at her tender age she was showing a remarkable attachment to her religion: by no means could she be persuaded to desert the faith of her fathers.

Fortunately the pious child was not destined to remain long under Lady Guilford's harsh tutelage, for in October 1660, Queen Henrietta Maria on a visit to England brought the young exile in her train. For a time Margaret lodged with her mother in the Savoy. A year or two later, the circumstances of the Blagge family were slightly relieved by the appointment of the eldest daughter, Henrietta Maria, as Maid of Honour to the Duchess of York. Readers of the entertaining pages of Count Grammont will recall his description of the eldest Mistress Blagge, and of the cruel practical joke played upon her by her fellow Maids of Honour.[39] However, marriage soon relieved poor Henrietta Blagge from the trials of life at Court, for early in the year 1664 she wed Sir Thomas Yarborough of Snaith in Yorkshire. "In the evening," records a Court news-letter dated February 8th, "the Duchess of York gave a great entertainment with comedy and ball at St. James's to their Majesties and all the ladies about town, as a respect to Mrs. Blagge, one of the maids of honour, married last week to Sir Thomas Yerbury, a person of very good quality and fortune."[40]

Thus no doubt Henrietta's youngest sister, whose reputation for piety was already becoming known, came first to be seen in Court circles. There she was destined to meet Mr. Godolphin, Page of Honour to the King. But whatever friendship existed between the young courtier and the poor friendless widow and her family was not yet suffered to mature, for the outbreak of the Great Plague drove the Blagges from London and Mrs. Blagge with her unmarried daughters* settled for a time with her late husband's relations in Suffolk. Not until 1666 did they return to the capital when the anxious mother was prevailed upon to place her youngest daughter, now aged fourteen, at Court as Maid of Honour to the Duchess of York.

Thus were the page and the young maid thrown into each other's company. Already Sidney had been shown signs of his Sovereign's favour, for some two years previously he had been the happy recipient of a generous gift from the King.[41] Already, no doubt, with the optimism of youth, he felt his feet firmly planted upon the lower rungs of the ladder of fame. Already, no doubt, he was beginning to think of his future and of taking a wife. Then he looked upon Margaret, the new Maid of Honour, sweet, demure and pure in a vicious Court. He looked, and he knew at once that he need look no further.

*Dorothy Blagge did not marry. Mary Blagge married Adam Colclough.

CHAPTER II

SIDNEY AND MARGARET

SIDNEY GODOLPHIN had not been long at Court before misfortune came his way. In the spring of 1667, the much-loved father died. "Yesterday morning Robin wak'd me with your letter and the most deplorable news for all our family that it was possible for them to heare," wrote Sidney to his brother William, "though I have all the affliction in the world which the losse of the best and kindest of fathers can cause in the heart of the most grateful child yett it does not equall that which I feel when I reflect upon my dear mother's grief. I beseech God almighty of his infinite goodnesse and compassion to send her and all hers that consolation which he alone is able to bestow." But even amidst his sorrows, the family interest must be maintained. "As soon as I had gott my selfe ready, I went directly to the King who being the tenderest natur'd man . . . seem'd to be much concern'd for the losse wee had all received in my dear father and made no scruple of promising me that his offices should be continued in you." He also took the precaution of hastening to Lord Bath, Lord-Lieutenant of the County of Cornwall, to enlist his assistance on his brother's behalf. He was well received, so that ". . . I never saw any man in my life more ready upon all occasions to do good offices to another than he has been for you. . . ." He therefore advises William to write to Lord Bath; but he is careful to add ". . . pray don't take it ill that I pretend to advise you in this matter, you may be sure that I will never doe it in any thing but when I know it is a thing fit for you to doe. for noe man living has more kindnesse and esteem for a brother than I have for you, and the more because I am very well satisfied that you love me extreamly." And he concludes pathetically, "Besides you are now to consider that we are now to be a father to one another or at least that you are to be soe to me, and as I am sure I shall alwaies have the respect due to a parent for you, so I doe confidently believe you will not want a fathers tendernesse for me."[1] The poor widow was equally distressed. "Next my selfe and my poore fatherless children," she wrote to her sister-in-law, Lady Fitzhardinge, "I know no body could have so great a share of affliction for our most grievous losse as your Ladyship . . ." though it appears that her late husband had not always been on the best of terms with her correspondent, whom she goes on to assure that ". . . this deare person was the worthiest husband and the tenderest father So he was the kindest brother that ever I knew how far soever passion might have transported him when he writ last to you." Unfortunately his affairs were involved "so that he was not able to leave any of his children ". . . more then annuities for their lives of which the greatest is but 6 skore lb. a yeare & ye least not 40. . . ." Then she moralizes sadly on the uncertainties of human existence, and reflects on ". . . how suddenly this most dear person was taken off from the world without having opertunitie of speaking one word concerning wife, children, friends or estate which will be an unspeakable griefe for me as long as I live.[2]

But if loss and disaster made Sidney a poor man, he could still have ambitions; and his one ardent desire was to enter Parliament. Early in 1667 his brother reported a possible vacancy in the West country. Sidney replied begging William to seek to gain the interest of Lord Bath.[3]

But a couple of months later, Sidney found a very different subject about which to write to William. The Dutch fleet had just sailed up the Medway, and a young man of spirit must join the army. "You must needs have heard something before this of the burning of some of our best ships in the river at Chatham by the Dutch fleet," he wrote, "wee depending too much upon the french promises of peace and having nothing in readiness to oppose them; in order to the preventing the most fatal consequence of this misfortune the King intends to raise a land army and I am resolved to take a Cornetts place in my Lord Sunderland's troop . . .": but money is wanting and, ". . . I shall be forc'd to think of parting with the annuity which my dear father has left me and if you think it may be more convenient for you to buy it of me than any other, propose your own conditions for I am sure what you doe, I shall think reasonable. . . . Pray let me hear from you as soon as you can and if you have any good men about you that will be glad to ride in our troup they need only to make hast hither to me and bring every one a horse, hatts, coats, boots and arms they shall be provided with here, but . . ." he adds excitedly, "the chief thing requisite is that they should make hast."[4] William's reply is not forthcoming; but clearly it was not enthusiastic. Sidney thanks him for his money and his good council, but to his brother's warning to think again before joining the army, the reply is definite that the matter is too far advanced for him to retire, even if he wished to. Nevertheless he admits that ". . . your reasons are extream good, for methinks your letter seems to expect a formall landing of an enemie and coming at least to one battel for itt when I beleive of the other side that there is no intention of any such thing . . ." for the French Ambassador at Breda and the Swedish Ambassadors have ". . . positively told the Dutch that the King of England's propositions were so reasonable that if they would not accept them they should think themselves at libertie to make peace without them and when wee have once peace with the French we have nothing to feare in land. . . ." Then follows some worldly wisdom. "Now granting this," writes Sidney, "'tis an even lay the troups now rais'd will be quite reduc'd; if they be not my employment will not oblidge me to be 3 days in a month from the King, nor to quitt that which I have neare him already till his majesty be pleas'd to bestow a better on me which time I doe confesse I can not imagine to bee very farr off nor I am sure will not bee the farther for the readinesse I have shew'd to engage in this matter but quite contrary I hope to receive benefitt from itt in my maine pretension; and as to what my mother's letter says that you thought it was beneath what I might well pretend to I take that to be the thing that in all reason ought to doe me the most good, for there is nothing better in the world than not to stand upon one's punctilios when the King's service once comes to presse. . . ." Nevertheless, he cannot join his troop immediately for "I am not able at the present to goe abroad," he adds, "having gott a bruise in my side yesterday morning as I was coming post from lee where our troup is quarter'd that make me void a great deale of bloud but Dr. Fraiser* has lett me bloud and give me glisters and ointments that have made me pretty well again so that I hope I shall bee able to goe abroad again tomorrow or next day."[5]

Fortunately the danger of invasion soon passed, and only four days later Sidney writes to William on the prospects of peace. Fortunately too most of the material points are agreed, and ". . . Mr. Coventry tells us the Dutch are extreamly low and at least as weary of the warr as their neighbours; the french are going to bisidge Courtray, a strong place and if it bee well garrison'd is like to hold them pray for a fortnight or 3 weeks. The Dutch fleet lies within sight of our coast seeming to threaten Harwich the next spring tide; our troop is there but my bruise does not yet suffer me to goe a horseback and recompenses the pain I felt by saving me a troublesome journey."[6] In a few weeks, however, he is able to write that all hostilities are to end on Monday next, ". . . so that when you please your regiment may goe home and take its rest. One of the consequences of the peace will (I hope) be the disbanding of your supernumeraries at Scylly. I intend to speake with Sr. Wm. Coventry about that matter and to make him understand that 500 men are not able to maintain the place in case of any resolute attempt. . . ."[7]

Whilst Sidney was thus pursuing his interests, Lady Godolphin was bestirring herself on behalf of her son Henry at Oxford, who was designed for the Church, "who his friends hope is no unworthy pretender to a fellowship in al soules where at present are two places vacant, if he could by the

---

* Sir Alexander Fraizer (1610?-1681), physician to Charles II.

favour of friends be recomended to the warden of that house or what were rather to be wisht to my Ld of Canterburie who we are told has great influence both on him and on those elections . . ." all might go well for Henry Godolphin, of whom "I may not speak of his learning being so incompetent a judg but for his modestie and sobriete may safely ingage. . . ."[8] The application was successful. "My most dear mother," wrote the delighted Henry, "I should not presume to trouble you yet, were it not to give you an account of my good success at All Soules, of which I have word brought me this minute. . . ."[9]

At the same time Lady Godolphin was busying herself in promoting other family interests. It appears that about this time one of her daughters became engaged to a Mr. Dryden, and the fond mother, anxious to provide a fit trousseau for the prospective bride, wrote to her courtier son in London for assistance. The projected marriage never took place, but Sidney's reply shows his growing influence in Court circles. He begins by apologizing for delay in dealing with the matter of clothes for his sister's wedding, but he has been away from London. "Since I cam home," the letter continues, "I have been in doubt whether I should get some made up new or endeavour to buy those of Mrs. Stuart"—that is la belle Stuart, the famous Court beauty— "which were sent her out of France just before the Court went into mourning and are now uselesse to her and therefore the more likely to be a good penniworth; your messenger is extreamly impatient or else for ought I know I would expect an answer of this before I determine this matter, as also whether you stay only for the wedding clothes, for there is a report however it comes to passe upon us not having your authority, that there is demur in the affaire; if so I would rather venture upon Mr. Dryden's anger at Robin when he comes home, and his at me here, than committt any more errors in this business. . . . I am my dear Mother's most dutifull Sid Godolphin."[10] The manner in which the young page nicely weighs in the balance the risk of annoying the prospective bridegroom against the alternative of laying out the family money on a wedding dress that will not be required is a foretaste of the statesman of the years ahead.

There is a significant postscript to this letter. "Concerning St. Mawes," it runs, "I should think my selfe extreamly happy if there could bee any thing done for me for love or money. But I refer it to you." We have seen something of Sidney's political ambitions which had been temporarily thwarted by the fears of invasion. Now that that danger was passed, his mind turned anew to the congenial career of politics. In 1668 died Sir Peter Killigrew who with Sir William Godolphin sat as one of the members for Helston in Cornwall: the surviving member hastened to advise his brother of the vacancy. Sidney was warm in his thanks; but unfortunately there was another candidate already in the field upon whom, however, Lord Bath hoped to prevail to waive his pretensions. Meanwhile, Sidney asked William to keep him informed as to how the matter proceeds, and concluded his letter with some significant words about his mother's health. "I am extreamly glad to heare my mother is so well again. Pray God continues her so and my deare brothers kindness to his affectionate S.G."[11]

We have already seen Sidney anxious to become a Cornet in Lord Sunderland's troop. Now, about a fortnight after writing the letter just quoted, we find him on a visit to the mercurial Lord Sunderland; "Before I came out of Town," he wrote to William from Althorp, "I have gott the speakers order to the clerk of the Crown for the writt and left itt to Mr. Bridgmans care to see it dispatch'd as soon as was possible and sent to you, who promis'd me faithfully it should be done; . . ."[12] So thus early had Sidney formed a friendship with that enigmatic statesman and his crafty wife, that was destined to have much influence on his own public career.

In the midst of these affairs, there was disturbing news of Lady Godolphin's health. "You may imagine I am extreamly troubl'd for the continuance of my mother's sicknesse," he wrote to William, "I pray God this may find you past apprehending her in any danger . . .": Then there were particulars of his affairs, there having been some delay in the issuing of the writ.[13] On Michaelmas Day, he sent his brother a draft election address to read and amend; ". . . and gett one of my sisters to transcribe it, for I suppose no body there knowes their hand any more than mine. I have defer'd my writing to you this week because I hop'd long past to have sent you the writt which Mr. Treasurer has undertaken to gett for me, but not yett perform'd. I must now leave it wholly to his care, being my selfe to goe to morrow morning to New market with the King who will not bee in town again till the end of Oct. . . ." Then he added significantly: "I would faine heare that my mother is perfectly recover'd. . . ."[14]

Some three weeks later the young page, in attendance on the King at Audley End, was still worried about his chances at Helston. "Pray try what may be done at Helston: iff I were apt to believe reports I ought not to bee confident of success."[15] On October 26th, King Charles returned to London with Godolphin in his train; and only then was it that Sidney learned that on October 15th he had been duly elected. Thus as a member of the Court party Sidney entered what came to be known as the Long Parliament of the Restoration, which was destined to continue for another ten years.*

* For *Members of the Court Party in the House of Commons, 1670–1678*, see *Bulletin of the Institute of Historical Research*, XI (1933–4), 1–23.

Swiftly on the heels of this success, however, came sorrow, for in the following month Lady Godolphin died.* "I confesse it was a very surprising affliction to me to heare of my deare mother's death when I did not imagine she was in any great weaknesse or extremitie," wrote Sidney to William. "Pray God almighty comfort you and my deare sisters, whose good nature I am so well assur'd off that I'll sweare I have more concern for their losse than for my self."[16]

At the same time that Sidney was beginning his political career, he was also making progress as a courtier. In March 1669 it was reported from France that Queen Henrietta Maria was dangerously ill; whereupon the King despatched the young page to enquire after his mother's condition. This separation from his Sovereign does not seem to have been altogether to Sidney's liking;" . . . wee are told," he wrote from Paris, perhaps to Lord Arlington—"that the King intends to begin his journey to New fforest the 5th of August, which I am troubled at very much because I am afraid I shan't be able to come soon enough to London to fitt my self with horses to follow him, which I confesse I would bee very glad to doe, because if I were ever in my life time the least serviceable to the king it was in those kind of jorneys, and I may say truely without intending to make my court that I have not so much pleasure in any thing as the hopes that I shall at some time in my life bee able to do him service. Your Lordship will know better than I doe whether Twill bee fitter to have any excuse made to the king for me and if you think it will, I must beg you to doe it for me." Then follows a little Parisian gossip. "Madame comes next Monday to St. Clou to stay till she lie in, the King of France makes her a great feast by the way at Versailles."[17]

The following month the impatient page returned to England on instructions from Arlington. "He has succeeded so well here with everybody," reported Ralph Montagu, our Ambassador in Paris, "that the longer he had stayed, it had been every day better for him. . . ."[18] This success soon prompted the King to send him on another mission. In the spring of 1670 Charles sent Godolphin to France to help to conduct his sister, the Duchess of Orleans, to England. The cost of Sidney's two journeys was £500.[19] Doubtless as some reward for his diligence, he was upon his return promoted to the position of Groom of the Bedchamber to Charles II at a salary of £500 a year.[20]

We must now return to Margaret Blagge whom we left immediately after her appointment as Maid of Honour to the Duchess of York. It was

---

* Lady Godolphin was buried at Breage on November 23rd. Marsh, *The Godolphins*, 8.

not long before she began to gain for herself a reputation for purity and
saintliness that was the more noticeable because of the vicious circles in which
she moved. Her mistress, Anne Hyde, was devoted to her, and Mr.
Evelyn of diary fame, who first made her acquaintance in the summer of
1669, was soon singing her praises. "My wife being gon a journey of
Pleasure downe the River as far as the Sea," he recorded in June, 1669,
"with Mrs. Howard, & her daughters the Maids of Honour, amongst whom,
that excellent creature Mrs. Blagge."[21] A few years later, "I entertained the
Maids of honour, (among whom there was one whom for her many &
extraordinary virtues I did infinitely esteeme) at a Comedy, this afternoone,
& so went home."[22] That is the first mention of "that excellent creature",
"my particular Devota"[23] in these pages; many were to follow, as we shall
shortly see.

Sorrow was to be Margaret's lot, for some time before June 8th, 1670 her
mother died.[24] "My mother Died, at first surpriz'd and very unwilling,"
recorded Margaret, "she was afterwards Resign'd, Received often, Pray'd
much, had holy things read to her; Delighted in heavenly Discourse;
Desir'd to be dessolv'd and to be with Christ; Ended her life cherefully, &
without Paine; left her Family in Order, and was much lamented."[25] Some
nine months later Margaret was to suffer another bereavement. On March
31st, 1671 the Duchess of York died from cancer of the breast; whereupon
Miss Blagge's services were transferred to the Queen. She thus described
events in words which to us seem more vivid than tasteful. "The D—esse
died, a Princesse honourd, in power: had much Wit, much mony, much
esteeme: she was full of un-speakable torture, and died (poor Creature!) in
Doubt of her Religion, without any Sacrament, or Divine by her, like a
poor Wretch:"—strange how her conversion to the Church of Rome the
previous year had been kept a secret even from those most close to her, and
that her devoted maid was ignorant of the fact that the Duchess received the
viaticum before she died!—"None Remembered her after one Weeke: none
sorry for her: she smelt extreamly; was tost, and flung about, and every one
did what they would with that stately Carcasse:— What is this World!
What is greatnesse! What to be esteem'd and thought a Wit! We shall
all be strip's without Sense or Remembrance. But God, if we serve him in
our Health, will give us Patience in our sickness."[26]

This awful indictment of human existence could only have been written
by one who, though so young, had already become acquainted with death.
She had lived through the Great Plague; she had recently seen her mother die;
and now she had watched the unhappy princess slowly waste away. These
painful experiences had given her a spirituality and unworldliness that lent
point and force to her morbid comment on the affairs of the flesh, and

enabled her to live up to the bitter moods she has herself recorded. Before many years were passed Margaret Blagge was destined to follow her royal mistress into the unknown: for the short time that remained to her, she served her God with a devotion remarkable at any time, but unique indeed in the England of the restored king. She drew up a code of conduct that she was determined to follow: early rising for prayer and meditation, to assure which when at Court she would instruct a sentry to call her by pulling on a thread passed through her bedroom keyhole and attached to her arm; self-denial, the reading of devotional works. Her calling she defined as "To entertain the Ladies, not to talk foolishly to men: more especially the King." Her moral courage was considerable. "Be sure never to talk to the King when they speak filthily, tho' I be laughed at."[27] A noble programme: yet harsh, and lacking much that makes life lovely. Music, the arts—these are rigidly excluded as irksome vanities. The joys of friendly converse are not for her, for "no *Raillery* almost, can be Innocent." Yet she had much more than her fair share of beauty, was naturally gay and an excellent mimic. But with all these vanities suppressed, where can that blessed thing, friendship, find a place?

Perhaps, indeed, it was a subconscious feeling of something missing from her life that caused the strange conversation that Evelyn has so vividly recorded. Visiting her one day in 1672 and finding her more thoughtful than usual, he sought to rally his young friend on her solemnity. The strange reply came that she had not a friend in the world. Evelyn answered truly enough that no one had more, for all who knew her loved her and those that loved her were her friends. He then put what we can only call a very leading question. "But I (who well knew where her Heart at that time was)," he records, "Asked her (smiling) what she Esteem'd a certaine gentleman beyond the seas to be? Alas! Replys she (guessing of whom I receiv'd that Seacret) He is very Ill, and that makes me very much Concern'd: But I don't speake to you of him, whom God will, I hope, be gracious to: But I would have *realy* a *Friend,* and in *that name* is a greate-deale more than I can Expresse: A *Faithful Friend,* whom I might trust with all I have, and God knows that's but little: For him whom you meane, cares not to meddle with my Concernes; nor Would I give him the trouble. . . ." A strange answer, we may think; yet Evelyn welcomed the opportunity to offer his services, and was gratified to find them welcomed. "Looke upon me henceforth," she said, "as your Child . . . and Calle me so."[28] Whereupon the delighted Evelyn took pen and paper and straightway drew something resembling an altar, beneath which he put a book and a cross and wrote these words: "be this the symbol of our Inviolable friendshipe." "Be it so," added his companion, "Margaret Blagge, 16 Octo.b.

1672." and beneath she appended these words, "for my brouther Evleyn."*
So Evelyn proffered his services. "I promised to do my best to serve her,
and from that time forwards, I reckoned her as my Child;" he tells us, "for
none did ever shew greater esteeme for a Father than did this incomparable
Creature to me, worthy of all the returne I could ever make, for the many
lasting obligations I received from her; a rare example of so much piety and
Virtue in so great a witt, beauty and perfection; This miracle of a young
Lady in a licentious Court and so deprav'd an age. She now delivered me
the ☆ under her owne hand, and it shall be Inviolable"† Henceforth, sometimes by name, sometimes by the pentacle, is she mentioned
in the famous diary. Thus commenced the strange friendship of John
Evelyn and Margaret Blagge.

But what of the "certaine gentleman beyond the seas" whose health
was causing the Maid of Honour so much anxiety? Exactly when Sidney and
Margaret became affianced we cannot tell; certain is it that it was some
years before 1672, the time of the conversation with Evelyn.‡ Probable
too, is it that in that year Sidney was already collecting things for the home
they hoped to make together. "I have yours of the 4th," he wrote to his
sister Jael, "and since Lady Sund(erland) had not yett taken her finall
resolution as to the parting with her bed, I shall not reckon any longer
upon itt, nor her hangings neither, but desire rather that all may be new, as
neare that Colour though, as if it were to match itt, because I like it better
than the lighter, for the inside, I submit it to your direction: my owne
bedding that is at the house I desire may not be stirred, for there I mean to
bee for some time, though I would not have the other out of my power..."29
In April of that year Godolphin had been appointed Envoy Extraordinary to the French Court with an allowance of £5 a day and £500 for
his equipage.30 In company with the Duke of Monmouth and others, he

* The drawing of the Altar of Friendship was placed between the pages of Evelyn's
MS. diary and is there still.

† Evelyn, *Diary*, October 16th, 1672. III, 628. Another symbol that Evelyn
frequently uses for Margaret Blagge in his *Dairy,* is ♎ This as the
seventh sign of the Zodiac represents the period between September 23rd and about
October 23rd, and may possibly celebrate the anniversary of their vows before the
Altar of Friendship on October 16th. For an explanation of the pentacle see Evelyn,
Mrs. Godolphin, Appendix A, 210–17.

‡ If Evelyn's reckoning can be relied upon they must have become engaged in
1666, the year of Margaret's first coming to Court, because at the time of the marriage in 1675 he wrote of their nine year engagement "... after a Passion of nine long
yeares, that they both had been the most inTire, and faithful Lovers in the World.
This was a space indeede of Sufficient Probation; nor will I presume to dive into the
Circumstances, which made them be so long in resolving; she being then very young,
and both of a Temper so very discreete." Evelyn, *Mrs. Godolphin*, 29.

had sailed on April 7th, Easter Day, in a high wind from Dover,[31] and they safely reached Rouen eleven days later.[32] On April 23rd, he reported his arrival in Paris and his favourable reception by the French King.[33] The great Turenne asked some pertinent questions about the state of our own fleet. "I told him," records the envoy, ". . . our Fleet would certainly bee out coming toward the Channell adding that I hop'd theirs would be as ready to meet itt . . ." a shrewd thrust! ". . . he said that 16 of their ships had been ready at Brest a good while and he hop'd the rest would be soe very soone."[34] In a subsequent letter from Paris, Godolphin recorded that he had informed Colbert of the Duke of York's arrangements to meet the Dutch fleet, ". . . desiring him to send away orders to Brest for their hastning out their Fleet with all possible speed." Colbert declined to add anything to his former statement that the French fleet had been ready since April 25th, and "as to the Dutch being soe forward, he said that their letters from Holland told them quite otherwise and that they found all the difficultys imaginable in getting out their Fleet. I confess . . ." shrewdly commented our Envoy, "nothing made me suspect their owne was not ready soe much as this for till now they have always said they were afraid the Dutch would bee at see before us. And I am veryly perswaded thay will hardly stir from Brest without a letter from the Duke (of York) telling them he is under saile and coming through the Channell to receive them."[35] Nine days later Godolphin announced his departure for Metz in the Duke of Monmouth's coach,[36] "the most magnifique I ever saw in France."[37]

But if the equipage was magnificent, the journey was tedious, eight days to Verdun and three more to Metz.[38] Three weeks later Sidney was in Wesel, whence he reported to Lord Arlington "I take it for granted that you have heard by some means or other that I have been a great while very sicke, it was my duty to have lett you know it from my selfe but neither my hand nor my head would lett me doe it sooner, and but very scurvily now. I shall bee obliged to stay some days in this towne to recover a little strength and then rejoyne the army . . . but at this houre I can hardly walke alone so low I have been brought by a feaver and griping of the gutts which are 2 inconvenient things to march withall. . . ." Then after some news of current events in France, he concludes, "My hand is soe weak that I feare you can scarce read it, but however sick or well I will always write to your lordship, when there is any conveniency of doing it."[39] But the next day he was able to write, "I recover my strength very slowly, however, after tomorrow I intend to goe to Emerick and next day to rejoyne The Army."[40] Three days later, we find him in Arnheim, whence he wrote to Arlington to announce the capture of Nimeguen and the investiture of Deventer; Duisberg was to be the next objective. Then with regard to himself he added: "I am yett soe very weak that I am afraid your lordship will find it very troublesome to read my hand."[41]

Very early on June 21st Godolphin writes to Arlington to announce the coming of a deputation from the States General;[42] and on the following day, that he has been informed by Pomponne that the envoys are actually on their way. Then he adds pathetically: "I have had a continued feaver ever since I came to the Army soe that I have been able to speak but once to the King who is alwayes a horseback, and when any thing is to be said to Mr. de Pompone, he is fain to give himselfe the trouble to come to me; I am extreamly afflcted that I should have the misfortune to bee sick just at this time when the employment wherewith the King has been pleased to honour me does require that one should bee a little more stiring than my health gives me leave to bee."[43]

On the following day the deputies from the States General arrive, sue for peace and ask for terms. These are high: France must retain all her conquests, but England and the princes of Germany must be consulted. Godolphin, familiar with Charles II's dilatory habits, urges his master not to delay his answer, which should be shown to King Louis "either by me or by some body more fitt to bee employ'd in a matter of soe much consequence, but certainly whatever resolution the King may please to take in this I think there ought to be no time lost in exposing his pretensions here that at least the pretext of ignorance may bee taken away from these people who are grown soe very high and are really soe very powerfull, that surely one ought to bee very nice and carefull in treating with them at this time. . . ." Then he reminds Arlington of the terms of our treaty with France, concerning the division of the conquests, quoting to him the Clause that gives a list of places that shall fall to England's share. "It does not say," comments Sidney, "that there shall bee noe peace made till the King bee possess'd of these places, nor that in case none of these places should be taken in this war, others should bee exchanged and these pute in the King of Englands hands, but however if I may venture my opinion of it to your lordship, it will not look at all honorably for the King to content him selfe with a lesse part of the spoile than is mentioned in the Treaty to come to his share."[44]

Five days later, Sidney writes again urgently to Arlington, "The King of France will have all and the King must be wholly at his mercy for his part, so that certainly my Lord with all kind of submission, there ought to be no time lost in sending hither . . ." In short, it is all a question of time, for the more conquests Louis makes, the more intractable he will be. If in this he is wrong, adds the writer, ". . . then all I have said and all I think upon this businesse is the grossest nonsense in the world and the greatest folly but if it should be soe I would rather chuse to expose it to your Lordship than bee wanting in what I think it my duty to represent to the king. . . ." Then in a postscript he has some pertinent remarks to make on the division of the spoils. Everybody agrees England shall have what Dutch ships she wants but not territorial gains which, it is feared, would give her too much influence. "I don't know but methinks if good ships may be had for the asking," is Sidney's sage comment, "I can't see what is more likely to strengthen the king or make him terrible to all his neighbours perhaps much more than places that may be taken from him in halfe a yeare considering what a neighbour he is like to have to them." If—that is—the King of France's demands are acceded to by the Dutch.[45]

Meanwhile negotiations were going forward secretly with the Dutch representatives. Nevertheless, Godolphin believed that all was agreed and that King Louis would be back in Paris within a month.[46] Three days later, Godolphin, informed by Pomponne that Louis XIV has dictated his terms, asked about Charles II's share. "I ask'd him," he recorded, "if he knew any thing of their intentions concerning their Fleet, and he said that Mr. de Groot had told him it was not intended that it should come in at all."[47] At this unsatisfactory stage in the negotiations, Lord Arlington arrived in France as Ambassador Extraordinary.[48]

In Arlington's ambassadorial train came a certain Sir Gabriel Sylvius, a Provençal who had long been in the service of the Orange family at The Hague. On the death of the Princess of Orange, Charles II's sister, Sylvius had come to England, and during the second Dutch war had been employed by Arlington as a secret agent. For this he was ideally suited, for he had many friends in the Orange party and could move freely about the United Provinces without creating suspicion. More recently he had gained the friendship and the confidence of his patron, the Secretary of State. What more natural than that he should be selected to accompany Lord Arlington on his mission to the Continent in the summer of 1672? The task assigned to Sylvius was to try to persuade the Prince of Orange that further resistance was futile. Inevitably he found the redoubtable William unwilling to listen. He would sooner perish than accept the peace terms, unless they were sensibly modified.[49] Sylvius subsequently returned to London bringing with him various offers from Orange, but these were no better received.

At about the time of Arlington's arrival in France, Godolphin heard from Henry Coventry, the new Secretary of State, of the report current in England that the French King had issued an edict that such of the inhabitants of the unruly province of Utrecht who do not forthwith return to their homes should have them razed. He was instructed to seek an audience with Louis to plead the cause of certain persons who had done Charles II "signall service . . . in his father's and his own Reigne."[50] Later in July Godolphin reported that Louis was leaving for Paris within two days,[51] and early in August he was in Paris himself. Here his friend Lord Sunderland met him and was alarmed at his appearance. "I found Mr. Godolphin heere who is yet very ill," he wrote, "and so that I thinke some staye in France necessary to recover him. It is not my owne interest which makes me say this but seeing him so extreamly weake that he is in danger without greate care and some rest."[52] But however ill he may be, duty called; and on August 9th, Sidney was received by King Louis at St. Germain. On the following day he reported none too optimistically of his audience.[53] But that seems to have taxed his strength to the limit. On August 12th, he recorded that he was on the morrow taking leave of the King, and then, ". . . shall have nothing to do but live very regularly for one fortnight or 3 weeks and afterwards I hope I shall bee well enough to come into England ..." meanwhile "I can not find any body here that will buy either a horse or a mule and next to making an equipage 'tis ye hardest thing in the world to be rid of one."[54] And again four days later, "I am yett but in very little better condition to make a journey than when I saw your Lordship. I hope a little rest and this good aire will att last overcome my distimper."[55]

In mid-September he was in correspondence with Arlington about books to furnish his library at Euston.[56] A week later he is advising Arlington that Colbert's library was being sold and that perhaps Oxford University would be interested. "As to your Lordship's owne books," he adds, "I have sent away one chest this morning to Calais and another I am promis'd shall bee ready by Wednesday next . . ." when ". . . I have directed they shall remayne till my lady Sunderland comes, and then bee put aboard her yacht which tis not impossible but I may see done my selfe. . . ."[57] But Sidney was pining for England: partly no doubt for Margaret, but also it seems for the pleasures of Newmarket, where he was to find his chief recreation for the rest of his life. "Mr. Godolphin has so greate a mind to be at Newmarket," wrote Sunderland in October, "that if it would onely have venter'd his Life, he would certainley have gone from hence a fortnight agoe, but he was at last perswaded to drinke the Waters of Forges, which agree so well with him I hope he will soone recover."[58] At length, on October 31st, he was pronounced well enough to embark on Lady Sunderland's yacht,[59] together with the books for the library at Euston.[60]

Whilst Sidney on the Continent was struggling against ill-health, Margaret at home was forming a resolution of the greatest importance—to quit the frivolities of the Court and in some secure retreat to devote her life to prayer and meditation. She had an old friend in Christian* Berkeley,

* Or perhaps Christina or Christiana.

wife of Lord Berkeley of Stratton, a cousin of Sidney's mother, the late Lady Godolphin. In 1668 Berkeley had purchased Twickenham Park, and had built a palatial pile fronting Piccadilly, which he named Berkeley House.[61] It was to a wing of this vast palace that Margaret Blagge betook herself in January 1672.[62] Here and at Twickenham she wrestled with herself for the rival claims of marriage and the cloister. The faithful Evelyn, anxious, so he tells us, to rescue her from her morbid thoughts, suggested a protracted visit to her sister, Lady Yarborough, in Yorkshire, but this, it seems, subsequently had the effect of turning her mind towards retirement at Hereford, there to live under the direction of worthy Dean Benson, who had long been her spiritual father.

The fierce struggle being waged within the poor girl's soul was fearful indeed. "The Lord help me," she wrote to her friend, "I know not what to determine: Sometimes, I think One thing; sometimes another: One day, I think it lesse Exemplary; and that the maried-state has more Opportunitys of exercising Works of Charity: And then again, That 'tis full of solitude and Worldlynesse: So as what I shall do, I know not:…"[63] And again: "Much afflicted, and in greate Agony was yr poore Friend this day, to Think of the Love of the Holy Jesus; and yet be so little able to make him any Returne: For, with what Fervour have I protested, against all Affection to the Things of this World! Resign'd them all without Exception; when the first moment I am Tried, I shrink away, and am Passionately fond of the Creature and Forgetfull of the Creator: This, when I consider'd, I fell on my knees, and with many Teares beg'd of God to Assist me with his Grace, and Banish from me all Concernes but Heavenly things, and wholy, possesse my Heart himselfe.…"[64] Evelyn, according to his own account, begged her earnestly to marry.* To his pleadings she replied from the Berkeleys' house at Twickenham, "Your Advise I like," she wrote, "and all you say on both Subjects; yet am still where I was; Wishing to Live *alone*, as a Thing most suitable to my humour, and the neerest Way to Heaven: Nor can yo blame one so weake as I am, to Choose that Path which will soonest bring me to my Journeys-End."[65] And so the struggle continued. Sometimes she was in London, sometimes in the country. From Evelyn's *Diary* we gather that he took her down to Twickenham Park on August

* This, be it noted, is according to Evelyn's own record in his *Life of Mrs. Godolphin*. We must not, however, lose sight of the fact that Evelyn wrote this for two persons only, for Lady Sylvius (the former Anne Howard) and for Sidney Godolphin; it was, therefore, to some extent written as a justification of the strange part he played in the friendship. Mr. W. G. Hiscock, working on the Evelyn papers now at Christ Church, Oxford, disputes Evelyn's chronology and gives a very different slant to the affair, which is much less favourable to Evelyn. Hiscock, *John Evelyn and Mrs. Godolphin, passim.*

26th, 1673; but she was certainly back at Berkeley House by the third week of September. So matters continued with little change until late in 1674, when something happened as unwished for as unexpected: she was summoned back to Court. A masque was to be acted before the King and Queen in which the princesses and the ladies in attendance were to appear. From this the ex-Maid of Honour could not be excluded: she was by far the best and most popular amateur actress in the royal circle. The King and the Duke of York laid their commands upon her. There was no refusing. So Margaret Blagge returned to Whitehall.

There was one advantage gained by Margaret's reappearance in London, for her lover could now see her regularly. During her stay at Twickenham, he had paid her constant visits but they only served to increase her mental confusion. "He came often to Visite her, and *that* broke her Heart:" wrote Evelyn. "If he abstain'd from Coming, she was still uneasy; and so she determined to leave the Berkeleys' house and was only dissuaded by the entreaties of her hostess." Thus it was not until the production of the play that Margaret made good her escape from her country retreat and returned to the Capital.

The play or masque to be performed by the Court ladies was entitled "Calisto: or the Chaste Nymph," and had been specially written by John Crowne, a young dramatist with little to his credit but three indifferent tragedies. The chief parts of Calisto and Nyphe were taken by the Duke of York's two daughters, whilst Margaret Blagge played that of Diana. Lady Anne Fitzroy, King Charles's eldest daughter by Lady Castlemaine and already at fourteen the wife of Lord Sussex, played Juno: whilst others taking part were Henrietta Wentworth, the future tragic mistress of the Duke of Monmouth, Sarah Jennings, soon to be the wife of John Churchill and one day Duchess of Marlborough, Lady Derby, Lady Pembroke, Lady Katherine Herbert, Carey Fraizer, Sir Alexander Fraizer's daughter, and Katherine Fitzgerald of Dromana. * In addition to the amateurs, professional players and singers were drawn from the public theatres, the Chapel Royal, and the King's Private Music.[66]

It seems that performances of the masque were given on Shrove Monday and Tuesday February 15th and 16th, and that at least one further representation was given the following June. John Evelyn reports having seen performances of the pastoral the previous December, but he must either have mistaken his dates or have attended dress rehearsals.[67] What a pity that the

* Readers of my *The House of Pitt* will be interested to recall that Katherine Fitzgerald, by her marriage to Edward Villiers, son of Viscount Grandison, became the mother of that Harriet Villiers who married Governor Pitt's son Robert. Robert and Harriet Pitt subsequently became the parents of the great Earl of Chatham.

garrulous Pepys was not present to give us an eye-witness's impression of the proceedings; what a pity, too, that we cannot be quite sure of the exact dates of all the performances.[68]   One thing, however, is sure; on May 16th, 1675, between the earlier and the later presentations of the masque, Sidney Godolphin and Margaret Blagge at the Temple Church in the city of London became man and wife.[69]

CHAPTER III

DEATH OF A SAINT

THE ceremony at the Temple Church was simple and secret. Lady Berkeley of Stratton was present; but, apart from Margaret's personal maid, Beck, it is not sure that there were any other guests. The Evelyns were certainly not informed and did not hear of the marriage for some time; nevertheless, two days later they were invited by the bride to a "colation", at which Margaret's sister, Lady Yarborough, and voluble Nanny Howard were also present.[1] A few days afterwards Margaret and her friends with Lady Berkely paid a return visit to Mr. and Mrs. Evelyn at Sayes Court.[2]

For some time yet the secret was kept and the young couple did not live together as husband and wife. Within a few months of her marriage Margaret Godolphin left England in the train of Lord Berkeley of Stratton, sent as Ambassador on a mission to France. At one time, curiously enough, it was thought that Sidney was to be the envoy, but rumour had it that at the last moment the King had changed his mind.[3] For once report spoke truly, and Lord Berkeley was duly appointed Ambassador Extraordinary to the Court of France: and at the urgent insistence of his wife, Margaret Godolphin arranged to accompany them to the French capital. Towards the end of June she visited Mr. and Mrs. Evelyn at Sayes Court, where she brought a Power of Attorney to enable him to look after her affairs during her absence abroad. Yet the Evelyns still knew nothing of the marriage.

Early in July, Evelyn, in blissful ignorance, wrote a truly remarkable letter to his wife on their relations with this saintly friend. "My deare," he wrote, "I set down my Friend and yr child (for so I pray you now esteem her with me), at my L. Sunderlands and went directly to Whitehall. I believe she is sincerely yours, and being so, you have the greatest jewell in the world, and at my heart I am glad you love her, for indeed she will make you love God, and our blessed Saviour above all things in this world, and so more and more indeare you to me: She shew'd me a little present you made her, which I find she tooke kindly, and I thanke you for it, 'twas a signe of yr love: I dare say she speakes her heart when she tells me the value she has for you, and askes me *why I would have a friend, who have so good a wife*: But you know (and so I have told her) that you yr selfe were the cause of it;

if you call to mind how incessantly you desir'd me to be acquainted with her, I say, *her in particular,* and propheticaly, and often told me, I should thank you for her, and so I do a thousand times, for the greate good which my soule has received from her piety, prudence, example and prayers both for me, and for you, and which I am sure she continues: she is now yours in spirit and the bond of friendship as she is mine, and how can I be happier, for if (as you pronounce) there were never two more alike in our way, and inclination, if it is possible you should long converse together, but you must contract something of that which in her resembles me, and so of necessity I must love you more, since resemblance is the motive of all affection; Be but like her, and you are perfect; make her like you, and she will be so; you both want something of each other, and I of you both; and I hope in God we shall all be the better for one another, and that this threefold cord shall never be broken . . . pray let the day you visite my friend be *Tuesday* next, which is as it were consecrated by us, not for idle conversation, but to pray, or reade, or discourse of holy things; and if you will put up a supplication together, I know you will both remember the absent, who never forgets either of you continualy (*sic*) : The Lord Jesus blesse you: you will likely find her at home immediately after Dinner, or about 11 in the morning if she be not at Twicknam. . . ."[4] Did ever a man of fifty-five write a more extraordinary letter to his wife ? Mrs. Evelyn, it is true, had encouraged the friendship. But what, one wonders, were her feelings on receiving this strange epistle from her lord !

Lord Berkeley's departure for Paris was delayed by an unforeseeable accident; he was seized with an apoplectic fit in the gallery of Whitehall.[5] Before his seizure, Berkeley had put all his affairs in Evelyn's hands, which responsibility his friend only accepted ". . . upon the great importunity of my *Lady* and Mrs. *Godolphin* to whom I could refuse nothing. . . ."[6]

At length, the Ambassador recovered, and on November 10th, he set out for Paris. Evelyn met the party with his coach at New Cross, for his son was of his Excellency's party, because Evelyn knew he would be safe in Margaret's charge. "Thus we set out 2 Coaches, 3 Wagons, and about 40 horses besides my Coach :"[7] So the cavalcade went by easy stages to the coast. At Canterbury, Margaret and Evelyn attended prayers in the Cathedral. At Dover, the party was joined by Frances Jennings, recently married to Sir George Hamilton, "a Spritefull young Lady," as Evelyn tells us, who was immensely popular with the Berkeley family.[8] Here too Mrs. Godolphin delivered to Evelyn her will, "which her *Husband* had given her leave to make, and absolutely to dispose of all her fortune, which was in value better than 4000 pounds . . . and so I parted with my Lord, my sonn, and the person in the world whom I esteemed as my owne life, Mrs. Godolphin;

28

being under saile, the Castle gave them 17 gunns, and Cap: *Gunman* answered with 11. Hence I went to Church to beg a blessing on their Voyage."⁹ On the evening of December 7th, "after a long and chargable iorny", the Ambassadorial party arrived in the capital; whereupon his Excellency announced his arrival to Pomponne. But "until my equipage be made I can have no publike audience: I suppose a private one will be obtayned upon my first intimation." To which announcement Berkeley added, ". . . I thank God I recovered much of my strength in my iorny, and eat and drink and sleepe as well as I ever did."¹⁰ The arrival of the party was witnessed by Sidney's elder brother, Charles, who wrote home to William that ". . . Berkeley was waited on yesterday by at least 4 score coaches with six horses, my coz. Nell not up soone enough to make one in that solemn cavalcade though she had her share of the magnificent treate which was prepar'd for you at St. Albans."¹¹

In Paris, the fame of Margaret's wit and beauty seems to have preceded her, and Louis XIV himself sent her a pressing invitation to visit him at St. Germain; but she would have nothing to do with the splendid vanity of his Court. Throughout the winter she remained in Paris, shunning all gaiety and acting as companion to her close friend the wife of the Ambassador. "I have seen nothing sens I cam to Paris but the hous I lye on, and shops which I thinke I live in, for I have hardly bin ever out of one sens I cam, not upon my own account I assure you:" she told Evelyn. Then she gave him news of his son John. "I have just bought your son a new suit of cloths, very gentil and fin, and today we begin to learn french together: he is to learn to dance also, which truly I thinke is very necessary for him: he is a very good husband of his mony and of his time, and I hope you will not repent his coming hither: he talks much more than he usd to doe, and is very chearfull as ever I knew any youth in my life, and as inosently merey as 'tis possable for anybody to be: we are to learn arithmaticke, in fin we entend to grow very wise: . . ." But when Evelyn expatiates on Godolphin's virtues in order to test her reactions, Margaret becomes "wary and evasive." "As for S(idney) being good," she writes, "I dout it not, as for his being worthy of me I believe him not only that, but worthy of anybody."¹²

Soon Margaret's services were needed to comfort the Berkeleys, for they were stricken with a family bereavement. "I have lost one of my greatest delights in this world my 3d sonne Maurice," wrote a sorrowing father early in the new year, "which hath sufficiently weaned me from the world: God grant me the spiritt of patience that I may beare it as I ought to doe."¹³ No doubt the faithful Margaret played her part in comforting the mourning family.

Early in the New Year, when the Berkeleys were due to depart for

Nimeguen for the treaty negotiations there,* Margaret made this her excuse for returning home. Escorted by Bernard Grenville,† on his way back from Italy, where he had served as an Envoy Extraordinary to the Duchess of Savoy, she reached Dover early in April, sadly missed, it seems, by the junior members of the Ambassadorial party. "Dear Grandfather," wrote young Evelyn, "I most humbly thank you for your kind letter, it came to me just before my Pretty Pious Pearly governess left me whose departure makes this place cease to be either Athens or anything else but a very melancholy abode to me, now my Minerva is gone I am as desolate as the Owl that used to sit on her Temple and almost in as great a Passion as Archilles for the losse of Briseis...."[14] Berkeley House being closed, Margaret went to stay with a relative in Covent Garden, and there she remained for several months. On April 6th, Mr. Evelyn welcomed Margaret home and on the 10th, she, Lady Sunderland, and the sisters, Dorothy Graham and Anne Howard, dined with him. Four nights later he dined at Lady Sunderland's, when Margaret Godolphin was of the party.[15] Not till April 26th does Evelyn disclose that the secret of the marriage has been given to him by the feckless Lady Yarborough.[16] He was clearly hurt, for he ". . . expostulated with her (Margaret) about the concealment, and was satisfied it was not her intention,"[17] Some ten days later Evelyn's son returned from France—to his intense satisfaction "for my deare friend Mrs. *Godolphin* coming thence I had no desire he should stay there any longer for many reasons."[18]

Now that the Evelyns knew of the match, rumours were beginning to spread, and on April 25th we find Jael Boscawen reporting a talk she had had with "Mrs. Blague," whom she attended "at half an hour after nine and made discoveries that has increased our familiarity, but you are not to make much reply to this nor imagine by it a marriage for I don't think tis soe yet...."[19] It was not, however, until towards the end of June 1676 that the Godolphins at last publicly proclaimed their marriage and went to reside together in Berkeley House.

It was about this time that the young couple purchased an apartment in Scotland Yard, ". . . just over against his Majesties *Wood-yard* : by the *Thames* side, leading to Scotland yard. . . ." This Evelyn helped the young couple to prepare for occupation. He and Margaret went to Lambeth to choose marble fireplaces and to inspect looking-glasses at the Duke of Buckingham's glass works. But Evelyn's help was not alone sufficient and they also enlisted the services of the eminent Robert Hooke.[20] In September and October, whilst her husband was at Newmarket in attendance on the King, Margaret visited the Evelyns at Sayes Court : and it was not until the

* As a matter of fact they did not leave Paris for several months.

† He was a groom of the bedchamber to Charles II.

Berkeleys return to England in the summer of 1677 that Sidney and Margaret at last took up residence in their own home. What a perfect picture does the diarist paint of the saintly young bride in the autumn of that year. "Lord says she . . . When I this Day consider'd my Hapynesse, in having so perfect Health of Body, Cherefullnesse of Mind: No disturbance from without, no griefe within: My Tyme my owne, my House quiet, Sweete and Pretty:[21] All manner of Conveniency for Serving God in Public and Private, How hapy in my *Friends, Husband, Relations, Servants; Credit;* and none to Waite on or attend in; but my deare and beloved God, from whom I receive all this! What a *Mealting Joy* ran thro' me, at the thought of all these mercys! and how did I think my selfe Oblig'd to go to the foote of my Redeemer and Acknowledge my own unworthynesse of his Favours! But then, what Words was I to make-use of? Truely at first, of none at all; but a devout Silence did Speake for me:—But after that, I pour'd forth my Prayers, and was in amazement, that there should be such a Sin as Ingratitude in the World; and that any should Neglect this greate Duty: But, why, do I say all this to you my Friend? Truly out of that *aboundance* of the *Heart, the Mouth Speaketh* and I am so full of it, that it cannot forbeare expressing my Thoughts to you."[22] And a few months later: "I thank *Almighty God,*" she wrote, "who has been so Infinitely gratious to me this yeare: For he has brought me back into my owne native Country in Safty and honourably: Prospered me in my Temporal Affaires, above my Expectation: Continu'd my Health, and my Friends: Deliver'd me from the Torment of suspense: Given me an *Husband,* that above all men—living, I Value: In short, I have *little to wish,* but a *Child;* and to Contribute something to my *Friends* hapynesse (which I most Impatiently desire) and then I must think, before I can tell what I would have more than I Injoy in this World; but the Continuance of a Thankful heart to my God."[23] To be a mother was what she longed for: and anxious lest that should not be, she took in a "poore Orphan-Girle," whom she tended and loved as a natural parent. Her profound wish was soon to be granted her, but, as we shall shortly see, with tragic results.

Meanwhile, the young husband had frequently to leave his wife for his Court duties. "My deare," he wrote to Margaret from Windsor, "I am just come hither and would not neglect to tell you soe because you desir'd it, I hope the post is not gone: if my Lady Sunderland comes or send to you in the morning pray lett her know that if she has any letters here, I will take care to send them to her; if you love me my deare, take care of your selfe, I will see you if it please God the Latter end of the weeke."* And to handsome Harry Sidney, he wrote at about the same time: "I know not why I give you the trouble of a letter from hence, unless it bee either to lett you see my own dulnesse, or else to convince you that other places have their share of itt as the Hague. . . ."[24]

Early in the following year, Godolphin had once more to set out for the Continent. In January, 1678, he went as Envoy Extraordinary to the Duke of Villa-Hermosa, governor of the Spanish Netherlands,† to demand that Ostend, which in French hands would exclude the possibility of our sending aid directly to Flanders, should as a precautionary measure be put into English hands until such time as peace should be concluded.[25] Two days later, about noon, he landed at Ostend. At Bruges bad news greeted him; he had taken two and a half days in his journey from London, and now he was informed that it would take him as long again to travel from Bruges to Brussels.[26]

At Godolphin's first interview with the Duke of Villa-Hermosa the envoy stated the proposal of Charles II to send over and maintain in Flanders a force of 12,000 men, horse, foot and dragoons, and also to send garrisons of 2,000 men each to Nieuport and Ostend, on condition that Ostend should be handed over for the duration of the war as a base for his supplies. The Duke demurred to this, and as an alternative suggested Nieuport; just as suitable, he maintained, and more in need of protection. Godolphin denied this, for Nieuport was suitable only for small boats and not even the yacht "Charles", in which he had sailed from England, could enter the harbour. So "there was but our no against his yea," as Godolphin put it. After further fruitless discussions it was settled that he should return next day to learn the duke's decision,‡ when Villa-Hermosa maintained that he had no authority to agree to his proposition with regard to Ostend. Of this the English envoy not unnaturally expressed incredulity; but the duke per-

---

* Godolphin to Margaret Godolphin, "Windsor 9 a'clock at night. (August, 1677)" Addressed, "For Mrs. Godolphin att her lodgings in Scotland Yard, Whitehall." Evelyn MSS., Christ Church, Oxford.

† Whence he reported to Henry Coventry, the Secretary of State, "From on board his Maj[ties]. yatch ye Charles neare Gravesend Friday 4 a clock." (January 21st. 1678). Endorsed by Coventry, "Mr. Godolphin. From on board the Charles yacht." Coventry Papers at Longleat, XLII, 293.

‡ An Account of the discourse yt passed between his Ex[ty] the D: de Villa Hermosa and me at ye first Audience I had of him att Bruxelles upon ye 15/25 of Jan: 1677/8." Coventry Papers at Longleat, LXIII, f. 41.

sisted that so it was, and thus, after further haggling, the conference broke down. So Godolphin demanded his passport and took his leave.*

In February Godolphin set forth again. This time his mission was to the Prince of Orange's headquarters in Flanders, where he was given the quality of Envoy Extraordinary.[27] On his way to the Prince, Godolphin was, through Laurence Hyde, our Ambassador in Holland, to demand an interview with Pensionary Fagel, and to refer to English reports of the serious condition of the Dutch forces in face of "the French King's falling into fflanders and sitting down before Ghent." At the same time the envoy was to explain the difficulties that Charles was labouring under with his Parliament, "from whence our supplyes come," to impress upon the sceptical Fagel that the ways of Parliament "are in their nature slow, and not capable of being brought so soon to effect, and that therefore we have not been able to do all wee would." At the same time he was to be careful to give the Dutch hope that more substantial aid could soon be expected.[28]

On the afternoon of March 6th, Godolphin arrived at Harwich[29] but was delayed by contrary winds.[30] During the passage he composed an account of his journey[31] and two days later announced his safe arrival at The Hague. Here he saw the Pensionary who enlarged upon his and the Prince's despair of sufficient aid coming from the allies and their longing for a speedy peace.[32] Sir Joseph Williamson wrote from London to assure Sidney that the King was making every effort to raise and equip his troops. But he had to admit that delay was being caused by the ill humour of the House of Commons. Yet in spite of all these difficulties the King is determined to proceed with all possible vigour, though Williamson admits that "things look very awkwardly here. I mean in the ill humour of the House of Commons since you left us."[33] Never has an Ambassador been given clearer instructions to walk the tight-rope than was Sidney Godolphin in the spring of 1678!

About the Middle of March, the envoy left hurriedly for Antwerp,[34] near which he had a meeting with the Prince.[35] That astute statesman of course saw clearly enough the horns of poor Sidney's dilemma and he stated with force and clarity that whilst he welcomed his Uncle's preparations, they were so dilatory and his own position was so grave that he saw small hope of saving the rest of Flanders. The alternatives, therefore, were clear; peace if it could be obtained; if not, an all-out war which ". . . might bring the ffrench to more reason." For the sake of peace, William thought that both the Spaniards and the States would agree that Tournai and Valenciennes should remain in French hands, and he requested Godolphin to

* "An account of ye discourse yt pass'd between his Ex^cy ye Duke of Villa Hermosa and me in ye 2d Audience I had of him at Bruxelles upon ye 16/26 of Jan: 1677/8." Coventry Papers at Longleat, LXIII, f. 43.

tell Charles that peace would be acceptable on these terms.[36]   Accordingly
Sidney hastened home to see the King.*   A few weeks later Godolphin
returned to The Hague.   On the evening of May 2nd, he and the Ambassador, Laurence Hyde, called upon the Pensionary, Van Beuninghen, to
whom they stressed the two main points of their instructions: that there
should be no separate peace and that trade should be prohibited with France.
The Pensioner agreed that these demands were reasonable, but pleaded that
his country was reduced to so dire a state of poverty that it was utterly
impossible for them to comply, a theme on which he enlarged with some
eloquence.   They had promised to send twenty ships to the Channel; but no
more than twelve or fifteen ships in all could be provided, and these were
needed for the security of the North Sea: therefore the safeguarding of the
Channel must be the sole responsibility of England.   From these embar-
rassing topics Godolphin and Hyde reverted to the two points they had
specifically raised, about which the cautious Dutchman became vague and
non-committal, only saying that they contemplated sending an Ambassador
to England to explain their difficulties to King Charles.   This evasive
answer was obviously unsatisfactory, and Godolphin and Hyde, whilst
welcoming the proposal to send an envoy to London, emphasized the
importance of Charles II receiving from his allies some definite statement on
the subject of war and peace.

From the Pensioner they betook themselves to the Prince, who was, or
affected to be, in a hurry to depart for the Assembly.   He spoke even more
vaguely than Van Beuninghen but to much the same effect.   That night at a
dinner given by Laurence Hyde to the Prince of Orange, William told them
that, contrary to his wish or expectation, the Assembly had determined to
dispatch the Burgomaster of Leyden, one of their most respected citizens,
to make formal request to King Charles that he would consent to the French
conditions of peace.   The Dutch, thought the Prince, were really not convinced that the English were averse to the peace; therefore he advised that
the King should leave him in no doubt that he would not agree to the terms.
Then, when the Dutch were convinced of this, they would apply themselves to making good their alliance.   In that case, asked Godolphin and
Hyde significantly, what assistance at sea and on land could England expect
from the States?   At sea, replied Orange, for protection of the Channel,
nothing at all; for protection of the North Sea, a squadron of small craft
and their fleet in the Mediterranean.   On land, further retrenchment was
inevitable, as already they were unable to pay their troops.   As to not
trading with France, the Prince did not think the States would agree to the

---

* His departure was so hurried that he missed his post. Hyde to Thynne.
"Hague, March ye 19/29, 1667/8." Coventry Papers at Longleat, XLI, ff. 335-6.

English requirement, and it would therefore be up to King Charles to compel this by seizing or sinking any Dutch ship that the navy might encounter. And what about the making of a separate peace? To this awkward question William returned an evasive reply, and though the envoys continued to press in Godolphin's words for a "positive answer or, indeed, any answer at all," they were not successful in extracting anything further from the cautious prince.*

The next day Orange left for Breda, and thence to Boome where Godolphin planned to join him six days after their abortive conference.[37] In spite of the lack of success, however, negotiations continued throughout the month of May and much of June, and a steady stream of joint dispatches from Godolphin and the Ambassador was sent home to Secretary Williamson.[38] But both men were heartily sick of their task, and Godolphin was suffering from his eyes, as Hyde told Thynne.[39] His health and anxiety for his young wife and her unborn child caused him to yearn for home, and he bombarded his friend Thynne with frantic appeals to secure his release. "I should scarcely be sorry for (almost) an occasion that would deliver me from being employ'd in any businesse here abroad . . . so that I assure you as troublesome and as angry as the Parl: is at this time I would rather be there than here. . . ."[40]

Towards the end of May, the Prince of Orange was induced to defer his departure from the Hague to the headquarters of the Dutch Army by rumours from Nimeguen that King Louis had expressed his willingness for a month's cessation of hostilities.[41] Meanwhile, there was talk of a general peace,[42] which, as Godolphin told Thynne, "I can tell you without the help of a Conjuror . . . will be receiv'd here with all the joy imaginable. . . ."[43] This disgusted Godolphin. "If the Generall peace bee made at last upon these shamefull conditions," he wrote to his friend, "what will become of us all I can't imagine, but I'me sure I'll come home if I can, and that's the only good I expect from it," and much more in that vein.[44] No wonder that, holding such views, he should be anxious to return. In the middle of June, he hears from Thynne that he will speak for him to the Duke of York: Godolphin is profusely grateful,[45] and three days later he assures his friend that he is anxiously awaiting a yacht in which he hopes to embark.[46] Towards the end of June, Laurence Hyde departs with many promises to do all he can for Sidney:[47] nevertheless the very next day the impatient Godolphin assures Thynne that he will continue to pester him until he is home.

* This is taken from the copy of Godolphin's official dispatch, endorsed, "Mr. Godolphin's account of his Discourse with the P. of Orange, May 3d 78. S.N." Hyde sent a copy to Thynne, "Hague, April ye 26th/May ye 6th 1678." Coventry Papers at Longleat, XLI, ff. 376-9, 382.

"Send for me therefore quickly if either you love your owne quiett or have any kindnesse for yrs. most faithfully S. Godolphin."[48] At last, a fortnight later, he is able to write joyfully of his release and is profuse in his thanks both to Coventry and Thynne for their help in having made this possible. Meanwhile, negotiations for the peace have been proceeding. "They are going to bee good boys here again I assure you," writes Sidney light-heartedly, "and if you would but clap their cheeks and stroake them a little no body knows what might come on't. . . ." But the States are still debating the matter, and Godolphin adds that he will stay till after the next day in the expectation of being able to give the King an account of what is at last resolved in the Assembly.[49]

And so at last Sidney Godolphin is enabled to sail for England. There can be no doubt that, though weary and disgusted with his fruitless mission, anxiety about his wife and unborn child made him doubly anxious to return. He had left Margaret in Thynne's charge, and was often sending her messages through the medium of his friend. "I hope you will excuse me to your charge that I doe not write to her till next post;" he writes in one letter, "tis late and I am sleepy already and I have yett to write the Coppy of this letter which you will find when you turn the Leafe."[50] "I dare hardly venture to lett your charge know," he writes on another occasion, "how much she is oblig'd to your care in acquainting me my letter came so late to her that I was not to expect any Answer of it till the next post. Soe many good offices may at last for ought I know produce ill consequences."[51] And on at least one occasion he writes half banteringly to Thynne of the obligations and duties of the absent husband: "For quietness sake & to avoyd all quarrels, I give you this trouble, which has no businesse at all but to give cover to the inclosed & to make you a Witnesse how I may pretend fairly to bee as good a husband in Absence as the best of them all; It may service too convince you yett more if it were needful what a terrible thing marriage is when a husband is obliged to such strict duty even while he is from his wife, but if I am not mistaken you are pretty well grounded in that faith as to this matter, & neither my good precepts nor my ill example will be able to adde much to your confirmation; all I desire of you, is that if I were able to counsell you in any thing, you would always believe I would advise you for the best as being ever your most faithfull humble servt. S. Godolphin."*

To his sisters, however, he showed a somewhat different mood. Writ-

* Godolphin, "For Mr. Thynne at Mr. Secretary Coventry's office in Whitehall, Hague, June 10/May ye 31, 1678." Coventry Papers at Longleat, XLI, f. 470. In her edition of Evelyn's *Mrs. Godolphin* Miss Harriet Sampson prints this letter but misdates it 1698 and quotes it as possible evidence of a second marriage (p. 377). But the original MS. at Longleat is clearly dated 1678.

ing to Anne, he sent greetings to Charles and Jael; and he begs for news "of what passes in the Parliament as to my coming back again."[52] And on Anne's birthday he writes to assure her how much he values her letters, for, as he assures her, "I am not soe agreeable entertained in this place, but that I have need of all the comfort my friends can send me out of England."[53] "I'me in an ill humour* you must know..." he adds, "or else I would not have shute my self upp to write at a time when the princesse and all her ladys are at play and just going to supper in the house, if I would take the paines to goe out amongst them, perhaps I might have some stories that would make you amends for your news; quarrells there were innumerable last weeke but Whitsontide ('Tis to be hop'd) has put an end to them...." To his brother-in-law's enquiry for news of the prospects of peace, he writes that nothing can be expected until the Dutch envoy sent to the French King to beg a cessation of arms has reached his destination...." Then he concludes bitterly: "Sure you are all mad in England, is it possible else that all sides could conspire to bee soe fatally in the wrong? forgive me this start, deare sister, indeed I am both troubled and asham'd for my Country. Yrs. most affectionately S.G."[54] A few weeks later there is sad news from home: the Boscawens' little boy is seriously ill. His condition is serious, "Yet Goddards droppes have done wonderful cures upon children of his age, and even upon men and women, in his particular disease of sharp humours and payne in the stomach..." he tells Jael. But he bids her take comfort from "the satisfaction of seeing your friends as much concern'd as if it were their owne, and I hope you will believe none of them can bee more particularly sensible of your troubles than, my deare Sisters most truly affectionate Servt S.G."[55]

These were the letters of a home-sick exile. Nevertheless, he improved on his enforced absence at the Hague by becoming more intimately acquainted with Prince William of Orange. That acquaintanceship, as we shall see, was to stand him in good stead in the years to come.

Sidney landed at Harwich on June 24th and hastened to London. A month later he purchased the office of Master of the King's Robes, thus substantially improving his financial position. On reaching Whitehall he found Margaret well advanced in her pregnancy. Yet her thoughts as always were for others. Only a few months previously she had forwarded the marriage of dear Nanny Howard with the now well-established Sir Gabriel Sylvius. On account of the disparity in their ages† there had been much opposition to the match, but the diplomatic zeal of Mr. Evelyn had

* Because of some scene between Lady Sylvius and his wife.

† Sylvius was over forty years old, Nan Howard about twenty-one.

been pressed into service to help to overcome these difficulties. "My friend *Mrs. Godolphin* (who exceedingly loved the young Lady) was most industrious about it, out of pity to the languishing Knight!" records the diarist.[56] Their united efforts were successful. At last all difficulties were overcome, and they were married in Henry VII's Chapel by the Bishop of Rochester.

And now Margaret was awaiting the fulfilment of her dearest wish: yet she had a vague morbid sensibility that she would not survive the adventure. On August 4th Mr. and Mrs. Evelyn dined with her in Scotland Yard. They found her well but strangely solemn and she admitted that she had been sorting her papers. There was a strange chill over the conversation. "When often wishing that she might (if so it pleas'd God) bring her *Husband One Child* (and leave him that Pledge of her intire Affection), she seem'd to *thirst* after nothing *more*, than to be with God; and verily, the estimate she took of these poore Satisfactions here; when I have sometimes reflected on yᵉ circumstances of her Youth and Chereful Temper (with the Prospect of as much worldly felicity as she could desire) I have extreamly wonder'd at her *Indifference*, not to say *Contempt* of it: Finding likewise, that it did not proceede from any Peevish discontent, or singularity of humour, but from a true *Philosophical, Wise, and Pious* Consideration of the vicissitude, and Instability of all Earthly fruitions; and an ardent Longing after that Glorious State where, (Says she) I shall be perfectly at Repose, and *Sinn no more. . . .*"[57] Margaret's time of delivery was now at hand. On May 16th, the anniversary of her wedding she dined with the Evelyns, when Sir Gabriel and the newly-wedded Lady Sylvius and her sister, now the wife of Colonel James Graham, were of the party. That, Evelyn records in his diary "was the last time that blessed Creature came to my house, now being also greate with Child, and seldome stirring abroad."[58] And a few weeks later she went with Evelyn to see Ashmole's library at Lambeth. This was her last outing,[59] for a few weeks later—on Tuesday September 3rd—her child was born.

That day Evelyn had called to see Margaret, though his Tuesday visits had been less frequent of late; and hearing that she was in labour and her husband absent at Windsor, had remained in the house. About an hour later the joyful news was brought to him that a boy had been born. He was shown the infant, and then very shortly was privileged to see the mother. "I hope," whispered Margaret to her friend, "I hope you have given thanks to God for his infinite mercy to me." Two days later the child was christened Francis."[60]

On the Sunday following, Mr. and Mrs. Evelyn were at morning service in their church at Deptford, when towards the end of the sermon an alarming note was handed to them. "my poore *wife* is fallen very ill of a *Feavor*, with lightness in her head & ravings: you know who says the effectual fervent prayer of a righteous man evayleth much, & the prayer of faith shall save the sick: I humbly beg your charitable prayers for this poore creature, and your distracted servant S.G. Lond: 9 a Clock——"[61]. Evelyn and his wife of course hastened with all possible dispatch to Whitehall to find the young mother delirious.

On the following day Evelyn wrote to an uncertain correspondent a detailed and heart-rending account of those terrible last hours. Portions of the letter can still be seen among his family papers. ". . . we were every moment expecting when this blessed one should expire . . ." he wrote. "So soon as you were gon, she fell . . . into one of her deliriums. Dr. Lower & Short being (with) her; yet prescribing nothing save Cordials, so soone as they had well examin'd the breaking forth of those pimples, which as yet had only invaded her neck to some degree. I staid 'till about nine o'clock when she seem'd to take some repose; but just as I was going into bed (about 11) was sent for to talke with Dr. Chamberlaine, who (upon yr recomendation) was call'd for; but he finding none of the Doctors there, and seeing now all her back very full of those uprisings, would by no meanes direct, without some other doctor, tho otherwise (being fully perswaded the midwife (to whom I perceiv'd he was no friend) had left something behind that might be the cause of these malignant vapours) he would have don something. Upon this, I sent for Dr. Needham (our Friend) both the other absolutely refusing to come out of their beds, it being now neere two o clock: The good Doc^r came, rising out of a Sweate, but when he had seene the poor Creature, was altogether averse from ordering any kind of thing, the malignancy of the distemper being (as he says) so high and dangerous; or indeed they were both agreed that there was no safe medling; whatever they should prescribe for one thing, being so repugnant to other accidents; so as besides a *Frontal* of Red rose cake Vinegar and Nutmeg;* they would direct no more; but leaving her to God's mercy, intended to call againe this morning at eleven a clock: In this Interim the two first physitians (Lower and Short) appear and find not onely all her back downe to ye wast, but all her breast to the navil exceedingly inflam'd with those pimples, as thick and fiery as you can possibly imagine, the pidgeons being changed, and blisters (which run abundantly) dress'd they are likewise departed without any thing at all don, but with purpose to meete Dr. Needham and Chamberlaine at the houre appointed. In this Interim, the poor Lady has after very small . . . restlesse . . . accesses of raving . . . convulsion, that one may heare her cry . . . to the farther part of Whitehall, as

* A preparation to be applied to the forehead in an attempt to reduce the fever.

far as a . . . of this nature is capable: so as it grieves our very hearts to be heare, and yet without great strength and company there is no keeping her in the bed: when she is out of these she sinks into a profound silence, and wonderfull patience, feable pulse, scarce perceptible; and in one of these, I feare she will go away: so as I can see my small hopes from any Crisis, but rather that she grows worse and worse."

Meanwhile, what of the husband? "The poore man," writes Evelyn, "being allmost dead with griefe, and lying for the most part flat on the boards, which he drowned with his teares, begs of me to stay; for that he is not able to speake to the physitians, and is allmost beside himselfe; I have mony for their Fees and have already given Dr. Needham and Chamb: each 2 guinnys: and now at the 3d consultation (which I presume will be the last) we shall see their utmost resolution: the Case I find being desperate: My Lady Mordaunt has send *Dr. Fabers aurum potabile*; but none of these Methodist physitians value it, nor will advise it; not withstanding Mr. Godolphin has sent to parsons Green for the doctor who makes it; and who, it seems is there. Dr. Ridgley (whom they much rely upon) being out of Towne: I have not been in bed at all since Saturday; but find my selfe very well in health, I blesse God: I am affraid I shall conclude this letter with the newes, who write it by snatches, being continualy call'd away upon some occasion or other; the rest being so tired out. . . ." There then follows much on his grief and on the vanities of this world. He is waiting for the doctors to pronounce their final verdict on the case.

"And so (as I feared)" he continues, "The physitians (physitians of no value) they came, but it was too late; she was now raging afresh; and with that impetuosity that the good man himselfe, no longer able to heare or brave it; with the silence tho (I cannot say) consent of the doctors, gave way that the famous (I must now call it something else) *Aurum* potabile, was given her; The Apothecurie in the meane time sent home, with a prescription of theires, wh was onely a forme, and to signifie they confess'd little; Imediately after she had taken 2 or 3 sponefulls o the Aurum, her raging, and convulsion abated; she wept abundantly, and thence falling into the Agonies of death, departed this miserable life, and is now an Angel in Heaven:* my teares suffer me to say no more, you will think it is because I truely cannot say enough to describe a losse, that is not to be express'd; for I am in sorrow unspeakable."

Evelyn now gives a distressing account of poor Sidney and his family.

---

* The cause of death was undoubtedly *puerperal sepsis* caused by the use of inadequate antiseptics. As in this letter, the acute Mrs. Evelyn also laid the blame on the midwife, and in this was probably justified. Evelyn, *Mrs. Godolphin*, 76. Evelyn, *Diary*, September 8th, 9th, 1678. IV, 148-50.

"And now here is another sceane that would draw pity from the heart; to behold the disconsolate, shall I say the miserablest man in the world; her Husband, with whose miserable Comforters, his brothers and sisters, none of them able to beare up against this torrent; the consequences of wh: are so distracting, that there is no Creature in the House who either gos about any thing, of I thinke minds what is necessary to be don; either with the corps, of the poor child, or any thing else: . . ." Some of the rest of this sad document is lost or indecipherable: it ends thus : "The Lord Jesus blesse us all, and ah that I were where my Friend is, for she is hapy; her part is finished. At 4 in yᵉ Afternoone: She departed just at halfe a houre after one." *

Thus it was that all the arrangements were left in Evelyn's hands. "The Fees to the Physitians, the intire Care of her funeral was wholly comitted to me," he records, "so as having closed the Eyes, and drop'd a teare upon the Cheake of my blessed Saint, Lovely in death and like an Angel, I caused her Corps to be embalmed, and wrap'd in Lead with a plate of Brass sothered on it, with an *Inscription* and other Circumstances due to her worth, with as much diligence and care as my grieved heart would permitt me; being so full of sorrow and tir'd with it, that retiring home for two daies I spent it in solitude, and sad reflections:" At her special request they carried her to Godolphin to be laid with her husband's ancestors. On the 17th they set forth, ". . . an herse with 6 horses, and two other Coaches of as many, and with about 30 people of her relations and servants. . . ." Evelyn himself "waited on the companie as far as *Hounslow* heath, with a sad heart," but "was oblig'd to returne upon some indispensable affaires:"[62] This seems strange, but may have been due to Evelyn's anxiety to retrieve his letters to Margaret before Godolphin should read them. If that is so, he was doomed to disappointment; not one of his letters came to light. What was found amongst her effects was a sealed packet which she directed to be burnt unopened. We can only conjecture what that packet contained, but may it not well have been the missing Evelyn letters or perhaps six of her letters to Evelyn that she had recovered from him shortly before her marriage and had resolutely declined to return?[63]

So the sad cortege went on its long journey to Cornwall without Evelyn. "The Corps," he tells us, "was ordered to be taken out of the *hearse*, and decently placed in the house with tapers about it, and her servants attending, every night during all the way to the foote of Cornwall, neare 300 miles, and then as honourably interred in the Parish Church of Godolphin."[64] The poor sorrowing husband was so stricken with grief that he was quite incapble

* Evelyn to uncertain correspondent. Parts are missing and much faded. It is endorsed, "From Mr. E. Monday the 9th Septr. 78." Evelyn MSS., Christ Church, Oxford. Mr. W. G. Hiscock states that the letter was addressed to Mrs. Evelyn.

able of making the long journey. A few weeks later, when he had regained sufficiently from the shock, he left London and followed his wife's body to Godolphin, where he remained alone with his thoughts and near his beloved's grave, until the following January. And there we must take leave of him for a while and intrude no more upon his grief.

Margaret had left with her sister-in-law, Jael Boscawen, a last letter to be given to her husband in the event of her death. This Jael had recently handed to her brother. Nearly three hundred years have rolled by since the words were written; yet even today we can scarce read them without emotion.

"My Deare," [she wrote]

"Not knowing how God Almighty may deale wth me, I think it my best Course to Settle my Affaires: So, as that in Case I be to leave this World, no Earthly thing may take up my thoughts:— In the first Place, my Deare, Believe me; That of all Earthly—things, you were and are the most deare to me; and I am Convinc'd that no body ever had a better, or half so good an Husband:— I Begg y^r Pardon for all my Imperfections, which I am sensible were many; but such as I could help, I did endeavor to subdue, that they might not trouble you: For those Defects which I could not rectifie in my selfe, was want of Judgment in the management of my Family and House-hold Affaires (which I owne my-selfe to be very defective in) I hope y^r good nature will Excuse, and not remember to my disadvantage when I am gon: I aske y^r Pardon of the Vanity of my humour, and my being oftener Melancholy and *Splenetick* more than I had Cause to be: I was allways asham'd of my selfe, when I was so, and sorry for it, and I hope it will come into the number of those faults which I could not help—Now, my Deare, *God b'uy*; Pray—*God Blesse you,* and keepe you his *Faithfull Servant for Ever*: In *him be all y^r* Joy and delight, satisfaction and Comfort; and do not Grieve too-much for me; since I hope I shall be Happy, being very-much Resigned to God's Will, and leaving this world with (I hope in *Christ*-Jesus) a good Conscience:

Now, my deare, (if you please) permit me to Ask-leave to Bestow a *Legacy,* or two amongst my *Friends and Servants:*—In the first place, (if it might be) I could wish when the *Child* I go with, grows of a fit bignesse, it might be either with my sister *Boscawen,* or my Sister *Pen*:* for I know they will be carefull of its *better-part*; which is the Chiefe thing I am Concern'd about. In the next place, I desire you will give B— an hundred-pounds; the use of which (being six po–'d a yeare) she may live at her Fathers house upon, if she will. For I feare she will scarce get any-body to beare with her want of good Service, as I have don: For my *mayd* (if she do not Marry) I

---

* Her sisters-in-law, Jael Boscawen and Penelope Godolphin.

MARGARET BLAGGE
AFTERWARDS MRS. GODOLPHIN
From the portrait by Mary Beale at Berkeley Castle

hope she will be kept to looke-after my Child, when it comes from Nurse :—
In the meane time you will give her Board Wages: For my two Footemen,
I hope you will get them places as soon as you can and—however, if ye be
not disposed to keepe them; you will give them at parting Ten-pound, a
piece:—I desire you will give my *sisters,* my share of the *Queens Lease:
fifty-pounds a yeare:* It is betweene them two, my un-married ones I meane)
and to my Cousin Sarah an hundred pounds in Mony. To my *Lady
Sylvius* my greate-Diamond Ring &c—

Now, my Deare, I have don : If you please to pay-out about an hundred-
pounds more in *Rings* for your *Five Sisters* (to Remember me by) I know
nothing more I have to desire of you, but that you will sometimes think of
me with kindness ; but never with too much griefe :

For my Funeral, I desire there may be no Cost bestow'd upon it at all,
But (if I might) I would begg, that my Body might Lie, where I have had
such a mind to go my selfe, (at *Godolphin*) among your Friends : I believe, if
I were caryed by Sea, The Expense would not be very greate. But I don't
Insist upon that Place, if you think it not reasonable : Lay me where you
please.

Pray my deare, be *kind* to that poore-Child I leave behind, for *my sake,*
who *Loved you so* well. But I neede not bid you, I know you will be so :—
If you should think fit to marry again : I humbly beg, that little Fortune I
brought, may be first settl'd upon my Child, and that as long as any of your
sisters Live (if they permitt) you will let it live with them ; For it may be,
tho' *you* will love it, my Successor may not be so fond of it, as They I am
sure will be :

Now my Deare Child, Fare-well

The Peace of God which passeth all Understanding, keepe your heart
and mind in the Knowledge and Love of God, and of his Sonn *Jesus Christ*
our Lord : and the *Blessing of God Almighty,* The *Father,* the *Sonn* and the
Holy-Ghost, be with Thee, and remain with *Thee* Ever and Ever, Amen."[65]

CHAPTER IV

THE WIDOWER

EXACTLY thirteen days after Margaret's death and before he left London for Godolphin, the bereaved husband wrote a pathetic letter in reply to an epistle of condolence from his friend.

"Deare Mr. Evelyn," [he wrote] " (for I hardly yett dare call you by that name which you had so much better bestowed) 'tis the desire of my soule to become more worthy of itt & the greatest consolation my condition is capable off, to see you soe desirous of my friendship & soe kind & good natur'd to promise me yours. A thousand things crowd into my mind to say to you, where shall I begin? most naturally, with my owne Interest; I lay hold them (to the greate joy & Comfort of my spirit) of the promise of your friendship & kindnesse; I lay hold of it in the manner you offer it to me, I desire to fill the place that she held with you & O if it were the will of the Almighty that I might doe it worthyly. I promise you mine most faithfully and inviolably as long as I live, & I will keepe your Letter for ever as the pledge of your constant friendship to mee. I will remember you constantly in my prayers; I must forget to pray when I forgett you, or her who (with your assistance & God Almighty's Grace, continually working with her) has taught me all that I know of God, & made such impression of my duty as any Soule, as I hope by the grace of God I shall always preserve there, especially now the Almighty has putt it into your heart soe kindly to offer me your assistance for the cultivating of them; 'tis that which I want, 'tis that which I would have wish'd of all earthly things, & if you will believe the first profession of your friend, I look upon your letter as a beame of God Almighty's countenance, & an earnest of his future care & protection of me; Remember then that from henceforth I look upon you as the Depository of all my concerns spirituall & temporall, to be wholly guided & directed by you in the former, to have always great regard to your opinion in the latter. And now you see I have putt you just in the place of her that I have Lost, Oh Losse! never to bee enough by me lamented, never to bee supplyd on this side Heaven, my heart has been divided, & almost rent between the submission that I owe to God Almighty, & the ease that I seeke (& for the present perhaps should find) in giving the rein to my griefe: & at those times when I strive to suppress it, there comes one thought very often into mind, which I confesse to you troubles mee; 'tis an apprehension I have least my sense of this losse (how great soever) will bee worne out by Time, as wee see all impressions of this nature are in most people; I have no patience to think it shall be soe; I am almost at an end of my paper & of my time, but nott of my matter: I must Contract; The worke which you meditate . . ." (writing an account of Margaret's life) "I doe not dislike, I commend it, I would not restraine you from the satisfaction & the entertainment of it: I would not bar my selfe the profitt & the delight of itt; but by no means let it goe farther, I conjure you, at least for the present, you & I will debate the matter when wee meet, in the meane while I hope I shall heare of you some-times, pray God blesse you & yours."[1]

"Oh Losse . . . never to bee supplyd on this side Heaven . . ." Poor Sidney's sense of his loss was never destined to be "worne out by Time," though rumours to the contrary were soon rife. "Mr. Godolphin, I be-lieve, will best like your saying nothing to him on the subject," cautioned Lady Sunderland to Henry Sidney, "for I dare swear there nether is nor will be any such thing as his marriage."[2] And so it was to prove. Sidney was never to find anyone to take his Margaret's place.

Having written his letter to Evelyn, Godolphin set out on his long, sad journey to distant Cornwall, there to remain alone with his grief until early in the following year. But even there family sorrows pursued him in the midst of his mourning. We hear no more of the Boscawen boy's illness, but soon Jael's daughter, Margaret, is causing anxiety.* "I pray God send her well and my deare sister much comfort of her," wrote Godolphin, "but if his will should be otherwise you have had too many letters of late to heed that I should preach patience and resignation to you." His other two sisters were with him, it seems. "Mrs. Katherine has been sick a little more than ordinary all this day, and yesterday Mrs. Anne and your humble servant very much . . . Pray, deare Sister," he concludes, "if any of the Exeter stage Coachmen will carry it hither lett George send me 6 quart bottles of my clarett wine to meet us at Exeter or 8 or 10 if they can carry so many. . . ." And again later, "Tis more comfort to me than I expected to find by yours of Sept. the 28th that the poor Little Peggie is still

---

* There is some doubt whether Margaret was in fact Jael and Edward Boscawen's child, as there is no record of a daughter of theirs having died at this time. I am grateful to Viscount Falmouth for the information that the Boscawens had a number of nephews and nieces, the children of Edward's younger brother Hugh, all but one of whom died young. One of their children was named Margaret and as she was born in 1665 she was about thirteen at this time. It may be, therefore, as Lord Falmouth suggests, that this is the child, living with her uncle and aunt, who is referred to.

alive, as long as there is life one may hope, especially in the Case of little children; my unworthy prayers for her and you, my deare Sister, shall never want:" But death stalks the Godolphins. "my last told you my Sister Katherine had been ill more than ordinary a day or 2, that very night she fell into convulsions, and the next day she died. . . ." Then he turns to other topics. "I don't know what questions you would aske concerning my coach but I can think but of one Caution to give which is that (in case the same man makes it) it may not have a hollow roofe as yours has, but flatter a top which if it bee high enough will give it a better shape. I hope by the time you have this Letter there may have been some more money receiv'd, and when you have it, I wish you would pay it away. . . . I left a great many bills behind me and would be glad to find them fewer when I come to you, which I hope will bee by the 19th. . . ."³

But in spite of these distractions, there is business to be attended to: the lodgings in Scotland Yard, where he and Margaret had found their brief period of happiness together, must be disposed of. His brother-in-law, Edward Boscawen, was attending to such matters for him. "I doe owne Mrs. Buckley has my first engagement if wee agree upon the termes," Sidney told him, "which you know is always necessary to a bargaine, and indeed I don't think it very likely I should agree either with her or Mr. Felton for them, because there are some obligations which I lie under concerning those lodgings which neither of them know of, and when they doe hear them, I doubt they will bee a little startled, and yett I can not consent to part with the Lodgings unless they that buy them of mee oblige themselves to pay the same rent that I have always before and since I built them to 2 people that had an interest in 2 roomes upon which I built; so much as this you may please tell Mrs. Stuart and when I come to town I will explayn the matter more at large to her. . . ." Then he closes with an affectionate message to his sister. "Deare Sister," he writes, "Excuse my last, I am very glad your poore little girl is yett alive, I hope in God she will recover, I wish you heartily all manner of comfort in this world."⁴ But this hope was not to be realized. "I have had no opportunity before, since I knew it to condole with you for the Losse of your pretty Little girle," wrote Sidney a week later, "I am sorry for her with all my heart, I assure you and the more for that I had hopes she would have recovered after having kept alive soe long: God almighty is able to send us Comforts equall to those he takes from us, if he sees it fitt, but tis better not to have our portion is this life; people are too apt in prosperity to forgett to whom they own it."⁵

Amidst these family distractions, at least one from the great world in London wrote to the lonely mourner in distant Cornwall, for soon Sidney's old friend, Thynne, sought to rally the sorrowing widower. "I see it is not possible for me to goe soe far as to bee out of the reach of your kindnesse to me;" came the reply, "though it bee not well bestowed in all sense, in one I may be bold to say it is, for no body living values more the markes of your remembrance and friendship than I doe, nor is gladder to be remembered by those whom I love and esteeme as I doe you;"—and what more natural, for had not his beloved Margaret been left in his friend's charge? the friend who now, it appears, had written to bid him amidst all his affliction to be of good cheer and return to public life anew—"for the advise it were well for me I think if I needed itt but my own temper which you mistake is sufficiently of proofe agaynst all melancholly impressions how reasonable soever, and I ought to be asham'd of letting you see when I come to town agayn how little I have been wrought upon by soe great a Cause of affliction as you very well know I have had." Brave words! But he had been more "wrought upon" than perhaps he knew. "The parlmt being putt off till the 21th [sic] I will endeavour to bee in town against that time . . . . if any letter for me comes accidentally to your hands, if you please to keep it, I shall have it sooner that way than by any others."[6]

Yet in spite of this promise it was not until January of the following year that Sidney returned to London. On the 14th Evelyn dined with him, "now newly return'd from the funeral of his deare wife, which he follow'd after some daies of its setting forth from *London* he being then not able to (have) accompanied (it) on the way, for very griefe."[7] It was to a very strange world that Godolphin returned from his mourning when he left the peace of distant Cornwall for the turmoil of the Capital—the turmoil of the Popish plot.

A few weeks earlier, the Sunderlands had returned from Paris, and it was natural enough that amid the confused welter of events, Sidney should look for guidance to his slightly senior and much more experienced mentor. Through the influence of this friend, Godolphin was soon appointed a Lord of the Treasury.[8] A few months later Sunderland's influence was to be exhibited in a still more remarkable manner. After the failure of the King's attempt to govern through a reconstituted council of some thirty members, which was soon found to be far too large and unwieldy to fulfil its functions with efficiency, a kind of inner Cabinet was speedily formed to transact the business of the State. The members of this Cabinet were Sunderland, his brother-in-law Halifax, Essex, son of the noble Capel who had died for the cause of Charles I, Lord Chancellor Finch, Henry Coventry, and Sir William Temple. In June, Halifax, Essex and Sunderland, the three most influential members of the Cabinet, took a momentous step. Genuinely alarmed alike at the rising influence of Monmouth and the pretensions of York, they turned their eyes in the direction of William of Orange. Accordingly, they sent over to The Hague as envoy Sunderland's engaging uncle, Henry Sidney, for the express purpose of making a treaty of alliance with Holland, and with secret instructions to invite William to England.[9] Godolphin, consulted by his friends, enthusiastically supported the plan.

Thus matters stood, in August 1679, when the King suddenly became ill. Soon everything was in confusion and wild rumours of poison were flying around. Godolphin was with the King at Windsor.* "God bee thanked, he is now pretty well," he wrote towards the end of August, "he has missed his fitt last night and slept very well, but he is weake still, having taken but little nourishment, now for a week together; it was an intermitting feaver that he had, which is a disease that reigns mightily at this time; I think the worst that is to bee feared now, is that it may perhaps turn to a lingering ague, some days afore that was the best hoped; he sitts up yett but very little, the Doctors are of opinion that he should goe to London when he has gotten strength enough to brave the journey; but the King is yett averse to that;"[10] Nevertheless, the public alarm was not unjustified, for it was soon apparent that the intriguing Shaftesbury was seizing the opportunity of Charles's illness and James's exile to thrust forward the Duke of Monmouth as heir to the Throne. Drastic action was clearly necessary. Thus driven fast by events, the three members of the inner Cabinet came to a swift resolve; they summoned Godolphin and Hyde to a secret conclave in the Duchess of Portsmouth's lodgings in Whitehall, where, after prolonged discussion, it was unanimously decided that James must be instantly recalled from Brussels.[11] So an anxious and imperative message was dispatched to the exile; and at the same time it was emphasized that the journey must appear spontaneous. James required no urging, and in a very few days, before anybody knew what was afoot, he waited on the King at Windsor Castle.†

But already the invalid had recovered and he received his brother with well-simulated surprise. Though James played his part by assuming full responsibility for his sudden appearance, this turn of events put the ministers in a quandary and they anxiously pressed upon the King the urgent necessity of sending the Duke of York about his business. Charles, nothing loth,

* Earlier in the month he had been detained in London by a fit of illness of his small son, which was sufficiently severe, it seems, for Evelyn to hurry up to see him. Evelyn, *Diary*, August 1st, 1679, IV, 178. By August 6th, however, he had recovered and was then staying with his uncle and aunts, Sir William, Anne and Penelope Godolphin in Suffolk Street. Evelyn, *Diary*, August 6th, 1679, IV, 179. September 3rd, 1679 would be the child's first birthday.

† For the French Ambassador's account of the Duke's sudden arrival at Windsor Castle see Barillon to Louis XIV, "Windsor, 19 Septembre, 1679." Archives of French Foreign Office. Campana de Cavelli, *Dernier Stuarts*, I, 295.

made it plain to his brother that once more he must retire to the Continent. But if the King's brother must be exiled, so in fairness must his illegitimate son, the popular Monmouth. Thus is the genius of the wily Sunderland demonstrated. A bargain is struck, and at one stroke the country is rid of both dangerous rivals; the thrusts that rid the country of these men were shrewd indeed.

In Holland the exiled Monmouth was received with kindness by the Prince of Orange, who, however, was careful to make it plain that he could not befriend an aspirant to the throne.[12] Orange's position was now clear. According to Henry Sidney, the monarchy was doomed unless William interposed to save it; on hearing which view, the dour prince remarked acidly that he did not expect his father-in-law to succeed to the throne, and that he, William, would not be averse from stepping into James's shoes.[13] He would, he declared, advise the King at all costs to come to some agreement with the Parliament, and would recommend the passing of an Act to exclude all Roman Catholics from succeeding to the Throne.[14] No advice could have been more distasteful to King Charles, who was above all anxious to be free of Parliament. Accordingly, the Whig triumph at the General Election of 1679 gave him his chance. The time for concession was ended. Against the advice of all his most timorous counsellors, he promptly prorogued the newly elected Parliament and then proceeded to adjourn both Houses by successive stages for a full year. The cultured Temple, disgusted at the latest turn of events, retired with relief to his nectarines at Sheen; Trimmer Halifax, ever a lover of moderation, was no less thankful to lay down office and seek the peace and quiet of his beloved Rufford; whilst melancholy Essex within a few months sought relaxation from the cares of state amidst his books and fish ponds at stately Cashiobury. So Sunderland, deserted by his colleagues, turned for aid to those same two men whose advice he had sought at the time of the King's illness earlier in the year; and Godolphin and Hyde joined him to form a triumvirate of comparatively young men soon to be dubbed with the contemptuous nickname of "The Chits", by a witty and satirical poet of the day.

Thus Sidney Godolphin, hitherto the holder of only minor Court offices, emerges at last into the full glare of public life as the friend and colleague of the brilliant, mercurial Sunderland. How the courtier turned politician acquitted himself in these new surroundings we shall shortly see.

The association of Sidney Godolphin with Lord Sunderland is often condemned; and nearly every writer on this period has been careful to remind his readers of the malign influence exercised by the leader of "the Chits" on the public men of his day. But to take that view of the happenings of 1679 is in fact to anticipate events, for there is no evidence whatever to show that the Sunderlands were looked upon askance by their contemporaries at that time; indeed there is evidence directly to the contrary. The pious Evelyn writes with respect, even with regard, of both the husband and the wife, and often records the hospitality that Mrs. Evelyn and he had dispensed to them or enjoyed at their hands.[15] And now he rejoices at Sidney's advancement. "My dearest Friend," he wrote in December 1679, "You employ all your moments, and dispose of your Selfe so profitably to the benefit of the public that I cannot regret the infinite losse I have lately made by being depriv'd of the most sensible effects of that indear'd Friendship I once enjoy'd, without envying the felicity of one that is now in Heaven, and injuring one of the best and most usefull men upon Earth, should I trouble you with my Impertinences but halfe to offer, as I think of you, and that blessed Saint. . . ."* And again some two years later, "That deare Lady was wont to tell me she came not to know you of a long time after you were intirely hers; because she daily discovered new excellences in you: How should I then not desire to partake somewhat of them, and after what you have declar'd to me, how can you refuse me? But you are, perpetually in public businesse, and I am glad you are so, because you are else too much *Soule*, that is (according to De Cartes) in continual *Thought*, which is prejudicial to you; and this would I have by any means diverted, tho at the price of suffering my Impertinencies. . . ." Some censorious folk, it seems, did not approve of the frequent visits the rising statesman was paying to Newmarket. "Tis, I assure you, on this account," continued Evelyn, "that I often justifie all your other Recreations (which some are pleas'd to judge less favourably of) because I am assur'd you preserve your heart intirely to God: give him as much of your time as you can, and often think of that blessed saint, who allways pray's you might do so. . . ."[16]

Furthermore, we have already seen something of the constant friendship displayed towards the Sunderlands by Margaret Blagge; and it is probably thanks to her and the Evelyns that Sidney first became acquainted with the much maligned pair. Can it be seriously suggested that a person of Evelyn's sensibility or Margaret's piety would have associated with people whose

---

* Evelyn to Godolphin, "Says Court, 17 Decr. 1679." Evelyn Letter Book (1678–97), p. 5. This letter book, which was formerly at Wotton and is now in the library of Christ Church, Oxford, with other Evelyn papers, has the heading in Evelyn's hand: "I did not enter any of these Lett^rs (or what are copyed in two other volumes), with the least intention to make them public, but for my owne satisfaction, and to look now and then back upon what has past in my privat concerns and conversations: many of them being Impertinancys and therefore may be dispos'd of as my Heirs think fit. J. Evelyn. 15 Novr. 99." Unfortunately, the other two volumes above referred to have not been found.

reputations were as black as those of the Sunderlands have been represented
to posterity? There is no doubt, of course, that for some years before 1679
both Sunderland and his wife had been paying assiduous court to the Duchess
of Portsmouth. Now that, according to twentieth century standards, may
well be regrettable; but in the seventeenth century to many people around
the throne the only approach to the Sovereign, the only avenue for advancement, was through the graces of the favourite. To some this may have
seemed undesirable, but those who were too sensitive to avail themselves
of this means of pushing their fortunes had their remedy—to quit the Court
and to retire into private life. Is Sunderland to be blamed if at this period of
crisis and danger, he remained at his post, and if in order to carry on his
work effectively he sought the powerful aid of an admittedly undesirable
woman? Are Godolphin and Hyde to be censored if they answered the
minister's appeal to meet him in the Duchess of Portsmouth's apartments,
there to concert measures for the safety and well-being of the State?

With what a terrible alternative were these men faced in the event of the
King's death, the choice between a Protestant bastard and a Catholic bigot!
Faced with this dilemma, the Chits took the only course that seemed open
to them. After much hesitation and uncertainty, they made their choice
by determining that they must secretly support the exclusionists; indeed,
Godolphin is reported by Barrillon to have expressed the view in the fateful
autumn of 1680 that if the Duke of York did not leave the country promptly,
both he and his brother would be compelled to go within a fortnight.[17]
At the same time, "the Chits," anxious to have a foot firmly planted in the
other camp, were careful through Henry Sidney at the Hague to cultivate
relations with the Prince of Orange, with whom all three Ministers, Sunderland, Godolphin and Hyde, were on friendly terms. And if anyone be
found to condemn the Ministers for playing a double game, let him put himself in the shoes of these young and inexperienced men living in troublous
times.* Thus "the Chits" took their precautions, and even as they did so,
the potential danger of the situation was exposed for all to see; the exiled
Monmouth suddenly returned to England without having obtained permission from his father.

Parliament stood prorogued, and petitions for its recall poured in thick
and fast. But these only served to provoke counter-addresses declaring
abhorrence of the activities of the petitioners. All the nation was divided
into petitioners and abhorrers. "You must needs hear of the abominable
disorders amongst us," wrote Sunderland's mother to her brother, Henry
Sidney, "calling all the women whores and the men rogues in the play-
houses—throwing candles and links—calling Lord Sunderland traitor, but

* They were all three under forty at this date.

in good company; the Duke rascal; and all ended in 'God bless his Highness the Duke of Monmouth. We will be for him against the world.'"[18] In the midst of this confusion and at the very time that his ministers were striving for an alliance with Holland, the wily Charles was privately importuning the French Ambassador for financial assistance, so as to render him independent of his Parliament. "He begged me for the love of God—that is the phrase the King made use of—to represent to your Majesty that it was in your power to relieve him of his embarrassments;" wrote Barrillon to Louis, "that you must heed him, and not think that he wishes to fail you when he takes new engagement. . . . The King of England said to me, 'Let us say no more about the past, let us think of the future. I beg the King my brother to make up his mind and not to be restrained by the fact of my not being able at this moment to be very useful to him. But if he will put me in a state of showing my gratitude to him, no one will be more attached to his interests.'"[19]

Meanwhile, the persevering "Chits", forcing on negotiations with Holland, dispatched Ministers to Denmark and the German Protestant Courts with a view to forming an alliance hostile to France; and Godolphin wrote from Newmarket in the King's name to Henry Coventry, the Secretary of State, requiring him to direct our envoy to notify the Duchess of Savoy of his Majesty's interest in the preservation of peace, and warning her not to do anything likely to disturb it.[20] Coventry thought the alarm unjustified. "Wee are all here in great calme," he replied, "and this end of the towne hath lesse people and less noyse then Newmarkett. I wish you good weather, and quick returne, and then I shall hope to take the ayre."[21] But there was to be no quick return. The King and Godolphin remained at Newmarket throughout March,[22] and only on the 28th did Sidney write to the Secretary of State instructing him that Charles would have the Council meet on the following Wednesday at 4 o'clock.[23]

Early in March, Monmouth had a secret interview with his father, and was reconciled to him. This caused dismay in Holland, which Godolphin did his best to allay. ". . . the Duke's return I find has given alarm in Holland, as it did here, but I hope a little time will undeceive the world in that matter, and satisfie their people and ours that it is not like to cause any alterations in the measures which the King had resolved upon, and in which he seems every day more and more confirmed . . ." Then he adds prudently, ". . . pray make my most humble excuse to the Prince that I doe not write to him by this post, there is noe need that I should trouble him, for I know he will have an account from all hands that everything here goes on to his satisfaction."[24] But Godolphin's efforts were not successful, and soon ugly stories were afoot to the effect that Monmouth's parents had been married, and that a mysterious black box would supply the needed proofs. Though no black box was forthcoming, Charles ultimately saw fit to publish a declaration denying before God that he had ever been married to any woman other than his queen.

On June 26th Shaftesbury, accompanied by fourteen followers, went to Westminister Hall to present James to the Grand Jury as a Popish Recusant and the Duchess of Portsmouth as a "common nuisance." Now Halifax, who had for some years been living in retirement at his beloved Rufford, was suddenly galvanized into action by the policy of Shaftesbury and the Whigs. So the illustrious Trimmer came forth from his retreat as the doughty champion of the Tory doctrine of Divine Right of Kings. The Exclusion debates were in effect a bitter contest between Shaftesbury, Sunderland and Essex against Halifax, and it was mainly due to the brilliant debating qualities of the Trimmer that the Bill was immediately rejected in the Lords. As a result, Sunderland and other prominent exclusionists were struck off the Council.[25] Thenceforth there was only bitter enmity between the brothers-in-law, and Sunderland's one thought was to recover his place.

Meanwhile in the Commons the attack was aimed at Halifax. Enraged at the verdict of the Lords, the lower House turned on their foes and voted an address to the King for the removal of Lord Halifax from his person and councils for ever. Sidney Godolphin was so moved by the intransigence of the Commons that he broke his habitual silence in the House to voice the view that as the good or ill success of the Parliament was of the highest consequence the debate should be discontinued.[26] In any case the fury of the Commons was of no avail, for the Lords and the King were against them. In consequence, only one exalted victim, poor old Lord Stafford, fell a prey to their malevolence.

Within a few weeks of the fall of Sunderland, the King struck a mortal blow at Shaftesbury by moving Parliament from Westminister to Oxford; and, when it was clear that they were bent on exclusion, he hastily sent members about their business. The wily King had been too much for Shaftesbury and the Exclusionists, and how he had enjoyed his triumph! Henceforth, thanks to the generosity of Louis XIV, he would rule without the pernicious aid of a factious parliament. A secret meeting with the French Ambassador in the Queen's bedroom had made this possible. Nothing was put in writing and no receipts were needed, for Louis knew his man; so when the King of England left his wife's apartment he was a pensioner of France, the French King having promised the payment of £400,000 within the next three years. Of these negotiations Shaftesbury and the Parliament were ignorant. A few months later the King followed up his advantage. On July 2nd, Shaftesbury was suddenly arrested on a charge of high treason and, though very ill, was lodged in the Tower. He was soon released however, the jury refusing to bring in a true bill; but though scarce more than middle-aged, he was worn out by faction and by a painful disease. He fled to Holland, and there he died in the house of a burgher of Amsterdam.

From all the obscure intrigues of this time, Godolphin kept himself aloof. At the fall of his friend Sunderland he did not lose the favour of his Sovereign, though one malevolent observer wished he would. "My Lord Sunderland and Mr. Godolphin did as treacherously desert the Duke's interest and underhand countenance it as much as they durst," wrote James in his Memoirs, "and, therefore, when the King declared his resolution in Council likewise to endeavour its being thrown out at the first reading in the House of Lords, those two and my Lord Essex opposed it, pretending that though it was not reasonable the Bill should pass as it was, yet in the Committee it might perhaps be modifyd with limitations and turn'd to a temporary banishment or the like, and so much they thought necessary to prevent an utter breach betwixt the King and the Parliament . . ."[27] "I am very glad to find his Majesty continues to be so ill pleased with Lord Sunderland and Lord Essex," wrote York from his Scottish exile to Laurence Hyde. "I think he is much in the right, and I know not why there should be any time lost in putting them both out of their places. And there is a third you have not named; I mean Mr. Godolphin: I think he should keep them company."[28] So far as Sunderland and Essex were concerned, no time had been lost in putting them out of their places. But Godolphin managed to ride out the storm, to retain his place, and within a few years, as we shall see, to receive remarkable promotion.

At the same time he remained on the best of terms with Orange, and when it was suggested that the Prince should cross to England in an effort to overcome the King's natural reluctance to break with France, Godolphin was one of the first people whom William consulted.* "For my part, I have wish'd for it"—the Prince's coming—"a great while," he wrote, "and I think it more necessary now than ever, for I am satisfied there's nothing that can soe infallibly restore that good understanding between the king and your highnesse which is soe necessary for you both, and which every day (to my great trouble) I see more likely to decline, and I am afrayd will be quite lost at last, if your highnesse will not please to make use of all your prudence, and all your temper, (and perhaps some of your adresse too) to prevent this misfortune; thus far Mr. Sidney and I were of a mind." But

* He also consulted Sir William Temple, who set out his views at length. Temple to Orange, "Sheen, June 28th, 1681." Dalrymple, *Memoirs,* I, App. to Part I, Book I, 67.

Godolphin had his own ideas, and was not afraid to voice them. He agreed with the envoy on the desirability of the Prince's visit; he disagreed with him on the pretext that should be given for it. "He seem'd to think it would be best for your highnesse to aske the King's leave that you might come over to wait, upon him, as a visit of complement [*sic*] only without pretending any businesse at all. . . ." But Godolphin preferred a more direct, straightforward approach. "I was of opinion," he wrote, "that it would look a great deale better, and I thought bee more agreeable to your inclination, to speak out plainly upon this occasion, and to write to the King that you found your selfe soe much troubled and concern'd for the dissatisfaction which his Majesty seem'd to have at your proceedings in the business of Mr. Skelton . . ."—Charles's anti-Dutch envoy at The Hague, with whom William had been carrying on something of a feud—". . . and soe apprehensive least any occasion might happen to increase itt, that you could have no satisfaction in your owne mind till you had begg'd his Majesty's leave to come and wayte upon him and endeavour to sett your self right in his good opinion, and if your highness would please to adde to this such assurances of your zeale for the King's service and his greatnesse as you shall think fitt; or your desire to bee acquainted with the measures he proposes to take that you might be able to assist him in them as far as lies in your power; and of your desire likewise to establish a good correspondence with those whom the King is pleased to trust and employ in his businesse; upon these advances to the King I am perswaded your highnesse might come over hither with great advantage, and the Countenance of your kindness which the King will shew you, finding you in this temper. joyn'd to the love and esteeme, and the naturell inclination which people have for you here would presently give your highnesse such an influence upon every body, even ye ministers themselves, that you would bee able to give what turn you pleas'd to most of our affayres here that are of the greatest importance. . . ."[29]

Within a few years he was writing anxiously to William lamenting his unhappy differences with King Charles. ". . . I am extremely and particularly sensible of our general unhappiness from the want of that right understanding between the King and your Highness," he wrote in the spring of 1684, "which is so necessary for both your interests, that I should hope, and most humbly beseech your Highness, that you would never lose any occasion of endeavouring to restore yourself to that kindness and affection which the King is so naturally inclined to have for you. . . . I beg only that you will be pleased to preserve me some small place in your favourable thoughts, which I shall study to deserve on all occasions. . . ."[30]

It has long puzzled historians to explain how Godolphin managed to keep himself aloof from the many intrigues of the day. Poor health seems to have been the main reason. In June, 1684, he was attacked with a fever at Windsor and was extremely ill. On the 27th, his friend Evelyn heard of it; two days later early in the morning he hurried down from London, when he found him very ill. After dinner that day he visited him again and found the patient "now somewhat better."[31] Obviously the crisis had passed; yet a fortnight later, there was still cause for anxiety. "Madame," wrote Evelyn to Jael Boscawen, who was with her brother at Windsor, "Tho I every day sent to Suffolke Street,* and heare that things grow better, yet I am at no ease, 'til I see that good man out of all danger, or (which is next it) that you were come home againe, which 'til you are, gives me apprehensions. . . . I am this day especially and ever day, beseeching God to spare and restore him to us all . . ."[32] Apparently Jael was able to reassure him, for soon we find Evelyn recording the recovery of his friend.[33] Thus Godolphin's illness enabled his friend, Laurence Hyde, the only survivor of "the Chits," to become for a short time perhaps the most prominent man in all England.

Hyde, raised to the peerage as Earl of Rochester, used his undoubted influence to bring about the return of Sunderland to office. This in itself offended some, and none more than the Trimmer. But Rochester's uncertain temper and overbearing demeanour made him many enemies. However, for a time, thanks to the support of Sunderland and the Duchess of Portsmouth, and possibly also to the influence of his brother-in-law, the Duke of York, he managed to ride the storm. But his position was precarious. Consequently, the dismissal of the aged Lord Radnor from the office of President of the Council offered the opportunity for removing the obnoxious Rochester from his post and giving him the dignified and comparatively unimportant office of Lord President. Whereupon, his delighted rival, Halifax, triumphantly declared that he had often heard of a man being kicked downstairs, but never before of one being kicked upstairs.

News of this change of office was conveyed to Rochester by, of all people, his successor, Sidney Godolphin. The choice of his supplanter to write the unwelcome news to the victim was presumably part of the subtle revenge of the King, who was weary of Rochester's somewhat presumptuous support of the dictatorial York. The unhappy Godolphin performed his difficult task with tact and discretion. He permitted himself not the slightest elation at his own advancement. He did not pity his friend and colleague but seemed to assume that the new post was congenial to him. Thus with exquisite urbanity he contrived to suck the poison from his noxious task.

"Not comming to London to-night, as I intended, when I saw you last," he wrote, "I would not deferre to tell you that last night, the King call'd

* To enquire from Sidney's brother and sisters, Sir William, Anne, and Penelope Godolphin.

mee into his Closett and told mee that having lately knowne you had beene for some time uneasy enough with your employment (at) The Treasury, and desirous to leave itt, upon any good occasion, and having a great deall of consideration of your services to him with much to this purpose, that he was resolv'd to make you President of the Counsell and att the same time to putt mee into your place at the Treasury, with many gracious expressions of the trust and confidence he had in mee, he knew very well, he say'd that the place I was in, was of much more advantage and that I must not, nor should not be a looser by this change, but that he thought itt of absolute necessity for his service, and could not think of putting any body but mee into this place; I told him, that if I were at libertie to consider either my advantage, or my inclination, I should most earnestly begge of his Majesty that he would bee pleased to lett mee continue where I was, but in the manner that he spoke of this thing, that I had nothing to doe but submit my selfe entirely to his pleasure with abundance of thanks for his favourable opinion of mee, wch I would still endeavour to deserve to the best of my power. I went this morning to the Duke to acquaint him with what the King had sayd to mee, and my Lord Sunderland was by, the Duke told (me) the King had told him the same thing yesterday evening in the drawing roome, and that hee had spoken to the King upon itt, that my Lord of Clarendon might bee Secretary of State, but that he found the King very averse to itt, yett, he desir'd my Lord of Sunderland to speak to the King of itt to, and he sayd he had already desir'd the same of the D: of Portsmouth, who had promis'd him to doe itt, I did not know this when the King spoke to mee, but he seem'd to mee very much at a Losse for somebody to put into my place, and sayd he could not like any one that had been nam'd to him, or that he could think of himselfe; he ask'd mee my opinion of Dr. Trumbull and of Mr. Blathwaite, and bade mee name such as came into my thoughts, I did not presume to put him in mind of any body but those that have the honour to serve him abroad at this time as my Ld. Preston, Mr. Cundleigh and Mr. Skelton; he seem'd not to like any of them butt to incline more to Mr. Blathwaite than any other that had been nam'd to him, and soe this matter remayn'd today at noone when I left Windsor; My Lord Sunderland made mee promise him to come back again to night, being in greate paine till he sees the King has fix'd upon some body that hee can *live with*, as he calls itt; soe that not being able to come to London my selfe, I hope you will excuse the trouble of this hasty account from

Yr. Lps. most obedient humble serv^t

S. Godolphin."[34]

Thus did Godolphin obtain his first important Government appointment; and at the same time he was raised to the peerage as Lord Godolphin

of Rialton.³⁵ ". . . This comes to congratulate againe the new accumula-
tions of your Merit," wrote his friend Evelyn. "Well I know you affcte
not pompous Titles; *But thus shall it be done to him whom the king will honor,*
and much more, whom God does honor . . . I wish you greate and hearty
and long and solid joy; Some theire Titles honor, *you* your Titles; and so I
reckon, that you do not so much Receive as *do* honor to his Majesty. . . ."
But the sad anniversary, September 9th, on which he was writing must
never be forgotten. ". . . Suffer me then, never to leave you out of my
dearest Thoughts, when I think of★ that saint so deare to you, and to me,
and whose memorie is as fresh, and Losse as sensible, as the most excellent
and most obliging creature can be to the most obliged of men." And lest
he had said too much, he reminded Sidney of "those *Indelible Lines* of a
Letter to me (22 Sep^tr—78) and know not that he had any way forfeited the
place you then gave him in your Heart, instead of Her; which he will never
part with to any living Soule, but to just such another, and so he thinks him
safe, tho he wish you such another with all his heart, that after all this sorrow
and joy, your joy may be full indeede."³⁶

But no sooner had Godolphin received these honours than clouds of
adversity seemed to obscure the sun of his prospects. On the morning of
February 1st, 1685, King Charles was seized with a violent fit of apoplexy.
Five days later he died. To the rising Godolphin, this must have appeared a
cruel blow. At once his future seemed obscure, even dangerous. Evelyn
was quick to see his friend's peril: "What is all this World! What is all the
glory of it! as a Dreame when one awakens, so passes it away, and is gon . . ."
and much more in that strain, which accords very ill, it must be admitted,
with the caustic comments he made in his famous diary on King Charles's
mode of life.† But he was genuinely concerned for Sidney's future.
". . . but sure I am, that besides the public, whatever touches you, adds
sorely to my affliction. As to your particular, I call to mind a little what
once you writ to a friend. . . ." That letter of September, 22nd, 1678 again!
—". . . Remember then, that from hence-forth, I took upon you as the
depository of all my Concernes, spiritual and Temporall, to be wholly
guided and directed by you in the former, to have allways greatt reguard
to your opinion in the latter." His friend, cast down, it seems, by this
latest stroke of ill-fortune, was thought to be contemplating retirement; and
that would never do. '. . . it was because the world tooke notice of yr abilities, and that I thought it your duty (as still I do) and that you may not wast
your selfe in thinking and Melancholy Reflections, when you may do good
in an active station by your Industrie and virtuous Example; this I speake,

★ Over the words "think of" there is written "contemplat."

† See page 3.

fancying that you are meditating a Retreate again, and think of pulling away the shoulder from the wright, after all the abilities, and experience you have acquir'd to be yet farther use-full to the public. . . ."[37] But in spite of these words of encouragement, Sidney's future prospects could not have seemed bright. He had lost a kindly master and a true friend; and what sort of treatment could he and his associates expect from the new Sovereign, the cold, calculating, vengeful York, who with rancour in his soul at the treatment he had received during the late reign now in triumph mounted his brother's throne as King James II?

CHAPTER V

THE GLORIOUS REVOLUTION

WITHIN a quarter of an hour of the death of King Charles, the new Sovereign assembled the Privy Council, and addressed them with some well-chosen words calculated to quieten the natural apprehensions of the nation.   In this he was successful.   His address was received with warm approval and Rochester begged that it might be published.   No record having been taken of the King's exact words, the Solicitor General took them down from memory.   James read over and approved the report.   One day he would repudiate what he had done and ignobly suggest that he had been tricked into strengthening in a permanent form words that he had uttered at a moment of great excitement.

Under such a Sovereign disgrace seemed the certain lot of Godolphin and his fellows.   Judge then of the universal surprise when these opponents of James, so far from being excluded from government, were actually given positions of honour and importance among the great offices of state!   Rochester was made Lord High Treasurer.   His brother Clarendon received the Privy Seal.   Sunderland retained his Secretaryship of State.   Godolphin became Chamberlain to the Queen.   Only Halifax was disappointed by a kick upstairs into the dignified post of Lord President of the Council.   Of these ministers, as Barrillon was quick to report to his Master, Rochester, Sunderland and Godolphin formed an inner cabinet of confidential advisers.[1]   To some the retention of the exclusionists seemed a sign of James's anxiety to forgive and forget the past; others attributed the rise of Sunderland and Godolphin to the influence of Barrillon, the French Ambassador.[2]   But perhaps James's true motives were most clearly seen by Louis XIV.   To the French King it seemed as if James, wisely hiding his resentment, counted on extracting faithful service from subjects anxious to purge themselves of the shame of their past conduct.[3]

Within a few days of his accession, King James, hitherto content to worship in private, went publicly to Mass in the Queen Consort's chapel.*

* According to a dispatch of Barrillon dated February 22, not published by Fox or Dalrymple, Rochester, Sunderland and Godolphin all advised James against this rashness at any rate until he had secured his throne.   Ranke, *History*, IV, 216.

This, the King told Barrillon, was because he was convinced that his enemies would be quick to take advantage of any hesitancy on his part or any discrimination in the exercise of his religion.[4] During the whole of the ceremony the chapel doors were left open and the anteroom was filled with courtiers, Catholic and Protestant alike. Upon the elevation of the host the Protestants retired in order to obviate the necessity of kneeling. This public worship, Barrillon reported, did not produce any dangerous effects on the minds of moderate and reasonable men, but he felt bound to add that the London populace looked askance at their King thus comporting himself.[5] Two months later, he is recording James's determination to go to Mass accompanied by the great officers of state with the same pomp as his brother had attended divine service before him; and that he had spoken on the subject to Rochester, Sunderland and Godolphin, giving them the choice of remaining at the chapel door and awaiting him there, or of returning after the service when he should be ready to leave. "Milord Sunderland ne fit point de difficulté, ni Milord Godolphin, qui est accoutumé, comme Chambellan de la Reyne, de lui donner la main jusqu'à la porte; mais Milord Rochester combattit avec véhémence la résolution que sa Majesté Britannique temoignoit avoir prise. . . ." Indeed, Rochester's fiery blood was up, and he told the King curtly that nothing short of a royal command would induce him to acquiesce. The dispute waxed bitter, and both Sunderland and Godolphin, "comme habiles courtisans", urged their colleague to comply; but Rochester was not to be moved by such arguments, and he set off for his country seat without further delay. Your Majesty may judge from this incident, concludes Barrillon shrewdly, "quelles oppositions le Roi d'Angleterre pourra trouver dans la suite à ce qu'il voudra entreprendre en faveur de la religion Catholique."[6]

Sunderland and Godolphin have been much censured for their complacency, but it is difficult to blame them. Most modern writers on this period, slavishly following in the footsteps of the great Whig historian, traduce Godolphin for doing what he certainly did not do. As the French Ambassador's dispatch makes it plain, he accompanied the Queen to the chapel door and no farther. Sidney was far too cautious a courtier to compromise himself. Had he heard Mass, everyone would have been convinced that he was either already a convert or very near to conversion; and that would not have suited him at all. As long as he kept to his duty as Chamberlain to the Queen he was safe. Outward forms and ceremonies had small meaning for him and for the sake of peace he would go a certain way in order to comply with them. But when things passed beyond the stage of mere show and he was expected to conform to the rites of the Catholic Church, he positively refused. Zealous priests, we are told, were always on the point of converting Lord Godolphin to their faith, but at the last moment there was invariably some difficulty that could not be overcome. We may not care much for this picture of the Queen's Chamberlain bowing her Majesty in at the popish chapel door, but little is left of the portrait, limned by the brush of a genius and embellished by a host of his followers, of Godolphin "bowing himself officially in the house of Rimmon."[7]

If the public were disquieted at the new King's popish proclivities, it was not long before they had cause for far greater alarm. It was evident that at the commencement of the new reign there was no escaping the necessity of summoning a Parliament: but, as James knew full well, that was the very thing the French King most dreaded, and Louis had long threatened or cajoled his brother monarch of England into neglecting it. Now that there was no avoiding the meeting of the Houses, the new Sovereign was painfully and indeed ignominiously anxious to make his apologies to France. He accordingly led Barrillon into his private room and there he made to the French Ambassador the most humble and abject excuses for having taken this step without the previous sanction of Louis. But, he insisted, a firm front to the nation was an absolute necessity; any show of weakness would betray him. "I know the English, and it will never do to let them see any sign of weakness at the outset," Barrillon reported James as having said. Furthermore, he added that he recognised the difficulties he would have to encounter, and he told of his brother's embarrassments when he suffered his ties with France to slacken.[8]

On the following morning Rochester called on the Ambassador to reinforce the ignominious excuses of his master. Then he turned to another and even more delicate matter. The King desperately wanted French financial help: would his Majesty of France oblige him as he had obliged his brother the late King before him? Rochester pleaded eloquently; the alternative, as he painted it, was alarming indeed, for if King Louis would not lend his assistance to the King of England, Barrillon reported Rochester as saying, King James would be at the mercy of his people and on the brink of ruin![9] What a shameful remark! What wonder is it that within little more than three short years the King who was so fearful of falling into the hands of his people was destined to be ignominiously hustled by those same people from these peaceful shores and never suffered to return?

But Rochester need not have pleaded so earnestly, for it was much to the interest of Louis that James should become his vassal. The bellicose foreign policy of Louis XIV had ranged half Europe against him, and the nations fearful of his power and arrogance were anxious for the aid of a united England. But England could only be united and powerful, as she had been under the Plantagenets and Tudors before the baneful hand of the Stuarts had in little more than half a century brought these humiliations upon her, if the King should be in accord with his Parliament. It was therefore the policy of Louis to ensure that the strife between the throne and the Parliament should continue. How better could that be brought about than by making James financially independent? The astute Louis had therefore anticipated the requirements of King James. Within a few hours of the demise of Charles II, a courier had set out from Paris bearing on his person the not inconsiderable sum of five hundred thousand livres.* Immediately upon receipt of this remittance, Barrillon hastened to Whitehall, where naturally enough he was received with transports of joy, and the subject Sovereign, with tears in his eyes, assured the Ambassador of his undying gratitude. "Il n'appartient qu'au Roi votre maître d'agir d'une manière si noble et si pleine de bonté pour moi," Barrillon reported James to have said. What had been done for him was the most wonderful thing in all his life. He saw clearly to the bottom of Louis's generous heart and he recognised how his good brother of France longed for his prosperity! No sooner had His Excellency retired than the abject monarch hastened to convey the good news to his Ministers. Subsequently, so Barrillon alleges, all three of them— Rochester, Sunderland and Godolphin—came severally to whisper in his ear that the glad tidings from France had given new life to their royal master.[10]

But if the gift of the most Christian King had been sufficient to give new life to his Britannic Majesty, it had been insufficient to satisfy his needs. Therefore, as Barrillon records, that evening his Excellency held a conference with the three Ministers, when Rochester, as President of the Council speaking for the others, was forced by delicate hints to convey to the agent of the generous benefactor that still more bountiful generosity would be greatly appreciated, and at the same time it was decided to dispatch Godolphin's friend, Lord Churchill, on a goodwill mission to the French capital. To the Ministers at home was entrusted the somewhat indelicate task of conveying to the French Ambassador the hope that their Master might be able to look forward to regular annual payments from his brother of France. To their importunities, Louis made some difficulties, probably to enhance the value of the gifts he had already determined to make: but in a few weeks he surrendered to the urgent requests of James and his Ministers and, nicely calculating the minimum that would be necessary to attain his object, dispatched to his Ambassador in London a vast additional sum, a portion of which was to be given to James "pour fournir aux gratifications que le Roi

---

* About £37,000. Louis to Barrillon. "20 Fevrier, 1685." Fox, *James II*, Appendix, p. xxi.

jugera à-propos de faire pendant cette assemblée"—in other words to bribe Members of Parliament—and the remainder was only to be parted with if James was forced to dissolve Parliament or on his finding so grave an opposition to the establishment of the Roman Catholic religion as to compel him to employ force against his own subjects.[11]   Whereupon Barrillon, with less than ambassadorial prudence, told James of the sum received but did not explain to him the limitations that had been set upon its expenditure.[12] The result of this indiscretion is obvious, and those who wish may read in the correspondence of Barrillon of the embarrassments of His Excellency begging to be allowed to disburse the largesse to the mendicants and the impatience of his master restraining the ardour of his too generous envoy.

But gratitude for past favours did not induce James's ministers to slacken their efforts to extract more money from Barrillon, who records a meeting towards the end of March, when Rochester, Sunderland and Godolphin were at pains to explain the King's imperative need of financial support. This assistance was required, they stated, to enable their master to conduct himself with the necessary firmness towards his Parliament who, it was affirmed, would require all manner of conditions prejudical to the royal authority before they would grant the revenue which the late Sovereign had enjoyed.   According to Barrillon, the ministers positively asserted that James was resolved not to accept any revenue granted by Parliament for a limited period, and that, rather than submit to such terms, he would prefer to try violent conclusions with his people and, in order to enable him to arm himself against his prospectively rebellious subjects, James needed French gold. The King himself reinforced the arguments of his ministers, when he told Barrillon plainly that he knew the English aversion to the Catholic religion, but that his sole aim was with French help to establish his religion in England regardless of his people's wishes: and Sunderland added that his Master was determined to maintain a show of cordiality to the Prince of Orange merely to prevent Orange from taking active measures against him.[13]   On these shocking, traitorous lines were the negotiations conducted with the French Ambassador.

Since the publication of Barrillon's dispatches, these disgraceful transactions have been universally condemned; and indeed it is quite impossible to defend them.   It must be with the deepest regret, therefore, that we find Lord Godolphin involved in such dealings.   But if we can believe the sagacious Frenchman, whose letters are our only evidence, the turpitude of Godolphin was far less than that of either of his colleagues.   Lord Rochester, whose religious scruples forbade him to go even to the door of the Queen's popish chapel, had not hesitated, as we have seen, to advance the outrageous argument that, if Louis denied James financial assistance, the English monarch would be at the mercy of his people and on the brink of ruin. Nor was Sunderland's attitude more nice. He was anxious that James should enter into formal alliance with Louis. He even descended so far as to advocate that James should deceive his Parliament by a show of friendship to Orange, and that, when this deception had yielded a dividend in the form of revenue granted to the Crown, he should throw off the mask and at one and the same time drop the Parliament and the Prince into the gutter.

Lord Godolphin, so Barrillon tells us, sided more with Rochester than Sunderland; but he was very obviously the junior of the three Ministers, and his object seems to have been to retain his position by pursuing a policy of prudence and moderation.[14] In short, Godolphin would tolerate the mere form of conducting the Queen to the door of her Catholic chapel: he would ask the French Ambassador for money to aid his master in his negotiations with Parliament and he would go with his colleagues to render thanks to Barrillon for the benefactions of the French King. But there were limits beyond which he would not go. He would not encourage James in his eagerness to dispense with Parliaments; and he would not break altogether with his old friend, the Prince of Orange. In short, the three Ministers "were cognizant of the secret money treaties with France, and yet with a difference. Rochester was playing the part of a meaner Danby, and Barrillon recognized that neither he nor Godolphin would ever entirely forsake their well-established relations with Orange, or cut themselves off from any chance of the co-operation with Parliament."[15]

Thanks to the success of the negotiations with the French Ambassador, thanks, too, to the failure of the abortive rebellions of Argyll and Monmouth, the sun of prosperity shone upon King James. In the autumn of 1685 he was at the height of his power. His vanquished enemies lay prostrate in the dust. His English and Scottish parliaments had granted him a larger revenue than had been enjoyed by any previous King in these islands. He had at his command a larger and better equipped army and navy than the country had ever before possessed in time of peace. Foreign powers were all competing for his friendship so that he bade fair to becoming the arbiter of Europe. In a few months he had achieved a position more powerful, and, as it seemed, more secure than his easy-going brother had obtained in a reign of a quarter of a century. All this King James now hastened to throw away. Pride, arrogance, and over-confidence were responsible for his fall, so that in three short years the powerful monarch of 1685 had become the friendless exile of 1688.

Feeling himself secure in his all-powerful position, James judged himself able to throw off the mask: at last his objects were clear. One of them was the repeal of the Habeas Corpus Act. Another was the formation of a vast standing army. But there was a third design far more compelling to James than either of these objects—the freeing of his Church from all proscription. And in furtherance of this design the King displayed the full measure of his folly. Against the advice of all the most moderate of his Catholic subjects, against the expressed wish of the Pope himself, James embarked on a course of blundering ineptitude that was later suspected to have emanated from the tortuous brain of Sunderland, deliberately guiding him to his doom. During the time of the rebellion, the King had appointed members of his Church to commissions in the army; and though this was contrary to the terms of the Test Act, little objection was taken at a time of crisis. But now that the crisis was past, James continued to grant commissions illegally; and he actually had the temerity to announce that he would be no longer bound by the Test Act, that he hoped to persuade Parliament to repeal it, but that if Parliament refused that would not alter his determination. It was at this unhappy moment that King Louis chose to revoke the Edict of Nantes, that beneficent statute by which in 1598 King Henry IV of France had guaranteed to his Huguenot subjects freedom to worship according to their ritual and civil liberty including the liberty to write in defence of their own doctrine; and immediately there started a steady flow of French refugee Protestants across the Channel. What a splendid example was thus shown to King James's subjects of Catholic toleration of other faiths! So this was what might be expected in these islands if the Catholic ruler once had his way. No wonder the great majority of Englishmen were disturbed, shocked, dismayed.

And to make matters worse, James was now in the hands of a new body of secret advisers, from whom indeed little either of wisdom or of virtue was likely to flow. One of them was Harry Jermyn, a little shrimp of a man, for whom, so the Grammont memoirs tell us, languished the Maids of Honour at King Charles's Court. For many years Jermyn had been renowned for his life of endless duels, lecherous amours, and ruinous play. More recently he had turned from pleasure to religion, had embraced the Catholic faith, and had recently been raised by James to the peerage with the title of Dover. With Lord Dover were associated his old rival, giant Dick Talbot, whom at his succession the new Sovereign had created Earl of Tyrconnel; and a Jesuit priest, Edward Petre by name, a man of good family and some ability, but vain and ambitious. Others of this group, but on a far lower plane, were Roger Palmer, Earl of Castlemaine, the husband of the Duchess of Cleveland, and an intriguing Irishman of the name of White, who had been rewarded for some secret services to the House of Austria with the high-sounding title of Marquess d'Albeville. To this ultra-Catholic clique was accorded the support of a man far abler than any of its members, none other than Lord Sunderland himself.

And so, urged on by these irresponsible advisers, the purblind and obstinate Sovereign now rushed to his doom. Not only did James at this time make numerous Roman Catholic appointments in the army, but he made such appointments to the Privy Council. He determined once and for all to settle the vexed question of the royal dispensing power. Having engineered a decision favourable to his right in the collusive case of Sir Edward Hales, James set to work with a will. He caused a special warrant to be issued whereby the Master of University College, Oxford, might hold his office without taking the Sacrament or the oaths of allegiance and supremacy. In December 1686, with the help of the dispensing power, he gave the deanery of Christ Church to John Massey, a Roman Catholic. About this time, the three sees of York, Oxford and Chester all became vacant. To Oxford and Chester, two sycophantic clergymen, Samuel Parker and Thomas Cartwright, were appointed though both men were suspiciously sympathetic towards the Church of Rome. Meanwhile, the Archbishopric of York was kept vacant for some months in the hope, it was believed, that James would prevail upon the Pope to consent to the appointment of Edward Petre to the See. To further this object and to improve relations with the Vatican, James determined to send a special embassy to Rome. For envoy he chose none other than Lord Castlemaine, better known for his wife's shame than for his own virtues. What a representative to send from the English Sovereign to the Holy Father!

There seemed no end to James's foolishness. At the suggestion, it is said, of Sunderland, anxious for the downfall of his rival, the King dismissed his brother-in-law, Rochester, for no better reason than his refusal to turn Catholic, and entrusted the treasurership to a board of Commissioners, one of whom was Lord Godolphin. At almost the same time as Rochester fell, his brother Clarendon was summoned to return from Ireland so soon as he had admitted Tyrconnel as Lord Deputy. With the fall of the Hydes, James threw discretion to the winds. He tried to insist that a Benedictine monk should be admitted to the degree of Master of Arts at Cambridge in deference to the royal mandate; and when this was refused as contrary to the university statutes, the Vice-Chancellor was summoned before the ecclesiastical commission and deprived of his office. In the spring and summer of 1687 occurred the shameful attack on the liberties of the fellows of Magdalen College, Oxford. In the autumn of that year King James nominated Petre to the Privy Council. This might be thought his crowning folly. But it was swiftly followed by other enormities rising to a climax in the trial of the seven bishops. This, coupled with the tidings that the Queen was pregnant, drove the majority of the nation to distraction; and the subsequent news that she had given birth to a son led to countless tales, long since discredited, that the infant was nothing but a changeling secreted into the royal bed by the hated Jesuits.

It was at this dreadful moment that the eyes of the unhappy people turned from their purblind monarch to that small, frail, taciturn prince, who had married their Sovereign's elder daughter. On June 30th, 1688, the very day that the populace were joyfully celebrating the acquittal of the bishops, a letter to William was drawn up and signed in cipher by Shrewsbury, Devonshire, Danby, Bishop Compton of London, Lumley, Edward Russell and Henry Sidney, * who, since his mission to Holland in 1679, had enjoyed to a marked degree the confidence of the Prince of Orange. This invitation, which begged the Prince to come over to England at the head of an adequate force with the utmost expedition, was entrusted to Admiral Herbert, who, garbed as a common sailor, crossed to Holland and placed the letter in the Prince's hands.[16] William hesitated no longer. He had required an invitation before taking action. Now that he had received it he could not with honour draw back, for to do so would be to desert those who had risked their lives in complying with his request.

The drama moved swiftly to its tragic climax. With the imminent risk of invasion, James at last saw his danger; whereupon ensued a bewildering series of concessions. On October 26, the King took a momentous step, which has never been satisfactorily explained: he suddenly dismissed Sunderland, undoubtedly his ablest, if also his most unscrupulous, adviser.† But the time for concessions had passed. All was confusion and rumours of impending invasion were bruited about the land. "heering the Doctour say by chance that he had sent to desire you to come to towne because the weather begins to grow cold," wrote Sidney Godolphin anxiously to his sister Jael, staying at his house at Windsor but thinking of returning to London, "I can't helpe putting in my word to you which is that considering the Dutch will probably land here in England within lesse than a week, I should think Cranborn a better and a quieter place for you and your children, than London. I pray God send us a happy meeting. Yrs. ever G."[17] How right he was. On November 8th, Prince William of Orange landed at Torbay.

For nine days little happened, and William began to think that he had been betrayed. Then events moved rapidly. On Saturday, November

---

* The cipher numbers for the names as set out in the text were: 25, 24, 27, 31, 29, 35 and 33.

† For one view of the real cause of Sunderland's dismissal, see Ranke, *History*, IV., 431–2, 441.

17th, James set forth from his capital to face the invader, and by the time he reached his headquarters at Salisbury on the 19th, the defections had become "a raging torrent. The two pillars of the royal cause, the army and the country gentlemen, were slipping irretrievably away.[18] Desertions had begun with Abingdon, Colchester, Wharton and Russell; and on the 14th Cornbury, Clarendon's fickle heir, went over to the Prince. Seymour joined him at Exeter, where a message was delivered from Lord Bath, commanding at Plymouth, that he placed the fortress and garrison at the Prince's disposal. Danby seized York in William's name. Delamere was in arms in Cheshire, Devonshire in the northern midlands. During Friday night, November 23rd–24th, Churchill, the commander-in-chief of James's forces, accompanied by the late King's natural son, the Duke of Grafton, and followed by a troop of horse fled to the invader. On the following day news was received of the defection of Ormonde and of Prince George of Denmark, husband of the Princess Anne.[19] Already James, discouraged by these defections, and debilitated by a bleeding nose,* was on the retreat back to London, when he heard of Anne's flight.† "God help me!" exclaimed the unhappy father, "my own children have forsaken me!" So he drank the cup of bitterness to the dregs.

James, now desperate, summoned a great Council of Peers, and on November 27th, some thirty or forty who were in or near London attended. The King asked their advice. There was much plain speaking, particularly from Clarendon. Four days later he followed his son's example and deserted to the Prince's camp. According to a dispatch from Barrillon dated December 3rd/13th, the counsellors were divided into two groups. The moderates, including Halifax, Godolphin, the two Secretaries of State, Preston and Middleton, together with Lord Belasye and other moderate Catholic peers, urged James that he must on no account think of leaving the country—which shows that the possibility of the King's flight was in men's minds before negotiations were opened with the Prince; that he must satisfy his subjects as to the security of the law and of the Protestant religion; and that he must call a Parliament. They furthermore assured James that, if he would act thus, he would gain wide-spread support and would suffer no personal risk. The other party, headed by Lord Melfort, the evil genius of the unhappy King, and many violent Catholics, urged James to escape. In their view, the Prince of Orange would find it difficult to form a government

---

* There can be no doubt that James was in very poor health at this time, and apparently was unable to sleep without opiates. H.M.C. *Rep. XII*, pt. 7, 220, 223.

† For Pepys's interesting account of the Princess's flight see H.M.C. *Dartmouth*, I, 214. See also Ailesbury, *Memoirs*, I, 191. Lord Chesterfield also accompanied the Princess part of the way. *Spencer MSS.* 31, (19.)

and to satisfy the ambitions and the jealousies of his supporters.[20] Torn between these rival factions, the King long vacillated, but it was agreed by the vast majority of those present that there was no alternative to sending Commisioners to treat with the invader. The men chosen for this task were Halifax, Nottingham and Godolphin.*

The reason for the selection of Lord Godolphin has been much debated, though in fact he was a remarkably good choice. Halifax and Nottingham were moderates among the opposition peers, and Godolphin was personally on excellent terms with the Prince of Orange. Indeed, there was probably no one in all England on such intimate terms with him, save only some of those who had signed the famous letter of July 30th, all of whom would be beyond the pale so far as James was concerned. Assuredly Godolphin, if any one, would be able to find a basis for agreement between the King and the Prince.

The three men entered upon their task with grave misgivings. According to Burnet, Halifax and Nottingham attributed their appointments to the Commission as the work of their enemies;[21] and Godolphin was no more sanguine than his colleagues as to any prospects of success for the mission. "The King," wrote one of them on or about December 1st, "has appointed the Lords Halifax, Nottingham and Godolphin to goe to the Pr. of Or. to acquaint him with his Majesty's calling of a parlt. and to adiust the freedom of it . . . a place which I doe not hear any of the 3 Lords desired but purely obeyed the king for in all probability this will have no effect. The affairs of the Prince being such as will admit little delay, especially since the K. of France troops have already advanced to Boisleduc and burnt 12 villages thereabouts."[22]

The instructions issued to the Commissioners by King James were clear and precise. They were to go with all possible dispatch to the Prince of Orange, to acquaint him that His Majesty "in order to the composing of the present distractions of this Kingdome" had directed writs to be issued for the calling of a Parliament to meet on January 15th, and to adjust with the Prince whatever may be necessary to secure the freedom of election and that Parliament may sit without fear of civil commotion. With this object in view the Commissioners were instructed to propose that the Orange troops should not advance nearer than forty miles from London; and, if William should refuse, they were to enquire what safeguards he thought necessary beyond James's assurances, and to transmit his proposals

* It is believed that the Commission as originally designed consisted of Halifax, Nottingham, Rochester, Godolphin and the Bishops of Ely and St. Asaph. Later the names of the bishops were omitted, and Halifax refused to serve with Rochester. Newsletter addressed to Roger Kenyon at Peel under date, "Nottingham the 26th instant" (November 1688). H.M.C. *Kenyon*, 209-10.

to the King.   In supplementary instructions issued by James later the same day, the Commissioners were further directed that if the Prince of Orange should take the view that there could be no security for the sitting of Parliament so long as the King's troops remained in or near London, they might express the view that "We will be content that our own fforces shall be removed some reasonable time before the sitting of the Parliament, at the same distance from the Towne, with the Prince's Army:" except only for a bodyguard to be allowed to the King and the Prince in equal numbers.*

It is hardly surprising if the Commissioners had little relish for their work, for, if their instructions were precise, their powers were meagre. "Visited my L. Godolphin, then going with the Marquis of Halifax and E. of Nottingham as Commissioner to the Prince of Orange," recorded Evelyn. "He told me, they had little power."[23]   According to one historian, Godolphin was in the secret of James's real intentions;[24] but his testimony is unsupported, and Evelyn's diary note, founded on what his friend had said to him, shows this as unlikely.   As a matter of fact, all three lords soon had ample reason to regret that they had been prevailed upon to undertake their thankless task.

On Sunday December 2nd, though the messenger who was to be responsible for their safe conduct had not arrived, the Commissioners each accompanied by ten persons, secretaries and domestics, set forth.[25]   The first night they passed at Windsor, the next at Reading, where they found their expected guide dead drunk.[26]   This caused some delay and is the true reason why James's representatives were not received earlier by the Prince of Orange.†   The passes arrived, however, two days later,‡ and on Thursday, December 6th, the Commissioners reached Ramsbury, where they took up their quarters.   On Friday, William betook himself to Hungerford and signified his willingness to receive the embassy there on the following morning.§   At 10 o'clock the three lords waited on the Prince,‖ and

* The detailed instructions "given at our Court at Whitehall this 1st Day of December, 1688 in the 4th year of our Reign, James R." issued to the Commissioners by King James can still be seen in the original documents. All Souls MSS. 273. These hitherto seem to have been overlooked. Miss Foxcroft, in summarizing the instructions, merely draws from the paper handed in by the Commissioners and dated "Hungerford ye 8th of December 1688." Foxcroft, *Halifax*, II, 23.

† The prince has often been accused of having deliberately delayed the audience.

‡ The originals can still be seen dated "Given at hyndon this 3d of Decemb. 1688." All Souls MSS. 273.

§ Not all thirty attendants on the Commissioners were allowed as far as Hungerford; a good many of them, not included in the passes, had to be left at Ramsbury.

‖ The Prince had previously refused the Commissioners' request for a private audience.

Halifax, speaking on behalf of the embassy, gave his Highness a verbal report of the Commissioners' instructions. William then requested James's representatives to embody their report in a written statement. In this document the Commissioners informed the Prince that King James recognized that the main cause of complaint referred to the calling of a free Parliament;[27] and that in consequence, although he himself would have preferred to have waited until the nation was more composed, for the sake of peace and good relations he was prepared to issue the necessary writs immediately, and also to consent to everything that could reasonably be required to assure the security of those attending Parliament. Meanwhile, King James suggested that their respective armies "may be restrained within such Limits and at such a distance from London as may prevent the apprehensions that the Parliament may in any kind be disturbed. . . ."[28]

That night the Commissioners dispatched to Lord Middleton, the Secretary of State, a full report on their audience. They recorded their reception by the Prince that morning at Hungerford, when his Highness had affirmed that he had little to add to his Declaration as to the reasons for his arrival in England, which were therein stated to be to maintain the Protestant religion and to preserve the laws and liberties of the people. He then bade the Commissioners retire to another room where they were speedily joined by Schomberg, Oxford and Clarendon, who desired them to put into writing what they had already said. This they promptly did, and the paper was carried back to the Prince, whose answer was expected to be delivered at Littlecote on the morrow. The Commissioners particularly marked that care was taken to avoid giving the English lords a chance to speak privately with them, lest this should cause jealousy, rumours being afloat that many of them were anxious lest an accommodation should be arrived at and their interests not properly safeguarded.

That night the Commissioners were William's guests at dinner, after which they had "preliminary discourse" with several of the English, from whom James's envoys derived small encouragement for the success of their mission. What they feared, according to their report, was that there was no intention of halting the onward march of the army, and that the Prince's demands would include the removal of Papists from all offices, both military and civil, and a declaration by the King that those who had deserted him had done so in defence of the laws of England and therefore required no pardon.[29] How could they expect King James to sign a paper such as that?

We may demur to the statement in this letter that the Commissioners had no more than "promiscuous discourse" with the English followers of the Prince after the dinner at Littlecot House. No sooner had the envoys arrived at William's headquarters than their leader was expressing the strongest desire to see Burnet, and to see him alone. This was in no way surprising; the two men had for long been friends and Halifax, anxious to learn the Prince's real intentions, knew full well that he would very soon hear all from the mouth of his Highness's garrulous chaplain. Orange, of course, knew this too. "If they get together, there will be fine tattling," he grumbled, and he forbade Burnet to see the Commissioners in private. But the astute Trimmer soon had his way. After the dinner, Halifax succeeded in having a few words apart with the worthy doctor. "What is it you want?" enquired the Commissioner, "is it to get the King into your power?" "Not at all," replied Burnet, "We would not do the least harm to his person." "And if he were to go away?" "There is nothing," replied Burnet, "so much to be wished." This, the doctor adds, he reported to the Prince, who approved of both his answers.[30] Thus the Commissioners learnt what was nearest to William's heart.[31]

The tenor of the Ambassadors' dispatch, it must be admitted, left little hope of an accommodation, and its receipt next day must have sent a wintry blast through the corridors of Whitehall. Yet the answer handed to the Commissioners on behalf of Prince William at a meeting called for the morning of December 10th, was surprisingly mild. In this Orange stipulated that all Papists and others disqualified by law should be disarmed, disbanded, and removed from all offices, civil and military; that all proclamations reflecting upon him should be recalled and any one who had been committed to prison for having been involved should be forthwith released; that the custody and government of the Tower of London and the Port of Tilbury should be placed immediately in the hands of the city of London; that the King and the Prince should both be either in London or absent from it, and, if absent, that they should be at the same distance from the capital; that their respective armies should remove thirty miles from London; that no more foreign troops should be brought into the Kingdom and, in order to prevent the landing of French or other foreign troops, that Portsmouth should be put into neutral hands; and lastly, that a sufficient part of the public revenue should be assigned to the Prince for the maintenance of his forces.[32] To this paper the Commissioners replied that some points were of a nature beyond their competence to answer and they therefore determined to return immediately to London to lay them before the King. Meanwhile, they proposed that the Prince should agree not to permit his troops to advance nearer than thirty miles from the capital.[33] The Prince, it seems, agreed to this important stipulation,[34] and on the same day the three lords set out.

On their arrival in London during the afternoon of December 11th, the Commissioners were greeted with the startling news that Orange's wish had already been fulfilled. On the 9th James had dispatched the Queen and the infant Prince of Wales to Paris, promising, so it is said, to follow within twenty-four hours. At three o'clock in the morning of the 11th, taking the Great Seal with him, the King fled secretly from Whitehall to Sheerness. On the way he dropped the Seal into the Thames,[35] thinking with puerile malice that its loss would cause civil commotion.

The first flight of James may be said to have terminated his reign; no Sovereign could survive the shame of such a pusillanimous retreat. True, much to William's annoyance and embarrassment, the fugitive was stopped and brought ashore at Sheerness by some over zealous local fisherman; but no sooner was James back in London than William asked or ordered him to retire to Ham House[36] and when the fallen monarch—no doubt with thoughts of flight uppermost in his mind—pretended a preference for Rochester, William assented with alacrity, and took immediate steps to ensure that the King's escape was not a second time impeded. Accordingly, early in the morning of December 23rd James boarded a vessel in the Thames; on Christmas day he landed at Ambleteuse on the French coast, whence he posted to St. Germain, there to be reunited with his family in the splended palace that Louis XIV had placed at the disposal of the royal exiles.

It has been long the fashion to place the responsibility for James's precipitate flight on Halifax and Godolphin, who, so it is said, terrified their befuddled Sovereign by alleging danger to his person. The injustice of this accusation is clearly established by Barrillon's dispatch of December 3rd/13th reporting the meeting of the peers in London,* and by the fact that James had determined on escape before ever he sent the three envoys to Hungerford. The French Ambassador, who was more in James's confidence than any of his ministers, is clear on that point,[37] and so, for what he is worth, is Lord Ailesbury, James's intimate friend, though his unsupported testimony on such a matter would admittedly be but poor authority.[38] This view is further supported by Francesco Riva, Wardrobe Keeper to the Queen, to whose graphic pen we owe a spirited account of the Queen's flight.†

So far as Godolphin is concerned, Lord Dartmouth tells us that he, Godolphin, had written to James advising him to withdraw so as to leave the kingdom in such confusion that his subjects would be begging him on bended knee to return:[39] whilst the Count d'Avaux, Louis XIV's Ambassador to the United Provinces, accuses Godolphin of having deliberately

* Not attended, it seems, by Godolphin or by Nottingham. *Hatton Correspondence*, II, 123.

† Riva's statement is dated, "Sunday evening 2/12 December." There are two copies, one in Italian, dedicated to his "dear father and mother," is preserved in the Archives of Modena; the other is in French. Hale, *Mary of Modena*, 217–20.

betrayed his master.* But it is easy to make sweeping accusations of this nature; and when, as in this case, they are unsupported by any evidence whatever and are in direct contradiction with other statements made by persons more likely to know the truth, they must be received with extreme reserve. D'Avaux's malicious statement may be quickly disposed of: he was alluding to events in the summer of 1688 and not to the months of November and December at all. And what of Dartmouth's note? If, in fact, Lord Godolphin wrote such a letter as Dartmouth alleges, where is it? Destroyed with King James's papers? Possibly. Who else, then, saw the letter and can bear any testimony as to its exact contents? In fact, no contemporary makes any mention of such a document, though many later writers repeat the accusation on the sole evidence of Dartmouth's note. And Dartmouth, be it remembered, was no contemporary. He was not the gallant admiral who had shown himself for so long the faithful servant of King James. The Lord Dartmouth of the caustic annotations to Burnet's *History* was the admiral's son, aged only sixteen at this time, who was writing from memory of events long past.† This evidence, therefore, was not first-hand, and is thoroughly untrustworthy.

Barrillon, on the contrary, tells a very different story; he reports a conversation that Godolphin had with Faversham after the King's first flight, when he expressed the view that, if James had not fled, the Prince would have carried out the armistice terms; though at the same time, with his usual caution, he declined to take the responsibility of advising the fugitive to return to London from the coast.⁴⁰ Whilst that perhaps hardly justifies the construction that Halifax's biographer puts upon Godolphin's words that he "severely blamed" the King for his flight, it does surely show that at the time of James's withdrawal this Commissioner had no fears for his Sovereign's personal safety at the hands of the invader.⁴¹ But there is one further point to be noted—the absolute silence maintained by James on the question of Godolphin's alleged betrayal. Is it possible to imagine that, if Godolphin had in fact served him as has been suggested, the loquacious and vindictive Sovereign would not have voiced his complaints far and wide, would not have vowed vengeance on his false servant in the most extravagant terms? Assuredly the Monarch's very reticence on the subject goes far to absolve Godolphin from this terrible indictment. The charge as formulated cannot possibly be sustained. Indeed, much the more reasonable

* "Dec. 9. I again repeated to the King the intelligence which I had the honour of giving him a long time ago, that Godolphin betrayed the King of England, that I was surprised he had chose him for confident, and that it would be necessary to give his Britannic Majesty warning of it." D'Avaux, *Negotiations,* IV, 272.

† The Admiral was George Legge, first Lord Dartmouth (1648–1691); his only son was William Legge, first Earl of Dartmouth (1672–1750).

explanation is that the Sovereign had determined on flight some days before December 8th, and that none of the Commissioners had anything to do with it.

The deliberate insult, as it seemed, that was offered to the Royal Commissioners by King James's flight was resented by no one more than by Halifax, who, together with other moderates, promptly joined the Prince. Very different was the conduct of Godolphin and Nottingham, both of whom remained loyal to the fallen King until his final desertion. We need not follow the long and somewhat tedious debates that followed the departure of James. It was known that he had left a paper behind him; and at the great meeting of peers called on Christmas Eve, some of his supporters, hoping that perhaps it might contain propositions upon which at even that late hour some happy settlement could be built, moved that the paper should be produced. But Godolphin knew better. "I have seen the paper," he sorrowfully declared, "and I grieve to say that there is nothing in it which will give your Lordships any satisfaction." No lesson, no shock, no misfortune, however decisive, however terrible, could move the obdurate heart of the fallen tyrant.

In the ensuing debates, both Nottingham and Godolphin supported Archbishop Sancroft's plan for a regency, which was only finally defeated in the Lords by the narrow majority of two votes. But Lord Godolphin took no very prominent part in the parliamentary proceedings, though he certainly did not dissent from the terms on which the Crown was offered to William and Mary; for, in spite of his loyalty to James so long as he remained at his post, it can be safely surmised that he would have been in general agreement with the summary of events of the great Whig historian: "For the authority of law, for the security of property, for the peace of our streets, for the happiness of our homes, our gratitude is due, under Him who raises and pulls down nations at His pleasure, to the Long Parliament, to the Convention and to William of Orange."[42]

CHAPTER VI

AT THE TREASURY

DURING Sidney Godolphin's short married life, he had, as has been noticed, a house in Scotland Yard. Whether he was successful in disposing of this after Margaret's death we do not know. But as the years passed and political advancement came his way, he began to sigh for a country home. Furthermore, his son Francis, all that was left to him of his beloved wife, was growing up; he was now about nine years old and fresh air would benefit the boy. This desire was satisfied early in James II's reign by the acquisition of a property close to one of the entrances to Windsor Park.

Little is now left of Cranbourne Lodge, but in Godolphin's day it was a mansion of considerable size, which had recently been extensively enlarged. It was not, it seems, a house to suit all tastes, and John Evelyn, an early visitor, wrote in his *Diary* in no very flattering terms of his old friend's choice: "to Cranburne," he recorded, "a Lodge & walke of my Lord Godolphins, in Windsor parke: there was one roome in the house, spared in the pulling-downe the old one, because the late Dutchesse of York, was borne in it, the rest was build & added to it by Sir Geo. Carteret, Treasurer of the Navy: & since the whole purchased by my Lord Godolphin, who spake to me to go see it, and advise what trees were fit to be cut downe, to improve the dwelling, it being invironed with old rotten pollards, which corrupt the aire." Evelyn did not hesitate, it seems, to be the candid friend, for: "It stands on a knowle," the *Diary* continues, "which though insensibly rising, gives it a prospect over the keepe of Windsore, which is about three miles north-east of it: The ground is clayy & moist, the water stark nought: The Park is pretty: The house tollerable & gardens convenient:" and then, showing that a visit to Windsor Park in those days was something of an adventure, "after dinner we came back to Lond, having 2 Coaches both going and coming, of 6 horses a-piece, which we changed at Hounslow."[1] Godolphin seems to have taken his old friend's remarks about the "old rotten pollards" to heart, for we find Treasury warrants for the felling of trees said to be spoiling the garden of Cranbourne Lodge.[2] In Sir George Carteret's day, the house was the scene of many merry parties that do small credit to Charles II's Secretary of the Admiralty, or to the courtiers around the throne.

Here is was that little Samuel Pepys, hurrying down from London with the ill news of the attack on Bergen, found that the only means of reaching his master's bedroom in his unfinished house was up a ladder, and that the only way of attracting the attention of the sleeping, and probably tipsy Secretary was by creeping into his bed: here too the King in drunken obedience to the demands of his armourer knelt to drink a health to his brother of York.[3] In grave Lord Godolphin's day, however, we may be sure the house witnessed no such scenes. His much loved sister Jael and her growing family were his constant guests. "I have receiv'd your Letter and am very glad you have such fine weather as to make you like riding," he wrote on one occasion, "but . . ." he added cautiously, "I am a little afrayd my niece should venture too often upon Spott, for to my certain knowledge he is not sure footed. . . ."[4] About the same time Sidney wrote to Jael that the Princess Anne was going to Windsor, and she must pay her respects. "Lady Marlborough, who is coming with the Princess, is going on to Eton to see her son, and as she comes back again from Eton, she will call upon you to carry you to the princesse, soe you may eatt your dinner in quiet and sitt at home in patience till she comes to you."[5]

The new King was not the man to harbour resentment at Godolphin's vote for a regency in the Convention debates; besides, he recognized in him a man of conscience and he respected his abilities. Accordingly, on February 14th, 1689, Sidney was appointed a Commissioner of the Treasury.* With him and senior to him were two Whigs: Mordaunt, now created Earl of Monmouth, who was destined as Earl of Peterborough to run a great but erratic course; and Delamere, created Earl of Warrington, a Chancellor of the Exchequer with small knowledge of finance. On one thing alone were these two agreed: they felt a common dislike for their Tory colleague. This perhaps was hardly surprising, for it was soon apparent

---

* I venture to join issue with Professor Keith Feiling. "No British sovereign ever so prized the royal prerogatives as did the Liberator, whose favoured ministers were silent automata, prepared to take his orders and do the work of the State, without thought of party or inherited prejudice. Hence his immediate resolution to employ Godolphin, hence the fatted calf prepared so early in the reign for the prodigal Sunderland, hence the political influence of men really outside party, like Henry Sidney or Portland." Feiling, *Tory Party*, p. 256. I do not understand how Sunderland, though certainly "prodigal" enough, could possibly be dubbed a silent automaton: he was in fact a man of the greatest ability and very far from being pliant. As for Godolphin, his correspondence with the King, shortly to be quoted, seems to me to go far towards disproving Professor Feiling's allegation. Of the other two mentioned, Sidney was a personal friend of William, but I should not have thought that his political influence was great, and Portland was a Dutch favourite who had come over from Holland with the Liberator.

that King William valued the financial acumen of the junior member of the Commission, whose calm, placid temper, very different from that of his superiors, was well suited to the Sovereign's dour personality. It was not long, therefore, before Godolphin became in reality first member of the Board and the only Commissioner whose views carried weight at Whitehall.

But such arrangements could not be expected to last, and when the General Election of 1690 resulted in a great Tory majority in the House of Commons, the King took the opportunity of dismissing both the Whig members of the Commission; having made these and some subordinate changes in the Ministry King William sailed to face his father-in-law in Ireland, leaving affairs at home in charge of Queen Mary assisted by a Council of nine, four Whigs and five Tories, of whom one was Godolphin.

The departure of Monmouth and Warrington from the Treasury was soon followed by that of their colleague. The reason why Godolphin retired we do not know: but probably ill health was the cause: ". . . I have been in paine more or less these 3 or 4 days," he wrote to Jael, "and this morning I voyded a great stone. I have not yett been at Cranborn, but I believe you will find mee there when you Come back, unless I bee at Tunbridge. . . ."[6] All we know for certain is that in March he resigned, and that in November he unwillingly returned. "Aug. 24: 90," records Lord Halifax, "Godolphin L^d told mee hee would do all that was possible to avoid imploy^t at the K^s returne, but hee was not sure it could be avoided."[7] Apparently it could not be avoided, and three months later, on November 12th, he was appointed as head of the Commission,[8] a position that he was to retain for the next six years.

To comprehend the difficulties with which Godolphin was faced when he became head of the Treasury in the autumn of 1690, we must understand something of the financial arrangements that had been made when the Crown had been offered to William and Mary.

Previous to the revolution, the medieval concept was in force that the King should live off his own—that is, that out of his own income he should govern the country, and that only on some such extraordinary occasion as the outbreak of war should he ask Parliament for financial assistance. In times gone by, the King's "own" was quite sufficient for what it was intended; but now that was so no longer. The method by which the Sovereign's income was supplemented by Parliament varied at different dates. At the Restoration it had been agreed between the Parliament and the restored monarch that all the noble tenures should be surrendered in return for a grant for life of the hereditary excise. In accordance with seventeenth century custom, it was the duty of Parliament to estimate the annual sum needed for the ordinary expenditure of the Crown—calculated to be £1,200,000—and to pledge itself to give the King an annual revenue to that amount for the whole of his reign. There the responsibility of Parliament ended. The principle of supplying annual estimates had not yet been evolved. Parliament did not expect them from the Sovereign; the Sovereign did not demand them from the Executive. After the revolution of 1688, the Convention Parliament contemplated proceeding in exactly the same way as at the Restoration or at the accession of King James II, but gradually a different conception of financial policy emerged. On February 26th, 1689, a Committee of the House proceeded to consider the settling of a revenue on the new King and Queen.[9] In the ensuing proceedings there was much debate whether the permanent revenue granted to James had lapsed with his departure or had automatically devolved on his successor; alternatively, whether it was constitutional for Parliament to re-enact or re-grant it to William and Mary, and whether the Convention, when converted into a Parliament, had power so to re-enact or re-grant. Such nice points as these, of course, gave full scope to the ingenious subtleties of the gentlemen of the long robe, and the debate waxed long and tedious. Perhaps the most sensible view was expressed by Sidney's younger brother Charles, the member for Helston. "I believe that Parliament that gave this revenue intended not to give it to King William," he said, "for there were no thoughts then of King James's abdication. If any doubt be in the House it is in your power to put it out of doubt." "'Tis our security," declared Sir William Pulteney bluntly, "to have the revenue in our disposition,"[10] That view prevailed. The House determined to originate a fresh grant just as if the new Sovereigns had succeeded on the death of King James.

In the ensuing debate Sir Robert Howard, Auditor of the Exchequer, was directed to bring before the House his computation of the annual value of the several branches of the revenue. This he did on March 1st, giving the approximate figure of £1,501,000; to this had to be added the value of certain special impositions granted to James II, which in the year ended Michaelmas 1688 had produced a further £415,500, making an approximate total of £1,916,500.[11] It was accordingly resolved that all branches of the revenue which had been due and payable by law in the reigns of Charles II and James II, should be collected for the use of the Crown until June 24th, 1689.[12]

On March 20th, Howard laid before Parliament an abstract of James's annual revenue and expenditure. The King's revenue, he said, had averaged approximately £1,916,000; his expenditure about £1,699,000, a figure which, after adding certain fixed and other charges, probably amounted to as much as £1,900,000 or thereabouts. Yet in spite of these figures, the Convention promptly voted William a standing revenue of no more than £1,200,000;[13] whereupon the Commons proceeded to vote a total of £718,680 for the fighting services and £600,000 for the civil government of the country.[14] In short, a total peace expenditure of £1,318,680 to be expended out of a revenue grant of £1,200,000! Having reached that ludicrous conclusion, the Commons promptly resolved that their figure of £1,318,680 fell short of the sum required by at least £400,000. Yet little was done, and it was not until July 15th that the Commons, spurred by frequent messages from the King, introduced a Bill for the settling of the revenue on William and Mary. Further barren proceedings ensued, in which there was much confusion between extraordinary supply for war and the permanent fixing of the revenue for the ordinary cost of government. At last on March 27th, the House voted a supply for the prosecution of the war with France, and on the following day went into Committee to consider yet again the settling of the revenue on their Majesties. As a result of these deliberations, it was at last decided that the hereditary revenues to which James had been entitled, except the hearth tax, should be vested in William and Mary; that a Bill should be brought in for settling that moiety of the Excise, which had been granted to Charles II and James II or either of them for life, on William and Mary for their lives and that of the survivor; and lastly that a Bill should be introduced to grant to the new Sovereigns for four years from the following Christmas the Customs which had been granted to Charles and James.[15] Thus to all intents and purposes was the right of William and Mary affirmed to all the fixed revenue enjoyed by either of their two immediate predecessors.

During April Bills were passed in Parliament for settling the Excise on the Sovereigns for their joint lives and that of the survivor, and for settling Customs and Tonnage and Poundage for four years. On April 21st, a Bill was introduced for declaring the hereditary revenue of the Crown to be vested in the joint Sovereigns. It passed both Houses expeditiously and on May 23rd was ready to be read a third time. But William, probably dissatisfied that the measure was restricted to the hereditary excise and omitted all that additional revenue which had been granted to James II and all miscellaneous small branches of the revenue still inherent in the Crown, suddenly adjourned Parliament until the following July. Thus the Bill was sacrificed.

This slight sketch serves to show the hopeless muddle made by Parliament, which had neither granted the King's revenue for life nor adopted the alternative principle of yearly grants.[16] Of the peace revenue, part had been granted for life, part for a term of years, and part had not been considered or granted at all. And amid all the confusion there had been no attempt whatsoever at the correlation of peace revenue and expenditure. Never perhaps has a House of Commons been so woefully misguided; never have members been so deplorably ignorant of the most elementary financial principles.

In administering his finances, William was mainly preoccupied with the pressing problem of finding ready money for the services and with scrutinizing the respective departmental debts. Similarly, the guiding principle of the head of the Treasury was administrative: he, like the King, was preoccupied almost exclusively with the twin problems of finding ready money to pay the troops and financing the departments of the civil government. Need we wonder that the wretched Godolphin, faced with these dilemmas, was soon agitating to be released from his onerous duties? Very soon we find Danby, now Carmarthen, reporting to William that Godolphin despaired of paying the money on the due day unless a loan of £200,000 can be raised from the States:[17] and at about the same time his friend Marlborough writing to William, absent in Holland for the Congress at The Hague, that in accordance with His Majesty's commands he had been doing what he could to dissuade Godolphin from his purpose, but he was forced to add, "I do not think that I prevail much on him, any otherwise than it makes him melancholy." Therefore he begs the King before returning to "tell him that you have so much personal kindness for him, that you deserve better than that he should abandon you at this time, when you have need of his service."[18]

Though this flattery serves to show the esteem in which Godolphin was held by the new Sovereign, it does not appear to have had much effect upon him, for we find Lord Sidney, his colleague in the Council, advising Queen Mary, writing a few days later to the King of Godolphin's determination to be done with public life: "He lays it most upon his wife, and saith it will not be convenient for a man of business that is not very young to bring a wife near the court."[19] This strange statement lacks any explanation. Many years earlier rumour had reported Sidney romantically attached to Mary of Modena, but as the acidulous Swift is mainly responsible for this we need not give it too much credence.[20] Nor need Dartmouth's note to Burnet's *History* much disturb us. "He was made lord chamberlain to the queen," it runs, "and more esteemed and trusted by her than any man in England. After the revolution he kept a constant correspondence with her to his dying day (which he managed by the countess of Lichfield:) notwithstanding Mr. Caesar of Hartfordshire was sent to the Tower for saying so in the house of commons in the reign of Queen Anne."[21] Some years later rumour had linked Sidney's name with Sophia Stuart, the beautiful sister of the better known "la belle Stuart" of King Charles's Court and now Duchess of Richmond. But Sophia had married a Jacobite spy, Henry Bulkeley, a son of the first Viscount Bulkeley, of whom we shall hear more; and thus marriage between her and Godolphin had become impossible. There had, as we see, been from time to time reports of the widower's inclinations, but never a reliable report of any marriage. What then means this reference to a wife? So far as is known Sidney Godolphin never replaced his beloved Margaret. Could it be that he had been joking with his credulous colleague, who swallowed all he was told and duly reported it as Gospel truth to his master?

Meanwhile, Godolphin was himself in constant correspondence with the King on financial matters. "The loans come in very slowly . . ." he told William in February; "for of the foure millions given by the parliam^t to bee applyed with the present yeare, our moyety is upon fonds so remote that no use can be made of them, other than by putting of them by Assignments into the hands of the Creditors to the Army, to the Navy, and to the Ordnance, as a security for what goods and commoditys have been furnished by them, either for cloathing the Army or for stores; now these people being trading men, and most of them necessitous, cannot stay till these tallys come in course of payment, and consequently must be obliged to part with them, at 5 or 10, or 12 pr cent losse, according as they can agree with the men that have money at their command." Therefore lenders of money were keeping back their funds, and unless a means could be found to destroy the profits thus earned Godolphin did not see how money would be forthcoming to pay the services. Could not the King, he asked, prevail upon his native Holland to allow the remainder of the money due to the States General to remain on loan a year longer at 8 per cent interest? With regard to the arrears of pay due to the army in England and in Ireland, Godolphin had a suggestion to offer: the former might be paid "in some degree by the remaynder of the money unappropriated upon the Land Tax"; and with regard to the latter, he suggested that William should agree to a quarter only being paid in cash and to the other three quarters being secured by debentures on the Irish forfeited lands. This expedient, states Godolphin, would ease the whole situation, ". . . and perhaps give. . . . more satisfaction to the Army than a Tally upon a remote fonds would doe. . . ." Finally he begs "that the King will on his return ". . . let me live this summer at least in the country; the occasion of it is in selfe indispensable; and in my case it admits of no delay. . . ."[22]

A second letter follows this up four days later, but it adds little to the first. Forty thousand pounds, he reports, have been borrowed upon the Excise, which sum is needed to pay the troops quartered at Chester.

Meanwhile "Wee have yett been very sparing to strike any Tally's from the apprehension of the ill consequences of it . . . but the services will not admit of delaying it much longer since funds are barely sufficient to pay the troops in England, and those in Ireland must not be forgotten."[23]

Small wonder that Godolphin, in poor health at this time, should be anxious to retire; but the King, overwhelmed with difficulties, could not bear the thought of losing one ". . . pour le quel j'ay une estime et amitie si grande. . . ." On no account must he abandon his Sovereign in his present difficulties. "L'amitie personell que j'ay eu pour vous, depuis que je vous ay cognu, me fait esperer que vous y vouderes repondre en cette ocasion . . ." so that he may have ". . . la satisfaction d'avoir aupres de moy une personne pour la quelle j'ay tant d'amitie personelle et dont j'ay une si bonne opinion. Si vous en avez le moundre pour moy," he continues pathetically, "je m'asseure que quandt vous aures bien considere la chose vous ne continuerea point en votre resolution, et voudres bien me donner cette satisfaction, ce que me sera asseurement un soulagement considerable en tous les affaires facheuses que j'ay sur le bras. W.R."[24] A few days later, the King acknowledged the Minister's letters of February 2nd and 6th, and agreed to all Godolphin's suggestions. Then he returned to the question of retirement on which he concluded ". . . . que je me flatte que vous ne vouderes pas refuser a donner des marques de votre amitie a une personne que en a autant que que [sic] j'en ay pour vous."[25]

Whilst William was writing thus to the Minister, Godolphin was repeating the request that he might be suffered to retire upon the King's return, if only for a limited period. He then turned to financial matters and particularly to the difficulty of paying the fleet. Before the fleet puts to sea, as Godolphin reminded William, no less than £200,000 will be needed; and only in the City of London can this sum be found for the City is always more ready to finance the fleet than any other service.[26] Several days later he informed the King that, the Queen having at yesterday's Council requested a loan from the City for the payment of the fleet, we must meanwhile strike no tallys "how pressing soever the occasions of them may bee. . . ." But he is able to report in conclusion, "All the money necessary for the recruits here, has been payed as fast as demanded; so that if there has been any defect in that matter, yett it will not reasonably be at our dore, where I expect most other faults will be placed."[27]

With the Minister in this mood, it is not surprising that Marlborough's efforts to dissuade his friend from retiring were not meeting with much encouragement. Indeed, towards the end of February we find him recording in his own curious orthography that—"I am sorry to tell your

Majistie that Ld. Godolphin continues very obstenant, soe that I have noe hopes, but your own prevalling when you speak with him. . . ."[28] Meanwhile, Godolphin continued to report on financial matters and particularly on the success of the loan. The City magnates had readily agreed to the request for £200,000 for the payment of the fleet; "it must bee our part," he added cautiously, "to quicken their performance."[29] And three days later he recorded the "good effect" the royal message had had, for in three days the City had raised sixty thousand pounds "which must all goe, and a great deale more as fast as we can gett it, for paying the seamen."[30] But there were many difficulties. In spite of William's promise to prevail upon the Dutch not to ask for repayment of their money for another year, it seemed that King William had not made the necessary arrangements. "The Citty loanes come in soe well," he was able to report in the same letter, "that we have issued £100,000 to the Navy this last week . . ." but "Wee are still in the last necessity for money to send into Ireland for the £300 a troop that should be pay'd here, and for the cloathing of the horse, all of which are extreamly pressing upon us at this time. . . ."[31] To the King's enquiry as to dates for repayment, Godolphin, was forced to admit that he could not estimate when funds would be available, but he definitely promised the punctual payment of the 8 per cent interest. At the same time, he was optimistic that the loan from the city might turn out to be more than the sum promised.[32]

Whilst Godolphin was thus corresponding with his master, the egregious Sidney was also writing to William though not on financial matters. Personalities were his theme. "Lord President hath been of late very peevish, and continually complaining; I am now his confidant, and he hath almost told me that he would retire in a very little time," he vouched. "My Lord Marlborough behaves himself much better than he did att first after your Majesty's going away; he is now pretty dilegent, and seldome fails the Committee's—My Lord Godolphin comes not often, but he hath a good excuse for it, which is the Treasury; . . . I hope your Majesty will thinke of comming quickly to us for you are wanted beyond expression."[33] And in an undated note of about this time, he tells the King ". . . that my Lord Godolphin's quitting your service is now no secrett, for my Lord Halifax told it mee the other day. . . . What My Lord Godolphin does in the Treasury I cannot tell, but I see his proceedings in other places are not with that zeale for your service as might be expected from him; he scarce ever comes to Councell and never to the Committees, upon the taking of severall ill affected persons and att the Examination of them he never was present; what the reason of it is I can't tell."[34]

At last on March 13th, Lord Godolphin became more precise as to his reasons for wishing to retire. The Queen had laid her commands upon the

Treasury in two matters of which he did not approve, first in the matter of the Lord President's pension for twenty-one years on the post office,[35] and secondly the necessity to find sixteen thousand pounds "Towards my Ld. Bathe's arrears." At the same time, the Minister was gratified to be able to announce the great success of the City loan for payment of the fleet—£200,000 had been paid up and a further £100,000 promised.[36] A week later, Godolphin was even more precise on the abuses to which he objected, and, he added, "I question whether some of my brethren will yett agree to countersigne the warrant which the Queen has signed for my Ld. President's grant...."[37] Early in the following month, he had more good news to report: a further £117,500 had been received and sent to Ireland, which was sufficient for four months' pay to all the officers of the army there. As to the rest of their arrears, Godolphin considered that most people would gladly accept debentures on the forfeited lands, so that fortunately "... the Army will bee pretty well enabled to goe cheerfully into the Campagne:..." As for the navy, almost the whole £200,000 had been issued to the seamen so that the fleet was now ready to put to sea.[38]

In May we find Godolphin asking for a place for his son, Francis, who "is now of an age to require some better education abroad than I am able to give him without your Majesty's favour...." A certain Mr. Thomas Howard was critically ill, and he sought his place for Francis. "I have not troubled your Majesty to aske many things of you for my selfe, and this is a thing, which I am very sure, I would rather lose than not owe it entirely to your Majesty's own favour and goodness to me."[39]

Three months later, Godolphin was at Tunbridge Wells, drinking the waters: during his absence, as he was careful to point out, Treasury business was in no way retarded; but he was anxious to retire on the King's return, "... especially since I can never hope by these waters or any other thing else, to be soe freed from the distemper that troubles mee as that the Attendance upon businesse myst not always increase it, and consequently bee extreamly uneasy to me;"[40] The poor man was suffering from the stone, a "distemper" to which he was destined to succumb more than twenty years later; but it was not sufficient to gain his release, and the following spring we find him still wrestling with Blathwayt, the King's confidential Secretary.[41] In June, Godolphin received orders to provide weekly returns for the maintenance of the Hanover troops. He hastened to inform Blathwayt that this was "still another new extraordinary," and as funds were short anyhow, it will be necessary to anticipate the revenue to find the required funds.[42] Then there was the money in arrear to the troops in Savoy, the funds that William was constantly requiring for the secret service,[43] and for his extravagant building projects at Kensington.[44] All this was leading to a financial crisis. "I beg of you to represent to the King," Godolphin told Blathwayt, "that the consequence of all this is loading his revenue with more Anticipation, and plunging it into such engagements as he will bee very sorry to see at his return. . . ."[45]

It is clear that Godolphin did not like the way he was being imposed upon by the exigencies of the King, and he did not leave the faithful Blathwayt in any doubt of his feelings. No wonder the Lord Treasurer was anxious to retire; and it is certain that the King was not unsympathetic towards his harassed servant. "Je vous asseure," he wrote quaintly to Godolphin, "que je *shrink* aussi bien que vous quandt je considere l'estat ou est la Treasurie et les facheuses affaires que nous aurons aparement cette hyver, j'espere que vous tous mes autres amis m'assisteront a surmonte tous les difficultes que l'on prevoit, et les cabales que se font deja pour me donner de la plene et nuire au gouvernement et toutte l'Europe, le bon Dieu vuillie que nous les puissions surmonte."[46] A year later there is still difficulty about finding funds to pay the fleet. "I need not tell you of the desperate straits we are in for money," he writes, ". . . j'espere que la ville de Londres en aura preste, sans quoy je ne scai comment vous faires. . . ."[47] Sympathetic the King might be, but he just could not release Godolphin, in whom he recognized a warm friend and a conscientious Minister: there were not so many such that this one could be spared.

Yet even whilst Godolphin was at the head of the Treasury and thus corresponding on familiar terms with his sovereign, he and other leaders of the revolution were involved in a mysterious conspiracy some account of which must now be given.

Early in January 1691 the busy Jacobite agent, Henry Bulkeley, reappeared in England after a sojourn on the Continent, whither he had fled at the Revolution. As the reader will recall, his wife was none other than "la belle Stuart's" equally lovely sister,[48] with whom rumour, though with little evidence, had long reported Godolphin to be enamoured,[49] and who, so gossip also had whispered in King William's reign, had recently been imprisoned in the Bastille for correspondence with her supposed lover.[50] In these circumstances, what could be more natural than that Bulkeley should within a few weeks of his return call upon Lord Godolphin, who, it will be recalled, had only a few months earlier resumed his seat at the Treasury? The two men were certainly old acquaintances and perhaps they were further united by a common admiration for the same woman, so it was probably not difficult for the agent to obtain an appointment with the Minister. Subsequently Bulkeley visited Lord Halifax, now in opposition, and in due course he issued a report on these interviews. According to the only account that has come down to us Bulkeley visited Godolphin twice. At the first interview the Minister made no mention whatsoever of the exiled King. But the spy was not discouraged, and in the second interview he tried a little flattery, saying that "He was in admiration to find his Lordship in imployment again, he haveing assured him before he left England, he was resolved never to take any for the future"; to which Godolphin replied that he had promised William—or the Prince of Orange, as of course the agent called him—to come in again upon his return from Ireland and that he had kept his word. Then he enquired after the exiled Court, "but with a seeming despondency." Bulkeley attempted to rally the Minister from his melancholy and "pressed him a little farther on the point to know what assurance he might give the King of his willingness to serve him: whereupon Godolphin sprang from his chair, and declared he would quit his employment at the first opportunity, and so broke off the interview by leaving the room." This was not too promising—"a coy beginning," Bulkeley terms it: nevertheless he determined to persevere; and he departed forthwith to see Lord Halifax. This cautious statesman, we are told, received him with open arms, and laying bare his breast, "sayd He would doe all that lay in his power to serve his Majesty and forward his return." He then gave his visitor permission to acquaint Lord Godolphin with his sentiments. This message from Halifax, we are told, made Godolphin bolder, so that at last he threw discretion to the winds and declared that so soon as William should return from the Congress at The Hague, he, Godolphin, "would quit all . . . for that he made a conscience (he sayd) of betraying his trust . . . he therefore resolved (he sayd) to disingage himself from any such tye, notwithstanding the Prince of Orange had writ to him from The Hague (which letter he shew'd Mr. Bulkeley) complaining how many difficultys lay heavy upon him at present, in reference to the Confederates as well as other affairs, but that nothing troubled him so much as his thoughts of leaveing his service in such a conjuncture, he being the person he had most confidence in, and most kindness for of any English man, and therefore charges him not to think of doing it; but he made shew as if all this weighed little with him in respect of his duty to his lawful Sovereign."[51]

A very touching scene! But there is more to come. One day, Bulkeley chanced to see Godolphin and Marlborough walking together in the park. He hailed them, and finding them responsive invited both to dine at his lodgings. There, doubtless under the mellowing influence of wine, at least one of the visitors began to talk. We are not told that Godolphin was communicative; but Marlborough was so loquacious that the host sent for Colonel Sackville who ". . . was hugely surprised to find him in apearance the greatest penitant immaginable; he beg'd of him to go to the King and acquaint him with his sincere repentance, and to intercede for mercy, that he was ready to redeem his apostasy with the hazard of his utter ruine, his crimes apeareing so horrid to him that he could neither sleep, nor eat but in continual anguish, and a great deal to that purpose. . . ." But Colonel Sackville, we are informed, was not to be too easily won. He determined to put him to the test; whereupon Marlborough ". . . without the least hesitation gave an account of all the forces, preparations, and designes both in England, Scotland, and Ireland, whither, he sayd, the Prince of Orange intended to go himself, if the French pressed not too hard upon the Confederates in Flanders, and he hoped to reduce Ireland so soon as to be able to bring back part of that Army into the Low Countrys that very Campaign, he gave likewise an account of the Fleet, and in fine of whatever was intended either by Sea or land. . . ."[52] Finally, he asked Sackville to be his intercessor with James, the best of Kings, to whose cause he did not doubt that he could bring over many great men dissatisfied with the new regime.

That is the pretty little romance as it has been handed down to us. It is the story that forms the basis upon which the greatest historian of this period founded his venomous attack upon Godolphin, Marlborough and Russell; and ever since he has been slavishly followed by lesser writers, blinded by the dazzle of the master's genius. But let us study the story a little more carefully. After his interviews with Godolphin and Marlborough, the agent wrote a detailed report of events as he saw them and sent it to James. Where is this report? It has never come to light: and it is not unreasonable to assume that it was lost, together with practically all of the exiled monarch's papers, at the time of the French Revolution. There is, then, no first-hand record of Bulkeley's dispatch: all we have to rely on is the second volume of the so-called *Life of James the Second collected out of the Memoirs writ of his own hand,* where the whole story of Bulkeley and his doings is in detail set forth.[53] It was upon this account of the affair that the Whig historian, on his own admission, mainly relied for his narrative of these events.[54] But it is now known that the real memoirs of King James II "writ of his own hand" ended at his accession to the throne, and that this second volume is nothing more than the work of a Jacobite clerk at Saint Germain, William Dicconson by name, writing some fifteen or twenty years after, and with no first-hand knowledge whatsoever of the events he purports to record.[55] Thus at one fell blow collapses the whole attack on the maligned leaders.

Now let us look a little closer into matters. It is not to be denied that Bulkeley had his talks with Godolphin, Marlborough and Halifax. Indeed, Lord Ailesbury in his *Memoirs* goes so far as to state that the interviews actually took place with the knowledge and leave of King William.[56]

That we may scarcely credit. Nevertheless, there is little doubt that the three Ministers bemused the agent with every kind of promise of what they would do if only conditions were favourable. What happens then? The eager agent hastens to write to James representing in the most favourable light everything that has been said to him partly in order to cheer the heart of the exile and partly in order to exaggerate his own worth to the Stuart cause. So far as Godolphin is concerned two "cautious entries" in the Devonshire House "note book" would seem to some extent to corroborate Bulkeley's account of his interviews with him, assuming, which is not quite certain, that B. stands for the agent. The entries run thus: "March 90. B. told mee, that L. Godol: had very lately given assurances &c. . . ." "May 91. B. said, perhaps some of L. Godolphins other friends &c. were content he should stay in . . . Lᵈ Godol: . . . shewed me a letter to him from the King out of Holland, expressing great trouble at his intention of leaving his imploymᵗ."[57] Very likely the letter from King William here referred to is the same as the letter that Bulkeley states Godolphin shewed him. Very likely Godolphin was in the habit of showing people the King's letters to illustrate his difficulties. Very likely, too, Godolphin gave "assurances". All the Ministers at this time were in the habit of giving the Jacobites "assurances." But that is very far from betraying King William.

But if we can believe the account thus far, there are some things that we really cannot accept. At Bulkeley's early interviews with Godolphin, the Minister, we are told, was "coy", but as soon as he heard of Halifax's sentiments, his whole attitude suddenly changed. Halifax, so Bulkeley reports, received him with open arms, laid his breast bare and immediately promised all possible help for the exiled Sovereign. Can we imagine the cautious Trimmer thus dangerously committing himself? Then he gave his visitor permission to acquaint Godolphin with his sentiments. But surely Halifax would be the last man living thus rashly to place himself at the mercy of a member of the Government, and of one on whom he was said at this time to be on bad terms.[58] And Godolphin? Would his whole attitude be likely to change at a mere word from Bulkeley on the views of the opposition leader with whom, so far as we know, he had had no consultation on the subject whatsoever? As for Marlborough, can we imagine that astute man acting the theatrical and ridiculous role for which he is cast in this absurd comedy? We can almost hear him grumbling out his habitual comment: "Silly! Silly!" In short, nothing could be less in keeping with all that we know of the characters of "timid" Godolphin, "crafty" Marlborough, and the illustrious Trimmer.

What then must we think of a story in which none of the chief participants plays true to type? So far as Godolphin is concerned we have seen the terms he was on with William. What on earth had he to gain from the restoration of malicious King James? He had felt in duty bound to support James so long as he was King, but so soon as he fled the country, Godolphin's duty to him ceased. Thus both conscience and self-interest pulled the same way. And there is nothing in the fabulous and absurd inanities of the Jacobite clerk, Dicconson, writing many years after the events he pretended to narrate, to make us think otherwise. On the flimsy evidence before us Godolphin must surely be acquitted from the shameful charge so long levelled at him by the malicious Jacobites.

CHAPTER VII

PLOT—COUNTERPLOT

THE Bulkeley affair was not the only intrigue with which the name of Godolphin was associated, nor was Bulkeley the only Jacobite agent to be busy in England during these critical years. At least two others, General Edward Sackville and an able and active spy, Captain David Floyd or Lloyd*—sent to Saint Germains elaborate reports of interviews and conversations they alleged they had had with Godolphin, Russell, Halifax and Churchill; and some account of the subterranean activities of these political moles must now be given.

The charges of treason which have been brought against Godolphin, Marlborough, and other leaders, are based upon certain documents now in the Bodleian Library, which previously formed part of the papers of David Nairne, under-secretary to Lord Melfort, then Secretary of State to James II at Saint Germain and subsequently in the confidential employment of Queen Mary of Modena. In 1775 a selection from the Nairne Papers was published by James Macpherson under the title of *Original Papers containing the Secret History of Great Britain from the Restoration to the accession of the House of Hanover*. Some forty-one years later, in 1816, the so-called *Life of James II* appeared, and on this work also historians relied. As has been stated, it is now known that the part of this work that concerns the reign and exile of James, so far from being "writ of his own hand", is the work of an obscure Jacobite clerk without any first-hand knowledge of the events he professed to portray. His fabulous writings, then, we may dismiss from our minds. But what of the publication of 1775? The credit of James Macpherson of "Ossian" fame stands so low that several authorities have actually suggested that he fabricated some of the documents he printed; but so far as the so-called "Original Papers" are concerned there were living at the time many persons who must have had a very full knowledge of the Nairne documents, and not one of them has ever uttered a word to suggest

* There seems some doubt as to whether the name was Floyd or Lloyd, but I have applied the former which seems to be the more correct. The D.N.B., however, calls him Lloyd.

that Macpherson had in any way garbled his texts.   This surely is sufficient to show that the charge that Macpherson forged the Nairne Papers cannot be sustained.[1]

We must now consider those of the Nairne Papers that implicate Lord Godolphin.

The first relative document is the only one written in English.   Dated "16 Oct. 93." it is in the hand of Lord Melfort, and consists of much corrected draft "instructions".   The relevant portion is headed "Instructions to E. Danby, L[d] Godolph: and Churchill* by C. Shrewsb:"—in other words, Melfort's instructions are designed to be transmitted by, or through Lady Shrewsbury, Shrewsbury's Jacobite mother.   It reads thus:

"It is his Majesty's pleasure that you desire Earle of Danby to Endeavour to gayne adml. Killigrue (Killigrew) to His service since his Majesty knows that he has an influence on him that is if he be to be imployed.

"That his Majesty Expects upon this conjuncture that the Earle of Danby will doe him what service he can and most particularly by giving him tyme now to act against the Prince of Orange and by letting him kno as near as he can what the princes designes may be and his opinione how to prevent them.

"E Sh: Dan: God: R[u] & C (Earl Shrewsbury, Danby, Godolphin, Russell, and Churchill). That they doe what in prudence they can to Hinder mony or retard it and to Hinder the going out of the fleet so soon as it might doe otherwiss.   That they send the K. this advice if it be for his service to send any thing to the par[t] in pursuance of his declaratione and if it will not be fitt that the M.C. King emitt some Declaratione nou that he is so victorus as to giv terror to all his neybours and it may be to England shewing that he has no intentione in relatione to England but the reestablishment of the lawfull King upon his thron.   Which done he will not medle in the Concerns but leav them to be Governed by thr own Laws and to Enjoy the Religious liberty and propertys which by there Lows they Hav right to."[2]

What a document on which to found a charge of treason, for there is no evidence whatever that these "instructions" were ever delivered, let alone obeyed.   Indeed, it would appear from the original manuscript, which is unsigned, as if they are merely sketched out in rough draft.   But even if by chance the "instructions" were delivered, what was there to prevent the self-deluded James from issuing orders to the empty air?   What was to prevent his partisans from using them to traduce those they were anxious to ruin?

* The Jacobites always called persons by the titles held before 1688, not recognizing those bestowed by King William.

Another document, undated but probably written about 1689, implicates Danby. It is even more absurd than the one previously quoted. In French throughout, it appears to be mainly, if not entirely, in Nairne's hand,* and has obviously been prepared for the French Government. It augurs well for the success of the enterprise because James's supporters include Danby, Godolphin, Shrewsbury, Russell, Churchill, and the sons of the Dukes of Beaufort and Bolton. "Tous gens que ont servy le Prince d'Orange avec zele tant quies ont cru quil pouvoit se soutenir en Angleterre et ont meprisé toutte correspondence avec le Roy : Ce qui fait voir quils ne sont plus de ce sentiment presentement, et par consequence que sa Majesté a plus desperance que jamais."[3] But because the original manuscript appears to be in Nairne's hand, it does not follow that he composed it. Indeed, it is quite unbelievable that he did, for this "tissue of absurdities"[4] shows quite astonishing ignorance of affairs in England since the departure of James. In fact, all that Nairne can have done is merely to have translated into French the report of some silly, ignorant Jacobite in England.

The next paper of importance particularly implicates Godolphin. Though in Lord Melfort's hand throughout, it purports to be a dispatch to James II from Floyd on his return to Saint Germain in the early summer of 1694.† Some time earlier, this same Floyd had written a curious paper, in which he shows doubts of being able to enlist the assistance of either Godolphin or Shrewsbury for the Jacobite cause. "As for thes two bailes you mention," he wrote in the strange secret service jargon of the day, "No 251 and No. 722 (Godolphin and Shrewsbury), for all I can yet learn there is not much more clearness here than you have ther and thefor I can saying nothing of positiv concerning them as yet."[5] But by May 1694, it seems, Floyd was no longer so pessimistic about his chances of seducing Lord Godolphin and other leaders. He begins by informing James that upon his arrival in London he had sent for Sackville, in order to facilitate meetings with Russell, Shrewsbury, Lady Shrewsbury, Churchill and Godolphin, and to consult with his fellow-spy on the best method of treating with these notables.

The first person Floyd saw was Churchill, to whom he showed his instructions and at the same time informed him that King James ". . . luy donnait son consentement pour L'accepter et luy laissa la liberte de se servir

---

* Mr. Churchill calls it "an undated, anonymous paper in an unknown hand." Churchill, *Marlborough*, I, 392. I think there is no doubt that about ten of its thirteen pages are in Nairne's hand, and I suspect that the opening pages were also written by him though they do seem to differ slightly from his customary style.

† The manuscript is headed by Melfort, "Relation du Capt. floyd nouvelment revenue D'Angleterre", and endorsed "Relation du Capt. Floyd porte a Versailles Le 11 May 1694."

des moyenns le plus propre pour L'Obtenir nayant null doute de sa fidelité.
. . ." What naiveté! The outcast and helpless monarch graciously gives
"Churchill" permission to accept service under "the Prince of Orange", in
order to betray him. How thoughtful! How kind! We can almost see the
flicker of a smile playing over the handsome features of the spy's bland,
inscrutable auditor. He contented himself, however, by replying in a few
words of empty compliment. The next evening, as Floyd reports, Churchill arranged for him to see Admiral Russell, who received him with much
friendliness. The agent brought Russell messages of goodwill from his
master, and he enlarged upon the gratitude King James would feel towards
the Admiral if he would apply himself seriously to his business. The reply was
typical. How delighted the Admiral would be to help ". . . mais que la
chose estant fort difficile d'accomplir, il falloit du temps. . . ." Excuses,
eternal excuses: things were difficult, time was needed. That ended the
conversation for the moment; but Russell promised in two or three days to
give the agent another interview.

Floyd's next appointment was with Lady Shrewsbury, who, so he avers,
vouched for the devotedness of her son to the cause of King James. At his
second talk with Admiral Russell, the agent pressed him on his promise to be
more precise. Once again, however, the Admiral returned a vague answer.
If only he were free to act as he wished, but alas, the times were out of joint.
The agent showed his disappointment: he would be reluctant, he said, to
report so unsatisfactory an answer, and he must know what Russell could
and would do to aid King James's cause. To this Russell replied with a
promise to endeavour ". . . de gagner les officiers de la flotte et quil feroit
savoir a My Lord Churchill de temps au temps le progres qu'il feroit. . . ."
"But, if you were in my position, what would you do?" asked Russell of
the agent, a former naval officer. "Je luy respondes quil y avoit plusiares
choses a faire comme eviter la flotte francaise et la laisser passer." To this
the admiral demurred; in any case he would not act alone. "Je luy pro-
posais," declared the agent, "que puis y aurat infalliblement quelque designe
sur la coste de france celle este necessairement . . ." to draw down troops to
Brest or elsewhere on the coast, ". . . quil en pouvoit avertir votre Majeste
et luy donner le temps de prepaper les vaissaux de transport elle este et que
vers lautumn quand il falloit disarmer les Grand Vaissaux et envoyer des
convoys en L'Amerique etc . . ." he would be a judge of those proper to
be kept in the Channel, and accordingly might retain those gained over this
summer, and either send the rest into the harbour, or employ them for
convoys; ". . . et estant par la devenu le maitre de se que restait si joindre au
francois pour transporter les troupes qui seroient necessaires pour accom-
pagner votre Majesté en Angleterre." The Admiral, we are told, interrupted

the agent several times, at last protesting, with many appearances of fidelity, that he would undertake the affair and thought Shrewsbury and Churchill should be judges of his actions.

And now it was Lord Godolphin's turn to receive Floyd. He, we are told, explained his feelings for King James, "dans la manière du monde la plus affectione." He told the agent that there was too much room to fear that a peace would be concluded that summer; and that that were sorry to believe, from the manner in which the Prince of Orange spoke of it, that the terms would be prejudicial to King James, "puis quinfalliblement"— infallibly, that same word again—the Prince would strive to oblige King Louis to send King James out of his dominions. This, Godolphin is represented to have said, he felt his duty to let the exile know. It was also his opinion that, if peace be not concluded this summer, King James "devoit passer en Angleterre Mais avec une force considerable; . . . que l'estait pas difficile aux francois de fair une decente en Angleterre sans russell . . ." who ought, nevertheless, to be treated with attention. Furthermore, it was Godolphin's view, we are told ". . . que Mr. Russell paraiteroit infalliblement devant Brest,"—that Russell and the fleet would infallibly appear before Brest, noteworthy words that we must not forget,—the military commanders believing that the place would be attacked, though the naval officers were of a different opinion: that this would give a just pretext to His Most Christian Majesty "d'envoyer des troupes dans de lieu et que celle este l'on pouvoit preparer les vaissaux de Armes fort necessaires etc. que les gros vaissaux rentreront vers le milieu de l'autumn et que les Matelots serout disperses et les convoys seront envoyes en toutes les . . . (illegible) . . . ou il y a Commerce, et que 30 vaissaux de force raisonable ceroint malaise a trouver pour les Anglais;" that your Majesty, ". . . pouvoit passer et le debarquement fait il ne croyoit pas," that a blow would be struck, because ". . . des dix de L'Angleterre faisant le prince d'Or: de tout leur coeur." Godolphin, we are told, then reiterated his protestations of entire loyalty to King James.

Finally, Lady Shrewsbury, according to Floyd, "m'informa que le Prince d'Or. passeroit incessement apres la prorogation du Parliament en Holland quil laiseroit le gouvernement entre les Mains de la Princesse mais quelle devout suivre entierment les Conseils de Danby et de Shrewsbury."[6]

What are we to make of this curious document? It has been pointed out by several writers that there are remarkable similarities in the text—the word "infallibly" used several times, some such phrase as that "he had said a great deal" or "all that could be expected of him," more than once—which lead one to suspect that the whole document was a fraud, perhaps secretly put together at Saint Germain by Melfort and Floyd and by them transmitted to

Versailles as the latest news from England. The truth more probably is that this paper is in fact no more than a translation into French of a genuine report in English. In rendering such a version, it would be not unnatural to repeat words and phrases; but if Melfort had been really composing a fraudulent account, he would surely have had sufficient sense to avoid making such a simple blunder. And if that be the correct view, where is Floyd's original report? Like so many of these supposed Jacobite documents, it has not been found. But that is not to say that it never existed. We have no reason to think that the agent did not have his interviews, or that his conversations did not run very much on the lines recorded. We may accept the account of his talk with Godolphin as being substantially correct without impugning Sidney's honour or loyalty. It is only natural that the four men concerned should consult together as to what they should say. It is noticeable, moreover, that what Godolphin said to Floyd is almost exactly the same as what the agent had said to the Admiral. May we not suppose that Russell had previously told Godolphin exactly what Floyd knew? Thereafter, all Godolphin had to do was to tell Floyd what he knew that he knew already! Too simple. Yet it is upon this unsure foundation that historians have raised their shameful charge of treason against Godolphin, Marlborough and the other leaders. Only in recent years has this unstable structure been completely demolished.

But we must not forget Godolphin's words to Floyd that Admiral Russell would "infallibly" appear before Brest. Neither Churchill nor Russell, whom the agent had seen previously, had, so far as we know, made any mention of an attack projected against the fortifications of Brest harbour. Yet Godolphin had not scrupled to suggest, though in vague terms, that something of the sort might be in the wind. What he did not add was that he had long known of the plans and had vehemently opposed them on the score of expense. As far back as April of the previous year, 1693, Godolphin was writing to King William about a Treasury paper estimating the cost of the enterprise. Some persons thought the report unfair, and that the officials had exaggerated the expenses involved. "I should bee glad they might prove to bee in the right," commented Godolphin, "but I doubt experience will show the contrary, and I must confesse . . . that I have not faith enough in the thing it selfe, to give easily into any expense, that the preparations for it doe require . . ."[7] And a week later, reporting that they had that day borrowed from the City the money needed to pay the navy, he added the hope that ". . . they may bee early enough at Brest to prevent the conjunction of the french fleet there, with the squadron expected from the Mediterranean which I should think is what our fleet ought principally to intend, and they need not apprehend, as formerly, the leaving the port of

Brest open, and giving liberty to the ships there, to come into the Channell for the french will never dare to venture that, while they know wee have a fleet soe much superior to theirs lying to the westward of theirs."[8]

Three weeks later Godolphin returned to the subject. "I believe your Majesty would not bee very pleased that there should bee a necessity of calling the parliament again before your return; I should hope therefore your Majesty would yett hinder us from throwing away money upon the preparations for a descent."[9] And three months later, Sidney wrote yet again to William bewailing the difficulties of raising money for war services as well as civilian needs, and concluding more in sorrow than in anger: "I trouble your Majesty as little as I can, but upon this subject, I have the misfortune to differ soe much from other in all the measures relating to the fleet, that I hope your Majesty will forgive mee if I am a little fuller of it than I ought to bee."[10] So Godolphin, vexed perhaps at having his advice ignored, hinted to the agent what was in the wind. In doing so was he guilty of the terrible charge that has been brought against him of having betrayed to the Jacobites a State secret of the highest importance?

With this in mind, let us now turn to the Nairne Paper that gives what evidence there is for the supposed betrayal of the expedition, the document generally known as the Camaret Bay Letter.[11] This document, dated May 3rd, purports to be the translation into French of a letter from General Sackville forwarding a letter from Marlborough to the exiled King. In this Marlborough is represented as stating that the bomb-ketches and the twelve regiments encamped at Portsmouth, together with the two regiments of marines, all commanded by General Tolmash (or Tollemache) are destined for burning the port of Brest and destroying all the men-of-war there. This information was communicated to the French Government, who took prompt and energetic action. Thus, so the story goes, Godolphin by his hints to Floyd at the end of April, and Marlborough by his letter to James early in May, betrayed the secret plans for the attack on Brest, and frustrated our efforts to seize the harbour.*

Let us consider this charge a little more carefully. We are not concerned with the defence of Marlborough: but to some extent the defence of Godolphin involves that of his lifelong friend.

During one of the last days in April, 1694, Godolphin had his talk with the Jacobite agent, when he is reported as mentioning in a somewhat casual

---

* Macaulay, *History*, V, 2450. It is significant that no letter in Marlborough's hand has ever been found to substantiate Macaulay's terrible indictment. All we have is the paper in the Bodleian Library, which is in Nairne's hand with one small addition by Melfort that the information given by the letter must be kept a secret "even from Lord Middleton," ("meme du Comte Midleton").

way that Russell would "infallibly appear before Brest." Of course, as we have already shown, this document is not be be relied upon. It may be a complete fraud; but even if it is, as we suspect, a genuine translation of a genuine report, there is plenty of room for errors in a translation, and it is unfortunate, to say the least, that the agent's original is not before us. But let us assume that the report gives a fair version of what Godolphin said. What then? In adumbrating in vague terms an attack on Brest, he was only repeating popular rumour. He only surmised what half England was surmising and what Floyd, who was in close touch with many persons over here, had no doubt himself surmised on many occasions. But even if Godolphin's words came as a complete surprise to Floyd, which we do not for a moment believe, could they have had any effect whatever on the fortunes of the expedition? According to its endorsement, Floyd's report was transmitted to Versailles on May 1st.[12] Churchill's Camaret Bay letter was sent to France by Sackville on May 3rd.[13] They could not have reached their destination in less than three days under the most favourable conditions, and the actual time needed was probably longer. Yet it was on May 1st that Louis XIV reported to Vauban the threatened attack on Brest and ordered him to take the necessary counter measures;[14] whereupon the engineer set about the construction of new batteries that would almost double the armaments and on May 9th he reported to Louis what he was doing. Two further letters from King Louis followed, one undated and the other dated May 18th, and, acting on the instructions contained in them, Vauban arrived at Brest on May 23rd. By that time his precautions must have been almost completed.* On these plans anything that Godolphin may have said to Floyd at their interview at the end of April and anything that Marlborough may have written on or about May 3/13th, could have had no effect whatsoever. In short, they were only stating what Floyd and half England knew already, they only made the statements because they knew they revealed nothing, and they therefore betrayed no secrets of any sort either to the Jacobites or to the French Court.

The year 1694 closed sadly. Early in December the Queen was indisposed. She rapidly grew worse, and in a few days gruff Dr. Radcliffe diagnosed small-pox. At first his colleagues were inclined to disagree. "Yesterday the Doctours Concluded the Queen had not only the small-pox but the worst sort of them;" reported Sidney on Christmas Day, "and now to day they think she will not have them at all, and that tis only measles, for she is extreamly well."[15] But all too soon the malady proved mortal. On

* All these dates are New Style except the Camaret Bay Letter which is Old Style or May 13th New Style.

December 28th, Queen Mary died. But William had little time for grief. Soon he must leave to take command of the army in the Netherlands, and in the face of the French force under Marshal de Villeroy to seize the great town and fortress of Namur. Before sailing he delegated his authority to seven Lords Justices, of whom it was noted that six were Whigs and Godolphin the only Tory.

Whilst William was abroad, his faithful Minister continued to labour at the Treasury at the difficult task of supplying funds necessary for the maintenance of the army in the field. By 1695 both sides were beginning to show signs of financial exhaustion and in England it seemed as if little more could be raised by taxation. Thus gradually it began to be realized that the whole requirements of a long and exhausting war could not possibly be met from direct taxes. Accordingly, in December, 1692, Charles Montagu, who earlier in the year had been appointed a Lord of the Treasury, proposed to the House of Commons that a million pounds should be raised by way of loan. This was approved by the House in Committee, and a Bill was rapidly passed by which new duties were imposed on beer and other liquors, on the credit of which a million pounds was to be raised by life annuities, which, when the surviving annuitants were reduced to seven, were to lapse to the government. This was the origin of the National Debt.

In the following spring Montagu went a step further. Adopting Paterson's ingenious scheme, he introduced a Bill for raising a loan of a million and a half to defray the expenses of the war, and in order to induce capitalists to advance the money, subscribers who should provide in the aggregate the total sum of £1,200,000 were to be formed into a corporation to be known as the Governor and Company of the Bank of England, and to be allowed to treat the loan to the Government as part of their capital, the interest on which, at £8 per cent, was to be secured by taxes. In spite of much opposition to these novel proposals the Bill quickly became law, and so enthusiastically did the City take up the new investment that in ten days the whole of the money had been subscribed.[16]

The astute Godolphin was quick to see the importance of the new bank, and in his correspondence with the absent King, we hear much of the difficulties to be found in its early days. The Lords Justices in Council, we are told, complained that the law did not permit them to authorize the Treasury to accept "the first 4th part in clipp'd money" and in consequence the Treasury officials were resisting. "Your Majesty is pleased to say," he added, "I make you a very ill picture of your condition here, but I assure your Majesty upon my word, I endeavour to make it exactly true, and as I am very far from aggravating on one hand, soe I think I should bee more wanting than I ever will bee in my duty to your Majesty if I did not represent this matter truly as it is.[17]   Later, however, Godolphin is able to inform him that the Commissioners "were perswaded to quitt their demands of clipp'd money to bee taken for one 4th of their payments. . . ."   As to the future, he was optimistic.   He and the Speaker were in agreement that at least seven million pounds would be necessary next year, and that this sum could only be raised by the restoration of the nation's credit, upon which everything depends, ". . . upon the whole if wee can hold out 2 months he adds, "I think wee shall in great measure weather this storm. . . ."[18]

This trouble of the depreciation of the English silver coin had become serious.   In the years immediately before and following the revolution, a vast part of the silver in circulation had been so clipped and filed that it was calculated that one hundred pounds sterling, which should weigh rather more than thirty-two pounds only weighed on average about half that amount.[19]   This evidently could not be tolerated, and Montagu, advised by Locke, Newton and Somers, determined to remedy the evil.   Accordingly, in December, 1695 he carried eleven resolutions providing that the new coinage should be according to the mint's established standard of weight, that the loss on the clipped silver should be borne by the public, that crowns and half-crowns should henceforth be milled, and that a day should be fixed after which no clipped money should be allowed to pass.[20]   The Bill, slightly amended, passed both Houses, and it was provided that the expense of re-coinage, estimated at £1,200,000, should be met by a window tax.

For a time, however, these measures rather increased than decreased current difficulties, for most of the clipped silver was withdrawn before sufficient of the new had been put in circulation.   Some echoes of this can be traced in Godolphin's correspondence with the King, whom he told that ". . . the want of current money in the Countrey makes the poor people disorderly in many places, but hitherto it has gon no further than complaints and I hope will not; tho to speak truth their condition is very uneasy."[21]   And again a fortnight later ". . . the scarcity of money at home, at a time when wee are soe much pressed to send money abroad distracts us."[22]

A week later we find Godolphin reporting that help may be coming from "the land bank" which has offered two and a half million for "a premium" of £300,000 "which is not 12 per cent whereas one must now give 18 pr Cent to discount Talley's at a years distance. . . ."   This sounded almost too good to be true; and Godolphin was anxious to make sure of this great sum.[23]   To understand what "the land bank" was we must follow something of the interplay of the Whig and Tory parties during recent years. The Bank of England, as founded by Montagu, was mainly supported by the moneyed interest; consequently, the Tories, who were mostly landed proprietors, affected to regard it as a Whig institution and as such something to be deplored. They accordingly hit on the idea of setting up a rival institution to be based on the ownership of land itself, and under the guidance of the mercurial Harley, they succeeded in forming a company to establish a National Loan-Bank. Furthermore, they managed to persuade Parliament to resolve that the loans needed for the next twelve months, calculated to amount to about two and a half millions, should under certain conditions be transferred from Montagu's established bank to the new bank. So far so good. But Montagu, the Whigs and the Bank of England directors took prompt counter-measures against their opponents' scheme. The result of their activities was the total collapse of the Tory bank and the triumph of the Bank of England over what might have been a serious rival.[24]

The death of Queen Mary was a great encouragement to the Jacobites, who could not believe that the dour, unpopular King could stand alone. Before long, therefore, all sorts of plots for armed rebellion were afoot. The majority had as their object no more than the capture of William and his replacement by James: but amidst these comparatively mild designs there was inevitably a plot far more sinister, far more ruthless, a plot that had as its object nothing less than the cold-blooded murder of the King. About the autumn of 1695, a certain Sir George Barclay with some twenty or more followers came to England with wide instructions from James, which encouraged them to hatch a plot whereby William should be waylaid on his way home from hunting and dispatched by a band of Jacobite desperadoes. The plot failed; but had it succeeded James would in fact have been no nearer to regaining his throne. With the passing of Queen Mary, the centre of interest had shifted from James to Anne, with whom the Marlboroughs and Godolphin had for long been in the closest accord, and other leading Ministers were at last coming to recognize the wisdom and prescience of these two far-seeing men. In fact, the murder of William would have been followed by no civil unrest, no panic, no riots. Anne would have mounted the throne as naturally and as unchallenged as if her brother-in-law had died peacefully in his bed. But the plot miscarried. Barclay himself escaped, but many of his gang were arrested and paid the just penalty for their crimes.

There was one plotter, however, who for a time escaped detection. Sir John Fenwick was deeply implicated in Barclay's plans; but he went to ground and it was some time before he could be secured. Of good birth himself, Fenwick was, through his wife, daughter of the Earl of Carlisle, closely connected with many great families: he, therefore, hoped for powerful aid from many quarters. In this expectation he wrote a confession which, whilst revealing no secrets of the Jacobite plot, contained grave accusations against Godolphin, Marlborough, Russell, and Shrewsbury. Their reactions were interesting and various.

The sensitive Shrewsbury broke under the strain; nevertheless he expressed himself as strongly in favour of extracting all the information possible out of Fenwick, which is not exactly the attitude of a man overwhelmed by a sense of guilt.[25] But William, who detested Fenwick, recognized quickly enough the value of this paper and the whole thing disgusted him. He wrote to Shrewsbury assuring him of his continual trust and confidence. "You will observe *the sincerity of this honest man*,[26] who only accuses those in my service, and not one of his own party"; he added disgustedly, "I replied to my lord Steward that, unless he proved what he had written, and that he moreover confesses all he knows, without reserve I will not permit his trial to be defended, which is his only aim."[27] "Sir Jo. Fen. story is as wonderful to me as if he had accused me of coining," wrote Shrewsbury to Portland.[28] And to the King, "I want words to express my surprise at the impudent and unaccountable accusation of Sir John Fenwick," he wrote, whereupon he proceeded to give William an account of his only recent conversation with his relative, Lord Middleton,[29] the Protestant Jacobite. Shrewsbury may not have been blameless,[30] but King William was determined to comfort him by an assurance that he was perfectly satisfied with his explanations. "And indeed you may be assured," he added, "that this business, so far from making on me any unfavourable impression, will on the contrary, if possible, in future, strengthen my confidence in you, and my friendship can admit of no increase."[31] In spite of this Shrewsbury's natural sensibility appears to have been entirely deranged by the terrible charges brought against him. His health broke down completely, he insisted on retiring from the public service, and nothing that William could say could alter him from that course.[32]

So much for Shrewsbury. What of the others? Of the attitude of Russell we know scarcely anything;* of that of Marlborough and Godolphin we know rather more. It has been often said that timidity drove Godolphin to resign. The truth seems to be rather that he was induced to retire by the machinations of the unscrupulous Sunderland. It will be remembered that

* Miss Gladys Scott Thomson, whose knowledge of the Russell archives is profound, has very kindly searched in the Muniment Room at Woburn Abbey; and she informs me that she can find none of Russell's papers there. For this she gives an interesting explanation. It seems that Russell's father, Edward, son of the fourth Earl of Bedford, was a royalist, and this would be sufficient to alienate the son from his Puritan father. It appears that Lord Orford was not *persona grata* at Woburn, and, in Miss Scott Thomson's view, this difference of opinion on political matters may very well account for the lack of reference to him at Woburn. I gladly take this opportunity of expressing my gratitude to Miss Scott Thomson for the trouble she has put herself to on my behalf.

Godolphin was the only Tory among the seven Lords Justices appointed by the King in 1696. This was doubtless distasteful to the vast body of Whigs, now the majority of the lower House, and they determined to take advantage of the Fenwick scandal to contrive his fall. "My lord Sunderland is engaged again in the old business of removing my lord G . . ."[33] wrote Lord Keeper Somers to Shrewsbury; and again four days later, he expressed the view that Godolphin was ". . . directly tricked in this matter, and has suffered himself to be cozened into an offer to lay down, and is surprised in having his offer accepted; and I have reason to think, sees it and repents it."[34] "I am pretty well assured," wrote Lord Wharton to Shrewsbury, "the noble lord that quitted his employment some days before, is sensible now that he was not very well advised in it; and I am apt to think there never was more management than in bringing it about."[35] What advice Sunderland tendered, what arts he employed, we cannot say: all that is certain is that his efforts were successful and Godolphin resigned from the Treasury."*

That Godolphin's retirement was ill-judged is certain, for it seemed to betoken guilt. Yet when Fenwick appeared before the House of Lords on December 1st, both Godolphin and Marlborough took strong lines: no sign of fear here. Marlborough roundly accused Fenwick of trying to save his head by implicating the innocent and in the strongest terms denied having had any sort of conversation with him during the time of the present parliament. Godolphin, as became a civilian, was milder, but hardly less cogent. He declared, according to Wharton, "that he found himself named in two places, first, as having been looked upon as being in King James's interest, from the beginning, and afterwards, as having entered into a negotiation, as was expressed in the paper. As to the first, he confessed he was one of those that had, to the last, continued in King James's service, and he did not know, but from that, King James and his friends might imagine him to continue in interest, but as to the latter part, there was nothing in the world so false."[36] Yet in spite of the great wrong done him by the accused's reckless charges, Godolphin showed less rancour than some of Fenwick's other victims. Whilst Marlborough steadily voted with the majority for the attainder, Godolphin took a more merciful view. But even this receives no approbation from the great Whig. "Godolphin as steadily voted with the minority, but with characteristic wariness, abstained from giving any reasons for his votes. No part of his life warrants us in ascribing his conduct to any exalted motive. It is probable that, having been driven from office by the Whigs, and forced to take refuge among the Tories, he

* Professor Keith Feiling says that the management was "rather improbably attributed to Sunderland." Feiling, *Tory Party*, 323. I should have thought that all available evidence tended to implicate Sunderland.

thought it advisable to go with his party."[37] Clearly some men can do no wrong, and Godolphin, in his eyes, could do no right.

All the wits of the prisoner, all the support of his friends, all the influence of his relatives, were unavailing to save his life. On January 28th, 1697, Sir John Fenwick was beheaded on Tower Hill.

CHAPTER VIII

LAST YEARS OF THE REIGN

THE death of Queen Mary was destined to have an important influence on Godolphin's future, for it brought him, through the Marlboroughs, into much closer touch with Princess Anne.

Sidney Godolphin and John Churchill, ever since their first coming to Court in Charles II's reign, had been close friends, and Sidney had the greatest respect for the abilities of his friend's formidable wife. This is borne out by their animated private correspondence over a period of years. He sends her fruit from Cranbourne. "I ask your pardon for sending you these Cranbourn peaches, because by their looks I doubt they are not good enough for a present. . . ."★ Sarah returns the compliment from Holywell. "I must give you abundance of thanks for the peaches you sent mee," Sidney replies. "Some were very large and ripe, and as good as ever I tasted, the nectarins were pretty ripe, but hapning to come upon a day that I had taken physick, I durst not tast many of them; . . ."[1] There is much of their ailments. "I long to heare how you bee, how the country agrees with you, if you have been soe kind to your friends as to take care of your health; if you have taken physick or when you intend to doe it, many more questions I would ask, but I feare you may think these too many. . . ."[2] Sidney, as ever, is careful of his health. ". . . the Doctour tells mee, the pain I complaine of is a sort of rumatisme," he writes, "occasioned only by cold which tho it be uneasy, is not quite soe bad as I feared it would have proved. . . ."[3] Another time he thanks Sarah for a letter ". . . which my Lord Marleborough gave mee in my bed, for I have been soe ill with a cold these 2 days I have not been able to stirr . . ." and he bids her ". . . take care of your selfe and not catch cold for they are more than ordinarily uneasy this yeare. . . ."[4]

There are in Godolphin's letters frequent references to his friend's eldest daughter. ". . . I hope it is very plain that Lady Henrietta will bee well before you come to her," he once wrote, "however I am sure you will bee easyer there than you could bee here while you are in any uncertainty of her

---

★ Godolphin "To the Countesse of Marleborough, Sunday one a clock." Blenheim MSS. E. 17. The packet is marked in the Duchess's hand, "very old letters of Ld. Godol. in King William's time."

Lady Henrietta Churchill
Eldest Daughter to John Duke
of Marlborough & Wife to Francis Earl of Godolphin.

LADY HENRIETTA CHURCHILL
AFTERWARDS COUNTESS OF GODOLPHIN AND DUCHESS OF MARLBOROUGH
From the portrait by Sir Godfrey Kneller at Blenheim Palace

condition. . . ."5   But whatever the subject, Sidney writes with a certain tenderness to the wife of his lifelong friend. "My Lord Marlborough went from my house at Windsor this morning very early to my Lord Shrewsbury's house in Gloucestershire, from whence they intend to bee at bath about Sunday or Munday next; . . . he tells me you are to stay at the Bath, yett a great while longer, which I am very sorry to heare because I had swallowed the hopes whenever that happend of seeing you here very soone, and I dare say you have no friend in the world that will be more pleased with it than your Ladyship's most obedient humble serv^t Godolphin."6 "I made all the hast to come home this evening that possible I could in hopes I should meet with the satisfaction of a letter from you by the Coaches, but to my great disappointment I find none, so I have nothing left but fruitless complaints, and the comfort of hearing by other people that you are well . . . they tell mee there is [a letter] come by the coaches today for Lady Harryett, but she is not at home; nor Lady Mary who is a most charming creature; and if you saw her every day as I doe now, you would have very little occasion to find fault with her looks; . . ."7 And when Sarah was at Windsor Castle, Sidney wrote to her: "I should bee very glad of the satisfaction of hearing from you, and that you continue well in that cold place, but you see I don't want that encouragement to continue troubling you; I have gott a great cold here in a warmer place than Windsor, which obliges mee to stay at home today, but that is no great inconvenience to mee that have not stirred out since my Ld. Marlb. went to St. Albans, but only to see La: Haryett." Then he adds quaintly "I was with her yesterday at least 4 hours in hand, she is very easy and sensible and I think entertayning enough, in short, wee are very good friends and I hope shall continue soe; . . ."8

Once he sends Sarah a mare, and writes in genuine anxiety for her safety. "By a letter I had from my Lord Marlborough last night I find you would have mee send your mare, I had done it as soon as I saw it good weather, but that having rid her abroad 3 or 4 times since I came to Cranbourn, I found she was fond of another mare that is her companion, and without that mare was before her she did not care to goe at all, and when that mare was before her she would bee too earnest to follow her: soe that I could never find her in a temper to be pleased enough with her to send her to you; however I send her now, but I must beg of you to promise mee you will not ride her till my Lord Marleborough has rid her first, or till some of your women has tryed her whether she will endure a woman's saddle; I must desire you besides never to ride her through the town of St. Albans where there are twenty things every moment that will make any horse shy, tho' they bee not apt to start; I have yett one thing more to beg, and that is that you would not ride her in 3 or 4 days after you have her, for all horses in the world are apt to bee fearfull in a strange place; . . ."⁹

Such was the friendship of Sidney Godolphin and Sarah Marlborough. It has often been stated that Godolphin was under the spell of the superior intellect of the Marlboroughs, but a study of their letters will demonstrate the falsity of that view. Both John and Sarah Marlborough regarded Godolphin in all things as an equal, and often the great soldier sought the sage and balanced judgment of his friend. "I am in so ill humour that I will not trouble you, nor dare I trust myself to write more," wrote John, harassed by the intransigence of the Dutch troops under his command, "but believe this truth, that I honour and love you, my lady Marlborough, and my children, and would die for the queen."¹⁰ And at Blenheim there is a note in the crabbed hand of the ageing Duchess, written long after Godolphin's death. "I used to send my Lord Godolphin my letters to the Queen before I sent them to her, to see if hee would add or alter any thing in them, after she came into hands that made it necessary for me to bee cautious, whoever knew him will easyly believe that hee could never have approved of any thing from me that was disrespectful to the Queen, whatever they may think of my own passion or unreasonableness."* These are noble tributes to their much loved friend.

Thus fostered since the days of their youth, the friendship between these two great men grew and ripened through the years, until it blossomed into a comradeship that was only to terminate with death; and early in 1698 the bonds that bound them were further strengthened by a domestic event of the highest importance to both families. On March 24th, Francis Godolphin, then aged twenty, was married to the near eighteen-year-old Lady Henrietta Churchill, the Marlboroughs' eldest daughter.

Francis Godolphin, all that was left to Sidney of his beloved Margaret, had grown up into a handsome youth of great charm, affectionately known in the family circle as Master. His education had been supervised by Mr. Evelyn, whom we find discussing the matter with Francis's father when the boy was only eleven. ". . . I totally agree with you in the preference of a publig Schole for many regards; The very method and Emulation of which

---

* There is also in the same box a note in Godolphin's hand reading: "Monday morning. I have read over the letter twice, which you did once the favour to send mee to see if I would propose any alteration to you, that was pertinent, but indeed I could not, and I think the letter is as right as can bee. . . ." On the same sheet is a note in the hand of the Duchess's secretary, which reads thus: "This is my Lord Godolphins own hand writting it has no date, but I believe it was wrote to me on my sending him a copy of a Letter I writ to the Queen. For at thee time I did not care to write anything to her without haveing my Lord Godolphin's oppinion." Blenheim MSS. E. 20.

will render him a thro-pac'd (not a superficial) Scholar; it will inure him to hardships, without austerities, and take off all that effeminate tenderness and fondnesse to home, with many other Advantages; and especially at Eaton, where he will have the Inspection of his Unkle,[11] the benefit and advantages of your often seeing him when you are at Windsor, or that sweete Retreate which I heare you purchase neere it :*   But with all this I think he is yet too young and tender (by a yeare or two at leats) to send him thither, until he be a little more grown, and sortable to his Companions there. . . ."   Meanwhile a tutor may "not onely teach him to Reade, write, and speake French, and give him the genuine Accent of a language so necessary, and yet so difficult to attaine, when elder; but Instruct him also in forming his verbs and nounes, and other parts of Latine Gramar, which will exceedingly advance and prepare him for the Schole: Besides he tells me, he understands Geographie, and Arithmetic, and the rudiments of Musig, all which will be diversion to the young Alumnus, as well as profitable."[12]

In the following spring, Francis had visited Godolphin in Cornwall, probably for the first time, and "grand-papa" Evelyn had written urging him to describe all he saw there.   "My deare child, Dos so *naturaly, prettily* and *particularly* describe *Suning-hill* and *Cranburn*," he wrote, "that I conjure him to oblige me with a diarie of his perigrination into Cornwall . . ." describing many things, but especially "*Godolphin,* how situated . . . and to be sure the *Church* of *Breague* and that he will drop a *Teare* for me on the *ashes* of a deare Saint there, whose memorie is most precious to *gran-papa.* And ah, how willingly should I now have made

> *A pilgrimage to that blessed shrine!*
> *And neare her Urne have placed mine:*
> *Since there, when 'ere from hence I part,*
> *At Breage (my Deare) you'l find my Heart.*

And so *God-almighty* Blesse my *Dear Child,* send him (Uncle Sr. Will: *Doctor, Aunts, Misse Dot, Squire Hugo,* and all the goodly Traine) safe back gaine."[13]

Not perhaps a very happily phrased letter to a boy of twelve, but Francis seems to have satisfied Evelyn's requirements.   "To my Deare Child Fra. Godolphin," he wrote in the following August, "Never did *Aldrovandus*[14] who writ of *Birds, Beast,* and *Fishes, Men* and *Monsters*; no nor *Ulysses* of *Ithaca* . . . in all his son-yeares *Errors* and *Ramblings* (himselfe so *transmographied* at his Returne, as no living Creature knew him but his *old* Dog) . . . I say neither of these have ever lett to posterity such an account of his

---

* This is strange, as in his *Dairy* Evelyn records visiting Godolphin at Cranbourne Lodge on October 23rd, 1686.   Evelyn, *Diary,* October 23rd, 1686. IV, 527–8.

Travells, as my deare *grand-child* has don . . ." and much more in this vein. Then he bids the boy pursue his studies. "That as he is the deserved *Darling* of his noble *Father,* and learned *Unkels,* so he may (like them) be qualified to serve his *Country* as a *Man* of honour: This I fore-see, and therefore Augure of my deare grand-son. . . ."[15]

Much of Francis's youth had been spent with the Boscawen family at Cranbourne Lodge, and much with the Churchills at St. Albans. From Eton he had progressed to King's College, Cambridge. "I left Master at Cambridge Sat. morning," Sidney wrote to Jael from St. Albans, "with more inclinations to see the fireworks than he uses to show for things of that kind, and here I find 2 young ladys ready to lose their witts for fear of missing the Ceremony at pauls upon the Thanksgiving day. I fancy you might easily learn from the provost what the difficultys are like to bee in getting of places upon that occasion, and by whom they are to bee disposed; he will also bee able to tell you, if the boys doe generally gett leave to come from Eton for this sight and if this be an allowable occasion to ask it; this is la: Ann's question in good nature to her brother and I am a good deal of her side in it. . . ."[16] A few days later he is off to Windsor. ". . . if I find Master there to night I shall think my Selfe in generosity obliged to bring him back to the fireworks, but I don't expect to bee soe put to it, nore have I heard yett that hee is free to the drawing room as you call'd it, which tho' a thing that may be dispens'd with is yett at least as necessary as Coming to Windsor to fetch fire."[17] At last the efforts of the Churchill girls on their brother's behalf are successful, but there are conditions. "The repeated attacks of the young ladys here have at last prevail'd for their brother to see the fireworks, but its upon Condition he goes back to Eton after Ch[ris] a week sooner than the other boys. I think I shall lay at Windsor till Monday sennight and goe thither Monday next when all this family goes to London," he wrote from St. Albans, "pray doe mee the favour to send the cook Munday morning and Chamberlain with him, and order them to take care my chamber bee well aired. I don't see that it can bee worth Master's trouble or indeed any body's to come for soe little a time as I shall bee at Windsor and which may possibly bee yett lesse than I now intend."[18] Lord Chesterfield has some slighting remarks to the effect that Francis went to the House of Lords to sleep and that it mattered not whether he slept on the left hand or the right hand of the Woolsack. Perhaps he was a little unfair, but certain it is that Francis Godolphin possessed more grace than force.*

* As early as 1698 we find his father writing thus of him: "Master is perfectly well, and perfectly lazy, or else he would write, for he has nothing else to doe this morning." Godolphin to Jael Boscawen, "Newmarket, 28: Octr." (1698). Evelyn MSS., Christ Church, Oxford.

Henrietta Churchill, on the other hand, was of more headstrong nature. Tall, slim and fair, she united the bland charm of her father with the impetuosity of her mother. Judging from her surviving letters, Henrietta's childhood and youth were the happiest periods of her life.* They reveal her as sweet, kindly, warm-hearted, though perhaps a little vain and impulsive. To this young girl, as to so many of her age, letter-writing was something of a penance. "I am in pain for fear my Dear mama should be angry yet this is ill writ, and spelt." she wrote in one early letter, "but if you will bileeve me, I am in such hast I hardly know what to do, and therefore hope that you will forgive all faults."[19] To her mother in London in attendance on Princess Anne, she wrote affectionately from St. Albans, "My dear Mama is allwayes ready to give, and I to ask, which shoud make me the more afraid, to abuse your goodness, but indeed I should be very glad to have ovid's epistles, sent me by the first opportunity. My sister and I, took physicke on Satterday, and are very well after it. pray mama, present my humble duty to the Princess. my sister presents hers to you, I bilive I have said a nough to tier you, and so will end, in assuring you that I am your most Dutyfull, Henrietta Churchill." Then she adds by way of postscript: "I thinke this letter very pritty, if you do too, pray let me know it."[20] All Henrietta's letters at this time are effusive pledges of her love and devotion. "I won't trouble you any longer now than to tell you that 'tis not in nature for mee to bee happy upon my word when my Dear Angell Mama is not," she wrote on one occasion: and on another that if her mother would write to her, she would be ". . . extream proud of it, and be the over joyest creature in the world."[21]

Intermingled with these pledges of eternal love, we find amusing domestic details. ". . . most part of the tea you gave me was used when Papa was here," once wrote Henrietta from St. Albans to her mother in London, "so if you don't send some when he comes their will be none when papa has a mind to have some, or my Lady Sunderland when she comes, for mine will be all gon . . . my sister Betty has a little horse given her by Mr. Seliock, which she is much delighted with, 'tis a great deall less then either of our

---

* A number of Henrietta's letters to her mother are preserved in the muniment room at Blenheim Palace. Most of them are undated and some unsigned, but they were written some before and some after her marriage. It is probable that these were the kindest letters that she wrote to her mother, and that many others were destroyed by Sarah in the same spirit as we are told she burnt many letters from her youngest daughter, Mary, Duchess of Montagu, "that I might never more see how she had used me." "An account of the Dutches of Marl. and Montagus behaviour before and after their fathers death." Blenheim MSS. F. I, 35, f. 7. The MS. which runs to over one hundred pages, is dated September 19th, 1722. In addition there is a five page appendix covering events of a later date.

little horses. prao my Dear Mama send word when you send the fans, which is to be mine, for I had rather you should chuse for me, then my Self. I am your most Dutyfull H. Churchill."[22] Yet even at this early stage, it is clear that young Henrietta was hard put to it to satisfy the exacting demands of her redoubtable parent. "Your kind message my Dear Mama has pleased me more then you can imagin," she wrote in one early letter, "I can't take any thing ill you do, and till I have a letter will bileeve that you have not time to writ one, and when it comes shall be extreamly pleased, as I shall have great reason to bee . . . I will do another letter for you very quickly and better then the other was, for I am a fraid it did not please you, I own when it was done I did not like it, but had not time to do another."[23] In a few years, as we shall see, there was to be bitter strife between indomitable mother and impulsive daughter; but for the present all is sunshine and sweet reasonableness.

This was the girl whom Francis Godolphin married in the spring of 1698. The Marlboroughs, Godolphin and his sister Jael were all, it seems, instrumental in forwarding the match. "When I talked to my sister at Windsor of our young people's affairs," wrote Sidney to Sarah, "she seemed to wish they might see one another sometimes and bee a little better acquainted, I make no great question but hee'l soon be as easy with her as he is with her father but I submitt that and everything else to you. . . ."[24] How "easy" Francis was with his Henrietta we shall see. His father had little money to settle on him, but his friend, the bride's father, provided a dowry of £5,000. Princess Anne, close friend of the parents of both bride and bridegroom, was anxious to settle £10,000 upon the young couple, but the Marlboroughs would not hear of it. This caused some delay. ". . . as to Master who is now with mee," wrote Sidney to his sister, "he seems not to be absolutely certain; I hope we are now near drawing to a conclusion of his affair, and doe design to talk with you about it, to adjust some matters that relate to that Ceremony. . . ."[25] Eventually the Marlboroughs were persuaded to accept £5,000; moreover, lucrative posts soon came Master's way, for in the summer of 1699, we find him appointed to the office of one of the four tellers of the Exchequer and a registrar in the Court of Chancery.[26]

The union of Francis and Henrietta was quickly fruitful. Within the year was born to the young couple a son, christened William but soon to be known in the family circle affectionately as "Willigo". "I can't help telling you how agreeably as well as unexpectedly la. Harryett surprised us yesterday morning with a boy," wrote a delighted grandfather to his sister at Althorp, "A very little one indeed, but the skilful say it is not at all unlikely to live; there seems to be no great certainty whether the child came

FRANCIS GODOLPHIN AND HENRIETTA CHURCHILL
AT THE TIME OF THEIR MARRIAGE
From the miniature by Charles Boit, in the National Museum, Stockholm

before time or not, she does not own to have had any fright or ill accident, but," he adds, "I need not be soe particular in this account which seems to bee more proper for your she-correspondents. I'me sure you are as glad of the news as I can bee, and I hope that will not hinder you from any uneasyness as being out of the way upon this occasion."[27] And some eighteen months later, Sidney, whilst staying with the Marlboroughs at St. Albans, reported to Jael: "All here are very well at present and Willigo begins to make a noyse which he is pleased with himself because he takes it for speaking, but its a language not much understood in the world hitherto; his sister is a great beauty, and I am always yrs. G."[28] In January 1700 the Marlboroughs' second daughter, the beautiful and gentle Lady Anne, was to wed Lord Spencer, the widower son of Lord and Lady Sunderland.[29] Thus were Godolphin, the Marlboroughs and the Sunderlands linked together by family alliances that brought much both of good and bad in their train.

During the closing years of the reign of King William there appeared on the political scene a new figure of the first importance. When we first meet him, Robert Harley has just been elected Speaker and practically Leader of the House of Commons; and, although an avowed Tory, he was contriving by adroit finesse to retain the goodwill of many of the opposing party. His whole manner betokened the man. His speech was halting, his letters were tortuous; nor did he care for his contemporary reputation. He was accustomed, he jokingly declared, "to howl with the wolves, and if his friends wished it, to call black white and white black." "It has always been my temper to go along with the company and not to give them uneasiness," he once declared to Godolphin, "if they should say Harrow on the Hill or by Maidenhead were the nearest way to Windsor I would go with them and never dispute it if that would give content, and that I might not be forced to swear it was so."[30] A candid friend did not hesitate with astonishing frankness to give the Minister his observations on people's opinions of him.[31] Universally dubbed "Robin the Trickster", Harley knew it and was not ashamed.

Though on intimate terms with Marlborough and with Godolphin, who in December 1700 had returned to the Treasury, as early as the autumn of that year we find Harley writing that Godolphin ". . . has not only promised entirely to comply with the Junto but also to sacrifice the Duke of Qu(eensberry) to them. For his going in to them I never had any doubt, he has for a long time been contriving to do it, though he at the same time exclaims against them, as they do at him. I think it fit that his grace should know of the intention regarding him though I will not have it known that the news comes from me. One way to prevent it is to let the design be publicly talked of, giving air to a mine."[32]   Yet Harley's future seemed assured; and this same autumn of 1700 Charles II's old friend, Henry Guy, a former Secretary of the Treasury, was reporting that it was the opinion of both Sunderland and Godolphin that he, Harley, would shortly be receiving a summons from King William, and ". . . that he must be positive and bold and rely upon his strength, for that will be sufficiently able to do it thoroughly."[33]

Early in the following year, Rochester and Godolphin and the King were all urging Harley to come to London to consult with them on the election results.[34]   "147 (Guy himself) was yesterday with 67 (King William), who asked when 104 (Harley) would come and desired him to hasten him," reported Guy to his friend.   "79 (Rochester) and 78 (Godolphin) did yesterday again enjoin me to write to you this night to come with speed; for they say that what you would chiefly see over is now past and there are several things of the greatest moment which do really want the opinion and advice of 440 (Harley); therefore I beg of you in your next let me have from you a short day for your setting forward on your journey."[35] But Harley was in no hurry to comply.   "When you come hither," wrote Guy five days later, "you will find a great deal more noise of the briberies and violences in several places.   Your friends do think that if 104 (Harley) were here now it would be but time enough for many important things; but 79 (Rochester) and 78 (Godolphin) are positive that if he is not here at least a week before the 6th, it will be of ill consequence."   Then he continued later in the day, "I wrote thus far in the forenoon, and I have since been with 67 (King William), who most earnestly enquired when 104 (Harley) would come.   And though 79 (Rochester) and 78 (Godolphin) enjoined me this morning to press 440 (Harley) to come, yet this afternoon they sent me a letter to press me to do it effectually.   I have written as far as I can at this time for my late illness still hangs heavily upon me."[36]

Towards the end of the same year, the elections were held, and Godolphin wrote to Harley in the country that he was glad "to hear the elections go so well in your parts.   I hope in the West they will do so too, but the North we hear will be otherwise."   But the important question of the choice of a Speaker is pending and Harley is urged to come to London, for this "will be a very decisive stroke in this ensuing parliament," and his presence is much desired.[37]   And again the following week: "I am very unwilling to pursue you with my letters; what I had written to you by Saturday's post of the necessity of your coming to town proceeded only from myself, but since that I have been pressed by the most considerable part of our chief friends to write to you again upon that subject, that though I told them all I had already done it as fully and decently as I could, yet nothing would satisfy but my promise to repeat it as from them all."[38] The result of the election was so close a balance of parties that neither could oppress the other. Godolphin was much distressed at the result of the polls, and on December 30th, 1701, much to Marlborough's annoyance, he resigned.

A month later came a hasty note from Godolphin suggesting that he and Marlborough should call on Harley the following night. It concluded with these significant words: "Lord Rochester has been dismissed this morning."[39] The fractious temper of the Lord Lieutenant had been too much for King William at last.

In September 1697, the war was brought to an end by the Treaty of Ryswick, under the terms of which Louis ceded Luxembourg and Lorraine, and recognized Orange to be King of England.[40] But the agreement thus come to could not be lasting, for the eyes of all Europe were turned on Spain, where the hapless King Charles II, after a life of mental and physical disease, was now fast sinking to his grave. Of the seven European princes who put forward claims to be the true successor to the last of the Spanish Hapsburgs, three were likely candidates, the French Dauphin, the Archduke Charles of Austria, the mothers of both of whom were Spaniards, and the nine months' old infant Prince of Bavaria. But with regard to the first two candidates, Europe could ill afford to see a son of the King of France as ruler of Spain nor a member of the House of Hapsburg on the thrones of both Spain and the Holy Roman Empire. Thus, by the First Partition Treaty of 1698 Louis and William came to an agreement to recognize the Bavarian baby as King of Spain. This plan seemed to suit everybody—except the Spanish people, who, of course, were never consulted; but unfortunately the infant prince succumbed to the prevailing scourge of small-pox the very next year. Consequently Louis and William had to renew their efforts to find a solution of the difficulty. By the Second Partition Treaty, they agreed that the Austrian Archduke should be recognized whilst the Dauphin should be compensated with two provinces in Italy. No sooner was this arrangement agreed upon than the sickly Charles II died, having on his deathbed made a will leaving the whole of his vast possessions to the Dauphin's second son; whereupon Louis XIV saw no alternative to accepting the will, though it obviously went entirely counter to his agreement with William, and dispatched French armies into Spain, Italy and Flanders. In a few weeks he was in peaceful possession of vast tracts of lands from which only a coalition of great strength and determination could drive him.

And no such coalition was in prospect. The English parliament was in its most pacific mood. The French King of Spain was recognized by both

England and Holland and the whole of William's life-work appeared to be falling in ruins. But just when things seemed most hopeless, William's old enemy came to his aid. When in 1701 the exiled James II was on his death-bed, Louis XIV had the temerity to recognize his son, the Pretender, as King of England. At once the whole country was aflame. That a king should be foisted on them by their old enemy was more than the proud islanders could bear. In a flash the most pacific of countries became the most bellicose. In November 1701 elections were held amidst scenes of martial enthusiasm. By the end of the year all Europe was ringing with preparations for hostilities. At last, as it seemed, Dutch William was to render his account to the tyrant of Europe.

But it was not to be. On February 20th, King William was out riding. His horse tripped over a mole-hill and threw his rider. The King's collar bone was broken. This was but a slight accident, but the shock on the exhausted frame was more than it could bear. In a few weeks William was in danger; in a few more he was dead. Thus at the supreme moment in our history, the dour Dutchman passed from the mortal scene. Never popular in England during his life, after death the Whigs contrived to make a hero of him; but the Tories preferred to drink toasts to "the little gentleman in black velvet," the mole which caused his fall. His epitaph has been written for all time. "Outside his own people and his own country of Holland, William never sought the love of contemporaries or of posterity, and he has not obtained it; but he sought their welfare and freedom, and these he achieved. His Calvinism was the garb in which his age and country dressed the temper of a Stoic, who serves God for duty, not for joy or fear. He scorned the popular. He scorned to be cruel. His wisdom was indefatigable. His patience was like the patience of the gods."[41]

BOOK II

Achievement

CHAPTER I

"A MOST GRACIOUS QUEEN"

"SIR, we have lost a great King, we have got a most gracious Queen." Thus spoke Sir John Packington, a West Country Tory, of the plain, dull, homely, semi-invalid who on the morning of Sunday, March 8th, 1702, replaced her gruff brother-in-law on the English throne. Totally inexperienced as she was, it was not unnatural that the new Sovereign should turn for guidance to the greatest of her subjects, whose wife chanced to be her closest friend. Honours were quickly showered on the Marlboroughs: he was made a Knight of the Garter, Captain-General of the Forces, Master General of the Ordnance; Lady Marlborough, Groom of the Stole, Mistress of the Robes and Keeper of the Privy Purse. Furthermore, the Rangership of Windsor Park was pressed upon her in affectionate terms.[1] Their two married daughters, Lady Henrietta Godolphin and Lady Spencer were appointed Ladies of the Bedchamber.[2] And with the rise of Mr. and Mrs. Freeman, as the Marlboroughs were known in their intimate letters with the Queen who was herself Mrs. Morley, it was only natural that they should rely for guidance on the prudence and sagacity of their old friend, Godolphin, who appears as Mr. Montgomery in this curious correspondence exchanged between the new Sovereign and her closest friend.

Anne at her accession had two objects in view, as in her soft, pleasing voice she told the Council on March 8th, the very day of William's death, to maintain the Protestant Succession and to reduce the power of France. On March 11th, Anne delivered her first speech to Parliament. She was so unwell that Godolphin hoped to save her the ordeal of going to the Lords. "She is very unweildy and lame," he wrote to the Speaker, "must she come in person to the House of Lords or may she send for the two houses to her."[3] Apparently, this suggestion was not well received; "I suppose the Queen will come to the House, but," he wrote the next day, "I doubt whether she has any robes."[4] Robes or no robes, the Queen delivered her speech, drafted, it is said, jointly by Godolphin, Marlborough and Harley;[5] in this she declared that everything possible must be done to encourage the Allies, to reduce the exorbitant power of France, and to promote an union between England and Scotland.

Two days later, on March 13th, Marlborough, accompanied by Godolphin, called upon Count Wratislaw, the Imperial Ambassador, to announce his new honours and appointments. He informed him that no official notification of the succession would be made to the King of France, and that he, Marlborough, had it in command from the Queen to depart forthwith for the Hague. During his absence, his Excellency should if need be have recourse to Lord Godolphin, who, though not yet a Minister, would in all matters act for him. The arrangement was subtle but effective. "Sarah was the link between Godolphin and the Queen. Mrs. Freeman reported to Mrs. Morley what Mr. Montgomery . . . mentioned in his talks with her. Never was the English Constitution found more flexible."[6]

At the Hague Marlborough found all in confusion at the news of William's death. He had a series of confidential interviews with the Pensionary Heinsius, whom he soon convinced that England had no intention of deserting the Allies; and such was his diplomatic skill that he quickly forestalled the insidious propaganda of Louis's agent, who was promising that France would make a separate peace with Holland if only she would desert the Grand Alliance. Thus fired with renewed enthusiasm, the Powers were emboldened to declare war simultaneously upon France and Spain.

During Marlborough's absence, the Queen vastly increased her growing popularity by the action she took over her Civil List. The Commons voted her King William's revenue for life, including the fifty thousand pounds a year that she had received as heiress presumptive. No sooner had this generous provision been made, than she informed a surprised and delighted parliament that for the current year she would forgo one hundred thousand pounds of the revenue voted to her. This, of course, evoked marked enthusiasm; but in fact it was hardly justified, for had Queen Anne accepted the full sum voted to her she would certainly have been expected to support the new heiress-presumptive, the Electress Sophia of Hanover, and her family out of the proceeds. By this gesture of apparent self-abnegation, the Queen had artfully freed herself from a hateful obligation. Who was responsible for giving this brilliant advice to the Crown? We can only guess. It could hardly have been Marlborough, for he was away at The Hague. It could hardly have been Sarah, or she would have surely mentioned it in her writings. Was it not then most probably "Mr. Montgomery"? Godolphin had the Queen's confidence. He was himself notoriously careless of money matters. He knew Anne's detestation for the Hanoverians. He was assuredly the very man to whisper this brilliant stratagem into the Sovereign's receptive ear.*

Marlborough's success at The Hague enabled him to return home in time to attend the late King's funeral and the Queen's Coronation. He was also in time to throw the whole weight of his influence into the task of forming a new Ministry and transferring the reins of Government from the Whigs to the Tories. Anne was a bigoted High Tory. Marlborough was a moderate Tory anxious only for a government that could be relied upon to support the war. Realizing, therefore, the paramount importance of having at home in a key position at once a financier of the first rank who would not fail to supply the funds needed for extensive operations on the Continent of Europe and also a statesman on whose loyal support he could implicitly rely, in May 1702 Marlborough stipulated as a condition of his own employment abroad that his lifelong friend Godolphin should be made head of the Ministry as Lord Treasurer.†

To Anne this could not have been unwelcome. She had long been on the best of terms with Lord Godolphin, and she was ever grateful for his support in the days of her frequent unedifying brawls with the late King. Only a few months before her accession, she had had occasion to write to Godolphin of King William the oft-quoted lines—"It is a very great satisfaction to me to find you agree with Mrs. Morley concerning the ill-natured cruel proceedings of Mr. Caliban."[7] At that time there were rumours of Godolphin's imminent return to power. "It has been much talked of," wrote Edward Harley early in 1699, "that Lord Godolphin is to be Secretary of State, but the report is looked upon but to be 'Hawking with a hobby'."[8] Apparently it was ill-founded, but it must have been long expected that with the new reign the fallen Minister would return to office. But there was one obstacle to this. To Godolphin himself the proffered post was most distasteful. At first he positively refused; and he

---

* Mr. Churchill senses a "truly feminine quality" in the act and suggests it was Queen Anne's own idea. Churchill, *Marlborough*, Book I, 531–2. Professor W. T. Morgan thinks the same. Morgan, *English Political Parties and Leaders in Reign of Queen Anne*, 74. It is, of course, pure guesswork, but it seems to me that the plan was far more likely to emanate from Godolphin's fertile brain than from Anne's torpid mind.

† In the days of Queen Anne, the functions of the Lord Treasurer were roughly analogous to the modern Prime Minister, and the actual phrase "Prime Minister" was occasionally used at this time. Thus by Sir John Clerk of Penicuik we find it used of Godolphin four times: *Memoirs of Sir John Clerk of Penicuik*, (ed. 1895, Roxburgh Club), 53, 56, 58, 63–4. It was also used by Lord Stanhope. Stanhope, *Queen Anne*, II, 88, 90. For the development of the functions of the Treasury from the Restoration to the end of Queen Anne's reign, see Miss Doris M. Gill's interesting article *The Treasury*, 1660–1714. E.H.R., XLVI, 600–22.

only yielded after a struggle when his kinsman made it plain that he was in earnest in his refusal to serve without him.

Godolphin's detractors have tried to substantiate the charge that his reluctance to accept the post of Lord Treasurer in May 1702 was feigned, and they point out that, having once assumed office, he showed no great eagerness to quit it, when eight years later he was compelled much against his will to surrender the White Staff at the bidding of the Queen. Indeed, the acrimonious Dartmouth has some very bitter things to say both of Godolphin and Marlborough in this respect.[9] But not a vestige of proof has ever been produced to support the charge. As all are agreed, Godolphin was a bashful, retiring man: might not such a one be excused for hesitating before assuming for the first time the post of chief minister at the outset of a new reign? And what has a hesitancy to accept a post in 1702 to do with a reluctance to quit that post in 1710? May not a man, who has occupied an important position for eight years and thereby acquired a self-confidence he did not previously feel, be justified in thinking that he is competent for his task and that his initial fears and hesitancy have been proved groundless by events? Furthermore, Bishop Burnet, who had no reason to look favourably upon Godolphin, does not support the charge. "The Lord Godolphin was made lord treasurer: this was very uneasy to himself, for he resisted the motion long; but the Earl of Marlborough pressed it in so positive a manner that he said he could not go beyond sea to command our armies unless the treasury was put in his hands; for then he was sure that remittances would be punctually made to him."[10] So much for the somewhat petty malice of Lord Dartmouth and his fellows.

Thus at last Godolphin's scruples were overcome. In the summer of 1702 he became Lord Treasurer, a post he was destined to hold for eight long years.

In considering the formation of what has come to be known as the Godolphin Ministry, the reader must first be familiarized with the state of the two great political parties in the opening days of the reign of Queen Anne.

The little Cockpit clique of the Marlboroughs and Godolphin stood midway between the High Tories and the Whigs; and as it was Anne's great fear that she might fall into the hands of either party, neither of whom she trusted, she looked to her three friends to see that the Government was carried on, as she termed it, without "faction". "All I desire," she wrote to Lord Godolphin a few years after her accession, "is my liberty in encouraging and employing all those that concur faithfully in my service, whether they are called Whigs or Tories, not to be tied to one, nor the other; for if I should be so unfortunate as to fall into the hands of either, I shall not imagine myself, though I have the name of queen, to be in reality but their slave, which as it will be my personal ruin, so it will be the destroying all government; for instead of putting an end to faction, it will lay a lasting foundation for it."[11] Nothing could be clearer. So long as the Ministry could maintain its middle position, all was well: as soon as events thrust it into the arms of the Whigs, as we shall see, it lost the Queen's confidence. Thenceforth she was bent on ridding herself of those who had formerly been her friends.

The High Tories on one side of this clique recruited their strength among the sporting landed gentry and their loyal tenants in the rural districts; likewise, many of the nobility and the lawyers were found in their ranks. The party was strongly imbued with the doctrine of divine right and passive obedience, which had placed them in considerable difficulties in King William's reign, and was to prove still more troublesome under Queen Anne. Indeed, early in the new reign they split into the extreme Tories, called Jacobites, the champions of the Pretender; the Highfliers, who were hardly less Jacobite than the Jacobites; and the Hanoverian Tories, styled by St. John "whimsicals", who supported the Protestant Succession. Their chiefs were Rochester, Nottingham and Ormonde, united by that acute sense of jealousy which they all felt for Marlborough and Godolphin. The Whigs on the other side found their main support in the wealthy merchant and shopkeeper class who looked for leadership to the great Whig houses of Cavendish and Russell. The party was managed, and indeed dragooned with remarkable efficiency, by the five lords of the "Junto": Wharton, an engaging rake, a true son of the Restoration; Somers, a former Lord Chancellor; Halifax, the financial genius who had founded the Bank of England and the National Debt; Orford, the victor of La Hogue; and Marlborough's able son-in-law, Spencer, who in September 1702 succeeded his crafty father as third Earl of Sunderland. *

But whilst Anne dreaded falling into the clutches of either of the great political parties, she composed her Cabinet and most of the lesser ministerial appointments of Tories. A few Court places, it is true, went to moderate Whigs, but not a single position of importance was offered to a prominent member of that party. To only two statesmen outside the Tory ranks did the Queen turn for guidance, to the politically unattached Dukes of Shrewsbury and Somerset.

* For the composition of the various political groups, see Walcott, *English Party Politics*, (*1688–1714*) in *Essays in Modern English History*, (Harvard University Press, 1941), 81–131. I am grateful to Mrs. Marjorie Cox for having brought this interesting article to my notice.

The cultured, witty Shrewsbury, known to all the world as "the King of Hearts", had long resided in Italy; and now he resolutely refused to return to England in order to serve the new Queen. On intimate terms with Godolphin, to whom he sent an interesting plan drawn by Italian architects for the rebuilding of Whitehall,* and with the Marlboroughs for whose abilities he had the greatest respect, he was a moderate and the ally of moderates. He hated the wild men on the fringes of both parties and, though a Whig, he was on poor terms with the lords of the Junto. Thus centrally placed, he would not return to the toil and turmoil of public life. An easy existence in Rome was much better suited to his not very robust health and his supersensitive nature. To the "proud" Somerset, though a man of insufferable arrogance and self-conceit, it was natural for Anne to turn, for when in the summer of 1692 she had been ignominiously ejected from the Cockpit by the late King and Queen and courtiers were forbidden to do her honour, it was Somerset who braved the royal displeasure by welcoming the almost friendless princess to his splendid mansion of Syon House. To both these magnificoes the new Queen looked for guidance; from both of them she was destined to receive loyal and faithful service ere her days were done.

All the ministerial positions, as has been said, were occupied by Tories. Sir Charles Hedges, a colourless mediocrity, and Nottingham, a leading zealot of his party whose gloomy temper had earned him the nickname of "Dismal", were the two Secretaries of State. Lord Normanby, soon to be created Duke of Buckingham and Normanby, was appointed Lord Privy Seal, Lord Pembroke, Lord President of the Council, and William Blathwayt, Secretary of War. For the great post of Lord Keeper of the Great Seal, no one more weighty could be found than Sir Nathan Wright. In the filling of the minor appointments, all the Lord Treasurer's large stock of patience and tact was needed. "I never took such paines in my life to satisfy anybody as Sir Ch. M(usgrave) in every thing from the first moment I spoke to him," he wrote, "but it's pretty hard to follow humours so changeable and uncertain. He would not be in the Ordnance, and when it was too late then he would be. At first he would not be a Teller because it was a

* Shrewsbury to Godolphin, "Rome 16 June, 1703 N.S." Brit. Mus. Add MSS. 28,156, f. 21. There are also in the Muniment Room at Blenheim Palace two amusing letters from Shrewsbury to Godolphin about his Whitehall plans. The first, dated, "From near St. Pauls a mile out of Rome, Feb. 9th, 1703 N.S." is endorsed by the Duchess, "A letter from the Duke of Shrewsbury at Rome to redicule [sic] popery. hee kept a correspondence with the Earl of Godol. & the Duke of Marl: & professed great friendship but afterwards joynd with Abigal [sic] & Harley to bring of [sic] Do: Sacheverall & to destroy the Ministry that had don so much good for England." The second, dated "Rome 7 July, 1703 N.S." is thus shortly dismissed by Sarah—"Duke of Shrews. to Ld. Godol of no use." Blenheim MSS. B. II, 33.

sinecure, and afterwards, when he had kissed the Queen's hand for it, he would not take it . . . I wish with all my heart that four or five of these gentlemen that are so sharp set upon other people's places had mine amongst them to stay their stomachs."[12] Doubtless there are still many Musgraves in politics today to pester their leaders; none the less, we may sympathize with the long-suffering Godolphin in his dilemma.

But there was one far more influential and important than Musgrave to cause trouble at this time, the Queen's arrogant uncle, Rochester. Both Anne's Hyde relatives, Clarendon and Rochester, had been unkind to her, and her elder uncle, having refused to take the oath of allegiance to the new Sovereign, had been sent from Court, though allowed a pension. But Rochester "a good natur'd Man tho' hot" as Cowper called him,[13] had followed a more prudent course. Although, after the revolution of 1688, he had opposed the election of William and Mary as joint Sovereigns, he had soon reconciled himself to the new order; and since December 1700 he had been Lord Lieutenant of Ireland. But with his niece's accession to the Throne, he had looked with covetous eyes on the post of Lord Treasurer, from which position, it will be recalled, he had been dislodged by Godolphin in the days of Charles II; and he was bitterly chagrined that his former friend and now his bitter rival should be advanced so far above him. Leaving the Government of Ireland in the hands of Lord Justices, he hurried to England, where he promptly vented his spleen at a Council held on May 2nd to issue the Declaration of War against France and Spain. This course he violently opposed, urging that the country should play only a minor role in the hostilities. Overruled in his first objective, he pursued his second aim, the exclusion of all Whigs from even the most subordinate offices. Such unreasonable prejudice was not to be endured, and it required all the exquisite urbanity of the Lord Treasurer to curb the zeal of this stormy petrel.

In view of the Queen's obvious preference for the Tories, it was not surprising that, at the election held in July 1702, their parliamentary strength was much increased. Bribery was rife. All manner of artifices were employed to influence the result. Yet we do not hear of Godolphin exercising any great influence on the contending parties, the rough and tumble of electioneering being ill-suited, it seems, to his placid temperament. According to common report, he had for long wished to retire and seek contentment in some rustic retreat.

"Granville shall seize the long expected chair,
    Godolphin to some country seat repair,
    Pembroke from all employments be debarred,
    And Marlborough for ancient crimes receive his just reward."[14]

But of course there was to be no country retreat for the new Lord Treasurer. Much of his time was occupied in attendance upon the Queen, and when, after the election she went on a tour of the West country, Godolphin accompanied her.[15]   During the last few days of August and most of September they remained at Bath, whence we find Godolphin busily corresponding with Nottingham, the new Secretary of State, on every conceivable subject.[16]   At the same time he was struggling with William Lowndes, the Secretary to the Treasury, to supply the necessary funds for our forces overseas.   On one occasion he was anxious to pay off as fast as possible ships that have been, or shortly are to be, laid up, so as to save public money;[17] on another, when £50,000 is urgently necessary for paying the wages of the Navy, he urged Lowndes to see whether money "may not be had upon the Tallys in the Treasurer of the Navy's hands", in which case the money in the Treasury would be used to meet whatever needs are most pressing.[18]

Towards the end of the month he went to stay with his brother, the Provost of Eton, but public affairs pursued him.   "I am come thus fare in my way to Newmarkete," he wrote to Nottingham, "the weather is so fair and settled, that I hope it will give my Lord Marlb : an opportunity in case his endeavours are well seconded, to make a good finishing stroak of this campaign, in Flanders, . . ."[19]   From Eton, too, he must write to Lowndes on financial affairs.   "I am going from hence towards Newmarket this morning, for one week," he wrote to him before leaving his brother's house, "if you have occasion to send for any directions from thence, to bee signed by me, you will consider I shall not have the assistance of Mr. Taylour"—Taylor, his private Secretary—"there as I had at the Bath, so that when you propose any warrant to be signed, you must send the Warrants themselves at the same time."[20]   By October 3rd he had reached Newmarket.[21]

It was clear that leisure was not to be granted to Godolphin.   This he had long realized, and towards the end of the late reign he had sold his house in Windsor Park to Princess Anne and had purchased from the Crown a lease of the great mansion that stood on the site later occupied by Stafford House.   This ugly red brick edifice, surrounded by a garden of ample proportions, he renamed Godolphin House.*

Whilst these events were happening at home, Marlborough was at The Hague, absorbed in the details for the preparations for war.   The Emperor was in urgent need of a loan, which "if it is not done quickly it will lose its effect," wrote Godolphin to the Speaker, "and if it be 'twill do more good now than treble that sum three months hence. . . ."[22]   Within a few

---

* Godolphin House stood next to St. James's Palace on the opposite side to the present Marlborough House.

months there were several secessions to the Grand Alliance, the Elector of
Brandenburg, bribed with the title of King of Prussia, the Elector Palatine,
the Elector of Hanover, and a number of minor princes were all induced to
join. Soon, largely through the dominating influence of the Pensionary
Heinsius, the superior genius of Marlborough was recognized, and he was
chosen to be General in chief of the British and Dutch forces, thus united
under a single command.

Yet, in spite of this seemingly satisfactory arrangement, the English
general was destined to be greatly hampered by the intransigence of the
Dutch "field-deputies", incompetent civilians attached to his staff whose
acquiescence in any project had to be obtained before it could proceed.
The pratings of these foolish muddlers were enough to try the patience of a
saint; but they were insufficient to ruffle the exquisite urbanity of the great
commander, though he was wont to complain bitterly to his friend.[23]
Indeed, it is remarkable that Marlborough, thus handicapped, made any
progress. Yet news of great successes were soon coming in. Setting forth
from his headquarters at Nimeguen at the head of some 60,000 men, he
crossed the Meuse and, following the retreating French troops, he invested
Venloo and Fort St. Michael, both of which soon capitulated. Then he
turned on Stephansworth and Rüremonde, neither of which could offer
more than faint resistance, and on the great stronghold of Liège, the fall of
which on October 29th gave the allies possession of all the fortresses of the
Meuse from Huy to the sea. "Lord Marlborough's affairs go on very
prosperously," wrote Godolphin from Bath, "I wish I could show you some
of his letters, but that must stay till I have the happiness of seeing you."[24]
And again a month later he reported the capture of Liège, adding that ". . .
they might have been able to carry their conquests further if the season did
not now oblige him to put the 40,000 men in the Queen's pay into winter
quarters, which he is doing as fast as he can, and hopes to be here by the end
of the month.... I am afraid," he added ominously, "Prince Lewis of Baden
has been worsted upon the Rhine."[25]

On Marlborough's return to England he received the thanks of Parliament for his services. This honour, however, was effectively marred by the
malice of the majority in the House, which joined the great commander's
name in the vote with those of the Duke of Ormonde and Sir George Rooke,
whose ineffectual handling of the recent expedition against Cadiz—"our
disappointment before Cadiz," as Godolphin termed it[26]— had only served
to lead to acrimony and bitterness. It was at this moment that Godolphin,
whilst taking his recreation at his beloved Newmarket, first heard the most
surprising news—that a detachment of our fleet having put into Lagos to
water, had there heard of the arrival at Vigo of French ships convoying

Spanish treasure galleons from the West Indies. To this he could scarcely give credit, "but supposing it to be true," he had asked Nottingham, "is it impracticable for Sr. G: R: or Sr. Cl: Sh:* or the most usefull part of bothe their squadrons to attempt something upon them there?"[27] But Godolphin was ever a landsman. He hoped the fleet would attack the enemy convoy and capture the treasure, but, he wrote to Nottingham three days later, "by all the acounts . . . our fleet seems to mee to be so desirous of losing no time in coming home that I am very apprehensive they won't goe out of their way to make any attempt upon that place or any place, wth out our express orders for it. . . ."[28] This view was most unfair, for the French ships were almost all either captured or destroyed, and the booty to the value of about a million was secured. But the credit for the feat belongs to subordinates rather than to Rooke, who was ill at the time; and the Queen, disgusted at such unreasoning partiality that sought to set Rooke's and Ormonde's services on a plane with those of her great commander, offered Marlborough a dukedom. The general was gratified, but Lady Marlborough was cautious: would it not be wiser to wait until their estate was better suited to so high a promotion? The wisdom of postponement was soon apparent. But it was not to be. On hearing of Mrs. Freeman's objections, the Queen promised to endow the title with a pension of £5,000 a year for her life; whereupon Sarah withdrew her opposition and her husband was duly created Marquess of Blandford and Duke of Marlborough. The new duke, so Godolphin tells us, was persuaded by his friends that it would not be difficult to get the grant confirmed by Act of Parliament. But they were soon seeking the Speaker's advice,[29] for it was apparent that the pension was most unpopular in the Tory House of Commons. Godolphin expressed his concern to Harley at the ill reception of the Queen's message, especially as the opposition "comes chiefly from those of whom I thought we had deserved better," and he begged for his advice.[30]

On the night following the writing of this letter, Godolphin and Harley held a consultation, and the Treasurer was emphatic that a division in the House on the proposed pension must at all costs be avoided, for the result would be ". . . that men will look upon themselves to be listed."[31] The upshot of this unfortunate affair was inevitable. The Commons refused their compliance and the pension had to be dropped. The generous-minded Queen, however, did her best to soften the blow; in order to make up for what had been "so maliciously hindered in the Parliament," she begged that Mr. and Mrs. Freeman would accept two thousand pounds a year from her Privy Purse. "This," she added, "can draw no envy, for nobody will know it. Not that I would disown what I give to people that deserve, especially

* Sir George Rooke or Sir Cloudesley Shovell.

when it is impossible to reward the deserts, but you may keep it a secret or not as you please."[32] The Marlboroughs declined the gift; but nine years later the Duchess, in the bitterness of her overthrow, claimed and received the pension with arrears from the date of the original offer.

No sooner had the Marlboroughs received this great honour than fate dealt them a cruel blow. They now had one surviving son,* a charming and promising lad of sixteen. John, Lord Churchill, since the creation of his father's dukedom Marquess of Blandford, had been at Eton and was now at King's College, Cambridge. He was anxious to serve in a campaign under his father, but his mother would not hear of it. There had been also, it seems, a project for him to go to Holland with his mother, but Sidney, consulted by the parents, was against the plan. "I begin to be convinced," he had written the previous year, "that if Ld. Churchill went wth you to Holland, he would not take much pleasure in his study's afterwards, for having been 2 or 3 days in ease at Windsor I find soe much to doe at my coming hither, that I take but scurvily to it;" then he ends quaintly, "I would beg the favour of you to assure dear Lady Haryett I am very much her humble servant."[33] Blandford must stay at college awhile.

Whilst at Cambridge, the young undergraduate was a frequent visitor at Lord Godolphin's house at Newmarket. ". . . I find lord Churchill very lean," he reported upon one such visit. "He is tractable and good humoured," he was careful to add, "and without any one ill inclination, that I can perceive. And I think he is grown more solid than he was, and has lost a great deal of that impatience of diverting himself all manner of ways which he used to have."[34] And again: "My Lord Churchill is now at Cambridg, but today he comes hither for 5 or 6 days. What you write about him is I think extremely just, and reasonable, and tho the small-pox has been in this town, yett he going into no house but mine, will I hope bee more defended from it by ayr and riding, wth out any sweating exercise, than possibly he could bee anywhere else."[35] Ominous words. On the following day all was well. "Lord Churchill is very well," reported Sidney to an anxious mother, "and at this time abroad with Mr. Godolphin; he had brought linnen enough wth him from Cambridg," he assured Sarah, "to serve him while he stays here; . . . I can't yett bragg of my better luck here than you have at Hazard. . . ."[36] And two days later he was able to write, "Lord Churchill is extremely regular and orderly, nor do I see the least objection (inclination?) in him to be otherwise, the good air & moderate Exercise at this place makes [sic] him look much better than when he came hither."[37] On the following Tuesday, October 13th, Godolphin returned to his house in London, whence he wrote to the Duchess "of your pretty son," he had

* Their younger son, Charles, had died an infant.

just left; "& I assure you without flattery or partiality," he told her, "that he is not only the best natured and most agreeable, but the most fore-thinking & reasonable creature that one can imagine of his age; he had twenty pretty questions & requests . . ." but ". . . will trouble you no longer but to tell you I will bring you a very little good fruit. . . ."[38]

No sooner had Lord Blandford returned to Cambridge, than he was involved in some scrape that infuriated his formidable mother. We cannot tell of what the poor boy had been guilty: all we know is that in February 1703 he wrote two pathetic letters to his parents begging for their forgive-ness, from the second of which it appears that his brother-in-law Francis had intervened on his behalf. "Dear Mama," he wrote, "I received a letter from Mr. Godolphin last post and the joy I had when I found I had some hopes of being friends with my Dear Mama is not to be expressed, but I can't think my self so happy till my Dear Mama can find some time to lett me have a letter from her, & I am sure there can be no greater pleasure than would be to my Dear Mama, your most Dutyful Son, Blandford."[39] We can only hope that Sarah responded to this appeal, for the ink had scarcely dried upon the letter before grave news came from Cambridge. Lord Blandford had small-pox.

His distracted mother hastened to his bedside, and Francis and Henrietta Godolphin, who were then at Godolphin House, set out hurriedly from London. Soon after their arrival at Cambridge, Francis wrote to his father in London the latest news of the invalid. His letter ". . . gives us the most grievous affliction imaginable," wrote his father to the Duchess. "Dr. Hannes and Dr. Cladon went from my house about 5 last night, in a Hackney coach & 6 horses wth orders to take one of the Queen's coaches to carry them onn, soe I hope they were this morning with you. God send their remedys may bee able to relieve the poor child, but it looks dismally by Mr. Godol-phin's Account."[40] But the doctors trundling through the night in the royal coach were of no avail. The victim was sinking fast. The poor father hurried from London, but arrived at Cambridge just as his son expired.

The unhappy parents retired to Holywell. Thence they were followed by a letter from the Queen. "It would have been a great satisfaction to your poor unfortunate faithful Morley," she wrote, "If you would have given me leave to come to St. Albans, for the unfortunate ought to come to the unfortunate. But since you will not have me, I must content myself as well as I can till I have the happiness of seeing you here. I know nothing worth writing, but if I did, I should not trouble you with it, being sure no sort of news can be agreeable to your dear heavy heart. God Almighty bless and comfort my dear Mrs. Freeman, and be assured I will live and die sincerely yours."[41] "The unfortunate ought to come to the unfortunate"! A cry from the wounded heart of one bereaved mother to the wounded heart of another; poor unfortunate, faithful Morley, indeed!

One other tribute offered to the sorrowing relatives of young Lord Blandford may here be mentioned. Hearing of the sad news from Cambridge, the great dramatist, William Congreve, hastened to compose a pastoral, which he entitled "Tears of Amaryllis for Amyntas," manuscript copies of which he sent through the agency of his patron, Lord Halifax, to members of the bereaved family. The poem itself he dedicated to Lord Godolphin. This simple act was fraught with strange consequences that none could foretell but which, as we shall shortly see, were destined to leave their mark upon our story.

But the Marlboroughs had small leisure for sorrow. The General must join his armies in the field. Before he left he made a new will, leaving his large property to his wife in trust for Francis Godolphin, his eldest daughter's husband.* Then, early in March, he sailed for Holland. Duty called and "Marlbrook s'en va-t-en guerre." Some eight months were to pass before he was destined to return.

* According to Archdeacon Coxe, Marlborough begged Anne to create his son-in-law, Francis Godolphin, Earl of Marlborough on condition he assumed the name and arms of Churchill. Coxe, *Marlborough*, I, 110. In fact he was succeeded by his eldest daughter Henrietta, at the time of her father's death Countess of Godolphin, as Duchess of Marlborough in her own right.

CHAPTER II

GODOLPHIN, HARLEY, AND DANIEL DEFOE

MARLBOROUGH returned to England in the autumn of 1703 to find the country in great political confusion. For months past there had been much animosity between the two parties and Godolphin had besieged his friend with letters full of his woes. Marlborough himself, wearied by all the slights to which he had been subjected by the Dutch, was in no mood for further humiliations. "There is nothing more certaine than what you say that either of the Partys wou'd be tyrants if they were lett alone, and I am afraid it is as true that it will be very heard for the queen to prevent itt . . ."[1] he had written to Sarah in June. In October he had written to Harley ". . . of the heats that continue between the two parties." If only he could allay them! If only he could retire from "these uneasy and troublesome broils." However, as he added wearily, he will do his duty to the Queen and country and that ". . . my greatest care and satisfaction is in the hopes I have from Lord Treasurer's and your abilities and prudent management of these matters, wherein upon my return I shall be ready to give my assistance and to be solely governed by yours and his Lordship's good advice. . . ."[2] And now he was back home and in the midst of the party heats in which his faithful colleague had been for so long embroiled.

The trouble had started in the previous year on the wording of Parliament's congratulatory Address to the Queen on Marlborough's victories, and when Jack Howe, a fractious west country Tory, proposed that the huge sum of £100,000—double what any Queen of England had ever had in jointure—should be provided for Prince George of Denmark, in the event of Anne's death. The Tories hesitated to offend the Queen by assailing a measure that no one could honestly defend. Instead they contrived to foster further trouble by moving that a clause should be inserted in the Bill exempting the prince from all disabilities imposed on aliens by the Act of Succession. This was an ingenious attack on that small body of peers of foreign extraction who had been rewarded for their services to the late King. Objection was taken to the clause that it was a "tack" upon a money Bill and as such unconstitutional.* The Queen regarded all opposition to the

* The Lords had no alternative to accepting or rejecting a money Bill en bloc. Consequently, if it became the practice of the Commons to "tack" other clauses on to a money Bill, it would completely destroy the Lords' legislative functions.

Bill as a personal slight and she pressed the measure upon the House with the full force of her influence. Godolphin saw the danger, that the clause added to the Bill might be used "to blow up the House of Lords into the thought that this is a tack . . . if they are kept up in this thought I doubt it may prove the loss of the bill, which would be very uneasy to the Queen; and I do not see how to prevent it unless upon the report so many other saving clauses be offered as will tire the House and give them a handle to leave out all the clauses of the bill and this among the rest."[3] And again six days later, "If the Prince meets with a disagreeable opposition in the House of Lords to his bill, he is obliged to his own servants for it. The whole proceeding of that House yesterday looks to me as if they were afraid the time were too short for madness and extravagance."[4]

It was clear to the Marlboroughs and Godolphin that the House of Lords must on no account be "blown up" nor the Queen made "uneasy", and they vigorously supported the Bill. Judge then of John and Sarah's chagrin at finding that they could not control their intractable son-in-law, Spencer, who had just succeeded his father as third Earl of Sunderland. He led the opposition to the measure, and when it passed by a narrow majority, added to his offence by joining with other Whig leaders in signing protests against the offending clause. Sarah was transported with rage and, a violent family quarrel ensued, that was only partly composed after an interval by the affectionate entreaties of Lady Sunderland. Queen Anne was deeply mortified. Her resentment was lasting and became of great public consequence a few years later.

The next matter to agitate the parties was the introduction of a Bill to disqualify occasional conformists from office. The position of Godolphin and Marlborough was delicate, for the Tory party, like the Queen, was for the Bill, and they did not wish to alienate either. But far more important to them than any such questions was the prosecution of the war, and they feared that the measure would divide the country at the very moment when national unity was imperative. In their dilemma, as they believed, Rochester saw his chance to use the measure as a wedge to alienate them from both their queen and their party. Two such experienced campaigners as Marlborough and Godolphin, however, were not to be so easily entrapped, and they proceeded to follow a course not unknown today of avowing their support for the principle of the Bill while taking steps to have it destroyed backstage. Sarah, who of course was violently against the Bill, was highly indignant when she heard that her beloved husband and her best friend were voting for it. What she wrote to John on this unhappy topic we do not know, for at her bidding he destroyed all her letters, but we have his remarkable reply, "I do own a great deal of what you say is right," he told her, "but I can by no means allow that all the Tory party are for King James, and consequently against the queen, but the contrary; I think it is in her power to make use of almost all, but some of the heads, to the true interests of England, which I take to be the Protestant succession, to the supporting of which, by the help of Almighty God, I will venture my last drop of blood." How he regretted this disagreement with his beloved Sarah! "But as I am firmly resolved never to assist any Jacobite whatsoever, or any Tory that is for persecution, I must be careful not to do the thing in the world which my Lord Rochester would most desire to have me do, which is to give my vote against this bill; but I do most solemnly promise that I will speak to nobody living to be for it; and to show you that I would do anything that were not a ruin to the queen, and an absolute destruction to myself to make you easy, at this time by what has been told me, the bill will certainly be thrown out, unless my lord Treasurer and I will both speak to people and speak in the House, which I do assure you for myself I will not do."[5]

Nor would the Lord Treasurer. To him the whole thing was crazy: ". . . the Queen's servants in both Houses are vying who shall be maddest,"[6] he told Harley, and "I doubt we have too many irons in the fire."[7] The two friends shoulder to shoulder withstood the brunt of Sarah's onslaught. Upon both the first and the second readings of the Occasional Conformity Bill in the upper House they "marched with Rochester."[8] So did Prince George, for Anne persuaded or compelled him, though himself an occasional conformist, to go to the House of Lords on the second reading and vote for the measure.* He went, however, most unwillingly and is said to have whispered to Wharton, the Whig teller, "My heart is vid you." But the "march" with Rochester was short-lived. Soon was the time to turn upon him. Godolphin and the Marlboroughs had a secret meeting with the Queen at which they told her clearly that it was impossible to work any longer with her tiresome uncle. Anne, delighted at the excuse to take action, ordered Rochester to repair to Dublin and discharge his duties as Lord-Lieutenant of Ireland.[9] He refused and promptly resigned.

In the midst of these excitements there appeared two anonymous pamphlets; one entitled *An Enquiry into Occasional Conformity* denounced the practice in violent terms; in the second and better known paper, *The Shortest Way with the Dissenters*, the writer parodied the extravagant language of the "High Flyers", the High Church controversialists. Unfortunately for the pamphleteer, his irony was taken seriously; and a reward was offered in the *Gazette* for the apprehension of the unknown writer. Speaker Harley told Godolphin that it was imperative for Nottingham to discover

* He was a peer with the title of Duke of Cumberland.

the author:[10] whereupon the Secretary of State bestirred himself. His activities soon bore fruit and the offender was discovered to be a certain Grub Street scribbler, Daniel Defoe, who promptly grovelled to Nottingham, promising that he would, if released, endeavour for the future to deserve her Majesty's favour.[11] In spite of his protestations he was tried at the Old Bailey, admitted the authorship and offered to betray his friends if he might escape the pillory, and not be called on as evidence against anybody.[12] Fortunately for the prisoner's reputation the Queen deemed his confession of no account and left it to the Lords of the Committee to determine whether or not the sentence should be executed upon him.[13] The Lords after some delay[14] sentenced Defoe to pay a fine, to stand three times in the pillory and to be imprisoned during the Queen's pleasure. And so the doors of Newgate close upon him and for a time we see him no more.

Now by this time the importance of political journalism had become recognized, and as far back as the previous summer the wily Speaker had written pertinently to Godolphin of the advantages of having ". . . some discreet writer of the Government side, if it were only to state facts right; for the Generality err for want of knowledge, and being imposed upon by the Storys raised by ill-designing men. . . ."[15] A "discreet writer of the Government side": what a boon he would be! Only of course, "to state facts right", for what else do propagandists ever do? "The Generality err for want of knowing"; how often politicians have uttered that cry! And so gradually, whilst pondering these profound truths, Harley's mind might turn to the poor denizen of Grub Street, now languishing in Newgate.

How did Mr. Speaker hear of this obscure man? Not so obscure, however, for when he had stood his punishment, the crowd had formed a guard, had covered the pillory with garlands, and with great heartiness had drunk his health! Fortified by this public enthusiasm the victim of malice and oppression had passed his imprisonment in composing a poem, *Hymn to the Pillory*, in which he expressed strong views as to his fate. So Mr. Speaker may very easily have heard of the poet and pamphleteer, may very easily have found that he had a wife and six children to support, and that he could only keep them by his pen. The person who seems to have put Harley in communication with the prisoner was William Paterson, who had first proposed the Bank of England, and had for some time acted the part of unofficial financial adviser to the Government, * for a paper is extant in which Defoe expresses to Paterson his unfeigned regret for his offence.

---

* However, Godolphin, it seems, did not think very highly of Paterson's financial ability: "I must own his notions seem to me for the most part very confused, not to say impracticable, and he talks still of *retrieving public credit,* as if money were still at 8 per cent." Godolphin to Harley, January, 1703-4. H.M.C. *Portland,* IV, 78.

"Tis vain for me to complain of the misfortune of my present condition," he wrote, "since you can render me no service for which you shall not receive reproaches from all parties. Nay, even the Dissenters, like Casha [sic] to Caesar, lift up the first dagger at me; I confess it makes me reflect on the whole body of Dissenters with something of contempt, more than usual, and gives me the more regret that I suffer for such a people." But there is nothing he will not do to gain a pardon for his offences. ". . . Nor is there anything so mean (which I can honestly stoop to do) that I would not submit to, to obtain her Majesty's favour." The last paragraph points clearly to Paterson having hinted that some distinguished person high in royal favour, presumably Harley, was likely to help him to employment; and he begs Paterson to "venture in my name in the humblest terms to ask his pardon . . . Let him know that I solicit you with more earnestness to convince him of my sense of his resentment and my earnest desire to be set right in his thoughts, than I do for the obtaining a recall from this banishment, forasmuch as I value the esteem of one wise man above abundance of blessings."[16]

Not much more was heard of Defoe for some weeks; but he was not forgotten, for in September, when Godolphin was at Bath in attendance on the Queen, he received a letter from the Speaker on this very subject. "Foe", it seems, was oppressed at his treatment and was anxious to serve the Queen. "Your Lordship can judge whether he be worth it; there is a private attempt amongst his friends to raise the 200 marks for his fine; he is a very capable man, and if his fine be satisfied he may do service and this may perhaps engage him better than any after rewards, and keep him more under the power of an obligation."[17] Apparently the Lord Treasurer thought that "Foe" was very much worth while, for he replied that "I have found it proper to read some paragraphs of your letter to the Queen. What you propose about Defoe may be done when you will, & how you will."[18] So Anne, Godolphin and Harley were agreed upon Defoe's potential value to them.

Two days later the Lord Treasurer left Bath for his beloved Newmarket,[19] where he remained until about October 16th, when he was due in London.[20] A few days after his return he informed Harley that "I have taken care of the matter of Defoe."[21] "Taking care" involved the dispatching from the Treasury of a sum of money to relieve the poor man's family. He was pathetically grateful. "Of all the examples in sacred story none moves my indignation like that of the ten lepers who were healed by our Saviour," he wrote to Harley, "I, like the one grateful wretch am come back to pay the tribute of thankfulness which this so unexpected goodness commands from me." It appears that Godolphin's name had not been disclosed, for Defoe begs "to know my benefactors", and to "know what I am capable of doing, that my benefactors whoever they are may not be ashamed of their bounty as misapplied."[22] But there were more benefits to come. A few months later, in the summer of 1704, Defoe was released from Newgate. In August he received a royal pardon. "I return you the blank warrant signed by the Queen for D's pardon," wrote Godolphin to Harley on the last day of the month; and referring to Godolphin's financial arrangements to relieve the Defoe family, he added, "Her majesty commands me to tell you she approves entirely of what you have promised him, and will make it good."[23]

No sooner was Defoe free than he was anxious to commence work for his new masters. He set out his misfortunes in eloquent terms.[24] Therefore he must work. And the work Harley and Godolphin had ready for him was to travel about the country to ascertain the views and feelings of the voters and to spread government propaganda far and wide. Or any other useful service he was very ready to undertake. At the same time he begged Harley to solicit Godolphin either that a branch of the Auditor's office might be bestowed upon him, or that the Lord Treasurer would appoint him "a convenient private allowance for subsistence on which I might comfortably depend and continue to be serviceable in a private capacity whether abroad or at home." If that be impossible, then he urged that he might be "delivered from the unsufferable disorders of my affairs, and that my going abroad may be as speedy as you please."[25]

Thus was Harley's and Godolphin's secret service system inaugurated. And soon the agent's reports began to come in. On September 16th Defoe wrote to Harley from Cambridge,* and on the 28th from Bury St. Edmunds, whence he gave an account of his activities in the Eastern Counties. In the postscript he asked for money. "Please to direct to Alexander Goldsmith at Mr. John Morley's in Bury";[26] and as Alexander Goldsmith, Defoe became known on his wanderings. In November, back in London, he wrote at length to his patron of the general feeling among the people about the Government. "They call the Duke of Marlborough, the Lord Treasurer and yourself, *the Triumvirate* who manage the State," he reported, "and that if the knot be broken in the House first, they will prevail with the Queen to continue the Duke of Marlborough abroad all this winter, under pretence of going to concert measures with the Princes of the Empire and so they will easily put by all this scheme of management. This ridiculous stuff had never reached your ears . . ." but for his enquiries.[27] "Ridiculous stuff" indeed, and hardly likely to deceive such experienced campaigners as the triumvirate!

Not much more is heard of the agent until the following summer, when

* This letter has not been found.

he embarks on a similar government mission of enquiry, this time to the west. In July we hear of him at Crediton,[28] in August at Tiverton,[29] whence he enclosed a warrant issued for his apprehension,* and in September at Kidderminster.[30] Thereafter his wanderings took him into Cheshire, Lancashire, Yorkshire and some of the counties of the midlands and the west.[31]

That Godolphin knew and approved of these proceedings is clear from two notes to Harley still extant in his hand; though neither is dated, both must have been written at about this time. "Not knowing where or how to send to Defoe," he wrote in one of them, "I trouble you with this letter, desiring the favour of you to let him know that I think it might do service if he could let us know the names of the persons concerned in carrying on these designs here in London, and the place of their abode." "As to De F," he wrote in the other, "I should think he might be made use of where he is without further charge to you, but I shall be glad to talk with you tomorrow, if you will call upon me as you go to Kensington; about him and some other things."[32]

Defoe's services were further rendered in *The Review,* a periodical which he had begun in Newgate. In this, every word of which was written by himself, he upheld the Godolphin government, discussed politics, finance and trade in vigorous terms; indeed, he supplied all the essentials of a modern newspaper, and offered a publication which, though meanly produced, was far above its predecessors, The *Mercurius Politicus,* the many outpourings of Sir Roger L'Estrange, and the productions of the rascally Tutchin. It was *The Review* that earned for Defoe the title that is so often applied to him, the founder of English journalism.[33]

Meanwhile, the two Ministers were faced with other problems in the solution of which the faithful Defoe could play no part. Rochester's removal from office had effected little to compose the dissension in the Tory ranks, for "dismal" Nottingham, had long adopted his views. Their objects were twofold: abroad, to restrict our participation in the war as far as possible to a defensive part;† and at home, to harry the Dissenters. Behind Nottingham were men holding office in both houses; Buckingham and Jersey in the Lords, Hedges and Seymour in the Commons. The political strife was becoming intolerable. "What you tell mee of 42

---

* "Hugh Stafford to all Constables and other officers in the County of Devon and also to Charles Sugg, August 9." H.M.C. *Portland,* IV, 218.

† This was particularly galling to Godolphin who was anxious to send aid to the Camisard rebellion that had recently broken out in the Cevennes. He advocated the sending of a fleet to the Mediterranean and a landing in the South of France. Memorandum in Godolphin's hand dated 1703. Brit. Mus. Add. MSS. 29,589, f. 327.

(Nottingham) concerning the Parke is very scandalous, but very natural to that person," wrote Marlborough to his wife; "I wish with all my heart the queen were rid of him, soe that she had a good man in his place, which I am afraid is pretty heard to find. . . . We are bound not to wish for any body's death, but if 14 (Seymour) shou'd dye, I am convinced it wou'd be noe great loss to 85 (the queen) nor the nation; and you may be sure the visset intended by 19 (Rochester) and his friend cou'd be for noe other end but to flatter 14 (Seymour) to doe such mischief as they dare not openly owne."[34] The attitude of Rochester was particularly galling. "I am of your mind, that if the Queen spoke to Lord Rochester in the manner you mention in your letter, I believe it would make him very cautious; not that I think it would make him honest, but he would be afraid. The conversation that was between Lord Rochester and the Speaker is no doubt the language that he entertains the whole party with . . ."[35]

Later in that same month of June, the Queen spoke to her uncle in the way Sarah had suggested, and the testy Rochester resigned. But things did not improve, and Godolphin and Marlborough were both becoming thoroughly sick of the impossible situation in which they found themselves. "The writer of the Letter in cypher, and the Gibberish language, ought certainly to be seized with all his papers;" wrote Godolphin to the Speaker, "perhaps it is the same gibberish language that Ld. Nottingham made so famous. . . ."[36] And again, "I have had this morning an account of a long tedious meeting betwixt the heads of the Whymsicall, and some Lords of our house. . . . Wee live the life of galley slaves."[37] By the autumn, both Godolphin and Marlborough had come to the end of their tether, and were beginning to talk of resignation. This alarmed the Queen, and towards the end of the year she wrote a letter to Sarah on this very subject. "The thoughts that both my dear Mrs. Freeman and Mr. Freeman seem to have of retyring gives me no small uneasyness, and therefore I must say something on that subject, it is no wonder at all people in your posts should be weary of the world who are soe continually troubled with all the hurry and impertinencys of it, but give me leave to say you should a little consider your faithful freinds and poor Country, wch must be ruined if ever you should putt your melancoly thoughts in execution, as for your poor unfortunate faithfully Morly she could not beare it, for if ever you should forsake me, I would have nothing more to do wth the world, but make another abdycation, for what is a crown, when the support of it is gon: I never will forsake your Dear self, Mr. Freeman nor Mr. Montgomery, but allways be your constant faithful servant, & we four must never part, till death mows us down with his impartiall hand."[38]

So matters dragged on during the last months of 1703 and the early months of 1704. After the Queen's pathetic appeal, the Ministers felt that they could not desert her. But the danger stood clearly revealed. Whilst at Bath in September, Godolphin had drafted the Queen's speech for the forthcoming session, and he sent it to Harley for his views. "I have drawn a line under such expressions where I am doubtful either of the expressions themselves, or that they are not proper in the paragraph where at present they are inserted," and he begged for the Speaker's "remarks and observations upon it with all freedom."[39] The speech closed with some significant words. "My interests and yours are inseparable; and my endeavours shall never be wanting, to make you all safe and happy."* It was clear that the triumvirate must keep closely united if trouble was to be avoided, and Godolphin suggested twice weekly meetings, if not oftener, "to advise upon everything that shall occur . . ."[40] and again "I think the meeting will be best on fryday morning for the reasons you give," he wrote, "& I will bee ready hard by to attend you upon Call, in the meantime I beg you to watch if any that passes in the H. of Commons tomorrow should require a meeting of those Gentlemen & cause it to bee appointed, for unless those meetings bee kept up constantly and those who are called come willingly to them & with a desire to agree, I can not think tis possible to proceed."[41]

It was this trying moment that Nottingham chose to threaten the Lord Treasurer that he must retire from the Government unless all the remaining Whigs were removed from office. To this haughty demand Godolphin seems to have turned a deaf ear: whereupon, the malcontent Minister, after carefully waiting until Marlborough had set forth for Holland, appealed directly to the Queen. He invited Anne to choose between the two parties: if she chose the Whigs, he told her, he and his followers would immediately retire; if, on the other hand, she could continue to give her support to the Tories, then he must insist on the removal of the Dukes of Somerset and Devonshire from the Privy Council.

But Nottingham had overplayed his cards. The Queen, affronted by his arrogance, and counselled by Godolphin to deal sharply with the malcontents, needed no second bidding: she promptly dismissed Jersey and Seymour from office. "I am just come to this place to get a little air and quiet," she wrote to Sarah from Kensington in her quaintest style, "I am told by a very good hand that the Queen has sent a message to Lord Jersey and Sir Edward Seymour which they will not like. Sure this will convince Mrs. Freeman that I never had any partiality to any of these persons; for if that had been so, this would certainly never have been done. Something more of this nature it is believed will soon happen, that will not be disagreeable to Mrs. Freeman."[42] The something more happened promptly.

* Delivered October 21st, 1702.

PART OF GODOLPHIN'S DRAFT OF A SPEECH FOR QUEEN ANNE

WITH SUGGESTED AMENDMENTS BY ROBERT HARLEY

From Welbeck Abbey, on loan to the British Museum

Nottingham, chagrined at the rough treatment that had been meted out to his friends, sulkily resigned.

Naturally Godolphin and Marlborough wished to fill up the vacancy thus created with their loyal supporter; and when for a time the Speaker seems to have been coy, Marlborough wrote impatiently from Vorst begging Godolphin ". . . to take no excuse from 47 (Harley) but that he must immediately come in."[43] No excuse was accepted, and after a short interview Harley was persuaded by the insistence of his friends. Nevertheless the appointment was not universally popular. "'Tis a pretty hard matter to please everybody and especially those who will neither lead nor drive," wrote Godolphin a trifle peevishly. "I speak now of some of the chiefs of Westminster Hall, who if they are angry may thank themselves . . . I doubt indeed the enemy may have been (more) industrious than we, but I cannot reproach myself for not having done my part. I never was near so industrious before in my life, and shall be very glad never to have occasion of being so again. If it be an objection that a Speaker should not be proposed by any in the Queen's services, I suppose that may be easily avoided by a meeting beforehand of those who will join heartily in carrying on the Queen's service, and the public business. . . ."[44]

The retirement of Nottingham and the dismissal of his followers was thought to show the great and growing favour in which Godolphin and Marlborough now stood with the Queen, which was further evinced by Anne standing godmother to their new grandson, the recently born child of Francis and Henrietta. The routing of the Nottingham faction naturally led to a number of governmental changes, the most noteworthy of which was the substitution for the plodding Blathwayt as Minister of War of a mercurial young friend of Harley's, the Alcibiades of his age, Henry St. John by name, soon to be better known as Viscount Bolingbroke.

Here we must pause awhile to consider for a moment the financial problems facing Godolphin upon his return to the Treasury in the opening year of the new reign.

At the accession of Queen Anne, the funded debt stood at approximately £10,000,000. In addition, there were £2,338,628 outstanding Exchequer Bills, borrowed at 7 and 8 per cent, and various other arrears amounting in total to something like £12,750,000.[45] On the other side, taking the average of the last three years of King William, the total revenue from both direct and indirect taxation amounted only to the annual sum of £4,650,000.[46] In 1697 a mortgage had been made of certain taxes totalling close upon a million pounds a year, to be continued until 1706, as a fund for the discharge of approximately £5,100,000. Early in the new reign this mortgage was extended until 1710 to meet a deficit of nearly three and a half millions; and Godolphin also allocated other taxes to constitute a further security for the floating Exchequer Bills.[47]

But the new Lord Treasurer was soon faced with the problem of how to meet the rapidly increasing expenditure necessitated by the war. For part of this he provided by the issue of annuities upon a loan of about £87,000 charged upon the Excise. The remainder he wished to meet out of taxation. He accordingly levied new duties on mum (a sort of German beer), cider, malt and perry; and by a one-third subsidy of fourpence in the pound *ad valorem*, with in 1704 a two-thirds additional subsidy, the whole amounting to a shilling in the pound, he increased the duties on wines and other commodities at the ports. In addition Godolphin raised the land tax from two to four shillings in the pound.[48] This disgusted the country gentry, and it is said that it was only their violent reaction from the unpopular measure that prevented Godolphin from raising the tax still further.

During the opening years of the new reign, stocks gradually rose, thus indicating the Government's improved credit, probably derived in part from the economies practised during the peaceful period of 1698–1701, when Parliament imposed a considerable disbandment of the forces on a reluctant King. But with the renewal of the war expenditure inevitably rose. Thus the national expenditure, no more than some three millions or rather less in 1700–1, between Michaelmas 1702 and Michaelmas 1703, rose to over nine and a half millions. A year later it was nearly ten millions and by Michaelmas 1705 it exceeded ten and a quarter millions. How was the Lord Treasurer to meet this vast increase in expenditure? In 1703 the Government's revived credit enabled him to tide over a temporary pressure by the issue at the low rate of 5 per cent of £1,800,000, of Exchequer Bills. But that was only stop-gap finance. In 1704 he levied additional duties upon tea, coffee, and the produce of China and the East Indies, and on these duties he effected a loan of £7,000,000 at 6 per cent.[49] In the same year annuities were issued to the amount of £878,000 secured upon the Excise,[50] and in 1705, £2,575,000 was raised upon the security of tonnage and poundage on wines, coals and other goods.[51] Unfortunately, however, part of the yield from these taxes was already pledged; therefore an additional £280,000 was borrowed to strengthen the security. In 1706 there followed two fresh issues of annuities to the total amount of two millions,[52] and a further million and a half was raised by Exchequer Bills secured upon the house duty.[53] Never before had such vast sums been raised for the public use.

Yet in spite of this huge increase in expenditure, Government credit continued to stand high: no wonder that King William's old friend, Bishop Burnet, should delight in the abundance of money and that the Government, even at the very peak of the war, could borrow at no more than six and a half per cent. Not a little of the credit for this happy state of affairs was due to the financial genius of Lord Treasurer Godolphin.

Meanwhile Marlborough was preparing his campaign. Prospects were gloomy. Austria was in imminent danger of collapse; therefore, Marlborough determined forthwith to march to the aid of Prince Eugene. His plan must be secret, lest the Dutch should cry out that they were being left to the mercy of France. The first time the Danube was mentioned in the General's confidential correspondence was in a letter written to Godolphin in early May, 1704; in this he set out his plans and asked his friend's advice.[54] But certain is it that the facts disclosed were no secret to Godolphin. Very probably the two comrades had the previous winter in the seclusion of Godolphin House discussed the possibilities of such a diversion. And now the great soldier's plans were ready. He artfully lured the French away from Flanders, and then, boldly turning his back on France, he headed for the Danube. His object was to seize Donauwörth on the northern bank. Here he routed a force of some 12,000 Bavarians, on the heights of the Schellenberg that dominated the town. It was a notable victory; and, though Rochester and the High Tories might try to disparage the General by dilating unduly on the allied losses, the only result of their malice was to make it clear to both Marlborough and Godolphin that no peace could be made with such factious men.

As a result of the battle of the Schellenberg virtually the whole line of the Danube from Donauwörth to Vienna was once again in allied hands. Some six weeks later, on August 13th, 1704, Marlborough and Eugene stood on the northern bank near the little village of Blenheim: together they barred the way to Vienna. When the sun sank to rest that night, Marlborough had proved himself the greatest general of the age. Not in living memory had a French army been so routed in the field. Not since Agincourt three centuries earlier had Englishmen won so great a victory.

even at the very peak of the war, could borrow at six per cent. falling to a half per cent. Even a billion the cost for this happy nation, which was then the financial centre of Europe. These are Gordolphin...

CHAPTER III

FAMILY AFFAIRS

ON December 14th, four months after his glorious victory, Marlborough landed at Greenwich. His return was a signal for general rejoicing, and practically the whole nation sought to do honour to the great commander. Early in the New Year the Queen informed the Commons that she proposed to convey to the Duke of Marlborough and his heirs the Royal Manor and Park of Woodstock, consisting of some 15,000 acres and said to be worth about £6,000 a year, and to build upon it a splendid palace to bear for all time the honoured name of Blenheim. But above the general chorus of approval, there was still to be heard within the Tory ranks a small but highly vocal element led by Rochester, Nottingham and Seymour, who were highly incensed against Godolphin and his Ministry; and the best method they could contrive of attacking the Government was to decry the General. With this object they sought to set the Tory Sir George Rooke's indecisive engagement at Malaga on the same plane as the glorious victory of Blenheim. The absurdity of this is clearly demonstrated from Godolphin's rating of Rooke's Pyrrhic victory. "Upon the whole it seems to have been a sort of drawn battle where both sides had had enough of it, though 'tis plain the fight was at a great distance."[1] What an event to set against the overwhelming victory on the Danube!

Whilst the High Tories were acting thus the Whigs were, with like injustice, striving to show that the Admiral had done nothing at all. So Marlborough became a hero of the Whigs. The attitude of the parties disgusted him. ". . . I know them both so well," he told his wife, "that if my quiet depended upon either of them, I should be most miserable. . . ." But, he added, "I will endeavour to leave a good name behind me in countries that have hardly any blessing but that of not knowing the detested name of Whig and Tory."[2]

This bitter party ferment had some results destined to be lasting. It drew Godolphin still closer to his friend—"I can believe in him against my own senses," he wrote once when he and Marlborough differed[3]—and it drew them both gradually towards the Whig camp. To Harley's secret agent, Defoe, this seemed not free from danger, for might not the extremes, —the Whigs and the High Tories—unite to crush the moderates? But to the Duchess of Marlborough it was supremely welcome. So thought Robert Harley who was busily engaged in making overtures to the great Whig magnate, Newcastle, soon destined to take the Privy Seal from the High Tory Buckingham. But there was one difficulty to be overcome, the antagonism of the Queen for the Lords of the Whig Junto, and especially for Somers, the obvious choice from the Whig ranks to succeed the Tory Wright as Chancellor.

Meanwhile, the indignant Tories were not slow to show their teeth. In this the High Church joined, and in a famous pamphlet, *The Memorial of the Church of England*, denounced both Godolphin and Marlborough in violent terms. Sidney was nettled; "a discreet clergyman is almost as rare as a black swan," he wrote testily to Harley in September, 1704,[4] and a year later, "I have heard since I came to town of several insolences of the clergy, which are really insufferable, and next door to open rebellion, and I don't find the least notice taken of it, or the least thought or disposition to reprehend any of them about it."[5] But he did not suffer as much as his friend, for soon commenced the final vendetta against Marlborough. He was represented to be an odious traitor who had by chance become a successful general, an illiterate ploughboy who could not spell his own tongue, a contemptible miser who could teach even Monsieur Harpagon his business, a vile trickster whom Volpone himself would have admired. The whole warped genius of Swift was concentrated upon the singular unworthy motive of decrying the national hero. And in this, unhappily, he was followed by another writer of genius, the great Whig historian himself.

The Godolphin Ministry, thus assailed, was soon making heavy weather. Early in the autumn session of 1704 a motion was proposed to "tack" the Occasional Conformity Bill to the Land Tax, and the fierce struggle between the "Tackers" and "Sneakers"* began. Godolphin was furious that either Bill or tack had been brought forward at all. The Queen's servants could so easily have kept out the Occasional Conformity Bill. "She has not much reason to thank them for it," he told Harley, "not that I apprehend they can carry a tack or put a stop to the money, but when the bill is thrown out in the House of Lords, they will make use of that handle to throw dirt and stones at whom they have a mind to bespatter."[6] Small wonder if Godolphin could write indignantly to Sarah that "I shall never think any man fit to continue in his employment who gave his vote for the tack."[7]

Towards the end of November, the tackers suffered a heavy defeat. This was far from rescuing the Ministry from its embarrassments, but it did serve to drive Godolphin and his colleagues more and more towards the

---

* The "sneakers" were those Tories who refused to support the motion for the tack.

Whig fold. In the Lords, Godolphin was threatened with a vote of censure for his handling of Scottish affairs, a predicament from which he was only rescued by Wharton, one of the Lords of the Junto. In the Commons, the Whigs showed signs of joining with the Tackers in sending an invitation to the Electress Sophia of Hanover to take up residence in England as heir to the throne. This would infuriate the Queen, Godolphin told Harley, adding ruefully that ". . . I don't know what way to prevent it, unless we can be strong enough to quash it in the House of Commons, which can scarce be hoped for, if all the Tackers and the Whigs join in it . . ." and he stated his intention of rallying the Whig lords to exert their influence on their friends in the Commons.[8] In this, it seems, the Lord Treasurer was not unsuccessful, but the feud between the two houses continued unabated until it reached its climax in the famous Aylesbury case of Ashby *versus* White. This dragged on until the spring of the following year, when Anne, weary of the eternal wranglings, brought the stormy session to a sudden end by first proroguing and then dissolving Parliament. Perhaps after a General Election the two Houses might be found to be in better humour. This seemed likely, for the new Parliament was distinctly more Whiggish than its predecessor,* and it was clear that Marlborough and Godolphin could rely on the strong force of Whigs and moderate Tories who now dominated both Houses.

But if the High Tories had been defeated, they had not been routed. To Godolphin, trying some months later to assess the strength of parties—not easy when the allegiance of so many was doubtful—it seemed that the Tories were still the largest party in the House, with the "Queen's servants" much less than the Whigs. "My computation runs thus," he wrote to Harley, "of the 450 that chose the Speaker Tories 190, Whigs 160, Queen's servants 100 . . ." but he reckoned that the last two could be counted upon in most cases to vote together.[9] From these results he might well draw satisfaction. But not so the Queen. "I must own to you, I dread falling into the hands of either party," she wrote to Sidney in July 1705, "and the Whigs have had so many favours showed them of late, that I fear a very few more will put me insensibly into their power, which is what I'm sure you would not have happen to me no more than I. I know my dear unkind friend, (the Duchess of Marlborough) has so good an opinion of all that party that she will use all her endeavour to get you to prevail with me. I do put an entire confidence in you, not doubting but you will do all you can to keep me out

---

* Among the casualties was Francis Godolphin rejected for Cambridge, where his fellow candidate, the great Sir Isaac Newton, found himself at the bottom of the poll. We get a brief glimpse of Godolphin's electioneering in the south-west in Sykes, *The Cathedral Chapter of Exeter and the General Election of 1705*, E.H.R. XLV, 260-72.

of the power of the *merciless men of both parties*."[10]   In fact she was objecting
to the replacement of the Tory and incompetent Wright by an able young
Whig lawyer, William Cowper, whom Sarah had long been pressing on her
notice.   Anne appealed over the head of Mrs. Freeman to Mrs. Freeman's
lord.   She might have saved herself the pains.   He begged her to rely
implicitly on Godolphin's counsel.   And the alternative?   To send for
Rochester and to lose the war.   Thus faced, Anne had no choice.   In
October Cowper became Lord Keeper of the Great Seal.   It was now clear
that the Godolphin Ministry would henceforth sail on smoother waters.*

The reader will recall the happy relationship that existed between mother
and daughter before Henrietta Churchill wedded Francis Godolphin.   It is
pleasant to recall that this state of affairs subsisted for some time after the
marriage.   "I can't tell my dear Mama what a pleasure her kind letter is to
mee, I have read it over and over and wou'd not part with it for any thing,
but have lockt it up with all my treasures."[11]   "Since my Dear Mama went
away I have had nothing to please mee so well as your kind long letter which
I made as much longer as I coud by reading it a hundred times over and with
more satisfaction than I can express because I think it looks as if you loved mee
as much as I can wish for, which is saying a good deall...."   Then follows
family news.   "my sisters and Willigo are very well, pray present my
duty to Papa and my Lord Godolphin and thank him for his letter which I
will do my self very soon but now I have three letters more that I must
write...."[12]   "... their is not two things I wish more for than that you
should love mee, and yet I would not desier you shou'd love mee at all
better then I do you, which indeed is extreamly, and I will never faill beeing
with a great deall of tenderness and passion, Dearest Mama, your most
Dutyfull, H. Godolphin."[13]   Of another letter from her mother she writes
this: "I am sure that line where you say your heart is so full of kindness for
mee has done mee more good then I can express, for tho I had no reason to
think otherwise yett tis what so much of my happiness depends upon, that
I should bee glad to have assurances off it a hundred times every day, I am
intierly off my Dear Mama's mind in thinking my self the happiest body in
the world..." but "... I can never know for any long time together any
thing like true satisfaction till I see my Dear Angell Mama again...."   She

---

* We may, I think, ignore the statement made by Lord Dartmouth that Cowper's
appointment was not made with Godolphin's approval.   Burnet, *Own Time*, V, 225.
All the evidence is to the contrary.   Lord Campbell suggests that Godolphin was
pretending in order to retain the support of the High Church party, who were
alarmed at Cowper's elevation.   Campbell. *Lives of the Chancellors*, (ed. 1857),
V, 251.

continues with no doubt welcome news of her sister Anne, who, it will be recalled, had recently become Sunderland's second wife. "I am now come to my sister who expects every moment to bee brought to bed," and concludes, "Dearest Mama, forgive this horrid scraull."[14] Three days later, Anne's safe delivery is recorded, but for the first time a mild note of jealousy is sounded. "I am very glad that I have any thing to tell my Dear Mama that will please her so well as that my sister is safe brought to bed this day for another son. She is very well, and has been so all day. I was mighty sorry not to have a letter last post, especially when my sister had one, my Dear Mama knows I can't help bee so when one loves any body to such a degree as I do you. . . ." Then she closes with some welcome news of her own boy. "Willigo is mighty well, he is now att St. Albans and says he wou'd give the world to come home to Mama. . . ."[15]

In the halcyon days of their early married life Francis and Henrietta had settled with the Marlboroughs, as Sarah "gave them my best appartment in my Lodgings at St. James's." There mother and daughter lived together, Sarah tells us, "like sisters"; but when Henrietta was about to have her fourth child, Marlborough suggested that they should live for a time with Francis's father, and so at about the turn of the century the young couple moved to Godolphin House. There Mary Churchill was a frequent visitor. "I am extreamly glad Lady Harryett has prevayled for lady Mary to stay with her," wrote Sidney from Godolphin House, "since all thee happyness I can hope for at present is the hope of seeing her half an hour while wee are at dinner."[16] Now Mary, it is said, was her father's favourite child, and in the spring of 1705 she married John Montagu, a son of that Ralph Montagu who years before had been our Ambassador at Paris. Ralph, an engaging rogue of vast possessions, was promptly created Duke of Montagu, and his heir, until he succeeded to the dukedom some four years after his marriage, was known by the title of Monthermer. Young Montagu was a welcome visitor to Godolphin House. But there were visitors there of whom the indomitable Sarah did not approve.*

It will be remembered that at the death of poor Blandford the worthy Mr. Congreve, the distinguished dramatist, had sent manuscript copies of his pastoral lament to members of the mourning family. By one of them at least these lines had been well received, and Henrietta had asked the great man to visit her. Three years later, in 1706, Congreve strengthened his attachments by composing a Pindaric Ode in honour of Lord Godolphin. This must have been particularly welcome to Henrietta, who was devoted

---

* I have rather assumed what seems to have been the case, that Godolphin's daughter-in-law had been given the role of hostess at Godolphin House and that therefore she issued most of the invitations.

to her father-in-law. Moreover, she would have been the more flattered by the compliment because she had long nursed a secret ambition to be herself numbered among the wits.* Judge then of her delight when Congreve and Vanbrugh, at the opening of their new playhouse in the Haymarket, referred to her as "the learn'd Minerva."† Small wonder that Congreve soon became a welcome visitor for cards at Godolphin House, where before long Henrietta's mother encountered him playing at ombre with her daughter and strongly disapproved. "When I cam to England, Did not I come to your House with all the kindness imaginable, but You always look'd as if you wanted to have me gone, and once I remember, I came in a very easy way, telling you that it was to consult you about Lady Harriot, whether she should have pinners with lappets or without, for tho' we thought it was better without, because She was low, we would not determine a thing of that consequence without your consent, (and in this manner I endeavour'd to be merry)." But Sarah's humour was not appreciated! "You were at ombre with Mr. Congreve and a Woman that I did not know. I thought He look'd out of Countenance but shew'd more willingness to talk to me than you did; I soon put you at ease, by going away; . . ." That settled matters for the moment, but the next morning Henrietta's mother called again. "The porter told me you were abroad," she recorded, "but an old Servant of the Family, thinking it was impossible You could be denied to me run after my chair, and fetch'd me back: It was so quick that I am sure it was not by your order, upon which I went back: You were above stairs in your dressing room writing: To this you Answer'd that one may be denied to one's Second self." "Being resolved to bear every thing in hopes of bringing Her to reason," continued Sarah pathetically, "I did not quarrel with Her, even upon these answers, but continued still expressing my kindness; and when she rise up to go away I took Her and hugg'd her in my Arms and wept over Her, begging Her still that she would love me, but all that I could get in Answer to This was, That she gave me a little squeeze with Her hand at parting, but I did not see her in some days after."[17]

* Her mother, it seems, had an aristocratic prejudice against her daughter associating with "wits" and such-like plebeians. "She has starts of giving 100 guineas to a very low poet that will tell her that she is what she knows she is not, which I think so great a weakness that I had rather give money not to have such verses made publick." Colville, *Duchess Sarah*, 312. "The very low poet" was, it appears, John Gay. Hodges, *Congreve the Man*, 110.

† The Lincoln's Inn Company moved to the new playhouse in the Haymarket, which was opened in 1705 with a Prologue written by Sir Samuel Garth and spoken by Mrs. Bracegirdle. Betterton, *History of the English Stage* (ed. 1711), 117–18.

Henceforth a new and harsher note may be detected in the correspondence between mother and daughter, and Sarah's endorsements of Henrietta's letters are tart and aggressive. At the foot of one we read in the Duchess's scrawly hand—"this letter was from Lady Godolphin before she was ruined by the very bad campany she kept;" and of another—"this was all she said for the trouble I gave myself in getting a Debt of [blank in MS.] from Lady Mohun not likely to have been paid." Yet a third bears this withering comment: "this letter was written by the Desire of my Lord Godolphin who seemed very much concern'd for what had passed, and owned to me that I had been the best and most tender mother that ever had bin."[18]

The truth is that Sarah did not approve of the sort of life her eldest daughter was living. She was far too fond of the theatre and of dancing—in short, of the frivolities of life. "Lady Haryett had a little of the chollick all yesterday and the night before," wrote Sidney anxiously on one occasion, "enough to hinder her from sleeping, but not from going to the play, wch. not curing her, I prevayled wth. her last night to take 4 of the Bishop's pills; I have not heard of her this morning, but I hope the physick will carry off the cause, wch. was eating too much sallad for three or four days together...."[19]

Then there was the company that Henrietta kept. The Gays and Congreves of this world were all very well in their place, wherever that might be; and doubtless the mighty Sarah did not mind very much, so long as it was not in the family circle at Godolphin House. Moreover, Henrietta had undesirable women friends of whom her mother was most outspoken. "I am sure their selldom passes a day that I don't do something or other upon your account," she told her mother, "and that Lady that you desired mee in particular to avoid I can bee positive I have severall times don it to a rudeness because you did desier it ... and tho my dear Mama reproaches mee so much about the company I keep I really know but off one that you your self can dislike and he is one that the people you think best off are very often with...." Then there is Lady Fitzhardinge, "as I said in my other I never do see her hardly neither her nor at London nor don't think off it...." Moreover she had been reproved for being fond of "country dances", one of which, it seems, "Lady F" had given. "... and for saying I don't love Country dances when I really do," wrote Henrietta with obviously rising indignation, "I could not think off denyeing such an inclination as that, but I bileeve it is a thing won't happen again with her" ["Lady F."] "or if it does I hope I shall find some way to avoid it which indeed I would have don this time but Mr. Godolphin thought it much better to go when he could think of no civil excuse...." Then in conclusion Henrietta deals her mother a shrewd blow. ". . . any thing that I can do as long as I live I shall never think too much," she writes, "if my Dear Mama were but satisfied which I cant but think she would easily be if she did but remember she was once off my age herself."[20]

But, Sarah, it seems, was far from satisfied with Henrietta's explanations. "Tho I must own in my one mind I thought their was a great deale off difference between having an intimacy with that Lady and once in a summer upon such an occasion as this to dance country dances att her house, yet however, affter my Dear Mama's letter till Mr. Godolphin came I had no more thoughts off going than to have but intended to send word I was not very well for nothing else could be said," but the mild-tempered Francis did not approve, thinking the excuse altogether too flimsy. Indeed, he seems to some extent to have championed his wife's cause against her formidable mother. "Mr. Godolphin intended to come to you yesterday and see you alone to say what he liked I should do in all this for I told him every think just as you told mee, and he would have mee go into the drawing room as I used to do twice a week and if it happens that I have a mind to it to a play once a week and both of these in such company as my Dear Mama shall certainly aprove off, and he hopes you won't take it ille he gives his opinion."[21]

It would be indeed interesting to know how Sarah did in fact take her son-in-law's intervention. Unfortunately, we cannot tell; but she has left for posterity a very clear record of her views on her eldest daughter's deportment whilst under the Godolphin roof. "Where she soon fell into very ill company, My Lady Oxford, and Her daughter, Mrs. Ramsey, & Mrs. Hamond, afterwards my Lady Sandwich, & at last having a great mind to be thought a wit, Mr. Congreve and several Poets, And in short the worst company that a young Lady can keep, but for many years this produc'd nothing worse to me than a cold and careless behaviour: I saw it, & dreaded the consequences of such company, but I never spoke to *Her* but once upon that Subject and in the softest manner imaginable, saying only, That I wish'd *she* would not go often to my Lady Fitzharding, for tho' she had a great deal of wit and Humour that was diverting, Her house was a dangerous place for young people, and that all the world knew, that there was not upon Earth so vile a woman as my Lady Oxford; That I knew *She* was good but that some time or other these people would wound Her, and that I was sure She would come to see That what I said was true." Nothing could be plainer than that! "She did not seem angry at this, and we parted very good friends," continued Sarah in this record, "but She went on in Her way and came to me now and then in Her usual manner: And I can be very positive That in Her whole life She never ask'd me once to go abroad with

Her, but once I desir'd Her to carry me with Her to Hyde-park, which She did in Her chariot, but she had so little pleasure in it, That She did not call me till it was almost dark, & I remember we met the company coming out of the ring, However, I never reproach'd Her, loving Her, & seeing her of a careless temper, and we sung all the way."[22]

And so the dispute waxed more bitter, and soon we find Lord Godolphin taking a hand. Sarah wrote a reproof to her daughter and sent it to Sidney to read. ". . . I delivered your Letter to Lady Harryett last night at the Thea table wch she went aside to a candle to read, so I could not observe what impression it made while she was reading it," he replied. "Yett tho she came back to us, & talked a little in answer to my questions, yett I could plainly see a good deal of uneasyness and concern in her Countenance ; . . ."[23] Marlborough too was drawn into the fray. "Upon your saying some thing to mee in one of your letters, of the Company 53 (Henrietta) keeps," he wrote to his wife, "I write to her of my self, not taking any notice of what you had urged, that she Cou'd never find any lasting happyness in this world, but from the kindness of 27 (Francis) . . . I shou'd be glad to know if it has had any effect, for I love her, and think her very good, soe that I shou'd hope if she Comits indiscresions, it is for want of thinking."[24] By this time, Henrietta's attitude to her mother was hostile, yet after this letter from her father she wrote a cold, unfeeling apology. "I was very sorry Madam to see you so much displeased with me the other day, for I think I have allways been very Dutyfull and always shall be so. And am your most Dutyfull H. Godolphin" : to which painful missive is added these words in Sarah's crabbed and almost illegible hand, "lady Godolphin's leter upon her father having talked a great deal to her to shew her how much she was in the wrong to me, & with great goodness shew'd her how uneasy it was to him to have her behave so ill to mee."[25]

Under such unpromising conditions budded the remarkable friendship of William Congreve and Henrietta Godolphin. It was to flower in the years ahead, and to wither only with the death of the great dramatist more than twenty years later.

"I do put an entire confidence in you, not doubting you will do all you can to keep me out of the power of the merciless men of both parties."[26] Thus the Queen to Godolphin in July 1705, when she saw how her Ministers were drifting towards the Whig fold. And two months later we find the Secretary of State writing to Godolphin in very similar terms. "I take it for granted," he opined, "that no party in the House can carry it for themselves without the Queen's servants join with them; That the foundation is, persons or parties are to come in to the Queen and not the Queen to them ;

Dr. James Drake, into his grave. Possibly Harley's lack of enthusiasm in tracking down the culprits was due to humanity and sweet reasonableness; but in the view of Godolphin and Marlborough it was nothing less than that trickery and double-dealing that had become associated with his name.

CHAPTER IV

THE SUNDERLAND CRISIS

WHEN the new Parliament met at the end of October 1705, the Queen addressed members in a speech, the first draft of which had been drawn up by Godolphin in his own hand;[1] this was definitely Whiggish in flavour, playing on the now familiar note of "war abroad and peace at home." In it Anne advocated a Union with Scotland, deplored the accusation of those who said that her beloved Church was in danger, and declared that the continued mastery over the Spanish monarchy by the King of France would utterly destroy the balance of power in Europe.

The Church in danger! In December, Rochester raised that cry. His niece, of course, was furious; and, listening "incognito", as it was termed, under the Lords' gallery, she was further affronted to hear her old beau, Buckingham, discuss the possibility of her shortly being physically incapacitated from reigning. The broad humours of the debate are vividly portrayed for us by a Tory eye-witness. The dispute was brought on, as Dartmouth tells us, by the passion of Rochester. "I happened to sit by Lord Godolphin, when Lord Rochester accepted Lord Halifax's challenge," he states, "and I said to him (not thinking it would go further) that I believed a scene between Hothead and Testimony would be very diverting. He was pleased with the conceit, and told it to all about him, knowing nothing damps a debate more than turning it to ridicule; and it had such an effect, that every body was ready to laugh, when either of them spoke." Whereupon, Lord Wharton, whose custom, it seems, was rather to insult than to banter, asked from what their Lordships derived their real apprehensions. Was it from the Queen? The Duke of Leeds, horrified at so provoking a query, particularly from a man of Wharton's ignoble character, replied indignantly, "No, but if deer-stealers were got into his park, he should think his deer in danger, though he had no suspicion of his keeper." Who then, asked Wharton, were "the rogues who had got into the park of the church?" To which the duke replied that, if there were any who behaved in a particularly disgusting manner against a Communion Table or in a yet more filthy manner in a pulpit, he would not regard the Church safe in such hands. "Upon which," commented Dartmouth, "Lord

Wharton was very silent for the rest of that day, and desired no further explanations."[2] No wonder! Let us hope that Queen Anne was not present in her usual place under the Lords' gallery that day! Though the motion was lost by an overwhelming majority, the Queen was much distressed at what she could only regard as her betrayal by the Tories; never in all her reign was she nearer to the Whigs. "I believe dear Mrs. Freeman and I shall not disagree as we have formerly done," she wrote angrily to Sarah, "for I am sensible of the services those people have done me that you have a good opinion of, and will countenance them, and am thoroughly convinced of the malice and insolence of them that you have always been speaking against."[3]

The Tories, whose prospects at the opening of the reign had seemed so bright, now felt thwarted. This alone can explain the desperation of their moves: for, led by the malevolent Rochester, they chose this moment to revive the proposal to bring the Electress Sophia to England. The plan was shrewd. Rochester, Nottingham and the Tory chiefs, seeing themselves completely out of favour with the reigning sovereign, thus sought to ingratiate themselves with her successor, who, it was generally thought, would very soon be in Anne's place. Alas for human calculations! The poor helpless invalid was destined to live for almost a decade yet, and she was not likely to forgive those who had so plainly demonstrated their expectation of her early demise.

But to Marlborough, Godolphin and the Whigs, the Opposition move was an artful trap, for if they accepted the proposal, they alienated the Queen, and if they refused to countenance it, would they not lay themselves open to the accusation that they were disloyal to the Protestant Succession? From this insidious dilemma the Ministers escaped only by prompt and energetic action. They declined to vote for an invitation to Sophia to visit England in the Queen's lifetime, but they proposed instead a Bill under which on the death of the Queen, Lords Justices were to form a regency until the arrival of her successor. The Queen welcomed the Regency Bill as infinitely preferable to an invitation to those hated Germans to come to England before her death: it was therefore easily carried. The Ministers and the Whigs had triumphed: the Tories "lay like beetles on their backs."[4]

In view of the Whig victory it was hardly surprising that the Lords of the Junto should determine that one of their number must be admitted to the Cabinet. They hardly minded, it seemed, which of them should be selected, but after some cogitation it was decided to press the claims of their youngest member, Sunderland, who as Marlborough's son-in-law might be thought to be especially acceptable. Unfortunately, however, his aggressive manner and radical views made him most distasteful to Queen

Anne. Nevertheless Sarah pressed his claims characteristically with much more ardour than tact. John, on the other hand, anxious not to antagonize the Sovereign, strove to moderate his wife's zeal.[5] Godolphin, too, pressed Sunderland's claims, not of course because he wanted him in his government; but because he realized that this was the price that must be paid for Whig support. But all was in vain; Anne would not be persuaded: and she wrote a long letter to the Treasurer, for at last the time had come, she told him, to speak her mind freely to her friends.

"I have been considering the business wee have so often spoke about, ever since I saw you," she wrote "& cannot but continue of the same mind, that tis a great hardship to perswade any body to part with a place they are in possession off [sic] in hopes of another [that] is not yet vacant." She need not have been so tender for Sir Charles Hedges, whose place as Secretary of State for the Southern Department was wanted for Sunderland; but here Anne was indulging in mere affectation and excuse! "Besides I must own freely to you that I am of the opinion, making a party man secretary of state when there are so many of their freinds in employment of all kinds allready is throwing my self into the hands of a party, which is a thing I have been desirous to avoid." These words have a more authentic ring—and a very familiar sound! "Maybe some may think I would bee willing to bee in the hands of the Torrys [sic], but whatever people may say of me, I doe assure you I am no(t) inclined no(r) (n)ever will bee to employ any of those violent persons that have behaved themselves so ill towards me." Here was the reward of Rochester, Nottingham, Buckingham and the rest for the way they had treated Anne! "All I desire is my liberty in incouraging & employing all those who concur faithfully to my service whether they are called whigs or torys, not to bee tyed to one, nor the other; for if I should bee soe unfortunate as to fall into the hands of ether [sic], I shall not imagine myself tho I have the name of Queen (to be) in reallity but their slave, which as it will bee my personall ruin so it will bee the destroying of all government; for instead of putting an end to faction, it will lay a lasting foundation for it." And now for Sunderland. "You press the bringing Lord Sun: in to Businesse this winter, & you think if this is not complyd with, they will not bee hearty in pursuing any service [sic] in the Parliament. But is it not very hard that men of sense & honour will not promise* the good of their country because every thing in the world is not don that they desire, when they may be asured Lord Sunderland shall com into employment as soon as it is possible." A shrewd thrust! "Why for god sake must I, who have no interest, no care, no thought but for the good of my country bee made soe miserable as to bee brought into the power of one sett

* So in original, but perhaps *promote* is intended.

of men, and why may I not bee trusted sence I mean nothing but what is equaly for the good of all my subjects? There is another apprehension I have of Lord Sun: being secretary, which I think is a naturall one, which proceeds from what I have heard of his temper. I am afraid hee & I should not agree long together; finding by experience my humour and those that are of a warmer will often have misunderstandings between one another. I could say a great deal more on this subject but fear I have been too tedious allready, therefore I shall conclude, beging you to consider how to bring me out of my difficultys, & never leave my service for Jesus Christ sake, for besides the reasons I gave you in another leter, that is a blow I could not bear."⁶ A *cri de cœur* indeed! Never leave my service for Jesus Christ's sake! Only four years were to pass before she was to dismiss Sidney without a farewell audience and to order him to break his staff. Such is life!

But for the present all was sunshine between them. Judge then of Anne's consternation on receiving the next day an uncompromising reply from her faithful servant. "It gives me all the grief and despair imaginable to find that your majesty shows inclination to have me continue in your service," he wrote, "and yet will make it impossible for me to do so. I shall not therefore trouble your majesty with fruitless repetitions of reasons and arguments. I cannot struggle against the difficulties of your majesty's business, and yourself at the same time; but I can keep my word to your majesty. I have no house in the world to go to but my house at Newmarket, which I must own is not at this time like to be a place of retirement; but I have no other. I have worn out my health, and almost my life in the service of the Crown. I have served your majesty faithfully to the best of my understanding, without any advantage to myself, except the honour of doing so, or without expecting any other favour than to end the small remainder of my days in liberty and quiet."⁷

This was the letter of a tired man, but Anne, though alarmed, was not yet prepared to yield. She accordingly suggested a compromise. She would nominate Sunderland to the Privy Council, allow him a pension, and confer on him an office bearing an emolument higher than that of Secretary of State, but which would not necessitate his being granted frequent audiences. Unfortunately, this was totally unacceptable to Sunderland. After dilating on the impossibility of contemplating such a proposal, to which only a fool or a knave would hearken, he told his mother-in-law that "Lord Somers, Lord Halifax, and I, have talked very fully over all this matter, and we are come to our last resolution in it, that this and what other things have been promised must be done, or we and the lord treasurer must have nothing more to do together about business; and that we must let our friends know just how the matter stands between us and the lord treasurer, whatever is the consequence of it."[8] The meaning of this was plain, and Marlborough was furious. He wrote indignantly to his wife. He wrote sympathetically to his friend. On no account must he retire, ". . . for without fflattery, as England is devid'd there is nobody cou'd execut your place with success."[9] ". . . without flattery, I am positively of the opinion, that should you quit the service of the Queen, you would not only disturb the affairs of England, but also the liberties of Europe," he wrote a week later, "so that I conjure you not to have a thought of quitting till we have obtained a good peace; and then I hope the queen's interest may be so well settled that she may allow of our living quietly. But as the affairs of Europe, and those of the queen in particular, are at this time, I think both you and I are in conscience and honour bound to undergo all the dangers and troubles that is possible, to bring this war to a happy end, which I think must be after the next campaign, if we can agree to carry it on with vigour. . . . I shall be very uneasy till I hear from you that every thing is easy between Mrs. Morley and yourself; for without that I shall have no heart to act in any thing, being sure that all things must go to destruction."[10] This from the greatest man in Europe was high praise indeed!

But high praise or not, poor Sidney was sickening of the whole troublesome business. "The uneasiness betwixt the queen and myself continues as it was," he wrote to his friend that same September, "nor do I see how it can ever be mended, unless you were here to do it, either by your credit with the queen, or by your authority and influence with Lord Sunderland and Lord Somers, and their friends. Not that I think them so much to blame, because they do really not see the difficulties as they are, and one cannot go about to show them those difficulties without too much exposing the queen. Now though I really think you might be able to ease all this, yet negotiation not being my talent, I doubt it may be past cure before you come, and there is no reason to hope for the least assistance from Mrs. Freeman in this matter."[11] And to the Duchess: "You are much better natured in effect than you sometime appear to be, and then you chide me for being touched with the condition in which I saw 83 (the Queen). You would have been so too, if you had seen the same sight I did; but what troubles me most in all this affair is that one can't yet find any way of making Mrs. Morley sensible of 83's (her) mistakes, for I am very sure she thinks 83 (herself) entirely in the right."[12] Of course Mrs. Freeman was far to ardent a Whig to be helpful ! "As for England," wrote Godolphin to Marlborough a few days later, ". . . the plain unwillingness in the queen to do anything for those who have shown themselves most forward and jealous in promoting all the present advantages, is a discouragement not to be overcome by me alone."[13] This shows clearly where Godolphin's sympathies lay. Yet Sunderland and the

Whigs strove to lay the blame upon him, when all men knew that the obstinacy of the Queen was solely responsible for the impasse!

Marlborough, alarmed at Godolphin's despondency, determined to make one more appeal to the Queen. He wrote with the utmost freedom.[14] He wrote in even blunter terms to his wife "that the jealousy of some of your friends have that I and the lord treasurer do not act sincerely, makes me so weary, that were it not for my gratitude to the queen, and concern for him, I would now retire, and never serve more . . . and this principle shall govern me for the remainder of my life, I must not think of being popular, but I shall have the satisfaction of going to my grave with the opinion of having acted as became an honest man; and if I have your 'steem and love, I shall think myself entirely happy . . . and since the resolution is taken to vex and ruin the lord treasurer, because the queen has not complied with what was desired for Lord Sunderland, I shall from henceforth despise all mankind, and I think there is no such thing as virtue; for I know with what zeal the lord treasurer has pressed the queen in the matter. I do pity him, and shall love him as long as I live, and never will be friend to any that can be his enemy."[15] "I have writ my mind with freedom to the queen," he assured Godolphin at the same time, "so that having done my duty, let what will happen, I shall be more easy in my mind. Allow me to give you this assurance, that as I know you to be a sincere honest man, may God bless me as I shall be careful *that whatever man is your enemy shall never be my friend*, as soon as You receive this I conjure you to let me have your thoughts freely, for till then I shall be very uneasy."[16]

Meanwhile the Queen determined to make yet another appeal to the Lord Treasurer. This lengthy letter, dated September 21st, contains all the arguments and suggestions that she had set out in her letter of August 30. Not one new proposition could she muster to advance her case. It ended with the words, ". . . I know very well that you doe not serve his (i.e. Sunderland's) advantage or ambition but with intire duty & affection which makes me that I can not bear the thought of parting with you & I hope after what the Duke of Marl: has said to you, you will not think of it again, for to use his words you can not answer it neither to God nor man nor in conscience nor honour doe it. Let his words plead for her who will bee lost & undone if you pursue this cruell intention & begs that you would nether think of it, nor mention it any more to one that is soe affectionately and sincerely your humble servant."[17]

Godolphin received this letter just as he was leaving Windsor for Woodstock, whence four days later he replied to the Queen. "Your Majesty seems to continue desirous I should stay in your service, and not retain a thought of quitting it. I never had such a thought, nor ever can have, for my own sake or ease, if I saw a possibility of supporting your service, to which, as I have often said to your majesty, I must be a weight and not a help, unless you would please to let me have the assistance of those who are able and willing to serve me.

"Your majesty is pleased in your letter to make use of some expressions in the Duke of Marlborough's letter to me, which I had the honour to read to you, that I could not answer it to God or man, that I was obliged both in honour and conscience not to quit your service. But you are not pleased to take any notice of those other expression, which he uses in the same letter, as that there is no doubt but the queen will do any thing you can desire to make your service easy, and the like. But I desire nothing to make my service easy; I propose nothing but what is necessary for carrying on your majesty's business, especially in this next winter, which is like to be the most critical of your whole reign, and when many things of very great import-ance will come to bear all at once. I doubt whether all we can do will be able to keep off the peace this winter. The peace will necessarily bring on the consideration of what fleet, and what army must be continued for your majesty's safety, and the safety of the government; besides all this, when the kingdom has been exhausted by a long war, your majesty's enemies, and mine particularly, which are not a few, will be grumbling at the greatness of your revenue. All these must be defended and supported. These are not slight things.

"These things make me much concerned to trouble your Majesty with repeating so often, that the future quiet and happiness of your whole life depends upon what is done in this winter, and you have an opportunity of making your government strong, which you will never have again.

"Your Majesty will have me think you are desirous of my advice, and of the continuance of my service, and yet you are not pleased to have any regard to it, in a time, and upon an occasion of the greatest consequence that can ever happen to you. By what your majesty says of some particulars in my letter, I find I have not expressed myself so as that your majesty seems to have rightly apprehended my meaning in them. I must therefore, endeavour to explain myself better as soon as I can: but since to go about it now would make this letter too tedious I hope you will allow me to do it in words, when I have the honour to wait upon you."[18]

The Queen's answer was short and curt. "Though I hope to see you on Wednesday," she wrote, "I cannot help writing a few words, to thank you for your letter, and I beg you would believe I am as sensible as any body can be, that the particular things you mention are of the greatest consequence imaginable, and that this is a very critical time; upon which subject I think there is a good deal could be said, but I shall defer telling you my poor opinion till we meet, and only now assure that I am with all sincerity, yours."[19]

Whilst Godolphin, Marlborough and Queen Anne were thus exchanging letters, the Duchess of Marlborough must needs intervene with an intemperate correspondence as ill-judged as it was untimely. A part of one letter only need be quoted here, for it involved the Lord Treasurer. After expressing the usual sentiments on Lord Sunderland and his claims, Sarah thus recklessly addressed the Queen. "But 'tis certain that your government can't be carried on with a part of the Tories, and the Whigs disobliged, who when that happens will join with any people to torment you, and those that are your true servants." What a picture to draw of the party of which she was a member! But more follows. "I am sure it is my interest, as well as inclination, to have you succeed by any sort of men in what is just, and that will prevent what has been done from being thrown away. Your security and the nation's is my chief wish, and I beg of God Almighty, as sincerely as I shall do for His pardon at my last hour, that Mr. and Mrs. Morley may see their errors as to this *notion* before it is too late; but considering how little impression any thing makes that comes from your faithful Freeman, I have troubled you too much, and I beg your pardon for it."[20]

That was bad enough. But matters were made worse by Anne reading the word *notion* as *nation*, a mistake that rendered the censure even more impertinent. The Queen was highly indignant. She declined to reply to the Duchess, and complained bitterly to Godolphin. Whereupon Sarah followed up her offending letter with a second, little calculated, one would think, to heal the breach, and commissioned the faithful Sidney to deliver it to the Queen.[21] How he performed this distasteful task we may learn in his own words. "As she was going to put it in her pocket, I told her that you have made me promise to beg of her to read it before I went out of the room. She did so, and then said she believed she had mistaken some words at the latter end of the former letter, which she seemed to think had a different sense from that which I had given her from you; but because you desired I might see it, she would look for it, and give it to me, which she did, and desired me to return it to her to-day. I come now from giving it back into her hands, and I think I have convinced her that her complaint was grounded upon her having misapprehended the sense of your letter, by not reading it right, that is to say, by reading the word *notion* for *nation*. To explain this the more clearly to you, I send you a copy of the conclusion of your first letter to her, taken as far back as I thought was enough to show the plain sense and meaning of your letter. At the same time I must own that in your original letter the word *notion* was not so distinctly written but that one might naturally read it *nation*, if the sense of the two or three lines together before did not fully explain your meaning."[22]

The breach was partly healed, but it was more than a week before Mrs. Morley replied to Mrs. Freeman. Then, excusing the delay, she continued, "I have obeyed your commands in showing your letter to my lord Treasurer, and find my complaint was not without some ground, a mistake any body might make upon the first reading: for you had made an *a* instead of an *o* which quite altered the word. I am very sensible all you say proceeds from the concern you have for my service, and it is impossible to be more mortified than I am, to see my lord treasurer in such uneasiness; and his leaving my service is a thought I cannot bear, and I hope in God he will put all such out of his own mind. Now that you are come hither again, I hope you will not go to Woodstock without giving me one look, for whatever hard thoughts you may have of me, I am sure I do not deserve them, and I will not be uneasy if you come to me; for though you are never so unkind, I will ever preserve a most sincere and tender passion for my dear Mrs. Freeman."[23] So it was "my dear Mrs. Freeman" once again; nevertheless "a friendship that is endangered by the mis-reading of a vowel may be held to have passed its prime."[24]

And so it was to prove. Yet Marlborough continued to do his utmost to conquer the Queen's obstinacy. He warned her that, if the Lord Treasurer should resign, she would be thrust into the hands of a party from which it would be difficult to release herself. "But madam, the truth is that the heads of one party have declared against you and your government, as far as it is possible, without going into open rebellion. Now, should your majesty disoblige the others, how is it possible, to obtain near five millions for carrying on the war with vigour, without which all is undone." That was strong meat indeed! "Your majesty has had so much knowledge and experience yourself of the capacity and integrity of the lord treasurer," the letter continues, "that you cannot but know you may safely rely on his advice, and if there be any opinion different from his, your majesty will allow me to say, they neither know so much of these matters, nor can they judge so well of them."[25]

But all Marlborough's efforts were unavailing. Anne was determined to stand out against the admission of Sunderland; and she highly resented the intervention of his mother-in-law. Mr. Montgomery sought to heal the breach, but in vain. "Mrs. Morley sent for me this morning," he wrote to Sarah, "and complained much of Mrs. Freeman's letter. . . . I went on to tell her that I knew very well all Mrs. Freeman's complaints proceeded from having lost Mrs. Morley's kindness unjustly, and her telling truths which other people would not; to which she said, as she had done forty times, how could she show her any more kindness than she did, when she would never come near her. I said, she had tried that several times, and complained it was always the same things upon that she said Mrs. Freeman would grow warm sometimes, and then she herself could not help being warmer than she ought to be, but that she was always ready to be easy with Mrs. Freeman. I said, I hoped then she would be so, for that I would die, with all my soul, to have them two as they used to be. Then she said she would send me a letter for you. . . . But when all this is done, you may see by her letter to Lord Marlborough, which he sent me, that she still leans to expedients . . ." to avoid Sunderland's appointment, ". . . though I have told her, that to satisfy her, I had tried how far that would go, and the thing was not capable of any expedient, and that I was convinced by what had been said to me by Lord Somers and Lord Halifax, that it was infinitely more for her advantage not to think of any such thing as an expedient. But she told me the other day, she believed I thought it strange that she said nothing upon my showing her Lord Marlborough's letter; but it was, that though she was very uneasy to see what he writ, she could not, for her life, be convinced but her expedient was better; and when he comes over she will certainly talk so to him; but if he holds firm to what he has written and said, as I do not doubt he will, I dare say she will do the thing."[26]

But though Sarah Marlborough's intervention in these disputes was often neither fortunate nor tactful, she sometimes had a clearer vision of political events than either her husband or her friend: and she it was who first realized that Anne's fortitude would not have been so protracted had she not received support and encouragement from some other quarter; for, as it suddenly dawned on Sarah, Anne was not the sort of woman who would for long assume and maintain unaided a strong, even a defiant role. From what quarter then could this unexpected encouragement be coming? From her husband? Assuredly not. Who then could it be but from Robert Harley, the only Tory now left in the inner circle of ministers. But when Sarah hastened to impart this news to John and Sidney, they were not much impressed; yet Godolphin had certainly had his suspicions of Harley back in the summer of the previous year.

But whatever the effect of Sarah's pronouncement, Harley was still entertaining hopes of winning over Godolphin and Marlborough to his views. In the middle of October he wrote a long letter from Brampton to the Lord Treasurer on party heats. His method of expressing himself is tedious in the extreme, but it is clear enough that he was tying to insinuate himself into Godolphin's and Marlborough's good graces. "As to home affairs," wrote Harley, "what I wrote to your Lordship was in the sincerity of my heart . . . but far be it from me to espouse any opinion of my own, or to differ from your Lordship's judgment; I shall always be ready, when required, and never but then, to give my poor thoughts and such reasons as I have, and when I have done that I know myself too well to be fond of any actions of my own. I have no other views but the Queen's service with that attachment to your Lordship and my Lord Marlborough which I shall always preserve." A little too much humility here! He then deplores "the attempting to bind everybody to one measure . . ." which always results in disaster. "I have often seen the foundation laid of blowing up each of the factions by that very method and the reason is plain; for those gentlemen who think themselves to be independent, and would be thought to be so, but yet would support the Queen and serve her ministers, expect their compliance therein should be accepted, and that they should be left to themselves in personal friendships and matters which they will always think remote from the government's observation. . . . This I am certain many of the most staunch Whigs (not Whimsical) have, and do frequently lament the fury of their leaders, and have rejoiced when their presumption was humbled; . . ." Thus he rambles on, until at last: "I have with grief observed," he writes, "that the leaders (or zealots rather) of both parties are frequent, even now, in their reflections on the Queen's ministers, I mean your Lordship and my Lord M. I cannot but apprehend danger from both sides in the extreme, and therefore I am humbly of opinion to increase the number of those who would devote themselves to the Queen's and your service would be best; and I the rather mention this because so many who have been lately obliged to pay their acknowledgement to and real dependence on other people. As to myself, I have made all the application imaginable to those who would be thought the chiefs of that faction, and there is nothing I will not do for the Queen's service and the support of her ministers. . . ."[27]

A month later he wrote again: "I do assure your Lordship I have no thoughts but for the Queen's service and for your Lordship's, neither would I ever mention anything disagreeable to your Lordship if I was not fully persuaded that the public interest were concerned in it: I have no obligation to any party, I have no inclination to any, one more than another, I have no animosity to any: but I think I should not do the Duty of a faithfull servant to your Lordship if I did not tell you what your Lordship may hear if you please from People of undoubted credity from Whiggs themselves, that al that has been done has not obliged the Party, whether it has their pretended Leaders they will shew hereafter; I have no concerne but only that what has been done, I wish the best of the Whiggs had been the better for. As for the violences of the other side, I hope I have shew'd myself as zealous against them as any one whatever; I think the distinction of the tackers was what they justly deserv'd; but my Lord, this is now carrying further not only the 134* are to be persecuted but al the rest; not only those who opposed them, but those with out whose assistance these gentlemen could not have been on equality, much less a majority, They have endeavoured their ruin, nay! they have proceeded so far as to proscribe, I use the words of a zealous Whig and no *whimsical*, many of their party, in short the Lay & Ecclesiastical policy is by an representation to make those they do not like disperate, they are doing their best to turne the Pyramide on its point: but I hope your Lordship will releve us from the violence of either party; & I cannot forbear saying I know no difference between a mad whig and a mad Tory: And as for their inveteracy of either Party; *Iliacos intra muros peccatur etextra.* There is no need of going back two years nor scarce four months, to hear the most inveterate malicious things said by their Leaders against the Queen my Lord Duke & your Lordship, that tongue could utter, besides what the last Parliam^t in its last Session could produce from their underlings; and this is so notorious that it is very common to match one malicious story from a Tory with another from a Whig; . . . ."[28]

What impression, one wonders, had all this cant on the shrewd Lord Treasurer? May he not have exclaimed with Caesar:

> "Yond' Cassius has a lean and hungry look;
> He thinks too much: such men are dangerous."

Be that as it may, certain is it that the return of Marlborough in mid-November had an immediate effect on these negotiations. At his first audience with the Queen, Anne reverted to the compromise proposal with regard to Sunderland, that she had made to Godolphin. But Marlborough would have none of it, and he told Anne in unequivocal terms, that there was no alternative to what the Lord Treasurer proposed. On December 3rd, the very day of the meeting of Parliament, Queen Anne surrendered: Sunderland replaced Hedges as Secretary of State for the Southern Department. Robert Harley retained the Northern Secretaryship, but with diminished authority. Such was his reward for the ignoble cabals to which he had lent his name.

To the victor of Ramillies every honour was paid. He received the thanks of both Houses of Parliament. The handsome sum of £5,000 a year was with universal acclamation settled upon him and his posterity for ever; and the peerage, the Manor of Woodstock and the rising palace of Blenheim were made heritable by his daughters and their male heirs in succession. The Treasurer too was suitably honoured. Two years ago had he been

* The number of persons who voted for the tack.

made a Knight of the Garter. Now he was raised to the rank of an Earl, taking the titles of Viscount Rialton and Earl of Godolphin. But though he was honoured, his position was far from secure. The Queen's heart was estranged. It was not long before Harley saw his opportunity. He was not slow to seize it.

CHAPTER V

THE UNION WITH SCOTLAND

In the days of Cromwell, England and Scotland had been united; and the union had "brought free trade, staple peace and equal justice, but at the price of religious laxity and heavy taxation";[1] at the Restoration the union was ended because it had rested on force and force alone. In the days of Queen Anne the time seemed ripe for a new union to be cemented by treaty instead of coercion. No mutual regard, no friendly feeling between English and Scots furthered these sentiments; indeed, the very hostility of the two nations forced the wiser statesmen both north and south of the border to see the necessity for a union of the two Parliaments as the only alternative to open hostilities.

At the accession of Queen Anne the Episcopalians and Roman Catholics, fortified with the knowledge that the new Sovereign was under the influence of Marlborough and Godolphin, who were believed to have kept up some sort of contact with the agents of the exiled Court, took heart. But they were doomed to disappointment, for England was at war with France; and, as Godolphin the realist clearly recognized, affairs were critical. He therefore agreed with the perspicacious Seafield, the Scottish Chancellor, that they should be well content in this first session to have the Queen's authority confirmed and not aim at anything further "which may occasion heats & disputes, but to gett it ended as soon and as smoothy [sic] as you can."[2] On no account must Parliament rise "abruptly & without effect," he told Seafield. Then he proceeded to utter a profound truth, not yet fully understood. "But," he added, "the Queen is Queen of Scotland upon the foot of the Revolution, & if that Cannot be maintained for her, I doubt nothing will bee maintained by her here." He emphasized our present critical situation in respect to other nations, so that ". . . all Europe must in some measure bee affected by the good or ill ending of the parliament of Scotland."[3] That was plain speaking. The blandishments of the Jacobites were all very well in time of peace. But amidst the perils of war Anne must rely upon the Whigs and Presbyterians of Scotland, who alone could be trusted to aid her in the event of open rebellion. The new Queen saw the wisdom of this view: hence her first speech from the Throne expressed a desire for a closer union with Scotland.[4]

While Godolphin was corresponding with Seafield, who was destined to be his first councillor in Scottish affairs, the Opposition peers were hastening southwards to pay homage to the new Sovereign and to beg her to dismiss her Scottish ministers and to dissolve Parliament, which in Scotland was still the Convention returned at the Revolution of 1688. At the head of the party came no less a personage than the Duke of Hamilton, violent, headstrong, overbearing, best known to English readers, perhaps, as the noble-hearted gentleman whose tragic end thwarted the ambition of Beatrix Esmond. But another councillor had been before him. The suave, ingratiating Duke of Queensberry was strongly opposed to the holding of a new election in Scotland. Though in England the Tories had been elected by a two to one majority, there was no certainty, he argued, that a similar result would follow an election in Scotland. After all, as Queensberry urged, the Convention in Edinburgh had voted sufficient supplies for the maintenance of the forces in Scotland for another twelve months; in a year's time, might not the nation be calmer, might not a more favourable result be anticipated? All this being reported to the Treasurer by Harley, too coy himself to advise, "having neither wit nor skill to reason upon these neads my self,"[5] Godolphin and the Queen were at first disposed to follow the advice of Queensberry. But the Tory Nottingham and others soon succeeded in impressing upon them the wisdom of dissolving the Convention, for if a Tory majority were returned the Government would be vastly strengthened. So gradually the Lord Treasurer was won round to this view. And as for the Queen, the more she saw of Queensberry, the more she disliked him.*

But there was one difficulty. In Scotland there was no Triennial Act, and the existing Convention Parliament, which many held to be of doubtful legality, had not met (in accordance with an Act of 1696) within twenty days of the Sovereign's demise.† It met in fact on June 9th, 1702, ninety days after King William's death. Immediately, Hamilton rose, read a solemn

---

* ". . . his last tricking behaviour, haveing made him more odious to me than ever; . . ." Queen Anne to Godolphin, "Windsor, June ye 6th." ". . . as to the Duke of Queensberry . . . it grates my soul to take a man into my service yt has not only betrayed me, but tricked me several times, one yt has bin obnoxious to his own country men these many yeares and one yt I can never be convinced can be of use. . . ." Queen Anne to Godolphin, "Windsor, June ye 14th." Brit. Mus. Add. MSS. 28,070, ff. 8, 10.

† The Act provided that the Parliament should meet within twenty days of the demise of the Crown, should sit for no more than six months and should only transact such business as might be necessary to secure the succession.

protest against the meeting as illegal, and forthwith at the head of some eighty peers and gentlemen, stalked out of the building.

Those who remained, soon designated "The Rump", "all one man's bairns", as Lockhart termed them,[6] passed Acts declaring the assembly to be a lawful Parliament and recognizing the Queen's authority. They passed several others of very little moment, and one of the highest consequence enabling Anne to appoint Commissioners to treat for a union with England on terms to be approved by the Parliaments of the two kingdoms. On November 10th, 1702, the Commissioners, twenty-three for England and twenty-one for Scotland, met at the Cockpit in Whitehall; they sat repeatedly through the next three months. On two points, concord was soon obtained; that there should be a common legislature, and that the succession should descend in accordance with the Act of Settlement upon the Electress Sophia of Hanover and her heirs. But when questions of trade and taxation came to be considered, difficulties at once arose, so that the Queen soon saw the futility of protracting the meetings further. Accordingly on February 3rd she adjourned them till October—that is to say, indefinitely. Three more years of tension and discord were to pass before union was to be effected on very much the same terms as were contemplated in the negotiations of 1702.

The ensuing General Election in Scotland seemed to sound the death-knell of Union policy, for widespread indignation had been roused against Ministers who were held to have sacrificed Scottish interests. Government supporters found themselves in a minority and the so-called Country Party, the strongest section of the Opposition, returned in aggressive mood to champion the wrongs of their oppressed countrymen. Never did the Union of the two kingdoms seem further off; yet it was this anti-English Parliament that was to pass the Union a few years later.

Following the General Election of the spring of 1703, Queen Anne made changes in her Scottish Ministry, increasing the Tory element. Thus, Marchmont, the Whig Chancellor, was removed to make way for Godolphin's friend Seafield. Atholl also took office as Privy Seal. These two and Queensberry, the Commissioner, sought support in the newly elected Parliament; and, if we can believe Lockhart of Carnwath, paid obsequious court to Godolphin and Marlborough. ". . . all parties," he tells us, "strove who should outdo one another in paying their respect and shewing their submission to the good will and pleasure of the Duke of Marlborough and Lord Godolphin: the Queen, indeed, for fashion sake, was sometimes addressed to; but such application was made to these two lords, that it was obvious to all the world how much the Scots affairs depend on them." Lockhart himself went out of curiosity to one of their levies and watched the

Scottish leaders "hang on near an hour, and, when admitted, treated with no more civility than one gentleman pays another's valet-de-chambre; . . ."[7] This disgusted the ardent Jacobite. But his account we can only regard as a distorted picture of the General and the Treasurer, who, whatever their failings, would never have acted in so ungracious a manner.

The uneasy truce between Anne's Ministers and the Jacobite element was, however, short-lived. The Opposition was far too strong and far too fractious. They promptly passed a measure depriving Anne's successors of the power of declaring war without the consent of the Estates, and the famous Act of Security, providing that the Scots Parliament should meet upon Queen Anne's death to choose her successor, who must be a Protestant of the royal line but not the same person selected as the English successor, unless England had previously given satisfaction to Scotland on many points.

Nothing could be more distasteful to Godolphin than these measures, for how could there be security without the peaceful succession of the House of Hanover and might not the day soon dawn when Scotland would be at peace with England's enemies?* Many of the Queen's Ministers, he told Atholl, the new Privy Seal, were extremely dissatisfied, for neither Scotland nor England could be secure unless they be under the same succession, and in that, he added, "both reason and experience seem to agree."[8]

The Act of Security had passed through the Estates and to become law only awaited the Sceptre's touch. Queensberry implored Anne to yield; but Godolphin, who saw clearly the dangers attendant upon a dual succession, bade her stand firm. He put the case clearly to his friend, Seafield. "England is now in warr with France," he wrote. "If Scotland were in peace, & consequently at liberty to trade with France, would not that immediatly necessitate a warr betwixt England and Scotland also? as has been often the case before the two nations were under the same Sovereign; and tho perhaps some turbulent spiritts in Scotland may bee desiring to have it soe again, if they please to consult History, they will not find the advantage of those breaches has often been on the side of Scotland; and if they will give themselves leave to consider how much England is increased in Wealth and power since those times, perhaps the present conjuncture will not appear more favourable for them; but on the contrary rather furnish arguments for enforcing the necessity of a speedy union between the

---

* The spiteful Jacobite Lockhart suggests that Godolphin supported the Hanoverian succession "because his enemies in England asserted he was an enemy to it, and that it might have been done, had he not secretly opposed it." *Lockhart Papers*, I, 94. Johnstone brings a similar charge. Ker of Kersland, *Memoirs*, Part I. There is no evidence whatever to support the charge and everything points to Godolphin being most anxious to secure the peaceful succession of the House of Hanover.

two nations, which is a notion that I am sorry to find has soe little prevalency in the present parliament of Scotland. And I hope your lordship will not bee offended with mee if I take the freedom to bee of opinion they may possibly be sorry for it too, when the opportunity is out of their reach."[9] Thus bitterly did Godolphin come to see the supreme necessity for a union between the two Kingdoms.

Scarcely was the ink dry on Godolphin's letters, however, than events forced his hands: he was compelled to advise Anne to pass the Act of Security; and he expressed his views to Nottingham in unusually forthright terms.[10] Amongst the Jacobite exiles returning at the change of government, there came a ruffianly Highland Chieftain, Simon Fraser by name, afterwards Lord Lovat. He had been outlawed for the rape of the Dowager Lady Lovat, Atholl's sister. Now he came back to his native Scotland, determined at all costs and with whatever villainy might be needed to obtain restitution of his estates. He had already in the previous year, through Lord Annandale, vainly offered his services to the English goverment.[11] Undaunted by this reverse, Fraser had crossed to France, turned Roman Catholic, and insinuated himself into the counsels of both St. Germain and Versailles. Thence he was sent back to Scotland to do their work Amongst his luggage was an unaddressed letter from Mary of Modena, James II's widow. On this potentially compromising document Fraser took it upon himself to inscribe the name of Atholl, whose sister he had outraged and whom he consequently knew to be his foe; and he handed the thus falsified and incriminating missive to Queensberry. Queensberry, none too scrupulous, listened to the false rogue, and Fraser's accusations were laid before the Queen. Atholl, thus attacked, embraced for a while the cause of the hostile Jacobites, and the Queensberry Ministry was rent from stem to stern. By the early months of 1704, Queensberry himself had become so unpopular that Godolphin was forced to advise the Queen to dismiss him from office. On the fall of the Government, Anne turned to the Country Party, which, headed by Tweeddale, brought in a group of nobles who acted together and later became known as the *Squadrone Volante*.

On turning to Tweeddale and his followers, Roxburgh, Rothes, Baillie of Jerviswood and James Johnstone, Godolphin relied on a promise they had lightly made that at the next session of the Edinburgh Parliament they would thrust through the longed-for settlement of the Crown of Scotland on the House of Hanover, provided Queen Anne would agree to certain limitations on the powers of her successors. Lockhart accuses Godolphin of conceding "a few deluding limitations," because they could afterwards be easily repealed when once the Hanoverian dynasty was secure on the Throne.[12] This charge, like his previous accusation that the Lord Treasurer only of necessity supported the Hanoverian Succession, entirely lacks proof, and only serves as an example of the irresponsible malice of Lockhart towards the English leaders. There is no doubt whatever that a genuine bargain was struck by Lord Godolphin with the Scottish leaders of the so-called New Party. It was only unfortunate that those leaders so singularly overrated their powers. Godolphin feared that "calmness and moderation" among them would be wanting,[13] and he even suggested in the Queen's name the formation of a Council to be composed of a small number from each Kingdom to advise the Crown. Something of the sort was successfully practised in King Charles the First's time, he told Seafield, adding "I can only say that, in my opinion, there never was any time, when some such method appears to be more necessary."[14] But all was in vain, and when in the summer of 1704 Parliament met, Tweeddale and his associates were soon in trouble. So were the Treasurer and the Queen, for the Godolphin Government lacked a majority in either the English or the Scottish Parliament. The position was truly desperate;[15] and Godolphin anxiously begged Seafield "to keep the Parlt in temper & moderation, & to bring on the matter of the succession as soon as possible."[16] Later in the month Godolphin was telling Seafield firmly that the Queen would not allow Ministers who refused to do her will to remain at their posts,[17] and in July he was repeating to him the old arguments that if the Scots really wanted trade concessions from England, they must obtain them through Parliament, and Parliament would only grant them on condition of their settling the same succession as England.[18] But he knew that if the Queen refused her consent to the Act of Security, the Edinburgh Parliament would withhold supplies, the Scottish army of some 3,000 strong would disband, and anarchy would inevitably ensue. Seafield suggested the adjournment of the House, which the Lord Treasurer approved; but faced as he was with the contingency of supplies being withheld, he knew he must advise Anne to yield.[19]

At the very moment that Queen Anne was signing the Act of Security, a dust-stained officer was galloping post across Europe. Five days later, he was ushered into her Majesty's presence at Windsor and delivered the most famous of all the messages that Marlborough ever wrote to his wife, the brief note that announced the victory of Blenheim. If five days earlier the Queen had known the glorious news that Colonel Parke now brought her, she would never have signed the Act of Security and the whole course of Scottish history would have been changed.[20]

The passage of the Scottish Act of Security, like the "tacking" of the Occasional Conformity Bill to supply, was hailed with delight by the High

Tories as a means of defeating the Godolphin Ministry. In December, 1704, accordingly, the attack was launched. Queen Anne, knowing that her faithful servant was in danger, attended the Lords in person; at first she sat upon the throne, but later, as it was cold, she moved to a bench near the fire.[21]

The debate was opened by Lord Haversham. Godolphin, obviously hesitant, nervous and in bad form, made small effort to defend the Act of Security which, he pleaded, he had advised the Queen to pass merely in order to avoid a revolt.* No sooner had he finished than Halifax delivered a forthright attack upon the Ministry. This was ominous, for it had been anticipated that the Whigs would come to the aid of the Government, the fall of which would shatter all hope of a reconciliation with Scotland. But things were not as bad as they seemed; for, whilst Halifax was speaking, Wharton crossed over to the Government side and was seen to be in earnest conversation with Godolphin. He was, we may surmise, striking his bargain for Whig support, for after the whispered colloquy was finished, the Whig leaders assumed a more moderate tone. They advocated that England should show herself prepared to negotiate with the Scots for the union of the kingdoms, at the same time warning their northern neighbours that their refusal would be attended by disagreeable consequences to their trade and commerce. The Government accepted this shrewd advice and it was embodied in the so-called Alien Act.

Thus Scotland was offered the choice between a union to be freely negotiated between the two countries, or the acceptance of the Hanoverian succession without any change in status for either country. If, however, Scotland refused this olive-branch, then certain very unpleasant consequences would follow: every Scot would be treated as an alien no longer enjoying the protection of the Crown of England; and many of the principal Scottish exports, as cattle, coal and linen, would no longer be importable into England or Ireland. "If that's done, we are ruined," declared Roxburgh bluntly,[22] and he only echoed what all the wiser Scottish leaders knew full well. And so it was that the Alien Act was steadily pushed through all its stages until it received the royal assent.

It was at this critical stage in Anglo-Scottish relations that occurred the unhappy affair of the *Worcester*. This ship, English owned and commanded

---

* His weakness, however, has been grossly exaggerated. Thus Lord Stanhope states—"His [Godolphin's] fire indeed was nearly burned out and it might almost be said of him that henceforward during the remainder of his life he played but a subordinate part in his own administration." Stanhope, *Queen Anne*, I, 166. Professor W. T. Morgan is equally off the mark when he writes that "Godolphin lacked influence in parliament and seemed sinking into his dotage." Morgan, *English Political Parties and Leaders in Reign of Queen Anne*, 153.

by Captain Thomas Green, homeward bound from the East Indies, put into the roads of Leith in the Firth of Forth; whereupon the Secretary of the African Company, erroneously believing that she was the property of the East India Company by which one of his ships was thought to have been seized, illegally boarded her at the head of an armed party and made prisoners of the crew. In subsequent conversations with the men of the *Worcester*, certain of them when in their cups spoke mysteriously of dark deeds of piracy they had committed on the high seas. Now it so happened that the African Company had a ship, the *Speedy Return*, long overdue, about which there was much anxiety. Thus the story soon became current that she was a victim of the men of the *Worcester*. Before long all Scotland was in a ferment; and as a concession to popular clamour, the Privy Council weakly ordered that Captain Green and all his crew should stand their trial. On March 14th, 1705, the Court of Admiralty sat in judgment; a week later they found all save one of the accused guilty. All were sentenced to death, as Seafield reported to Godolphin, "and I find all persons I speak with convinced that they are guilty, and, since the sentence, two have confessed that there was a pyracy committed but they were on shoar [*sic*] at the time and know not the particulars. It is thought that more will confess."[23] It was upon the condemnation of Green and his men that the tension between the two nations reached its height, for in England it was universally held that the verdict was wrong. "This business of Green, &c. is the devil and all. It has spoilled all business. I am told it was two hours in the Cabinet," reported Secretary Johnstone from London. "10 (Somers) says he knows not the laws of Scotland, but that the proceedings are illegall, according to all other laws that he knows . . ."[24] and Queen Anne was advised that, regardless of the consequences, she should grant a reprieve. There was no time to be lost, for the condemned men were due to be hanged in batches at intervals of a week, and the first executions had been fixed for April 4th.

Before the fatal day, however, there arrived in Edinburgh from the Duke of Argyll, the Royal Commissioner, a letter expressing her Majesty's pleasure that the men should be reprieved. Unfortunately, for the reprieve to be effective the letter should have been addressed to the Privy Council. The importance of these seeming technicalities was more than appears at first sight, for if the letter had been addressed by Anne herself direct to the Privy Council, its members could have used it as a pretext for granting the reprieve and would thus not have unduly exposed themselves to public indignation. Deprived of this pretext, as Seafield explained to Godolphin, all the Privy Council dared do in reply was to send Anne a petition that the reprieve should not be granted.[25] In consequence, a direct communication from the

Queen ordering a reprieve was immediately dispatched, and the execution fixed for the 4th was postponed for one week.

According to an arrangement made the previous night,[26] at 8 o'clock in the morning of April 11th, the day fixed for the postponed executions, all available Privy Councillors assembled at Lord Seafield's house in Edinburgh. In fact, only some ten or eleven attended, bringing ugly accounts of tumults in the streets; and the *Squadrone* Ministers were particularly careful to absent themselves. A flying packet had just arrived from Lord Godolphin in London. When the seal was broken, this was found to contain a letter from the Queen dated April 3rd and a bundle of documents which proved to be sworn affidavits from two sailors of the *Speedy Return* to the effect that their ship had been seized not by the *Worcester*, but by a notorious pirate named Bowen, and to have been boarded off the coast of Madagascar on a date when Captain Green's ship was in far distant seas.

What course should be taken by the timorous statesmen assembled at Lord Seafield's house? It was clear that the men of the *Worcester* ought not to die. It was equally clear that the mob howling in the streets were determined that they should. If the blood of Green and his crew were denied them, the blood of Seafield and his advisers might well be forfeit. But there was an even worse probability than that; for if the condemned men were now to be reprieved, the Union would be doomed and civil war might easily ensue. The terrible dilemma was one to daunt hearts far stouter and minds far nobler than those of the timid statesmen assembled that April morning in the Scottish capital.

The slaughter of Green and two other selected victims served as sufficient sacrifice to pacify the mob. The rest of the *Worcester*'s crew were soon afterwards reprieved and set at large. England, of course, was furious, but she could only demand the removal of the cowardly *Squadrone* ministers. The Duke of Argyll, the Queen's Commissioner, emphatically concurred, and he was supported in this by the English Whigs, upon whom the Godolphin government was becoming daily more dependent. But Godolphin himself was disgusted. "How can we hope to succeed in our public affairs," he asked Seafield, "if leaders cannot prevail with themselves to lay aside private animositys." Concessions on both sides were needed. But he added bitterly, "by all I hear from Scotland neither party seems inclined to this sort of temper."[27] The moderate Seafield seems to have been impressed with Godolphin's arguments, for he frequently wrote to the Lord Treasurer advocating "the conjoining of the two parties,"[28] or, as we should say, a coalition; but nobody seems to have paid much attention to him. Yet he was not altogether daunted, and he, Argyll, and Queensberry, the three leaders in the reconstituted Ministry, now combined in their joint task to settle the Hanoverian Succession or to initiate negotiations for a Union with Scotland.

Time was short because the Alien Act was due to operate at Christmas; and Argyll's uneasy temper was a further danger. "... knowing his warmth and temper as I doe," wrote the Lord Treasurer, "I am very apt to suspect he may bee so unadvised as to persist in demitting, in which case, my Lord, it is absolutely necessary you should think, as well as the shortness of time will permit, into what method and into what hands the Queen should put the conduct of her affairs ..." and at all costs Seafield must stay on and have no thoughts of resigning.[29]

When the Estates met on June 28th, 1705, the Ministry had still not determined whether to urge a settlement of the succession question or to treat for a union; and for a time there was further wrangling.[30] Lord Godolphin expressed himself to Seafield in strong terms. "The sincerity of those who pretend to be friends to a Treaty will easily appear in this point;" he wrote, "for unless they are content such an Act should goe single and upon its own foot, it will be plain that at the bottom their design is only to obstruct what they pretend to be for."[31] And again a few weeks later, "... for nothing can be with submission, more against reason and common sence than the barefaced arguments of your opposers, viz., when the matter of succession is in question. No. There must first be a previous Treaty; when the Treaty is brought onn, No; there must first be Limitations on the successor. What can bee more preposterous? In short it looks to mee as if that nation desired to bring things to extremity, in which I am not sure they are very well advised; England is not now in the condition it was when Scotland used to make inroads upon us. Wee have the power, & you may give us the will to return those visitts, & supposing the French more able to assist the Scotts, than I hope they are, or like to bee, the French have the character of being very good servants but the worst masters upon earth."[32] Some too were complaining of the influence of the English counsellors round the Queen. As to that, asked Godolphin pointedly of Seafield, "how can the Queen but bee influenced by her English servants when she has no Scots servants near her person, at least during a sessions of Parliament, which is the time when the greatest affairs of that kingdom are transacted? And if the Scots have a mind to obviate that objection," he added seriously, "why don't they make an address to her Majesty that she would appoint a certain number of her Counsell of Scotland to bee always attending upon her person."[33]

At length the wrangling somewhat abated, and it was decided to consider proposals for a treaty of union. On the first day of September the Act for the appointment and instruction of the Scottish Commissioners was

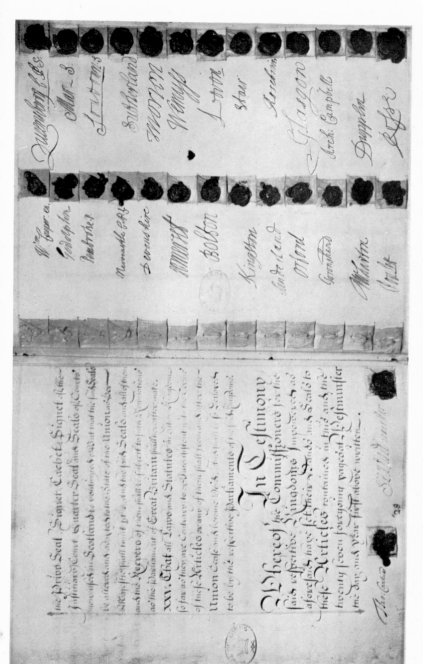

ARTICLES OF UNION OF ENGLAND AND SCOTLAND

SIGNED BY THE ENGLISH COMMISSIONERS ON THE LEFT AND THE SCOTTISH ON THE RIGHT

read and approved; but it was not until February that the Scottish and not until April that the English appointments were made. ★ They first met in the Cockpit on April 16th, 1706 and in nine weeks they had completed their task. On July 22nd, the Articles were signed by all but some half-dozen of the Commissioners. The next day they went in procession to St. James's Palace to be received by the Queen. It was indeed a great occasion. The Battle of Blenheim and the Union with Scotland are the greatest achievements of the reign of Queen Anne.

In the days immediately following the Union, all those, both Scottish and English, who had laboured in the cause were regarded as having sacrificed the interests of their country; and Godolphin, Marlborough and other English statesmen have been accused, often in the most extravagant terms, of having bribed the Scottish leaders.[34] What justification is there for the charge?

The accusation was first brought by the Jacobite Lockhart, who asserts that, after the Union had been concluded in London, the Scottish Ministers, realizing that they would have to face considerable opposition, represented to the Queen that she should advance from her Treasury the sum of £20,00 to pay in part the arrears of salaries and pensions to Scottish leaders; and that subsequently, on the representation of Queensberry, Seafield, Mar, Loudoun and Glasgow, Lord Godolphin waived the right of the Treasury of England to receive from the Scots Lords of the Treasury a public security for the repayment of the money. He further alleges that of this sum, which he computes not at the round sum of £20,000, but at £20,540 17s. 7d., no less than £12,325 found its way into Queensberry's own pocket for official expenses, and that the remainder was distributed among some thirty different persons whom he names.[35] According to Baillie of Jerviswood, Godolphin paid Queensberry the sum of £10,000 to obtain his support for the Union, and he quotes a letter addressed to him by Secretary Johnstone as evidence for this charge. "225 (Queensberry), till two days before he left us," wrote Johnstone, "railed at 15 (Godolphin); said he was not for 58 (the Union) &c. but at last 102 (a sum of money) quieted him. I believe 103 (this sum of money) is ten thousand pounds; the thing itself is no secret. 16 (Godolphin) told 273 (Johnstone) that 103 (money) was advanced to 89 (Scottish Ministers) upon 38 (Scotland's) revenue to pay 38 (Scotland's) debts, particularly to 241 (Tweeddale).

★ For a full list of both the Scottish and English Commissioners who sat "At the Council Chamber in the Cockpit, Tuesday the 16th of April 1706," the opening meeting, see Defoe, *History of the Union between England and Scotland* (ed. 1786), p. 113.

Your friend asked Why not 243 (Roxburgh)? He say'd he knew nothing of it. And why not 273 (Johnstone)? He laugh't and bid him do for himself. He talked much of 98 (for the Union); said positively 21 (the English Parliament) would be for him (it), and if 39 (the Scottish Parliament) was not, they must try whose heads were hardest."[36]

These are vague and unconvincing charges, and coming from violent acrimonious Jacobites may well be mistrusted. Furthermore, no historian of these events has ever endorsed them.[37] Nevertheless, there can be no doubt that certain sums were paid to the impecunious Scottish lords from the English Exchequer. Of this we have abundant proof, and it is admitted by Godolphin himself in a letter to Seafield. After stating that if "honours or other advantages" were conferred upon Scottish lords "while they continue against setling [sic] the protestant succession it will be looked upon as a sort of compounding . . ." he continued, "As to the allowances to my Lord Atholl & others on account of their expense, I agree they have not been well bestowed, at least upon his Grace, who was so farr from being satisfied with having 1,000ll that he was very much unsatisfyed it was no more; but as to that matter, & all others of that kind, your lordship will please to reflect, the business is to establish Her Majesty's affairs & restore her authority in Scotland. Those who have the meritt of that work will bee sure of having the favour & all the advantages which are necessary consequents of it."[38]

Similar evidence from other quarters can also be produced. The meaning of these words from the Lord Clerk Register to Lord Mar cannot possibly be misunderstood: "His Grace (Queensberry) wishes his Lordship to remind the Queen of some secret disbursements he made when Commissioner, for which he had secret instructions, but which because of their nature could not be stated in the accounts with the Treasury. Her Majesty may trust him and order payment or not as she pleases."[39] Equally compromising is a little known letter addressed jointly by Seafield and Glasgow to Queensberry in the summer of 1707. "May it please your Grace," it runs, "you have ane accompt signed by the Earl of Glasgow, how the twenty Thousand pounds advanced by my Lord Treasurer was disposed off, wee would doe any thing that is in our power, to procure it to be reimbursed to his Ldp. and for a considerable part of it, it may be done and stated upon the Equivalent. Your Graces Equipage and dayly allowance will amount to betwixt Twelve and Thirteen Thousands pounds and it is already stated as owing to your Grace, and that being a preferable debt to most of the debts in the Civil List, my Lord Treasurer may reckon upon it, but it is impossible for us to doe more, for what was given to the Duke of Atholl, Marquis of Tweeddale, Earles of Roxburgh, Marchmont, Bellcarras, Dunmore, Cromarty, and sixty or seventy others in small sommes, its impossible to state these sommes without discovering the haill (whole) affair to every particular person that received any part of the money, which hath been hitherto kept secret, and its more than probable, that they would refuse to give assignations if they were demanded of them, so the discovering of it would be of no use, unless it were to bring discredit upon the managdement of that parliament; and all that will be Loosed about Seven Thousand pound, if your Grace please, you may lay this before my Lord Treasurer with that secrecy that this affair requires." Then follows this significant postscript: "Your Grace may be pleased to burn this letter when you have read it to my Lord Treasurer."* But Queensberry did not heed this advice. He did not burn the letter: and so we can produce it today as conclusive evidence that payments were made to the Scottish leaders.

But this does not betoken the carrying of the Union by widespread bribery. It is doubtless true that Godolphin, convinced that only by the Union of the two Kingdoms under one Crown could the interests of both be best served, was prepared to go to considerable lengths to forward his policy. And in this many of the wisest Scots were in agreement. Thus, Lord Cromartie, though, as he says, "a man without doors can say little to purpose of the publicke transactions . . . Yet," he adds, "I may say over ane old prayer of mine—God send a solid union in and of Brittaine; for I am sorly afraid and firmly perswaded that such only will secure Brittaine and deliver old Scotland from its many complaints."[40] And the *Squadrone* chief, Baillie of Jerviswood, expressed a like sentiment. "After all, considering the temper of this people, how unfit to govern ourselves, how likely to weary of Limitations, were they got, and for other reasons mentioned in your's," he wrote to Roxburgh, "I must be convinced that the Union is our onlie game. But . . ." he is forced to add, "it will not be so easie as you

---

* Seafield & Glasgow to Queensberry, "Edr. 20 Jully, 1707." Brit. Mus. Add. MSS. 34, 180, f. 1. Seafield himself was not above giving a broad hint of his needs. "I hear the Duke of Athol has got a thousand pound and My Lord Cromartie fifteen hundred. I doe not at all complain of it but I shal only say.—that the station I serve in and my expense and trouble Has been verie great an al I got was but six hundred but I submitt and shal spair neither pains nor expense in Her Majesties service and depend upon Her favour. . . ." "edr. May the 30. 1704.": and again a few days later," . . . the Marques of Anandale Has this day presented in the Treasurie a Letter in His favours [sic] for a thousand pound ann the accompt of His jorney so that now none wants this alouance bot the Earle of Eglintoun and my Selfe. I am unwilling to desire any thing for my selfe bot I trulie think it for the Queens Service that Her Majestie give me at least the same alouence. I am the first officer of State and was expresslie called and I am sure spent more then any of them having indeavoured to support my Character and to spair no expence [that] might be for Her Majestie's Service." Seafield to Godolphin, "Edr. June the 9th, 1704." Brit. Mus. Add. MSS. 34,180, ff. 40, 48.

imagine; for all you reckon upon will not be of that opinion in Parliament."[41] Therefore, widespread bribery was not necessary; and if a moderate element of inducement was required to influence those who were not "of that opinion in Parliament," this was not looked upon as in any way a dishonourable transaction. Loyal service was entitled to its just reward.[42]

In the early years of the union there was much discontent; consequently exaggerated reports were soon rife in France of a great revival of Jacobite feeling throughout Britain. These were so far credited in March 1708 as to induce Louis XIV to send from Dunkirk a squadron of nearly thirty sail with the Pretender and six thousand French infantry aboard on an invasion of Scotland. In spite of constant warnings early in the year, England was ill-prepared and Scotland virtually defenceless. For this state of things Lord Godolphin must be held in part responsible, though prevalent suspicions, often expressed in unbridled language, that he and Marlborough were secretly in touch with the exiled court and were disloyal to the Queen were quite unfounded.[43] Indeed, in March of the fateful year, on the advice of one Elkin,* he made the interesting suggestion which was actually adopted in the first World War, of blocking the harbour of Dunkirk by the sinking of ships and ballast in its channel.[44] Soon pilots, flag-officers and captains were busily engaged demonstrating how it could not possibly be done. But it serves to show that the Lord Treasurer was zealous for the safety of the country and that suggestions that he was disloyal to the Queen are without foundation.

More by good fortune than by skill, the invading force was never able to land on the shores of Scotland. When the danger was passed clemency was shown to the arrested Jacobites. This was in part due to the humanity of Godolphin, Marlborough and the Queen. But other considerations induced them to be merciful. A General Election, the first for a Parliament of all Britain, was about to be held, and Scottish support for the government was anxiously canvassed. In these circumstances undue severity would have been most impolitic.

---

* Perhaps Alexander Ekins, Master of the *Warspight* in 1690, and First Lieutenant to Leake in the *Prince George* in 1705. *Byng Papers,* II, xiii.

CHAPTER VI

THE FALL OF HARLEY

THOUGH the Whigs had certainly achieved a notable success in foisting Lord Sunderland on the reluctant Queen, their victory was less complete, their position less secure, than might at first appear. For some time now the Duchess of Marlborough's ungovernable temper, haughty manners, and violent pro-Whig partisanship had been gradually alienating her from her lifelong friend, but the presence in the circle around the Sovereign of an insinuating rival was a completely fresh phenomenon of the highest consequence.

The new courtier, Abigail Hill, was a distant and impecunious relative to whom and to whose family the Duchess had shown much kindness.* How this plain, sly, red-nosed woman obtained her influence over the Queen does not appear—no doubt her very contrast to the fiery Sarah was her greatest asset—but certain is it that by the middle of 1707 her position at Court had become established. The Marlboroughs knew something of this, but they hardly as yet realized the danger. "If you are sure that 256 (Abigail) does speak of business to 42 (the Queen) I should think you might speak to her with some caution, which might do good," wrote John early in June, "for she certainly is grateful, and will mind what you say."[1] But he was ignorant of the truth. Earlier in the year and without a word to the relatives who had befriended her, Abigail Hill had been secretly married in the Queen's presence to Samuel Masham, a Groom of the Bed-Chamber to Prince George of Denmark.

But quite apart from the personal complexion of the matter, the rise of Abigail had a profound political significance. Mrs. Masham was a staunch Tory, and it was soon clear that the directing power behind her was none other than Harley, anxious, not so much for the dismissal of Marlborough or the advent of a Tory Government, as for the continuation of a moderate Ministry dependent on neither party but supported by the favour of the Queen. The obvious danger was that Harley might succeed in driving

---

* For the Duchess's own account of the Hills and what she had done for them, which has never been seriously disputed, see Duchess of Marlborough, *Conduct*, 176, *et seq.*

Godolphin from office, a contingency that would surely be followed by a Whig revolt. This would mean either the fall of the Ministry or the replacement of Tories in the Government by Whigs. The Duke looked askance at both these alternatives. He dreaded having to rely on a Tory Government under Harley's control; equally distasteful would be a Whig Government controlled by the Junto. Neither Harley nor the Duke wanted a completely Tory or completely Whig Ministry. How well they could have worked together if only Harley had not aspired to displace Godolphin! But it was just that very fact that drove the Queen and Harley into the camp of the High Tories and Godolphin and Marlborough towards the tents of the Whigs. Thus it was that the non-party Ministry dependent on the Queen's choice was destroyed, and something like party government in the modern sense was gradually established.

The alarm of the Whigs was first raised by Anne's nomination of two Tories to the bishoprics of Exeter and Chester. Against these choices, Sir William Dawes and Dr. Blackall, nothing could be alleged save their politics. But that alone was sufficient to flutter the Whigs, who immediately assumed that her Majesty had acted on the advice of Godolphin and Marlborough. This was quite unwarranted; as also was the belief, which Godolphin expressed to Marlborough, that Harley was behind the Queen. That alarmed the general. "But you know my opinion was, and is yet, *that you ought to take with you Mr. Secretary Harley*, and let the queen see, with all the freedom and plainness imaginable, her true interest," he replied, "and when she is sensible of that, there will be no more difficulty, if there should, you will have performed your duty, and God's will be done."[2] To his wife a week later he urged the view that Godolphin must write frankly to the Queen stating his views ". . . without offering to quit, or expecting any answer; but as in duty bound, to leave it to her consideration. I should hope this would do it; but if it should not, the last and only thing must be, that the solicitor-general speak very freely to Mr. Harley. . . ."[3]

Meanwhile, the Lord Treasurer was employed in detailing to Marlborough all the tribulations of his office, ". . . especially since 42's (the Queen's) proceedings in some things will give 89 (the Whigs) a handle to bee uneasy & to tear every thing to pieces if they can't have their own terms, and 208 (Harley) does so hate and fear 5 (Somers), 6 (Sunderland), and 7 (Wharton) that he omitts no occasion of fillng 42's (the Queen's) head with their projects and designs, & if Mr. Montgomery should take him with him upon any occasion of that kind he would either say nothing or argue against what the other says, as he did upon some subjects some months since when Mr. Freeman himself was present."[4] "Since you think it will be no use to take Mr. Harley with you to the queen," replied Marlborough to his friend's anguished cry, "you must find some way of speaking plainly to him;...."[5] And to his wife, who had evidently been writing to him in her usual unbridled language, "I am very sorry that you think you have reason to believe that Mr. Harley takes all occasions of doing hurt to England," he wrote. "If lord treasurer can't find a remedy, and that before next winter, I should think his wisest and honestest way would be, to tell the queen very plainly which way he thinks her business may be carried on; and if that be not agreeable, that she would lose no time in knowing of Mr. Harley what his scheme is, and follow that; so that the lord treasurer might not be answerable to what might happen. If this were said plainly to the queen and Mr. Harley, I am very confident the latter would not dare undertake the business and then everything might go quietly."[6]

Side by side with the commotion about the two new bishops, further trouble was brewing about the administration of the Admiralty under Prince George of Denmark. The grievances were real enough, but the true object of the attack was Marlborough's High Tory brother, who presided over the Admiralty Board in the name of the Prince. "One of the measures which I fear is laid down by 89 (the Whigs) is to disturb 182 (George Churchill) as soon as ever they have an opportunity," Godolphin told Marlborough.[7] Churchill himself was fully alive to this and had thoughts of retiring. Godolphin too was seriously perturbed at the conduct of the Whigs, though, he is careful to add, "... I know 38 (Godolphin himself) will not neglect any thing that is possible to prevent the inconveniences that threaten, yett the difficulties hee meets with are such, & particularly in the unwillingness of 209 (the Queen) to do any thing that is good & necessary for Mrs. Morley, that unless he (I) may hope for Mr. Freeman's assistance even before the winter, there must be the greatest confusion imaginable in all the affair of 88 (the parliament)."[8]

All this was most worrying to Marlborough. How he wished that his friend had not dissuaded his brother from retiring! How he wished that Godolphin and he could both quit and live in retirement together; "... but I fear neither of us can have any till we are at Woodstock, so that I could wish some practicable scheme could be made, by which her majesty might be well served, and we both out of the ministry."[9] He wrote with equal frankness to his wife of being "mortified by the prosecution of my brother George." But "My greatest concern is for the queen, and for the lord treasurer," he added. "England will take care of itself, and not be ruined because a few men are not pleased. They will see their error when it is too late. . . . The union you mention between the lord treasurer, yourself and me, for the good of the queen, and England; can there be a difficulty in that union? But I will own to you my apprehensions are, that somebody or other, I know not who has got so much credit with the queen, that they will be able to persuade her to do more hurt to herself than we can do good."[10] He wrote also to the Queen, sending a copy of the letter to Godolphin, "tho' I own to you," he admitted to Sarah, "I am desponding as to the good it may do; however, I have done my duty, and God's will be done."[11] "Mr. Freeman's letter to 42 (the Queen) was as right & as full as is possible & was no more than was extreamly necessary;" responded the Lord Treasurer, "& it will bee as necessary to continue in the same style upon all occasions both before and after 39's (your) return."[12]

As the weeks passed and Marlborough was more and more embarrassed by cares abroad, he was continually harassed by the news from home. "I do assure you I did not mean 89 (the Whigs) when I spoke of ingratitude," he wrote peevishly to Sarah, "but I meant it in general to England. . . ." How heartily sick he was of both parties. The Whigs had attacked his brother. And the Tories? They "will do all they can to mortify the queen and England;" he told his wife, "for I am now both at an age and humour, that I would not be bound to make my court to either party, for all that this world could give me. Besides, I am so disheartened, that when I shall have done my duty, I shall submit to Providence." But, he warned Sarah, if the Whigs persist in mortifying Godolphin, he will retire and Harley will take his place. "This I know will hurt both the queen and England, and I see no remedy."[13] A week later in reply to a letter from his wife emphasizing the close collaboration between Anne, Abigail and Harley, he wrote to express the view that, if the Queen will not listen to their warnings, he and Godolphin should retire and leave the others to do what they please, for if they had lost the Queen's confidence, it would be madness to let the world think that they still had influence. "I shall always be ready to sacrifice my life for the quiet and safety of the queen," he wrote, "but I will not be imposed upon by any body that has power with her; for as I have served her with all my heart, and all the sincerity imaginable, I think I deserve the indulgence of being quiet in my old age."[14]

Meanwhile the Lord Treasurer bombarded his friend abroad with his anxieties at home. "I reckon one great occasion of Mrs. Morley's obstinacy & of the uneasyness she gives herself & others, especially about the Clergy, proceeds from an inclination of talking more freely than usuall to 156 (Abigail Masham)," he wrote, "and this is sayd, told of & improved by 199 (Harley) upon all such matters. . . . I am apt to think he makes use of the same person to improve all the ill offices to 89 (the Whigs), which both hee and that person are as naturally inclined to, as 42 (the Queen) is to receive the impressions of them." How to avoid the ill-effects, which will be apparent by the winter, if "a timely remedy" is not found? This can only be achieved ". . . by Mr. Freeman & 38 (Godolphin himself) speaking very plainly at the same time to Mrs. Morley, both of 199 (Harley) & a good many other things, & settling a rule for preventing, before it is too late, all the uneasyness for the future; . . ."[15]   "What you write concerning the queen, Mr. Harley and Mrs. Masham, is of that consequence," Marlborough replied, "that I think no time should be lost in putting a stop to that management, or else to let them have it entirely in their own hands."[16]

It is clear that the tidings that Sarah sent of the increasing influence of Harley and Abigail with the Queen were treated with the utmost seriousness by the two friends, so that Marlborough told Godolphin that the sooner they spoke seriously to the Queen, the better for all concerned. If in the face of that Anne should remain obdurate, let them impress upon her the impossibility of carrying on her business under such circumstances. "I shall always be ready to sacrifice myself for the prosperity of the queen; but I will not be thought to have credit, when her business is managed in a way, which, in my opinion, must be her ruin."[17]   From Godolphin's reply we learn "that both Mr. Montgomery and Mrs. Freeman have thought it best to read to Mrs. Morley 37's (your) later letter to 209 (me), all except one word, which was the name of a person not fitt to be mentioned." But though they did not mention Harley's name, the Queen's reactions were not quite what they had expected. "They did very well foresee," he continued, "this would certainly have the consequence of making yett more uneasyness in Mrs. Morley towards Mrs. Freeman, but did hope it might bee of so much use another way, as to over-balance it; whether their thoughts will prove right in the latter of these, I cannot tell but in the former I am sure they have not been mistaken, & I believe 39 (you) will soon be of the same mind in that matter, by a letter which I am told he (you) will have from 42 (the Queen) as soon as this, & I can't but think it is of so much consequence that 42 (the Queen) should not bee countenanced & encouraged in complaints of 240 (Sarah Marlborough) when you have the opportunity of talking with 38 (Godolphin himself) of these matters, you would advise him to take great care of his answer in that particular."[18]

The letter from Queen Anne to which Godolphin refers, was dated the same day. ". . . as to what you say, I must either put my business into the hands of 4 (Harley) or follow 10 (Godolphin's) measures. I should be glad (if) you would explain yourself a little more on that;" wrote the Queen, "for I know of no measure 10 (Godolphin) has but what were laid down when 40 (you) were here, and I do not know I have broken any of them; for I can not think my having nomi(na)ted Sir William Daws or Dr. Blackall to be bishops is any breach, they being worthy men, and all the clamour that is raised against them proceeds only from the malice of 18 (the Whigs), which you would see very plainly if you were here. I know this is otherwise represented to you, and I believe you have been told, as I have, that these two persons were recommended to me by 4 (Harley), which is so far from being the truth that he knew nothing of it till it was the talk of the Town. . . . Now I must give some answer to a long letter from 10 (Godolphin) read to 17 (the Queen), which he (I) received by the last post from 40 (you).★ In that I find 41 (the Duchess of Marlborough) has said 17 (the Queen) had an entire confidence in 4 (Harley). I know so much of 17 (the Queen's) inclinations that I am sure she has a very (good) opinion of 4 (Harley) and will never change it without she sees cause; but I wonder how 41 (the Duchess of Marlborough) could say such a thing when she has been assured from 17 (by me) that 17 (the Queen) relied entirely on none but Mr. Freeman and Mr. Montgomery. 40 (Marlborough) seems very much concerned at this thing that 41 (the Duchess of Marlborough) said, and upon that tells 10 (Godolphin) Mr. Freeman and Mr. Montgomery should speak their minds freely to 17 (the Queen). It is what I desire of all things they would do, for I can't see any other measures to be taken than what has been already laid down, and I am sure 17 (the Queen) has no thought of altering them. I can think of but one thing to be added, which is a resolution to encourage all those that have not been in opposition that will concur in my service, whether they are 18 or 19 (Whigs or Tories), which is a thing I wish might be put in practice, believing it would do a great deal of good, and I am sure it is not for 17 (the Queen's) service to disoblige anybody. . . . In the meantime continue your justice to 17 (the Queen) in believing her intentions are honest, and be assured she will be to her last moment most sincerely your humble servant."[19]

Marlborough replied to the Queen without delay; but before she received his letter, she heard from Godolphin, who struggled to put things in their true perspective. "The liberties of all Europe, the safety of your Majesty's person and of the Kingdom, the future promotion of the Protestant religion, and the glory of your reign, depend upon the success of the next session of parliament, and indeed upon every session of parliament while this war lasts, to which, except it please God to give a favourable conclusion, your Majesty can never hope to enjoy any settled quiet during your whole reign." Winning the war is all that matters. How often have we heard that in our own time! "This being truly the case what colour of rason [sic] can incline your Majesty to discourage and dissatisfy those whose principles and interest led them on with so much warmth and zeal to carry you through the difficulties of this war? . . ." In the face of that, what do

★ She means, of course, Marlborough's letter of August 29th, read to her by Godolphin.

these petty Church appointments matter, what does it signify "whether Dr. Blackall at this time be made a bishop, or a dean or a prebend ? . . ." "Your Majesty I am sure will remember how uneasy the Parliament was about the extraordinary expenses of the war in the last year, tho' that was a year of greater success than had ever been known before; the present is a year of great misfortunes and disappointments, and yet the extraordinary expense . . . is greater than in the last; how then can one hope to be supported in unsuccessful irregularities against an inveterate number of men who will hearten and encourage one another from the mark of your Majesty's favour to their friends and adherents, unless there be a considerable majority in either House that will show a warmth and a spirit to support your Majesty and your administration in all your zealous endeavours towards a good and speady conclusion of the war."[20]

No sooner had Anne received this bombshell than Marlborough's reply to her letter of August 25th reached her. "I beg the justice of you to believe, that I am no ways concerned for the power that the Whigs may have with you, but the great concern that I must always have for your quiet and safety; for if you are served to your satisfaction and security, I am very indifferent who the persons are. And as you desire that I would speak freely, I do protest in the presence of God Almighty, that I am persuaded that if you continue in the mind that I think you now are, and will not suffer those that have the honour to serve you, to manage your affairs agreeably to the circumstances of the times, your business must inevitably run into confusion, and, consequently, make it impossible for my lord treasurer to serve; for if he is thought to have the power, when he has not, both parties will be angry with him; though both would admire him and his friends if he were out of the service. If I were with your majesty, I believe I could let you see the trouble and distraction you are like to be in this winter, which you must prevent before the meeting of parliament or it will be too late." He then reverts to affairs on the Continent, and concludes with a spirited defence of his wife. "I pray God to direct you in all things for your own good, and that of all Europe, that your own affairs may prosper and be glorious, as they have been for some years, and I shall then enjoy all the happiness and quiet that this world can give me."[21]

This letter he sent under cover of one to Godolphin, leaving it to his discretion either to deliver or to burn it. Of the conduct of the Whigs he wrote bitterly, ". . . for the truth is, they are jealous that you and I have inclination to try once more the Tories. You and I know how false this is. However, if the queen will be governed by Mr. Harley, they will have just reason given them to be angry; and if you and I continue in business, all England will believe what is done is by our advice, which will give power to the Whigs to mortify whom they please; so that I think ye must speak very freely to the Whigs and the queen, and if they will not approve your measures, have nothing to do with either; and if we were well out of this war we should then be happy."[22] He was desperately sorry for Godolphin, as he told his wife, "for were I used, as I do not doubt but I shall, as he is by the Whigs, who threaten to abandon him, whenever the Queen displeases, I would not continue in business for all this world could give me; and I believe they would be the first that would have reason to repent. . . ."[23]

At about the same time Marlborough received a letter from Godolphin announcing an early reply from the Queen and an audience he had recently had with her Majesty. "By a long conversation between Mrs. Morley and Mr. Montgomery, of which I have had some account, I find they both agree that for 37 and 108★ (you and England) to see one another before the naturall time, might bee liable to many great inconveniences . . . one cannot at this time depend upon the fruits of it with any certainty, 38 (Godolphin himself) having lately spoken very fully upon all those subjects of which Mrs. Freeman's head and heart seem to bee so full; and tho there has yett appeared but very little encouragement to think the arguments used upon that occasion are like to prevail, yett one may conclude, in this case, as the Scriptures say, in the very words of our Saviour; *if they hear not Moses & the prophets, neither will they be perswaded tho one rose from the dead.*"[24]

Towards the end of September, the Lord Treasurer went for a month's holiday to Newmarket.[25] Whilst he was away Marlborough wrote anxiously to Sarah for news of his intentions, for, as he told her, if he stays in office and cannot influence the Queen, he will be duped by Harley; on the other hand, if he resigns, it will be fatal to affairs both at home and abroad. "I do with all my heart pity the queen," he concluded, "being very sure she does not know the fatal step she is going to make."[26] The same day he wrote to the Lord Treasurer announcing the receipt of the expected letter from the Queen. He was much worried about the news from England, where ruin seems inevitable if her Majesty will not listen to his friend's advice; in that event, he added, ". . . I hope you will take such measures that it may appear very plainly to England that you do not approve of the measures now taken."[27] Later that day he wrote a second letter displaying his anxiety for his friend if Whig intransigence and royal obstinacy should give the Tories an opportunity to show their malice; and he put to Godolphin very clearly the alternatives, as he saw them, of his resigning or remaining at his post. "If you stay in your place, though you are in no ways consenting, yett all that shall be amiss you must be answerable for;" he told him, "and on the other side, I am very sensible that if you do quit, the

★ He writes thus, of course, to conceal the cipher.

business both at home and abroad must very much suffer. For whatever the queen and these new schemers may think, the allies will expect nothing good from England when they shall see that you and I have lost our credit, after having served with so great success. I hope your answer to this will let me know your positive resolution, so that I might govern myself; for whilst you are in I shall send my opinion."[28]

The campaign on the Continent being now well-nigh over, early in October Marlborough determined after a brief visit to the Hague,[29] to sail for England. From The Hague he wrote to his son-in-law, Sunderland, on affairs at home. "I believe the last year no argument could have prevailed with the queen to have had a thought of parting with me and lord treasurer," he wrote a shade bitterly, "but I have good reason to think that is much altered." Nevertheless, they must stand firm! "However, I believe when it is very plain that I and the lord treasurer are in earnest, I am a good deal of your opinion that the queen will not part with us; so that I think there should be no time lost in trying this experiment. If it does not, at least the lord treasurer and I shall have nothing to reproach ourselves with, and shall be blessed with a quiet life, which in my opinion, is preferable to all this world can give. I do from my soul wish so well to the queen, that I hope those that shall succeed may be more lucky in giving content than we have been; but I am sure they can never be more sincere, though we could not cure jealousies."[30] Sunderland in his reply affected to agree. He admitted that his father-in-law and Godolphin were not so much in the Queen's favour as in the past. "But I must beg on this occasion to say that if you and the lord treasurer would have believed what some of your friends and servants have told you in relation to Mr. Secretary Harley, this had never happened. But be that as it will, without looking back to what is past, I am sure it is high time to try to retrieve them before they are past recovery—and I can't but believe, as you say, that when it is very plain that you and the lord treasurer are in earnest, the queen will not part with you; since what is insisted on is so reasonable in itself, as well as what has been promised over and over."[31]

On the afternoon of the day on which he wrote to Sunderland, Marlborough left The Hague for Antwerp; thence he wrote again to his friend on the political situation at home. He despaired of achieving anything by his presence in England, but he was in favour of postponing the sitting of Parliament until the Queen should make up her mind what she would do, ". . . for if the Whigs will not support, and the Tories will be malicious, what must be the consequence but ruin? But if any body has a good scheme which is like to succeed, the sooner they meet the better."[32]

While Marlborough was thus writing home to his kinsman, Godolphin determined to follow his advice and to have a heart-to-heart talk with Harley. This took place at Windsor, and could not have been a pleasant interview. The Lord Treasurer, speaking both for Marlborough and himself, taxed Harley with deceit and desired a categorical answer as to whether he would support them or continue to influence the Queen by the backstairs. In reply to the charge Harley, affecting humility and surprise, answered more in sorrow than in anger, in terms of injured innocence; and he followed up the interview with a letter which conveyed what he had intended to have said at Windsor. He recognized the difficulties that faced them during the coming winter, but he would regard it as "very impertinent" on his part to trouble the Lord Treasurer with his "poor thought of the true occasion of them." Nevertheless, he wished to say just one thing, ". . . that I am resolved to do everything to the utmost of my power (if required) to make the Queen's service and her minister's easy, and I will be under your lordship's directions and be active or passive, to do anything or nothing, to meddle with business or to let it alone, as your lordship shall think best and shall be pleased to let me know your pleasure."[33] To this effusion, Godolphin returned the typically blunt answer ". . . that if we who have the honour to serve the best Queen in the world can't agree upon the proper measures for her service at home, whatever we do abroad will signify very little."[34]

Harley's well-known letter in reply portrays him at his trickiest! "As to the last paragraph of your lordship's letter," he wrote, "I have leave to profess to you most solemnly, that I have made it my study to serve the Queen upon an honest principle, that I have no attachment to any other person in the world but your lordship and the Duke of Marlborough." He then let drop some dark hints of the malice of the Whigs and continued, "I know your lordship is too just to admit any insinuations of that kind, and I am so little fond of standing in any one's way, that any endeavours of that sort give me no disquiet, because I depend upon your lordship's goodness to let me know when I am thought a burden to the service, or uneasy to anyone, and the least hint of that nature shall meet with a very ready and cheerful compliance in me by a willing retreat." To Godolphin's query as to his future conduct, Harley replied in singular terms. "I had much rather be directed than not," he wrote, "and shall never be inquisitive to know anything but how to do my duty. It has been always my temper to go along with the company and not to give them uneasiness; if they should say Harrow on the Hill or by Maidenhead were the nearest way to Windsor, I would go with them and never dispute it if that would give content, and that I might not be forced to swear it was so." One wonders how Sidney Godolphin greeted this self-revealing avowal! There then followed more of his sincerity and devotion to his two patrons; after which he concluded with these words: "I am satisfied to a demonstration there can be no other centre of union but the Queen, by the ministration of your lordship and the Duke of Marlborough; and there the bulk of the nation will fix themselves if they may be suffered, all other expedients are very wretched things and will end but very ill; and I dread the thoughts of running from the extreme of one faction to another which is the natural consequence of party tyranny, and renders the government like a door which turns both ways upon its hinges to let in each party as it grows triumphant, and in truth this is the real parent and nurse of our factions here. It is time to relieve your lordship's patience and by pardon for this tedious letter and withal to desire to assure your lordship that you have not a more faithful servant nor a truer nor more zealous friend in the world than myself to the utmost of my capacity."[35] A week later he wrote again to Godolphin in similar strain.[36]

Thus Harley! At the very moment that he was maintaining the external profession of respect for Godolphin and Marlborough, at the very moment that he was proffering to them the most solemn and abject assurances of his attachment and support, he was taking every measure available to destroy their influence with the Queen. Small wonder that his asseverations did not dissipate the Ministers' suspicions. Marlborough, in particular, was affected by Harley's evident ingratitude, and spoke more and more of his resolution to retire. Godolphin, it seems, was more hesitant. He would only retire jointly with Marlborough and he continued to clamour for his friend's return. Then he loyally defended the Queen. "In several of 39's (your) letters to Mrs. Morley I find he (you) often repeat(s) *that the rashness of some people's schemes may prove fatall*, but there is really no such thing as a scheme or any thing like it from any body else, nor has 42 (the Queen) as yett any thought of taking a scheme, but from Mr. Freeman and Mr. Montgomery. The misfortune is, I think, that 42 (the Queen) happens to bee intangled in a promise (over the two bishoprics) that is extreamly inconvenient & upon which so much weight is layd, & such inferences made that to effect this promise would bee destructive & at the same time 42 (the Queen) is uneasy with every body that but endeavours to shew the consequences which attend it; . . ."[37] But all would be well if only Marlborough were home. "I long extreamly to see you here, for till you come I doubt nothing will goe right . . . 38 (Godolphin himself) labours as much as he can, and trys every way that can bee thought of, to prevent 42's (the Queen's) spoiling every thing, but I am much afrayd twill bee too late, unless Mr. Freeman helps to make a Solemn Treaty, from which there is to bee no parting upon any terms whatsoever, without which it will bee next to impossible for Mr. Montgomery to continue where he is and the consequence of that, I need not enlarge upon to you; . . ."[38]

In his reply Marlborough depreciated the value of his presence in England; but he promised to be governed by Godolphin's advice, and added sadly ". . . it looks as if it were resolved by destiny that nothing should go well this winter."[39] The same day he wrote to his wife, who had been posting him with the enormities of Abigail Masham. "What you say of 256 (Mrs. Masham) is very odd;" admitted John, "and if you think she is a good weathercock, it is hie time to leave off struggling; for believe me, nothing is worth rowing against wind and tyde, at least you will think so when you come to my age."[40] Excellent advice! If only Sarah could have taken it! But he might just as well have addressed his words to a stone!

When at last, later in the same month, Marlborough set foot on English soil, he found all in confusion. The indignant Whigs had come to a secret understanding with the more violent Tories, and the unhappy Lord Treasurer stood between the crossfire of the two parties. The proceedings in Parliament were violent and uncontrolled. Peterborough was attacked for his conduct in Spain: the administration of the Admiralty was subjected to a minute and hostile investigation; and, though Admiral Churchill defended himself and the council with warmth and ability, it seemed as if the Godolphin administration, buffeted on the rocks of confusion, must needs go down amid the swirling waters of party strife.

Amid the welter of these events, it gradually dawned upon Godolphin and Marlborough that their only way of escaping from the storm was to regain the confidence of their former supporters in the Whig party. They accordingly looked hopefully in that direction, and were gratified to find that their advances were not too coolly received. After much palaver, therefore, some sort of temporary reconciliation was patched up between the warring factions. The Queen, of course, was indignant, but she had to bow before the storm. True, she had gone too far to recede from her promises in respect of the two Tory bishops; but she gave a definite undertaking that she would not repeat the offence, and as some evidence of her future intentions she bestowed the see of Norwich on Sunderland's ex-tutor and lifelong friend, Dr. Trimnell, and the office of Regius Professor of Divinity at Oxford on Marlborough's Whig candidate, Dr. Potter, destined one day to be Archbishop of Canterbury.

The reconciliation between the Ministers and the Whigs rendered inevitable the fall of Harley. Yet for a time both Godolphin and Marlborough hesitated, and in their vacillation the intended victim thought he saw his chance. He accordingly wrote asking Godolphin to receive him at his house at 8 o'clock the same evening, and requesting the presence of the

Duke of Marlborough at the interview. Godolphin agreed; but his reply clearly displayed his surprise and suspicion.[41]

It is doubtful if the meeting had any beneficial effect for Harley, for the Secretary's credit was further damaged at this moment by the arrest of Greg, a clerk in his office, and of two smugglers, all of whom he had employed as spies, on charges of conveying secret information to the enemy. Furthermore, though we have no certain knowledge as to what passed between Harley, Godolphin and Marlborough at their secret meeting on the evening of December 8th, it may be surmised that Harley sought to rock the Government by threatening that his friend St. John intended asking some awkward questions about the number of British troops in the Iberian peninsula at the time of Stanhope's defeat at Almanza in April 1707, well knowing that the numbers of those present would be very much less than those voted by Parliament. If that form of political blackmail was in Harley's mind, the threat completely failed. Godolphin and Marlborough stood firm. Three days later the Commons passed without a division an order that an account should be laid before the House of what troops were present at the battle and what other forces were in Spain and Portugal at that time. The figures were duly given and on January 29th the Commons debated the matter. The fact that it was that very night that Godolphin, his patience at last exhausted, sent the Attorney General to Harley to inform him that he no longer possessed his confidence has led to the deduction that this was the result of Harley's conduct in promoting the debate.[42] This, however, appears not to be the case. The Ministers had plenty of evidence against their colleague, and the resolution to force Harley out had been taken some weeks earlier.[43] All that the debate on January 29th did was to enable the Whigs to reveal the price of their support—the removal of the Tory Ministers. Godolphin and Marlborough perforce agreed to their terms.[44]

When Harley received Godolphin's message late in the evening of January 29th, he pretended to be in no way disconcerted, and he appealed to Marlborough whom he affected to look upon as his friend. The General no doubt spoke clearly and to the point; whereupon Harley wrote one of his usual letters to the Lord Treasurer. "Last night Mr. Attorney acquainted me that I had fallen under your Lordship's displeasure;" he wrote blandly, "he would not tell me any particulars. This I could not but receive with the utmost grief, and had it not been so late I had given your Lordship the trouble of a letter to desire leave to wait upon you, to clear myself. This morning my Lord Duke of Marlborough gave me permission to attend him upon a like occasion, and his Grace was pleased to tell me the particulars. I know it is impossible to ward against misrepresentations or misconstructions, or the applications of things said generally to a particular purpose which was never thought of; for I do solemnly protest I never entertained the least thought derogating from your Lordship or prejudicial to your interest. I am confident in my own innocency, and I know no better way to clear myself than to desire your Lordship will let me by my actions demonstrate the uprightness of my intentions, and my zeal and duty for your Lordship's person and service."[45] Godolphin's reply was shattering. "I have received your letter," he wrote, "and am very sorry for what had happened to lose the good opinion I had so much inclination to have of you, but I cannot help seeing and hearing, nor believing my senses. I am very far from having deserved it from you. God forgive you!"[46]

The reluctance of Queen Anne to part with her favourite minister had still to be overcome. In spite of everything she remained adamant; indeed, if need be she would form another Ministry and plans for this were actually circulated. It was now clear to Marlborough and Godolphin that they must not waver. They accordingly informed Anne that if Harley was not dismissed they would straightway resign. On the principle of divide and conquer, Anne showed little concern at the prospect of losing Godolphin's services, but she implored the General not to forsake her. But Marlborough was not to be moved; he would stand by his friend.

The Cabinet Council met at the appointed hour. Her Majesty presided and Mr. Secretary Harley proceeded to open the business of the meeting. But two seats at the Council were empty, and the members present, at first seemingly absorbed in reflection, gradually began to murmur beneath their breath. Harley paused; and after an awkward silence, the Duke of Somerset rose. "I do not see," he said, "how we can deliberate, when the Commander-in-chief and the Lord Treasurer are absent." No one moved. The Queen sat silent, and Harley shuffled in his place. Then Somerset repeated his remarks. The spell was broken, and Anne, hurriedly breaking up the meeting, withdrew in anger and dismay. The next day she told Marlborough bitterly that Harley was resigning his place.

Thus were the Whigs triumphant, and Godolphin and Marlborough came in on the flood. Only some two years were to pass before the tide was to turn, and they were destined to go out on the ebb.

CHAPTER VII

THE WHIGS TRIUMPHANT

THE fall of Harley was followed by the retirement of St. John, Harcourt and
Mansell. Henry Boyle, a moderate Whig, replaced Harley as Secretary of
State, and John Smith, the Whig Speaker, became Chancellor of the Exchequer. For the post of Attorney General Godolphin pressed the claims
of Sir John Montagu, Halifax's brother, but the Queen refused to agree
and the post was long left vacant. Perhaps Anne was supported in her
stiff-necked attitude by her fallen favourite, for it is certain that Abigail
Masham was still at her elbow. Through her agency, "while she lived at
her Little House over against the gate that goes into Windsor Castle,"
wrote Sarah Marlborough many years later, "Harley and his friends saw the
Queen as often as they pleased. Those that saw the Queen that were not to
be known, came in from the Park into the garden, and from thence Abigail
carried them a back way to the Queen's closet, which kept this correspondence secret for some time."[1] But by far the most interesting appointment
made at this time was that of the gifted son of a Norfolk squire to replace
Henry St. John, for young Robert Walpole, already noticed by both
Godolphin and Marlborough for his remarkable abilities, was made Secretary at War. He was destined to run a great course ere his day was done.

It was soon apparent that the triumphant Whigs would not for long be
satisfied with these appointments to the Ministry, and ere long they were
pressing for other of their leaders to be taken into royal favour. Their
first choice was the mild-tempered Somers, to whom neither Godolphin nor
Marlborough had the slightest objection; and even before the General's
return to the Continent, the patient Lord Treasurer was striving to make
Anne see the necessity for placating the Junto by his appointment as President
of the Council. But the Queen reacted sharply to Godolphin's submissions:
she had been made to accept Sunderland and others she detested; nothing
would induce her to accept yet another from the same camp. Meanwhile, the Whigs were becoming impatient, and Godolphin, relaxing at
Newmarket for a few days early in April, implored Marlborough to return
from The Hague at the very first opportunity to ". . sett things upon a

tolerable foot, which otherwise are like to come to great Extremitys next winter in the opinion of your humble servant. . . ."[2]

Unfortunately, Marlborough was forced to visit the Elector of Hanover and it was not until early in May that he returned to The Hague. There he found further urgent letters from home. In one Godolphin anticipated seeing him in London shortly.[3] In another he was less hopeful. This depressed him for ". . . I had much sett my heart upon the hopes of seeing you & endeavouring once more to have sett Mrs. Morley's affaires upon a right footing. . . ." But he had just learnt of his friend's intention to go to Hanover. Nothing could be more vexing, for he felt himself helpless without him. "It will bee looked upon here," he wrote querulously, "as a very full conviction that any place is more agreable than England; . . ."[4] And again a few days later he wrote, ". . . Mrs. Morley continues so very difficult to doe any thing that is good for her self, that it puts us into all the distraction & uneasyness imaginable." Then he put his finger on where the responsibility for Anne's obstinacy truly lay. "I really believe this humour proceeds more from her husband then from herself, and in him it is very much kept up by your bro: G: (Marlborough's brother George), who seemed to mee as wrong as is possible, when I spoke to him the other day, & finding him so, I spoke so freely and so fully to him, if things were to goe on at this rate; he appeared to bee much less resolute, after I had talked awhile to him, & thanked mee for speaking so freely. If he did not do this out of cunning, I believe your taking notice to him that Mr. Montgomery seemed to fear he putt Mrs. Morley upon wrong measures, might possibly have no ill effect, but you are the best judg of this."[5] Marlborough, thoroughly irritated at the vagaries of brother George, was sympathetic. Six months later he was to write him a blistering letter, as Sidney now advised; but the time was not yet.

Whilst the friends were thus corresponding, Sarah was striving to avoid further disagreements with the Queen by absenting herself from Court. Both Godolphin and her husband doubted the wisdom of that course. Was not that the very thing that Harley and Abigail most wanted? Furthermore, as Marlborough told his wife, he did not propose to return that winter, because he could do no good in England so long as the Queen would not listen to his advice. So much for the pleadings of the hard-pressed Lord Treasurer!

Meanwhile, the Whigs continued to press Lord Somers's claims and early in May the moderate Whig Dukes of Newcastle and Devonshire were closeted with the Queen in an effort to make her yield. But Anne pleaded with stolid obstinacy that it would be a great hardship to remove Lord Pembroke. The two Dukes parried this by proposing that Somers should be called to the Cabinet Council without holding any office. This took the Queen by surprise; but she quickly recovered her poise. Was not the suggestion unusual? Precedents were quoted to her: whereupon she averred that the Cabinet Council was full enough already. This terminated the audience: the two Dukes left "in much discontent." But Anne too was "very uneasy", and the next morning she summoned Mr. Montgomery to tell him her troubles. ". . . he told her that the matter was much changed by this proposall, & that he could not but think it entirely for her service to accept of it, that it was a very small condescension, if they would bee satisfied with it, that it gained her poynt absolutely in relation to Lord P(embroke), that it would make all her affairs easy at once, & that if Mr. Freeman were in town he was sure it would bee his mind as much as it was Mr. Montgomerys. She seemed still very uneasy and very unwilling, but she said she would write to Mr. Freeman about it tonight or to-morrow. I hope therefore you will endeavour to prevail with him to make such an answer to her, as this thing may bee no longer delayd; for as it stands now you will give me leave to say the refusall is of much worse consequence, & exposes her much more than as it stood before; if Mr. Freeman has no mind to enter into particulars, why might not he answer in generall that hee begs her to comply with Mr. Montgomery's desires in this affaire who he is sure will never propose any thing to her, but what shall bee as much for her honour as for her advantage. . . ."[6]

The Queen was as good as her word. She wrote to Mr. Freeman the very same day, giving him an account of the visit paid her by the Lord Privy Seal and the Lord Steward, and the arguments they had marshalled against her. These, she told him, did not convince her. She then reverted to the Lord Treasurer, who had supported the Dukes' proposals ". . . using a great many arguments to persuade me to comply with it, and I must own to you, did not convince me any more than what I had heard before on the same subject; though I have a much greater respect for him than for either of the others looking upon it to be utter destruction to me to bring Lord Somers into my service. And I hope you will not join in soliciting me in this thing, though lord treasurer tells me you will; for it is what I can never consent to."[7]

Marlborough was evidently annoyed at the Queen's letter and on May 8th he assured Godolphin that he would reply to her in accordance with his wishes, for her obstinacy "is a plain declaration to all the world that you and I have no credit, and that all is governed underhand by Mr. Harley and Mrs. Masham."[8] The next day he replied to Anne, sending a copy of his letter to Godolphin and Sarah.[9] First he dealt with foreign affairs. With regard to affairs at home he hastened to disabuse the Queen of her anticipation of a

Tory victory in the forthcoming election, for the party's support for the Pretender would be fatal to their electoral prospects. In these circumstances, he begged Anne, "for God's sake" to consider the consequences of her refusing the two Dukes' request; ". . . it will be," he told her, "a demonstration not only to them, but to every body, that lord treasurer and I have no credit with your majesty, but that you are guided by the insinuation of Mr. Harley." Finally, he begged her earnestly to "let no influence or persuasion hinder you, not only in this, but in all your worldly affairs, to follow the advice and good counsel of lord treasurer, who will never have any thought but what is for your honour and true interest."[10]

In face of all, however, Anne remained as hostile as ever to the Whigs, as evidenced by her shameful neglect of Sir George Byng, the Whig Admiral, in spite of his great services to the Crown. On other matters, too, she was "extreamly obstinate", as Godolphin told Marlborough, not only in the way she stood out against Lord Somers, but ". . . in the matter relating to 41's (Halifax's) brother, (she) is as inflexible to all that can bee said upon that subject by all those who have access to 237 (her) & are concerned that 89 (the Whigs) should not bee divided; for tis most certain 42 (the Queen) might yett easily prevent it by a very little compliance with Mr. Montgomery's advice in the matter of 5 (Somers)."[11] And a few days later, when Marlborough's letter from Ghent of May 9th was handed to her ". . . she layd it down upon her table, & would not open it, while I stayd in the room," Godolphin reported, "by which I am afrayd, it is not like to have any more effect than some other representations of the same kind have had from your humble servant. . . ."[12]

There followed two conversations of two hours apiece between Mrs. Morley and Mr. Montgomery at the end of which Anne remained "inflexible" as Godolphin put it, ". . . & disclaims any talk or the least Commerce with Mr. H(arley) or first or second hand & is positive that she never speaks with any body but 41 (Prince George) upon any things of that kind. From whence 41's (Prince George's) notions come is not hard to conjecture; . . ." From George Churchill of course! "Upon the whole Mr. Montgomery's life is a burthen to him, and like to bee soe more & more every day."[13] Whilst Godolphin and his Sovereign were thus arguing, the general talk was of the forthcoming elections. "Every body here is busy at present about Elections, & the talk of them," Godolphin told Marlborough, ". . . & there is little reason to doubt, but the next parliament will bee very well inclined to support the Warr, and I hope to doe every thing else that is reasonable, if they can have but reasonable encouragement, all seems to turn upon that. Mrs M(orley) continues to bee very inflexible. I still think that must alter, my only fear is that it will bee too late."[14]

In the event Godolphin and Marlborough proved far better election prophets than Queen Anne's secret advisers. Indeed, it is strange how the Tory chiefs could have given Anne any hopes of a victory, for their party fought the election under a grave disadvantage. Only a few months previously had the attempted invasion been thwarted. What splendid electoral ammunition this supplied to the Whigs, who in speeches and manifestos strove with conspicuous success to confound their opponents with the Jacobites and the French. No wonder that the Whigs secured a majority of more than a hundred over their opponents and that the Lords of the Junto, jubilant at their victory, returned in no very happy mood for compromise. One of their number, the outspoken Sunderland, did not moderate his words. "I heartily Congratulate with your Grace upon the Elections throughout England, being so well over as they are," he wrote delightedly to Newcastle, "I think one may venture to say it is the most Whig Parliament has been since the revolution, so that if our friends will stick together and act like men, I am sure the court must, whither they will or no, come into such measures as may preserve both us and themselves; . . ."[15]

In spite of the Whig triumph, however, Anne still would not yield. She summoned the Lord Treasurer. An awkward interview ensued. ". . . I am now going to give you an account of one (conversation) this morning betwixt Mr. Montgomery & Mrs. Morley, which ended with the greatest dissatisfaction possible to both. They have had of late, many great contests, I am told upon the subject of 4 (Halifax's) brother but without any ground gained on either side. This day it held longer than ever. The particulars as they have been repeated to mee* are both too tedious and unnecessary to trouble you with them. In short, the obstinacy was unaccountable & the battel might have lasted till (now) if after the clock had struck 3 41 (Prince George) had not thought fitt to come in and look as if he thought it were dinnertime."[16] Even the otiose Prince George, it seems, had his uses!

The attitude of Sunderland not unnaturally infuriated the Queen. It also profoundly disturbed his father-in-law and Godolphin. Indeed, it was unpardonable, and clearly showed him to have loyalty only to the Junto. What an opportunity for Harley up the backstairs to fan Anne's dislike of him! He had made use of her name in the Election for party purposes; he had been disloyal to his colleagues in the Government: this was the man who had been forced upon her, contrary to her wishes and better judgment. The first charge he denied, so Anne told Godolphin, "but at the same time owned he had writ his own thoughts about the election to some Lords of the Squadron, as they call them; and I find by all his discourse on that subject he

* So worded to conceal the cipher.

intends to continue in opposition to what I think for my service. . . ." Then she reminded Godolphin of his promise made at the time of Sunderland's appointment, that in the event of his offending her he should be removed from his post.[17] ". . . it is such a behaviour, I believe, as never was known," she wrote bitterly to Marlborough, "and what I really cannot bear, nor what no other I dare say would one minute: . . ." Nevertheless out of consideration she will defer Sunderland's dismissal for the moment. "I have told all my thoughts pretty freely to 10 (Godolphin) on the subject," she added, "and I do not doubt but what he will give you an account of what passed between us, and what his opinion is, and therefore will not say more upon a subject, which must be so disagreeable to you, only that it is impossible to bear such usage; and I am sure you are too reasonable, if you consider this matter impartially, to blame me when I send for the seals, and be assured I shall ever be the same sincere and faithful friend to you as ever."[18]

All this was too much for the long-suffering Lord Treasurer, and at last in desperation he tendered his resignation to the Queen. He announced this in a letter to his friend. "42 (the Queen) continues so averse to every thing Mr. Montgomery can propose for the support of Mrs. Morleys affairs," he wrote, "that he is soe tired out of his life at present, and has so little prospect of any tolerable ease in the Winter, that he has been obliged once or twice to begg of 42 (the Queen) either to follow his notions or to dismiss him, & not let him bear the burthen & load of other people's follys, but all this hitherto has been to no purpose & seems to make no manner of impression." Then there was the trouble over Prince George and the administration of the Admiralty, which did not mend. "He is sometimes uneasy at the apprehensions of what he shall meet with, but unadvisable in what is proper to prevent it, whether from his own temper, or made so by 82 (George Churchill) I cannot judg. But 82 (George Churchill) is not, at least seems not to bee without his own unhappynesses too, in which I always confirm him when Wee talk together, and he appears to bee upon those occasions very much of my mind, but, however, he has great animosity's, & partialitys, & he either cannot, or will not prevail with 41 (Prince George) to doe any good." In view of all this, it seems impossible to carry on. "This being the case here, at present & not very likely to mend before 88's coming to town (the meeting of parliament), I had a mind . . . to prepare you to expect that it will not bee possible for 38 (me) to continue as he is (I am) till 88's arrivall (the meeting of parliament) unless it may consist with Mr. Freeman's affairs to see 108 (England) and settle measures both with 38 & 44 (me and the Queen) before the arrival of 88 (the parliament), for at least 15 days."[19]

The thought of losing Godolphin's services alarmed the General on the point of defeating the French at Oudenarde. He had ignored the Queen's two last letters, having greater anxieties to fill his mind; but if the Lord Treasurer should go, he was determined to go also. Anne knew this perfectly well and she dreaded to lose the two greatest of her servants. She early got wind of Godolphin's intentions, for at the very moment that Marlborough was harvesting the spoils of victory on the Scheldt, she wrote a mollifying letter. She was sorry he should have thoughts of retiring; but until he can see how things are at home, she was sure he could come to no settled resolution. "What you desire concerning Lord Treasurer was not at all necessary," she added, "for I have so true a sense of his friendship to me, and so real a value and esteem for him; that if ever anybody should endeavour to do him any ill office, it would have no effect upon me ... great care must be taken that no cause be given to our friends abroad to think that there is any fear of business going ill in England, and you may be sure I will advise in everything with those you desire; the partys are such bugbeares that I dare not venture to write my mind freely of either of them without a cypher for fear of any accident. I pray God keep me out of the hands of both of them."[20]

Even as the Queen was penning these words, Marlborough was winning the great battle of Oudenarde. From the camp, he hastened to write a few hurried lines to his beloved Sarah for her to show to Anne. He concluded them thus: "I do, and you must, give thanks to God for His goodness in protecting and making me the instrument of so much happiness to the Queen and Nation, *if she will please to make use of it*"[21] These words clearly nettled the Queen. "... I was showed a letter the other day, by a friend of yours, that you writ soon after the battle," she replied, "and I must beg that you will explain to me one expression in it. You say, after being thankful for being the instrument of so much good to the nation and me, *if I would please to make use of it*. I am sure I never will make an ill use of so great a blessing, but according to the best of my understanding, make the best use of it I can, and should be glad to know what is the use you would have me make of it, and then I will tell you my thoughts very freely and sincerely."[22]

Marlborough's reply to this letter was a grave but dignified protest at the treatment he had received at her hands. He was particularly reproachful of her attitude to his son-in-law, and he earnestly begged her to suspend judgment on the matter until such time as he could return and meet her face to face. "For God's sake, madam," he continued, "consider, that whatever may be said to amuse or delude you, it is utterly impossible for you to have ever more than a part of the Tories: and though you could have them all, their number is not capable of doing good. These things are so plain that I don't doubt but your majesty will be convinced nothing can be so fatal to your service, as any way to discourage the Whigs, at this time, when after the blessing of this victory, you may be sure, that if you show a confidence in their zeal for your interests, they will all concur very cheerfully to make you great and happy, as I wish. God Almighty bless and preserve you." In a postscript* he dealt in a very frank manner with the phrase that had nettled the Queen. "What I then meant," he explained, "as I must always think is, that you can make no good use of this victory, nor of any other blessing, but by following the advice of my lord treasurer, who has been so long faithful to you; for any other advisers do but lead you into a labyrinth, to play their own game at your expense. Nothing but your commands should have obliged me to say so much, having taken my resolution to suffer with you, but not to advise, being sensible that if there was not something very extraordinary, your majesty would follow the advice of those that have served you so long, faithfully and with success."[23] Plain speaking on a well-worn theme!

And still the Queen remained obdurate: and still, though she must have known that neither Marlborough nor Godolphin would believe her, she continued to asseverate that she had no backstairs advisers. "I am very sorry to find you persist in your resolution of not advising me concerning my home affairs;" she wrote, "but I would beg your pardon for disobliging your commands in that particular, it being impossible for me, who have on all occasions spoke and writ my mind very freely, as I think every friend ought to do to one another, to forbear doing the same still, and asking your opinion in every thing; there being nobody but you and lord treasurer that I do advise with, nor can rely on, which I will yet hope you will believe, since I tell you so, you having more than once or twice assured me you would credit what I said." Alas, vain hope! Much had happened lately to strain her servants' credulity! "Though I must confess, by what I am told every day of my being influenced by Mr. Harley, through a friend of his, and your saying you are sensible that if there were not something very extraordinary I should follow the advice of lord treasurer and you, I fear you have not a thorough good opinion of me, and if that be so, it is in vain for me to say any thing." Alas for her credit with posterity that she said so much! "However, I can't help asking, why my not complying with some things that are desired, and which you know I have ever been against, should be imputed to something extraordinary? Is not one body of your

---

* The draft of the body of the letter appears to have been written by Marlborough and corrected by Sarah and Godolphin. The copy of the letter actually sent is in the Duchess's hand, with the parts omitted underlined. The postscript is entirely in the Duke's hand.

opinion, and *one of another*:* and why then should it be so wonderful that you and I should differ in some things, was well as other people, especially since my thoughts are the same of the Whigs that ever they were from the time that ever I have been capable of having notions of things and people; and I must own I can see no reason to alter mine."[24]

This reply from the Queen made the most painful impression upon Marlborough. "I have had a good deal of struggle with myself whether I should burn it, or send it you to show lord treasurer," he wrote to Sarah on August 9th. But in the end he decided to let them see the letter: but he conjured them to keep the contents secret "which has thoroughly convinced me that there is no washing a blackamoor white"—a phrase the Queen had used—"and that we must expect this next winter all the disagreeableness imaginable; for the Tories have got the heart and entire possession of the queen, which they will be able to maintain as long as Mrs. Masham has credit. I do earnestly beg," he continues, "when Mr. Montgomery has read Mrs. Morley's letter and this of mine to you, that they may both be torn to pieces, so that they may never hurt Mrs. Morley, whom I can't but love and endeavour to serve as long as I have life; for I know this is not her fault, otherwise than by being too fond of Mrs. Masham, who imposes upon her."[25] Alas for the Queen's credit that Sarah did not obey her lord's injunction in this matter!

Meanwhile, Sunderland continued to cabal against the government of which he was a member and against his fellow Ministers, including his own father-in-law. Early in August he wrote to Newcastle from Althorp, where he was confined with a sprained foot, an accident that prevented him from visiting the Duke at Welbeck. This he regretted, as he was anxious for a discussion of public affairs. Our fortunes abroad had somewhat mended thanks to the victory of Oudenarde and to Admiral Wager's successful action against the Spanish treasure galleons from Porto Bello about which Sunderland had written enthusiastically to Marlborough only three months earlier;[26] but at home things "seem to grow worse and worse every day," he wrote, "for without running over all the Particulars, such as the villainous management of Scotland, the state of the fleet which is worse than ever, the Condition of Ireland in which the Protestant interest is lower, and the Popish higher than ever; their late management in relation to the invasion, and in particular the pardoning Ld. Griffin, is a declaration to the whole world, as far as in them lies for the Prince of Wales, and against the Protestant succession, there are such proceedings that if there is not a just spiritt shewn in Parliament we had as good give up the Cause, and submitt

* The Queen's italics.

to My Ld. Treasurer's and My Ld. Marlborough's bringing in the Prince of Wales; . . ."27 No wonder Anne disliked Sunderland!

But indeed, the Whigs had become so inflamed at the Queen's evident hostility that there were scarcely any lengths to which the impetuous Sunderland and his associates would not go to advance their cause; and during this summer of 1708 they revived with enthusiasm the proposal of inviting the Electoral Prince to take up his residence in England. This of course infuriated Anne, who implored Marlborough to see the Prince in order to put any such idea out of his mind . . . "that the difficulty may not be brought upon me of refusing him leave to come if he should ask it, or forbidding him to come, if he should attempt it; for one of these two things I must do if either he or his father should have any desires to have him see this country, it being a thing I cannot bear, to have my successor here, though but for a week."28 This pathetic appeal moved Marlborough to indignation, and he assured his wife that as to the Queen he would never do anything . . . "that looks like flying in her face."29 And again: "You and Lord Sunderland may be assured that I have no intentions or thoughts but that of deserving well from England, and consequently must and will depend on the friendship of the Whigs; and if my good intentions are not seconded with success, I think I shall have nothing justly to reproach myself withal, so that I may retire with quietness and honour."30

This theme of retirement "with quietness and honour" is much in the letters of both Marlborough and Godolphin throughout these critical August days. For a time Anne affected to be unmoved by their embarrassment: indeed she ignored it as if they had nothing of which to complain. At length, however, she became alarmed. How could she spare the great general who had brought so much glory to her arms? How could she spare the great Lord Treasurer whose financial and administrative genius had made those victories possible? They must at all costs be dissuaded from fulfilling their threat. She would not yield one whit in regard to her trusted Harley or her faithful Masham, but she would employ fair words to allay the suspicions of her two tiresome Ministers. Prevarication should be her weapon. Anne was a Stuart indeed!

And so the Queen wrote to Marlborough. She could never consent to his retirement and she appealed to his sense of duty to his countrymen not to desert them. A master stroke! Then she turned to Godolphin. "Lord treasurer talks of retiring too, and told me, not many days ago, he would do all he could to serve me, by advising with people, and settling a scheme for the carrying on my business in the parliament, before he went to Newmarket; but that he would not come back from thence. I told him that must not be, that he could not answer it either to God or himself; and I hope you will both consider better of it, and not to an action that will bring me and your country to confusion. Is there no consideration to be had for either? You may flatter yourselves that people will approve of your quitting; but if you should persist in these cruel and unjust resolutions, believe me, where one will say you are in the right, hundreds will blame you." Meanwhile, Godolphin has, she told Marlborough, gone off to a meeting of the lords of the Whig Junto, who do not wish her well and ever since parliament has risen ". . . have been disputing my authority, and are certainly designing, when the new one meets, to tear that little prerogative the crown has to pieces." In the face of the manifest hostility of the Whig chiefs, how can one, she asked, "when one knows and sees all these things, as plainly as the sun at noon-day, ever (to) take these people into my bosom? For God's sake, save me from the five lords of the Junto! For God's sake, do but make it your own case, and consider then what you would do, and why a handful of men must awe their fellow-subjects. There is nobody more desirous than I to encourage those Whig friends that behave them- selves well; but I do not care to have anything to do with those that have shown themselves to be of so tyrannising a temper; and not to run on farther on those subject, to be short, I think things are come to, whether I shall submit to the five Tyrannising lords, or they to me. This is my opinion on the disputes at present, which could not be, if people would weigh and state the case just as it is, without partiality on one side or the other, which I beg, for the friendship you have ever professed for me you would do; and let me know your thoughts of what may be the best expedient, to keep me from being thrown into the hands of the five lords."[31]

We do not know precisely what answer the Duke returned to Queen Anne's pressing appeal, but there is extant a draft in Lord Godolphin's hand, which gives us the general tenor. It is undoubtedly in the style of the Lord Treasurer, but it may be regarded as embodying both his and the Duke's views on this matter.

"As to the reflections your majesty is pleased to make upon my *real* inclinations to retire, tho' it be very natural and very desirable, after one has lived a great many years in a hurry, to enjoy some quiet in one's old age; yet I will own freely to your majesty, my inclinations to retire proceed chiefly from finding myself incapable of being of any further use to your majesty. The long and faithful services I have endeavoured to perform to your majesty, and the goodness you had expressed to me upon several occasions, had created a general opinion, both abroad and at home, that your majesty placed entire trust and confidence in me; and upon that foot I was the more capable of doing many great and effectual services, both here abroad and in England. But your majesty will give me leave to say, with all imaginable duty, that is now reduced singly to serving you at the head of the army this campaign; for your majesty having shown so publicly, last winter and this spring, that you have no more trust and confidence in me, nor any reliance upon my opinion, but much more upon the opinion of those who have neither honesty nor capacity to serve you, and who visibly ruined your service last winter in several undeniable instances, it is no longer possible for me to be of any further use to you; and to continue in your council to advise, without credit enough to prevail with you to follow good advice, would only expose myself and my reputation in the world, by making myself answerable for other people's follies or worse."

"And by what your majesty is pleased to say in your letter of the lord treasurer, tho' I have nothing so far as that from himself, I believe his opinion, and his reasons for that opinion must be the same with mine. Your majesty is pleased to think we shall be blamed for quitting; but, not to reflect upon that coldness, and that behaviour in yourself, which forces us to quit, by withdrawing your trust and confidence from us, to give it to insinuating, busy flatters, who can't serve you one month this winter without danger of being torn in pieces in the streets. I don't doubt but these things are very sensible to the Lord treasurer, as I am sure they are to me. However, I shall not trouble your majesty any farther with the consequences that must follow, since I find plainly by your majesty's letter, that all I have said and written hitherto is to no purpose, nor indeed, ever can be, while your majesty's heart is possessed by all the false and malicious insinuations which are possible to be suggested by your enemies; and therefore, I shall conclude this head, with wishing your majesty may find abler servants than we have been; more faithful and affectionate, I will beg leave to say you never can."

This draft was submitted to the Duchess, and we find several small emendations in her hand. What follows is on a separate sheet, also in Lord Godolphin's writing and without alteration: it is evidently a continuation.

"As to the tyranny of the five lords, which you seem so much to apprehend, and so much to desire that you might be kept out of their hands, if your majesty were disposed to hearken to the advice of those who have supported you for almost seven years upon the throne, and much more before you came to it, you would be in no danger of falling into their hands but ours, whom you did not, till very lately, used to think dangerous; and certainly we have not altered. But a maxim I have often heard, that 'interest cannot lie', we have no other interest but your majesty's, and to make your throne powerful and your government strong. But your majesty will allow some people may have an interest to our prejudice; they may have an interest to create difficulties every day in your majesty's

THE EARL OF GODOLPHIN, K.G.
LORD TREASURER
From the portrait by Sir Joshua Reynolds at Blenheim Palace

mind against us, and by that means to force us out of your service, and then, indeed, I am afraid you may be in very dangerous hands. But as to these five lords, if your majesty will be inclined to do such things only, as in themselves are not only just and reasonable, with regard to all that is past, but useful and necessary, for all that is to come, your majesty needs not to apprehend falling into any hands but ours, who have done you many faithful services, and who, whatever return we are like to have for them, will never fail to pray for your majesty's long life and prosperity."

"I have written this in a good deal of haste and disorder, and therefore I believe it wants no little correction; but you may omit or alter any part of it just as you please."[32]

Whilst these bickerings were being exchanged between Queen Anne and her Ministers, the indomitable Sarah was having a violent quarrel with her royal mistress. It arose over the Thanksgiving Service for the victory of Oudenarde. It was the duty of the Duchess of Marlborough, Mistress of the Robes, to lay out at St. James's the jewels for the Queen to wear on this great occasion. It was her duty, too, to drive with her majesty in the royal coach to St. Paul's Cathedral. On the way the Duchess noticed for the first time that her Majesty wore no jewels. We may surmise that thoughts of her husband, whom she had left upon what she must have known to be his death-bed, had prompted Anne to discard the finery that had been arranged for her adornment. To Sarah, however, things looked very differently. This was the way the Queen had chosen to demonstrate the handiwork of the hated Abigail. This was the way the Queen had chosen to show to the whole world that her beloved "Lord Marl's" favour was waning, and so it would be reported by the Ambassadors to their Courts. This was the way the Queen had chosen to wound her upon the Duke of Marlborough's festival. And so with bitter words she reproached her mistress as they drove in state through the thronged, cheering streets to give thanks to God for victory. What passed between them on that tragic drive we do not know: probably the Duchess did all the talking. But at the top of the Cathedral steps, where all the functionaries of state were arrayed to receive her Majesty, the Queen began a heated reply to these bitter reproaches. "Be quiet—not here," whispered Sarah, or words to that effect; and thus the two women passed into St. Paul's. Subsequently an acrimonious correspondence passed between them. The Duchess sent the Queen a letter from her husband, and accompanied it by an unseemly effusion of her own.[33] This drew a blistering reply from the Queen.[34] "After the commands you gave me in the church, on the thanksgiving, of not answering you, I should not have troubled you with these lines, but to return the Duke of Marlborough's letter safe into your hands."[35] A further outburst from Sarah[36] drew yet another reply from the Queen. It denied the charges of having withdrawn her favour from Marlborough and of having shown undue favour to Abigail; and it ended with these mollifying words; "I have nothing further to trouble my dear Mrs. Freeman with at this time, but that whatever opinion she may have of me, I will never deserve any that is ill but will always be her faithful Morley."[37] Was there still hope of an accommodation? Who can tell? But the position was not promising. Behind the Queen stood Harley and the Tories. Behind the Duchess stood Marlborough, Godolphin, and the Whigs. The Tories were for Peace; the Whigs for the Grand Alliance and the War. And facing them all stood, still proud, still erect—the mighty power of France![38]

As the weeks passed, the Whigs became more and more insistent in their demands for office and more and more resentful against the two Ministers who had done all in their power to advance their interests. Their sin was failure, and the Whig chiefs were determined to make them pay in full.[*] Towards the middle of October, Godolphin had an interview with the leading malcontents, including Devonshire, Bolton, Dorchester, Orford, Wharton, Somers and Halifax, assembled as guests of Sunderland at Althorp. There they delivered their ultimatum to the Lord Treasurer. They would not give any further support to the Court unless their grievances were met: they enumerated mismanagement and Tory bias in every branch of government; they demanded the retirement of Prince George from the office of Lord High Admiral, because they considered him to be under the thumb of the odious Admiral Churchill. If we can believe the obviously jaundiced account of this interview left to us by Sunderland, Godolphin strove to pacify the Whigs by affecting to agree with them, "as his way allways is in words," but enlarged on the difficulties which could only be overcome by the return of the Duke of Marlborough to England. This, it seems, went nowhere towards satisfying the malcontents, who demanded as a first step the appointment of their choice as Speaker. To all this, the Lord Treasurer made a proposal, "which was as ridiculous, as it shew'd the unsincerity of their intentions, to do anything that was right," that Prince George should be allowed to retain his post as Lord High Admiral, but to act solely through his Council. "It would be tedious to repeat all the objections the Lords made to this proposall as absurd, ridiculous, and ineffectual, and what no Parliament ever would hear of." Again according to Sunderland, Godolphin protested that he had already discussed this suggestion with the Lord Chan-

---

* According to one story Wharton had evidence of Godolphin's correspondence with St. Germain and blackmailed him in order to force an entrance for his colleagues and himself into the government. Hamilton, *Transactions during the Reign of Queen Anne,* 110–21. But no evidence has ever been produced in support of the statement.

cellor, and that he entirely approved; but that Cowper denied all recollection of any such conversation with the Lord Treasurer. "This extraordinary proceeding," continued Sunderland in his account to Newcastle, "has been a further Confirmation to these Lords of the reason they have to declare against the Court . . . and I am Confident when the Court see this, that the wigs [sic] will no longer be fool'd, they will then do all reasonable things, which they will never do, whilst they hope that words and promises will pass; . . ."[39]

The position of Admiral Churchill was highly vulnerable. Even if his financial record was pure, even if his administration was above reproach—and the Whigs suspected both—his politics were highly obnoxious to them. He was an extreme Tory, and he had had the bad taste to excite the Toryism of his chief, Prince George of Denmark. Furthermore, he had been instrumental in circulating a report that his brother had, at the instigation of Harley, given a regiment to a certain Colonel Jones, and he had cited Walpole, the Secretary at War, as his authority for the statement. This had been a considerable embarrassment for both Godolphin and Marlborough. It was clear that Churchill must go. Sarah had long been convinced of this and she had not been silent on the subject. This pained Marlborough, who seems to have had a strange affection for his brother. Several months previously Godolphin had been forced into the fray. He had had the unpleasant task of writing frankly to his absent friend, answering questions about the erring Admiral. He did so with great reluctance, "but since you required an account of the noise about 82 (Churchill) & Mr. Walpool [sic], I cannot but think he (i.e. Churchill) was very much to blame in that whole affair from the beginning to the end, but nobody is able to give so exact an account of the particulars as 85 (Craggs), who was himself a witness to the most materiall part of it. I must needs add, upon this occasion, that 82 (Churchill) does certainly contribute very much to keep us both in 41 & 42 (the Prince and the Queen) the naturall but very inconvenient averseness they have to 89 (the Whigs) in general, and to Sir G: Bing [sic] in particular, tho' Mr. Montgomery took all imaginable pains to reconcile them, & to give promises & assurances to each other, and nothing is more certain than that the generall dislike of 82 (Churchill) in that station is stronger than ever, & much harder to bee supported but nothing less than your Express Command should have made mee say so much to you upon so disagreeable a subject. . . ."[40] This indictment must have shaken the General: yet it was not till three months later that he wrote to his brother in uncompromising terms. By that time, as it seemed, the retirement of Churchill was the only hope left of saving the Queen from the mortification of a Parliamentary attack upon her beloved husband.

But it was nature that relieved her from this humiliation. All the summer the Prince had lain grievously ill of his asthma in the little house occupied by the Queen in Windsor Park. There Anne, assisted by Abigail, nursed him with wifely devotion. There Harley was frequently admitted in secret to see the Queen. There at last the Queen was forced to yield to the Whigs' demands. "42 (the Queen) is at last come to allow 38 (me) to make such condescentions, which if done in time, would have been sufficient to have eased most of our difficultys;" wrote Godolphin bitterly to Marlborough. If only the Whigs would be reasonable; if only his friend were in England for a short forty-eight hours, all might yet be well![41] His old cry. There was some delay in fulfilment of the Queen's promise, and the Junto were becoming impatient and angry. Then they learned the cause. Their enemy was dead. "Nature was quite worn out in him, and no art could support him any longer," wrote Godolphin of the Prince's end. "The Queen's affliction and the difficulty of speaking with that freedom and plainness to her, which her services requires, while she has soe tender a concern upon her, is a new additionall inconvenience which our circumstances did not need, and will make it still more necessary than ever that 39 & 109 should not delay their meeting (that you should not delay your return to England) for I really foresee that unless that can be compassed very very soon, it will bee next to impossible to prevent ruine."[42]

How the death of Prince George was viewed by the Junto is clearly expressed by the callous Sunderland. "Since I writt last to your grace,[43] and had the honour of your Answer, the Death of the Prince, has made so great an alteration in every thing, and particularly in what was most at every Body's heart, the affair of the Admiralty, that as soon as it happen'd those of our friends in the house of Commons, that were in Town, and that were the most zealous with us . . . begun to Press us to accommodate the matter, and nott to make a Division, since by this accident, there was room to have every think [sic] still right; since that My Ld. Treasurer has acquainted us, that the Queen had agreed to make Ld. Pembroke Ld. high Admirall, Ld. Somers President and Ld. Wharton Ld. Lieutenant of Ireland."[44] In short, the crisis was ended. The Junto Lords "marched into the conquered citadel of power."[45] The Whigs were triumphant indeed!

CHAPTER VIII

THE TURN OF THE TIDE

THE resignation of Churchill and the death of the Prince completed the triumph of the Whigs. The claims of the Junto could no longer be denied, for a refusal of their demands would mean that supplies would not be voted in the new House of Commons. This no doubt was extremely distasteful both to Godolphin and Marlborough, who had been nurtured on the theory that the Crown's servants were above party, but gradually it was becoming recognized that the party that had won the election must have its reward. This was met by the appointment of the moderate Pembroke to succeed Prince George at the Admiralty, Lord Wharton to the Lord Lieutenancy of Ireland, and, at Marlborough's especial request, the amiable Somers to the Presidency of the Council. Anne in her mourning was in no condition to continue the struggle, and the appointments were accordingly made without any further opposition.

But even in her hour of sadness the poor Queen, in whose weary body dropsy was beginning to manifest itself, was not vouchsafed any peace by the two women about her person. On hearing of the Prince's serious condition, Sarah had hastened to Kensington Palace. Though Anne's attitude was somewhat cold, her old friend strove manfully to play her part, and successfully pressed upon the Queen the advisability of removing from Kensington to St. James's: and even when Anne showed some partiality for the hated Abigail, the Duchess for once kept her head and her temper. For this she had her reward. After the departure of Lord Godolphin, summoned to make arrangements for the royal funeral, Anne went to Sarah's apartment and not finding her there left a pathetic little message that wafts a note of sadness down the centuries. "I scratched twice at dear Mrs. Freeman's door, as soon as lord treasurer went from me, in hopes to have spoken one more word to him before he was gone; but nobody hearing me, I wrote this, not caring to send what I had to say by word of mouth; which was, to desire him, that when he sends his orders to Kensington, he would give directions there may be a great many Yeoman of the Guard to carry the prince's dear body, that it may not be let fall, the great stairs being very steep and slippery."[1]

For the moment it seemed as if Sarah might regain at least some of her former influence over her mistress. But this was not to be. To the intense annoyance of both Sarah and Abigail, Anne shut herself up in her late husband's room, because, so the Duchess wrote many years later, "the back stairs belonging to it came from Mrs. Masham's lodgings, who by that means could secretly bring to her whom she pleased."[2] Abigail gives a somewhat different version, and her memory is likely to be the more accurate, for her complaint was written only a few days after the Prince's death. "I hope in God," she wrote to Harley on November 6th, "this affliction will have no ill effect upon her health, there is care taken she shall not be alone, for since the misfortune the Lady Pye (Sarah) has hardly left her so long as to let her say her private prayers but stays constantly with her. My Lady's friends say it is fit she should (and they hope she always will), to keep that jade my cousin Kate (Abigail herself) from her. Oh my poor aunt (the Queen) is in a very deplorable condition, for now her ready money (courage) is all gone, because I will not trouble you with a melancholy story (give me leave to repeat your own words) she has shut and bolted the door upon herself."[3] Probably the poor Queen's real object was to avoid the attentions of both these tiresome comforters!

The new Parliament, the first to be elected since the Union, met on November 18th, and the lower House promptly passed a vote of thanks to the Duke of Marlborough for his eminent services to the nation. In the Lords, however, things were very different, and Lord Haversham accused both Marlborough and Godolphin of negligence or treachery in connection with the recent invasion. It was clear that the Tories were seeking to revive the old charges against the two kinsmen of having corresponded with the exiled royal family. In their time of need, Marlborough and Godolphin might have expected to receive support from the Queen whom they had so faithfully served; but Anne, still smarting from the parts they played in forcing the Whig chiefs upon her and from the intemperate zeal of the Duchess, treated them with marked coolness. This disturbed Godolphin. All may look well from abroad, he told his friend; nevertheless, the credit of the government at home was in a "precarious condition;" "but what gives the greatest occasion for the present ferment at this time is that 42's (the Queen's) intimacy & present conversation seems to lean only to those who are enemies to all that are most usefull to the public service; ... That creates endless jealousy. But worse, it makes others who are willing to support the Government and are friends to the Administration uncertain to whom they should apply or upon whom they shall depend." And the remedy? "I know nothing so capable of remedying it, as your being here, whose authority, when it appeared plainly, would bee of so much weight as to extinguish much of this uneasyness if not remedy the whole."★ "I don't use to trouble you with complaints of my own circumstances," he wrote impatiently, "but soe much advantage is taken of your absence, and I suffer soe much, that I must give myself the vent of saying, the life of a slave in the galleys is paradise in comparison of mine; but at first the length of the campaign would not let you come, afterwards the States would not let you come, and now God Almighty won't let you. So I must yield to fate."[4]

Marlborough was distressed for his hard-pressed colleague. But what could he do to aid him? He was far from the scene of these brawls. He was immersed in continental affairs.

Whilst in the summer and autumn months of 1709, the indefatigable Duke was capturing Tournay, winning the battle of Malplaquet, and seizing Mons, the political feuds in the Cabinet were growing apace. Hostile Tories with unpardonable exaggeration began to denounce the "butcher's bill" that had to be paid for the Duke's great victory.[5] Meanwhile, the news from Portugal was not good, though this did not surprise Godolphin, who had long foreseen trouble there; but, as he told Marlborough, he did not see why it should affect the general war, save that ". . . it may encourage the Spaniards to flatter themselves, as they are apt enough to doe, that they are the bravest nation in Europe, & can defend Spain against the whole world, but it gives no ease to France, nor can any thing doe that but Peace; and even peace itself will scarce doe it, unless it bee imediat; . . ."[6] Towards the end of the month news arrived of France's rejection of the preliminary Treaty. Though many found fault with the peace when it seemed a certainty, wrote Godolphin, on news of it being broken off, ". . . the stocks fell 14 pr. cent in one day; tis true they had risen 20 pr. cent upon the news of the peace; I own however that it vexes one to have them fall so much, since I can see no ground to think the condition of France so much altered but that wee must quickly bring them either to the same Treaty, or a better one for the Allys. . . ."[7] But if England was certainly satisfied with the preliminary Treaty "tis also certain that we shall bee less able to support the Warr every year . . . but I believe wee shall always bee better able to doe it, than either of our Enemys or our neighbours; & surely tis better for us to continue the warr in conjunction with them at any rate, than to make such a peace with France, as will sett them wholly at ease, & have the weight of the warr with Spain

★ Godolphin to Marlborough, "Decr. 24. Christmas Eve." (1708). Blenheim MSS A. II. 38. Four days later he wrote to Marlborough specially to send him a letter from Willigo, their joint grandson. "The enclosed to you, from Willigo, is a piece so very particular that you will excuse the trouble of a second letter to send it." Godolphin to Marlborough, "Tuesday ye 28th 9 at night." December 1708, Blenheim MSS. A. II. 38.

wholly upon ourselves. . . ."⁸ In July came news of the fall of Tournay. This encouraged the Lord Treasurer to think that peace negotiations would soon follow, for the English fleet was having great success in stopping supplies of corn to France, and the misery amongst the French was reported to be widespread.⁹

At home, meanwhile, things were delusively quiet, but as Godolphin told his friend, ". . . great stress will be layd pretty soon about putting the Admiralty into some other management, I can easily agree the present is not to be supported next winter, but I am pretty sure 42 (the Queen) will not bee brought to doe what only will be liked, & if it bee not done the blame will be layd where it uses to bee in such cases. . . ."¹⁰ The Whigs were demanding that the Admiralty, over which Pembroke had presided since Prince George's death, should now be given to Orford, the only member of the Junto who had not regained office. But he was objectionable to Anne because of his attack upon her husband's administration, and she strongly resisted his appointment. Both Godolphin and Marlborough would have willingly obliged the Queen in this matter had they been able, but the Whigs were insistent, and they both had to advise her Majesty to yield. She did, and seemingly with a good grace; but the Lord Treasurer knew his mistress only too well, and he was certainly right in saying that the blame would be laid in the usual quarter.

But if on the surface politics seemed quiet during these summer months of 1709, the secretive Harley was laying his plans, and his activities were not unknown to Godolphin. Towards the end of July he wrote to Marlborough a remarkable letter recording a conversation he had had two days previously with Somers, who spoke to him with the utmost candour. "Hee told me," Godolphin recorded, "he had newly had a good deal of talk with an old acquaintance of his, to whom 199 (Harley) used to tell as much of his mind as to any body, & that having lately seen him 199 (Harley) had said enough to him to lett him see plainly what were the schemes and designs of him & of 84 (the Tories) when 88 comes to Town (Parliament meets). In the first place he layd it down for a foundation that Mr. Freeman and Mr. Montgomery were absolutely against 80 (the Peace)." He also declared "that he did not doubt but that 43 (Harley) would yett be able to fence so, this Summer, as to hinder 39's (Marlborough's) hopes of making 80 (the War) agreeable to 108 (England), if those were really his hopes. . . ." Furthermore, he was certain "39 (Godolphin) was as fond of 80 (Peace) as was possible . . ." but that in order to prevent awkward investigations ". . . they must have 81 (war) at any rate (cost), for that there was no attacking of Ministers, nor no naming maladministrations of any kind while 81 (war) was in being . . . and therefore, as formerly Mr. Caliban (the late King) had been forced into 80 (peace) so they must now force 42 (the Queen) by refusing necessarys for 81 (war) . . . and in case 43 (Harley) can bustle so, as he hoped, that 81 (war) should not in the mean time bee to the liking of 108 (England), then to impute that to 38 & 39 (Godolphin and Marlborough), but chiefly the latter, from which, he sayd, they could never gett off; . . ."[11]

So Harley's plottings were revealed. No wonder Godolphin should write a few days later, ". . . at home the politicians are buzyer than ever, especially 199 (Harley) who omitts no art nor industry to strengthen his party, or to spread all the malicious insinuations imaginable against Mr. Freeman and 38 (Godolphin), if one would believe 10 (Rivers), who is very deep in all their treasons & designs, I mean 84s & 199s (the Tories and Harley's) 10 (Rivers) seems to take it for granted that 28 (Shrewsbury) is very farr engaged with them, whether this bee really soe, or whether 10 (Rivers) finds he will not bee so much engaged as they desire, this is a little too deep for mee to penetrate, but so farr is certain, that 10 & 28 (Rivers and Shrewsbury) joyn entirely in open dislike of 5 & 6 & —(Somers, Sunderland and ?) &c; tis certain besides that 28 (Shrewsbury) has lately been with 42 (the Queen) upon pretence of speaking about their relations, but as 10 (Rivers) says, encouraged to it by 199 (Harley); to give Mrs. Morley right impressions, as he calls it; . . ." Then he adds: "10 (Rivers) professes to Mr. Montgomery more deference and concern for Mr. Freeman & 38 (Godolphin) than for all the rest of the world together, my opinion of that is, that he had endeavoured to gain his poynt by 199 (Harley) and finds it won't doe; . . ."[12] Thus the political world in July 1709!

In other quarters, however, wiser and more honest heads prevailed. In February £5,200,000 was voted by Parliament for supply. This was below the estimate, but if they could get but half of it, said Godolphin, they should be content and wind up the session as soon as possible.[13] A few days later we find him reporting to Marlborough that the subscription to the Bank was completed in two hours "with all the crowding & eagerness imaginable. . . .[14] A few months later he tells of a memorable interview he had just had with Sir Gilbert Heathcote, the Governor of the Bank of England. ". . . upon the strength of your victory I spoke yesterday to the bank," he wrote a few days after Malplaquet, "that, pursuant to the latitude given in the last Sessions of Parliament, they would now contract with mee for the circulation of 600,000£ more in Excheqr bills to the carrying on the public service. What I sayd seemed to bee pretty well received, & I hope it will succeed, but upon that occasion Sir Gilbert Heathcote, who is Governour, says to me, 'pray My Lord, don't lett us have a rotten peace;' 'Pray tell me,' I answered, 'what you call a rotten peace;' 'I call any thing,' he sayd, 'a rotten peace unless wee have Spayn,' 'But, Sir Gilbert,' I said, 'I want you a little to consider the circumstances of the Duke of Marlb: and of mee, wee are railed at every day, for haveing a mind, as they call it, to perpetuate the warr, & wee are told wee shall bee worryd next winter, for refusing a good peace, & insisting upon terms which it was impossible for France to perform.' Hee replied very quiet, 'They are a company of rotten rogues that tell you so. I warrant you, we'll stand by you. . . .' The Chancellor of the Exchequer & Mr. Gold Deputy Governr. of the Bank were both present at our discourse. . . ."[15] A week later he contracted with the Bank of England for another £1,000,000 in Exchequer Bills, which, he told Marlborough, "is one other good effect of your battell."[16] All this in spite of the fact that our affairs in Spain had sadly deteriorated during the year. But it shows the spirit of the City and the goodwill there felt for the government in this troublous time.

Meanwhile, the feud between the Duchess and the Queen reached its climax when Anne accused her former friend of having nothing so much at heart as the ruin of her rival, Abigail Masham. After all that had happened, Anne frankly told Sarah, their friendship was dead, though the Queen promised to treat the Duchess "as the Duke of Marlborough's wife, and as my groom of the stole."[17] In spite of the hopelessness of the position the unteachable Duchess, stung by the expressions in the Queen's letter, drew up a long and dreary narrative detailing the origin and progress of their intimacy: this she sent to Anne together with extracts from *The Whole Duty of Man*, the writings of Bishop Taylor and the directions in the liturgy that no one not at peace with his fellows should receive the Sacrament. Of this provocative epistle the Queen took no notice, beyond a brief promise to read it when she had the leisure. Nevertheless, one day as she went to Communion, Anne cast a good-natured smile at her erstwhile friend: but "The smile and the pleasant look," declared Sarah roundly, "I had reasons afterwards to think were given to Bishop Taylor and the Communion Prayer Book, and not to me."[18]

With relations between the Queen and the Duchess in this shape, it is hardly to be wondered at that Anne turned with renewed confidence and partiality to her young favourite, who never lost her temper, never wrote intemperate letters, and never disagreed on politics. And with the pliant Abigail in the closet, there was the insinuating Harley mounting the backstairs. As the influence of Godolphin and Marlborough waned, so the influence of Harley increased. And with solid Tory backing, Robin was a power in the land. Nevertheless this was not enough: and now Harley began to woo some of the more discontented elements among the Whigs. By a combination of charm and insinuating talk he won over Lord Rivers, hitherto an ardent party man. Then he turned his attention to that magnificent grandee, the "proud" Duke of Somerset, offended with Marlborough for not having conferred a regiment on his son. The self-important Duke in this mood was as clay in the hands of the potter. He was flattered by long audiences with the Queen. He was admitted to secret meetings at Harley's house, to which he rode in his sedan with all the mystery and furtiveness so dear to both intriguers.[19] Already he saw himself a great man at the very summit of affairs. At the same time Harley sought the aid of the other great Whig lord, the Duke of Shrewsbury, who had long been Robin's friend and made no secret of his burning desire for place.[20] But Shrewsbury was timid or cautious, and for the present declined to declare himself. Before long he was to play a decisive role.

Meanwhile, Mrs. Manley, in her *New Atalantis*, regaled the public with spurious stories about the Whigs and especially Godolphin and the Marlboroughs.* According to this low woman's story, Sarah was Godolphin's mistress and her husband complacent. With stories such as this to regale the public this contemptible work soon boasted a second volume, and ran through several editions. With the atmosphere thus charged, Harley let it be known that in his view Louis XIV was invincible; that, were it not for the selfish machinations of the Lord Treasurer and the General, peace could be had for the asking; and that the Queen was, as he put it, in bondage to a single family, who shared between them the honours and wealth of the State. Harley spoke thus to Mrs. Masham. Mrs. Masham spoke to the Queen. The favourite's stories made a profound impression on Anne's torpid mind. It must have been clear to every Whig that the tide was on the turn. Yet it was this of all moments that Marlborough chose to ask that his post of Captain-General—or Commander-in-Chief, as we should say—should be secured to him for life. The Queen, shocked and troubled at the imprudent suggestion, curtly and indignantly refused: whereupon the Duke had the temerity to write to her an intemperate letter complaining bitterly of her attachment to Abigail Masham. The country was genuinely alarmed. The Tory leaders roundly declared that he was seeking to make himself "perpetual dictator" and they shouted of Cromwell and the military power. All that the General had really done was to strive to set his relation to the army above the cut and thrust of party politics, but his ill-advised action was represented to the people as an attempted treason.[21]

In November 1709, Marlborough returned to England to find the Junto lords, now in triumphant mood, constantly bickering amongst themselves.

---

* In the *New Atalantis*, false names were used to veil thinly the persons libelled. The key to the names in the first volume can be found in *Hearne's Collections*, II, 292

In all this Harley and his associates saw their chance: they were not slow to grasp it with both hands.

Their opportunity came early in the new year, when the death of Lord Essex rendered vacant the Lieutenancy of the Tower of London and a Regiment of Dragoons. Though it was the custom for the Sovereign to be advised on all military appointments by the Commander-in-Chief, Anne, on the backstairs advice of Harley and Abigail, promptly nominated Earl Rivers to the Tower* and offered the Regiment to Colonel Jack Hill, Abigail Masham's worthless brother. The Duke of course was furious, for he had his own candidates for both preferments, and he expostulated warmly with the Queen. It was a studied insult. But worse; the appointment of the young untried Hill, whose only claim to advancement was that he was a brother of the Queen's favourite waiting-woman, over the heads of older and more experienced officers would be a clear indication to the Army and to all Europe that the Commander-in-Chief no longer enjoyed the confidence of the Queen. He therefore absolutely declined to countenance the promotion. On retiring from the royal presence, he rallied his Whig colleagues and told them firmly of his unalterable resolve. They all promised their support. Sunderland went so far as to advocate an address in Parliament for Abigail's dismissal, and Somers offered to intercede with the Queen himself or to join Marlborough at his second audience.

On the following day, the Duke again repaired to the Palace and remonstrated once more with Anne. To appoint young Hill over the heads of others far better suited for advancement was ". . . to set up a standard of disaffection to rally all the malcontents in the army." There was no misunderstanding the significance of that; but Anne showed no sign of comprehending what was at stake. She looked upon her greatest subject with cold disdain; and she closed the audience with the words, "You do well to advise with your friends."

Marlborough was both distressed and angry: and he resolved that her Majesty should be given the clear-cut choice of retaining either his services or Abigail's. Now was the time for action: he refused to temporize further, and on January 14th he left London without the ceremony of leave-taking and retired with his wife to Windsor Lodge. There he drew up a letter to the Queen explaining his views in the strongest terms and giving her the choice between the general and the serving-woman. This he submitted to the Treasurer and the Whig lords. But the Junto, who had hitherto seemed so strong and so united, were now in the face of crisis; and they wavered. Only Sunderland remained resolute. Godolphin laboured for a com-

---

* To which appointment Marlborough had been previously tricked into saying that he had no objection.

promise. On the 16th, two meetings were held at the Duke of Devonshire's house to concert plans; but confusion was only worse confounded by the absence of Godolphin and Somers from both and of Sunderland from the second. Somers, following the advice of the Lord Treasurer, preferred to act on his own; and he expatiated to the Queen on the great services that the Duke of Marlborough had rendered to his Sovereign and on the inconveniences that would inevitably follow an open breach. But he failed to move the stony heart of Queen Anne. "I have a full and lasting sense of his long and great services," she replied, "and no one dares attempt to do him ill offices with me, because if they did their malice would recoil on themselves. This I will confirm when I see him, and then I doubt not I shall have the satisfaction of hearing him own that, after mature reflection, he has changed his opinion, and will not continue to deem my proposal unreasonable."[22] We can well imagine Anne's defensive attitude, her cold, repulsive words, her strong, firm jaw, her face impassive, her eyes glinting—a Stuart on the warpath!

The attitude of Godolphin is lamentable. He was anxious for compromise, for he dreaded the accusation that they were coercing the Queen. He was clearly in a state of great agitation. "I am in so great a hurry," he wrote to Marlborough, "And my thoughts so much distracted with the confusion I see coming upon everything, and everybody equally, that I have neither had time to write nor a mind enough composed to write with any sort of coherence, since I do not see any disposition in those most concerned, on either side, to delay coming to extremities, though to the irrecoverable ruin of the public, nor even to do so much as is necessary to put themselves in the right, when those extremities come. I have done, therefore, with advising, and shall second, as well as I can, the methods you think most proper, be they never so differing from my too little sense; but I have too much experience, as well as too great concern for my friends, to have any quiet thoughts on this matter."[23] Extremities must be avoided at all costs, for in his view ruin would inevitably follow.

Now this attitude of Lord Godolphin is liable to serious misinterpretation and in at least one instance bred a story much to his discredit. There is in existence a curious paper, purporting to give an account of the events of this time. It was drawn up in later years for the benefit of King George I by an eccentric Irish peer, Lord Coningsby.[24] According to this document, Godolphin's passion for compromise caused him, whilst his friend was out of London, to consult with Somers, Boyle and Smith the Speaker, as to whether an accommodation could be arranged on the lines that neither the Duke's candidate, a certain Meredith, nor Jack Hill should have Lord Essex's Regiment, but that it should go instead to Sir Richard Temple, an intimate of the Lords of the Junto, and that Hill should be fobbed off with a life pension. If we are to believe Coningsby's story, this proposal originated in Harley, who imparted it to Somers from whom it reached the Lord Treasurer; and it was through the influence of Harley that the Queen was prevailed upon to agree to the scheme. The proposal from the point of view of Harley and his friends might well be most acceptable, for if, as Coningsby states and as seems likely, they did not as yet feel themselves to be sufficiently strong to face the consequences of an open breach with Marlborough the compromise of giving the Regiment to an outsider might seem a partial victory, for it at least avoided the necessity for an undignified withdrawal. But Coningsby is not altogether reliable. Though a distinguished soldier and a brave man—he had done yeoman service for King William at the Battle of the Boyne—he was not in the innermost counsels of the leading statesmen of Queen Anne's reign. Indeed, though throughout the reign he acted consistently with the Whigs, his services received no reward even when his friends were in office, until at last in October 1708 he was sworn of the Privy Council: and though a lifelong friend of the Marlboroughs,* it seems as if he bore something of a grudge against the Lord Treasurer, to whose lack of appreciation he ascribed his failure to achieve office. Furthermore, he drew up his paper some years after the events he records, when his memory of them may well have been uncertain. In details he is inaccurate: thus he states that the Marlboroughs, when they left London, withdrew to Woodstock, whereas in fact they retired to their Lodge in Windsor Park. If mistaken in small matters, he may well be faulty in greater. And his condemnation of Godolphin lacks evidence from any other quarter. The thing is unsupported; it is intrinsically unlikely. But of course it may have been.

But even if we do not credit this story, we may condemn Godolphin's vacillating attitude. By his absence from the Devonshire House meeting he had helped to divide and confuse Ministers. By not venturing to mention the subject of his friend to the Queen when he saw her and by sending the far less acceptable Somers to expostulate with her Majesty on Marlborough's behalf, he did ill service to the General's cause. Finally, he had successfully persuaded Marlborough to delete the last sentence from the letter he proposed to write to the Queen—the decisive sentence that said in effect, "Dismiss Mrs. Masham or dismiss me"—and this gravely weakened the ultimatum and spoilt much of its effect. "By what I hear from London,

* About a year after Marlborough's death, Coningsby, having divorced his first wife and lost his second, proposed marriage to the widowed Sarah; but in common with other suitors he was refused. At this point in 1723, their correspondence, which had continued for some years, abruptly ceased. Churchill, *Marlborough*, Book II, 1038.

I find your Majesty is pleased to think when I have reflected, I must be of opinion that you are in the right in giving Mr. Hill the Earl of Essex's regiment. I beg your Majesty will be so just to me, as not to think I can be so unreasonable, as to be mortified to the degree that I am, if it did proceed only from this one thing; . . . But this is only one of a great many mortifications, that I have met with. And as I may not have many opportunities of writing to you let me beg your Majesty to reflect what your own people, and the rest of the world must think, who have been witnesses of the love, zeal and duty, with which I have served you, when they shall see that after all I have done, it has not been able to protect me against the malice of a bedchamber woman. . . ."[25] A strong letter no doubt, but how very much more effective it would have been if its last decisive words had not been omitted!

The letter was duly dispatched. But before it reached her the Queen summoned Lord Godolphin to her presence late on Friday night, to say that after due reflection she would not insist on the disposal of the regiment to Hill. "I desire you to communicate this to the Duke of Marlborough, and tell him that I shall say so to him in person, when I see him, which I hope will be soon." "I wish, madam," replied Godolphin, "that your Majesty had communicated this to the Duke of Marlborough at an earlier period, as he would then doubtless have been satisfied, but as I am afraid that at present it will not have so good an effect, I must request your majesty to write to him yourself." To this Anne only said, "I will tell it him myself when I see him."

No sooner had Godolphin left the presence chamber than Marlborough's missive reached the Queen; and on the following day, when the Lord Treasurer again waited upon her, Anne showed him the letter. "It is a very good letter," he said. "Do you think," retorted her Majesty, "the conclusion of it good?" "It shows, madam," replied Godolphin, "that he is very much mortified, and I hope your majesty intends to answer it." "Yes," Anne assured him, "but should I not stay for an answer to the message which I sent by you?" "With humble submission, I think not." After a pause the Queen closed the audience by saying, "I will write to the Duke, and send the letter to you tonight." On receiving the letter* Godolphin opened and read it before forwarding it, as the Duke had authorized him to do. This made it essential for Marlborough to return to London without delay. He had gained a great victory: his position in the army was now secure, and no attempt would ever be made again to undermine his authority. Thus argued Godolphin. But to the Marlboroughs,

---

* Mr. Churchill states that the Queen did not write. Churchill, *Marlborough*, Book II, 568. But this is not correct.

that was not enough. So long as Abigail Masham remained at the Queen's side, so long would last Robert Harley's opportunities for making mischief. Therefore Abigail must go.

But even as the Commander-in-Chief was voicing his views on these lines, the Whig chiefs were meeting once again at Devonshire House, where after long debate it was decided that in the opinion of the majority the Queen had made substantial concessions, and the Duke ought to be satisfied. This opinion was duly communicated to Marlborough, together with a note from Secretary Boyle congratulating himself upon the happy termination of the affair. The General saw that he must yield. To remain firm in the face of this opinion might lay him open to the charge of bullying the Queen. He therefore returned to London on Monday, January 23rd, and the following day had an audience of her Majesty. Anne, having won her point and saved Abigail, was of course delighted, and she received the Duke with greater favour than he had enjoyed since Ramillies. But however much she might smile upon and flatter her great subject, she could never forgive him for having attempted the overthrow of her favourite. Henceforth she would be more circumspect, would employ greater dissimulation; but for the moment she would bide her time. Meantime Harley and Masham laid their plans. Soon they would be ready to strike. The Queen's hour was nigh at hand.

CHAPTER IX

THE EBB TIDE

THE triumph of the Whigs determined Harley and the Queen to prevail upon Marlborough to return to Holland. Whilst detained at Harwich by adverse winds, he received a letter from his son-in-law which shows that at least one person fully recognized the dangers of the political situation at home. "It is very unfortunate for our home affairs," wrote Sunderland, "that you were obliged to go away so soon; for lord treasurer has a slowness and coldness about him that is really terrible, and therefore all that can be must be done to keep him up, and to animate him. But I am sure it will be impossible to do it without Lady Marlborough, and, therefore I must beg of you, in the name of all our friends, that you would persuade her to come straight to town when you are embarked, to keep lord treasurer up to do what is right, for without her I know we shall all sink. I don't mean be out of our places, for that I think will be no mortification to any body of common sense; but besides the danger to the whole none of our heads are safe, if we can't get the better of what I am convinced Mrs. Morley designs; and if lord treasurer can be persuaded to act like a man, I am sure our union and strength is too great to be hurt."[1] Perhaps we may be excused for thinking that the "slowness and coldness" of Godolphin are to be preferred at times to the heat and passion of Sunderland and his mother-in-law; but judging from the remainder of the letter, that was not the view of Somers, Devonshire or Orford, all of whom joined in pressing for Sarah's speedy return to town. No wonder Godolphin wrote to his friend that his last letter "seems pretty full of spleen. I think I have use enough for my share of it, but I am thorowly satisfyed ther's no putting an end to it, but by getting a good end to this warr. . . ."[2] No wonder that Godolphin himself had the "spleen" for he and the Whigs had embarked on the ill-judged prosecution of Dr. Sacheverell.

It is constantly asserted that Henry Sacheverell was a man of no consequence, attacked by the Whigs owing to the malice of Godolphin. This needs further examination.

By the autumn of 1709 there was great discontent throughout the war-weary country. The taxation necessary to meet the expenditure was oppressive and financial difficulties were accumulating. In 1707, to the cost of the war which showed no sign of decreasing, had to be added the Scotch Equivalent of £400,000. Additional resources, therefore, had to be found. The Government accordingly created fresh annuities to the amount of £640,000 upon the surplus of the Excise after the discharge of its prior liabilities,[3] and raised a further sum of £1,280,000 on duties, a part of which was applicable to pay interest on the annuities just created.[4] In addition, certain duties on wines, vinegar and tobacco were set aside as security for the raising of a further sum of £730,000.[5] The amalgamation at about this time of the Old East India Company with the new or English East India Company, which the brilliant Montagu had created in 1699, gave Godolphin an exceptional opportunity for raising a new loan, and as the price for renewal of the united Companies' charter to March 1726, the Companies advanced the welcome sum of £1,200,000.[6]

Indeed, the more Godolphin relied on the Whigs the more successful were his financial operations. In 1708 a further £645,000 was borrowed at 7 per cent upon the security of the duties on wine, vinegar and tobacco.[7] In the following year, a supply of seven million was voted, but the yield from taxes was estimated to fall short of this by some two million. In these circumstances, the Whig financiers saw their chance of improving their position by rendering the government more dependent on the Bank of England. The Bank had at its foundation advanced £1,200,000 to the Treasury,[8] and in 1706 had undertaken to circulate one million and a half of Exchequer Bills.[9] These Bills the Bank in 1708 offered to pay off and cancel, together with the interest due, at a total cost of £1,775,000, upon the assignment of an annuity amounting to 6 per cent out of the house duty until such time as the principal had been redeemed. The Bank further undertook to advance £400,000 without interest until August 1st, 1711, and thereafter to accept interest upon the original debt of £1,200,000 due from the Government and upon the £400,000 at the reduced rate of 6 instead of 8 per cent per annum. It also agreed to circulate future Exchequer Bills up to two and a half millions at 6 per cent secured upon certain assigned duties. In return for these services, the Bank obtained permission to double its capital by issuing fresh stock at a premium of 15 per cent, which, with a call on the proprietors of 15 per cent amounting to £656,000, brought the Bank's capital up to the figure of five million pounds.

Great success attended the Bank's operations. Its subscription lists, opened at 9 o'clock in the morning of February 22, 1709, were closed four hours later when the entire amount had been subscribed, and its stock rose from 15 to 17 per cent. The Tories, mindful of the complete failure of Harley's Land Bank in 1696, raised all manner of objections to the new arrangement by which, they complained, the Bank was incorporated with the State; and their pamphleteers worked day and night to brand it as a corrupt monopoly, which raised interest rates, obstructed trade, and lowered the value of land.

In 1709, towards the end of which year expenditure approached thirteen million, the precariousness of Godolphin's tenure of office rendered the raising of money far more difficult. In these circumstances, recourse was had to a lottery, as a means of raising £1,500,000. Unfortunately, however, this was not fully subscribed and a sum of £1,300,00 was borrowed upon the security of the old Excise and Customs duties;[10] furthermore, the Government proposed a loan of £900,000 upon new Excise and Customs duties, derived mainly from beer, vinegar and spices. By the autumn of 1710, after the dismissal of Godolphin, annual expenditure exceeded thirteen and a half million; and though £7,700,000 had been borrowed, there still remained a deficit on the year of over half a million pounds.[11] No wonder that at Harley's elevation in August 1710, his brother Edward, the Auditor of the Exchequer, should write of Robert's embarrassments. "When he came into the Treasury he found the Exchequer almost empty," he wrote, "nothing left for the subsistence of the Army but some tallies upon the third general mortgage of the Customs; the Queen's civil list near £700,000 in debt; the funds all exhausted and a debt of £9,500,000 without provision of Parliament, which had brought all the credit of the Government to a vast discount. In this condition the nation had to pay 255,689 men … Besides these difficulties the Bank, stock jobbers and moneyed men of the City were all engaged to sink the credit of the Government, which they did so effectually that Navy Bills and others were sold at 40 and 45 per cent discount."[12]

In all these circumstances, it is not surprising that the Tories should denounce the war as an unjustifiable waste. Their complaints were taken up by the High Church Clergy, prominent among whom was Henry Sacheverell, Fellow of Magdalen College, Oxford, Doctor of Divinity, and since 1705 chaplain of St. Saviour's, Southwark. That Sacheverell was a man of small ability is true enough; but that he was of little consequence is by no means the case. He was a powerful, if platitudinous, preacher who rejoiced to play upon public feelings at a time of great discontent by the delivery from the pulpit of polemical attacks on nonconformity. One such diatribe he had delivered in the University Church at Oxford in the summer of 1702.[13] On December 23, 1705, taking the text "in perils among false brethren,"[14] he delivered from the same pulpit a vigorous attack against latitudinarianism in Church and State. In August 1709, he preached before the judges at the summer assizes at Derby a sermon he called *The Communication of Sin*. Three months later, on November 5th, he preached in

St. Paul's Cathedral before the Lord Mayor and the Aldermen of London, and this discourse he entitled *The Perils of False Brethren both in Church and State*. The first of these sermons was directed against those, especially the clergy, who countenanced dissent. In the second he vigorously denied that resistance could ever be lawful to any form of tyranny and he gave vent to his hatred of those in high places who were for comprehension and toleration as a political expedient, applying to them the language of the Psalmist. "In what moving and lively colours does the Holy Psalmist paint out the crafty insidiousness of such wilely volpones? Wickedness (he says) is therein, Deceit and Guile go not out of their Streets. For it is not an open enemy that has done me this dishonour, for then I could have borne it: Neither was it mine Adversary, that did magnify himself against me, for then peradventure I would have hid myself from him. But, it was even Thou! my Companion, my Guide, and mine own Familiar Friend. We took sweet counsel together, and walked in the House of God as Friends. There is no faithfulness in their mouths, their inward Parts are very wickedness; their throats are open sepulchres, and their words are smoother than oil, yet be they very swords. Like Joab, they pretend to speak Peaceably, and smite us mortally under the fifth rib." And much more unctuous rhetoric on these colourful lines!

The Whigs, of course, were incensed. Early in December the Ministers met to consider what action should be taken. It was clear that to ignore the matter would be to show intolerable weakness. The cautious Somers, it is said, favoured a prosecution according to the ordinary form of law, but the impetuous Sunderland advocated a trial before the House of Lords. To this latter counsel the Lord Treasurer gave his support because, so say most historians, he was enraged at the temerity of the preacher who referred to him in opprobrious terms by the name of *Volpone*, the odious chief character in Ben Jonson's famous comedy. This view was first expressed by the malicious Swift,[15] who is the authority on whom so many writers have relied; yet there is no evidence to support the view. The nickname of Volpone had for some years been applied to him and he had never been known to show the slightest impatience. It occurs in a poetic lampoon as far back as 1705;[16] by 1709 it has become well known.[17] Why then should Godolphin be so much annoyed at the speaker's impertinence? His true motive, to which so many writers of this period have been blind, was clearly seen by Edmund Burke. "The impeachment of Dr. Sacheverell," he wrote, "was undertaken by a Whig ministry and a Whig House of Commons, and carried on before a prevalent and steady majority of Whig peers. It was carried on for the express purpose of stating the true grounds and principles of the Revolution; what the Commons emphatically called their

foundation. It was carried on for the purpose of condemning the principles
in which the Revolution was first opposed, and after calumniated, in order
by a juridical sentence of the highest authority, to confirm and fix Whig
principles, as they had operated both in the resistence to King James, and in
the subsequent settlement; and to fix them in the extent and with the
limitations with which it was meant they should be understood by posterity."[18] Those were undoubtedly Godolphin's true motives in advocating the prosecution of Henry Sacheverell in Westminster Hall.

But whatever Godolphin's motives, the unwisdom of the prosecution
was soon apparent; and he was among the first to show anxiety as to the
outcome. He complained of ". . . having not time during this troublesome
tryall of Dr. Sacheverell, either to eat or sleep in any regularity, the worst of
it is, that tis like to last yett 4 or 5 days longer."[19] And again ". . . this
uneasy tryall of Sacheverell does not only take my time, but very much
impairs my health, & how it will yett end I am not at all certain, but I certainly wish it never had begun for it has occasioned a very great torment, &
given opportunity to a great many people to bee impertinent who always
had the intention but wanted the opportunity of showing it. . . ."[20] Meanwhile, the Duke of Somerset "labours hard against us, and makes full use
of the Queen's name." "I doubt he is pretty sure of not being disavowed,"
is the Lord Treasurer's comment, "and I believe him entirely linked with
the opposite party upon the foot of knowing 42's (the Queen's) inclinations
and flattering them but is so vain & so simple as not to bee sensible he is
incapable of being any thing more than what he is. . . ."[21] In the great trial
Somerset's attitude was equivocal. Sacheverell was found guilty by a
majority of seventeen votes. "The Duke of Somerset did not vote, some of
his friends sayd he was sick, but I fancy twas only his profound Wisdome
that kept him away from the house. . . . Tomorrow we are to goe upon the
consideration of the punishment. . . ."[22] This on March 20th. On the
morrow: "Our sentence against Dr. Sacheverell is at last dwindled to a sus-
pending him for 3 years from preaching, which question wee carry'd but for
six;" Godolphin reported, "and the 2d which was for incapacitating him
from during that time, to take any dignity or preferment in the church wee
lost by one, the numbers were 60 to 59. So all this bustle and fatigue ends
in no more but a suspension for 3 years from the pulpit, and burning his
sermon at the Old Exchange. . . . The conjunction of 13 (Somerset) and 10
(Rivers) with 24 (Argyll) & his brother, has been the great occasion of this
disappointment."[23] The conduct of the lordly Somerset was particularly
galling. "42 (the Queen) shows a great deal of weakness," wrote Godolphin
in disgust, "in countenancing & supporting the folly and impertinence of 13
(Somerset), to give it no worse name."[24]

The trial of Dr. Sacheverell was a Whig disaster, and about this time Marlborough wrote to Godolphin a confidential letter "for yourself," the cipher address for his friend, which shows clearly his growing alarm at the passage of events. "By the different accounts I have from 108 (England)," he wrote, "it will be a great ease to mee to know from you how far 38 and 39 (you and I) may safely depend upon the sincerity of 28 (Shrewsbury). The encouragement 221 (Argyll) has received by the favour 42 (the Queen) has shown him, makes it absolutely necessary for 38 (me) to countenance 37 (Orkney) in opposition to 221 (Argyll), which makes me beg of you that you will use your interest with 42 (the Queen) that they [sic] wou'd be pleased to allow me to give assurance to 37 (Orkney) that when any of his Countrymen (the Scots) are made Pears [sic] that he should be made an English Baron, if it is the intention of 42 (the Queen) that I shou'd serve Her which I am ready to do with all my heart, she must in order to bring the discipline of the army back to that happy posture in which it was some time ago for her Service, let me have in my power to oblige the officers, and not to have any body incoraged to think they can meet with preferment by others. If 42 (the Queen) dose not think this absolutely necessary and good for Her, I shall be as well contented to be quiet, and retier, which may make mee happyer, if I were not morally sure that her service can't succeed any other way, pray lett me have your mind freely, and your advice as a faithfull friend, for I can't be at ease in my mind, til I have fixt my resolution, as to my behaviour, for the remaining part of my life, which will bee very much guided by what I shall hear from you."[*] This remarkable outpouring shows, not only Marlborough's perturbation, but also his implicit trust in his friend.

But whilst Marlborough was besieging Douay in the spring months of 1710, events were passing at home calculated to cause him even greater consternation than the trial of Dr. Sacheverell. His wife was having her final bout with the Queen, which ended with the fatal audience of April 6th. Eight days later, against the advice of the outspoken Burnet, now Bishop of Salisbury, her Majesty summoned the Marquess of Kent, deprived him of his office of Lord Chamberlain, and consoled him with a dukedom. The next morning, within only a few weeks of his hostile vote at the Sacheverell trial, the Queen appointed the Duke of Shrewsbury to succeed Kent. To Godolphin, ill at Newmarket,[†] the Queen wrote curtly to announce her decision.

[*] Marlborough to Godolphin, no date. H.M.C. *Morrison*, 470. The original letter is in the possession of Dr. G. M. Trevelyan. Trevelyan, *Queen Anne*, III, 44.

[†] He had been taken ill during the Sacheverell Trial "with very great pains of the gravell. I hope before the post goes out to be able to tell you I am a little more at ease." Godolphin to Marlborough, "Monday 6th of March" (1709/10). He attended the House of Lords within a few days and left for Newmarket on April 6th. Blenheim MSS. B. II. 8.

The Lord Treasurer, of course, was furious. "Your Majesty is suffering yourself to be guided to your own Ruin and Destruction," he told Anne, "as fast as it is possible for them (the Harley-Abigail faction) to compass it, to whom you seem so much to hearken..." Of Shrewsbury he wrote not unkindly, "There is no Man of whose Capacity I have had a better Impression; nor with whom I have lived more easily and freely for above twenty years ... (but) to bring him into your Service and into your Business at this Time just after his being in a public open Conjunction in every Vote with the whole Body of Tories and in a private constant Correspondence and Caballing with Mr. Harley in every Thing ... must have the most fatal consequences." Then he made two requests. "The one, that you will allow me to pass the Remainder of my Life always out of London, where I may find more ease and Quiet. The other, that you would keep this Letter and read it again about next Christmas, and then be pleased to make your own Judgment, who hath given of the best and most faithful advice."[25] He also unburdened himself to his friend, whose victories, he told him, "were needed to keep up the spiritts of 89 (the Whigs) who are mightily mortified and dejected, at what has been done for 28 (Shrewsbury), as 38 (Godolphin) has reason to bee ... I hope 38 (I) will bee able to keep 89 (the Whigs) from flying out upon this occasion into any measures that would ruin all the affairs abroad irrecoverably, & doe no good to those at home..."[26]

On the following day, the Treasurer, back from Newmarket, waited on the Queen. She at once reproached him with having shown more uneasiness at the new appointment than had any of his colleagues. "If that be true," retorted Godolphin, "the reason is, because they will not suffer themselves to be provoked by the folly and madness of others, to draw irrecoverable ruin on those who had not deserved it, as well as those who had. But I believe that my letter, when it is too late, will be found a true prophecy of what will happen." To this the Queen replied in a confused and awkward manner that she intended no further changes. "The reports of the town," was Godolphin's laconic rejoinder, "run high on that subject." On that unhappy note the Minister took his leave.[27]

Yet in spite of his chagrin Godolphin had to admit that the new Lord Chamberlain seemed anxious to be on good terms with the Ministers. "He was extreamly full of professions to 38 (you), 39 (me) and 240 (Duchess of Marlborough)" he told the General, "and that by whatever dore [sic] he came in, it was always with an intention & a desire to live well with those three, and not only so, but with all others they would have him live well with, not doubting, he added, but that it would have been done much sooner, if 38 & 39 (you and I) had been entirely masters of it, & that, perhaps it was as well for them (us) that it had hapned in this manner, considering the jealous humour of 89 (the Whigs)." To all this Godolphin returned a complimentary answer. "28 (Shrewsbury) protested most solemnly to me that he never had spoken one word to Ab: (Abigail Masham) in his life; then he says, the only sore place was, the difference betwixt 240 (Duchess of Marlborough) & 42 (the Queen), and that all the rest might presently be sett right; . . ."[28] A few days later he wrote again in similar strain about Shrewsbury's intentions. "I believe him really inclined and disposed to live well with Mr. Freeman and 38 (me), and also a good deal apprehensive of doing otherwise. . . ."[29]

Whilst Godolphin and Marlborough were mortified at Shrewsbury's appointment, they were soon involved in further trouble with the Queen. After the fall of Douay, the Commander-in-Chief submitted a scheme for the promotion of those officers who had distinguished themselves in the field. Unfortunately, the Duke's list of brigadiers stopped short at the name immediately before Colonel Jack Hill and that of the Colonels at the name preceding Masham, the husband of Abigail. The Queen naturally bridled at these pointed and deliberate omissions; whereupon the General agreed to the promotion of Masham, but to that of Hill he for a time maintained his objection in uncompromising terms. Very likely Marlborough would have stood out longer but for the fact that he was soon to realize that he could not count on the consistent support of the Whigs. "I find by Mr. Walpole, that you have not been easy in the matter of Abigail's brother," wrote Godolphin anxiously on June 2nd. That was to be regretted. "The question is not so much what is wrong and what is right, but what gives a handle to the duke of Somerset to tell lies, and make impressions, where nobody has the opportunity of setting it right, or so much as of knowing it till it is too late."[30] Faced with this sage argument from his friend, Marlborough determined to yield; but though he did so with a good grace, the iron had entered into his soul.

Some have described Godolphin's attitude as weak and timid; as a matter of fact it was actuated by a profound sense of duty, as is shown by a remarkable letter he wrote early in May. Already there were rumours of the Queen's intention to put the Treasury into commission, but when taxed with it ". . . she gave a sort of scornfull smile, but did not think fitt to say a word to mee upon it, & perhaps it is not yett in her intentions or thoughts, but what she may be brought to in time, by a perpetual course of ill offices & lyes from 199 (Harley) & his friends . . . but this I know, that as long as you are abroad in the field, & that your Army can not bee regularly paid, but by my particular care and endeavour, no slight provocation shall prevail with me to quitt my post though it is uneasy enough in it self, nor would, in any circumstances bee intolerable, but that I know the publick would suffer, both at home & abroad if I should not contain my self till your return, which is therefore my present resolution; but the insolence of 199 (Harley) and his creature are inexpressible; 221's brother (Argyll's brother, Ilay) & 10 (Rivers) & that sort of cattell [sic] have as little management here, as they say he has abroad."[31] How unfair to dub this timidity and weakness!

But if the Marlboroughs and Godolphin felt outraged over the affair of Hill and Masham, a worse mortification was soon in store for them; for Harley, Abigail and the Queen designed no less than the disgrace of the General's son-in-law, Sunderland, the Secretary of State.

We have already seen something of the Duke of Shrewsbury's cautious approach to the Harley-St. John faction. Argyll, too, though on foreign service, was showing himself increasingly hostile to the Ministry.[32] And now the Duke of Somerset, ensnared by the smiles of Anne, the crafts of Harley and the encouragement of Newcastle, the Lord Privy Seal, began to fancy himself a great party leader. As we have seen, he held clandestine meetings with Harley that must have delighted him. Only in a sedan chair with the curtains drawn would the Duke come to Harley's house, where the porter had instructions to admit the mysterious visitor without asking any questions.* And soon this little group of minor figures acquired the distinction of a name of its own. The Whig Lords had been called the Junto. Somerset and his clique became known as the Juntilla.

It was, it seems, largely at the instigation of Somerset that the attack on Sunderland was launched, with Shrewsbury working for moderation: at any rate that was the view expressed by the Lord Treasurer towards the end of May. So long as Somerset was away from London, all remained quiet, he told Marlborough. "I am every day more and more confident in my opinion, that as 13 (Somerset) is the driver of everything against 240 & 39 (the Duchess of Marlborough and you), so 28's (Shrewsbury's) consideration for the latter (you) and the fear of justly *choquing* [sic] him (*you*) has been the only reason that has hindered the affair of 6 (Sunderland) from being brought to a conclusion. . . . At the same time I don't think that he has any thoughts of living well with 89 (the Whigs), or of trusting them so as to lose his hold with the others, or not make his court to 42 (the Queen); but as farr as it is possible to him to keep off violent extremitys till Mr. Freeman's arrival, I think he will try to do it." Therefore, suggested Godolphin, why not write to Shrewsbury pointing out clearly and frankly

---

* Somerset to Harley, "Kensington, May 24, 1710." "Sunday night, six o'clock, July 30, 1710," the same date, "Sunday night ten o'clock." H.M.C. *Portland*, IV, 543, 545, 553.

the dire effects that the fall of Marlborough's son-in-law would have on the General's prestige abroad? Meanwhile, so Godolphin warned Marlborough, Halifax, Somers, Sunderland, and most of the Whigs seemed ready to court Harley's favour, and he to receive their advances and those of any Whig well disposed towards his faction. Not even the Lord Treasurer himself, it appears, has been quite immune from this pressure. "Mr. Montgomery stands stock still," he assured Marlborough, "and makes the same answer to abundance of applications of all sides, & even from the very best of 84 (the Tories); viz., that while Mr. Freeman is absent, he can only thank them but not enter into any engagement without him."[33]

A few days later, Godolphin wrote of a conversation he had with Lord Poulett, a minor Tory politician generally known as "Swallow". According to this informant, the chief opponents of Sunderland were Somerset and Rivers, with Shrewsbury working for a compromise. Godolphin, returning Poulett's frankness with equal candour, told him that in his view the dismissal of Sunderland would be such a mortification to the General as to have the most serious consequences. Furthermore, Godolphin made it abundantly clear that, if Marlborough resigned, he would retire also. Poulett was impressed and he warned the Queen.[34]

Meanwhile, Marlborough, following the Lord Treasurer's advice, wrote a somewhat undignified letter to Shrewsbury deprecating the dismissal of his son-in-law and also the dissolution of parliament.[35] This was without effect, for, as Shrewsbury had told the Lord Treasurer a week or so previously, the Queen was pressing hard for the removal of the obnoxious Sunderland. On hearing this Godolphin went straight to Anne to remonstrate. He told her with the utmost bluntness of the effect that the dismissal of his son-in-law would have on the General. "As for my part," he added, "I have so much dread of the effect which this will have upon the Duke in particular, and upon all the other officers in general, who are abroad, that I do think I should not do my duty without saying this much on the subject." The reply was shattering. "The Duke of Marlborough is too reasonable to suffer a thing of this kind to do so much prejudice to himself and to the whole world, by taking it to heart; and surely nobody knows better than the duke and yourself the repeated provocations which I have received from Lord Sunderland." In reply to this sally Godolphin could only repeat his fear of the ill effect that would be produced by any precipitate action before the General had been informed. This plea made some impression on the Queen, who thereupon authorized Godolphin to apprise the commander of her intentions.

But if the Queen showed a bold front to the Treasurer, she and her Tory advisers knew full well that they were playing with fire and they thought it well to tender explanations to the Foreign Ambassadors. Thus Count Galles, the Imperial Envoy, apprised of the intended dismissal of Sunderland, reported that "... I was to assure the Emperor and the King of Spain that the object was not at all to diminish the prestige of Marlborough, which the Queen wished to preserve. The queen was, moreover, resolved not to weaken the position of England in the international sphere. The affair was a purely personal one, affecting Lord Sunderland only: the Queen had kept him in her service till now merely out of respect for Marlborough."[36] But Galles was no fool. He knew that the Tories were for peace. He saw the French Court take courage from these events. Both he and Hoffman, the Imperial Resident in London, took a gloomy view. "The Tories," Hoffman reported, "intend to secure the dissolution of the present Parliament and the summons of a new one. If they succeed, this gives them control of the Government; thus the Queen will no longer be able to select moderate men of both parties. . . . It is difficult to be able to foresee the attitude which Marlborough and Godolphin will take. As long as the war lasts both of them will be needed; for if the Treasurer were dismissed, the credit which is the real basis of the wealth of the country at this moment, would simply collapse, and everything would be plunged into the utmost confusion. Events here have already had the result that France is stiffening."[37]

In telling Marlborough of his audience, the Treasurer urged his friend to write a bold and strongly worded remonstrance to her Majesty. Meanwhile, they must try to gain time; with which object he would seek the co-operation of the Duke of Shrewsbury, ". . . but he is pretty mysterious," he warned, "and seems in every conversation, as if he wished for help, & wanted help from us, but without ever explaining against whom that help is wanted; only he said today that he believed 13 (Somerset) stayed away on purpose, in hopes the affair of 6 (Sunderland) might be ended before his return, that he might have room to impute it to other people, and tell as many lies upon it as he thought fitt. . . ." And he concluded his letter by once again begging his friend to "write plainly to 42 (the Queen) or 28 (Shrewsbury) that it is not right to presume too far upon a man's good temper . . ."[38] In spite of all that has been said ". . . the affair of 6 (Sunderland) hangs over us still, like a cloud ready to break upon our heads . . ." he wrote two days later; and again he begged the General to write to Shrewsbury such a letter as he must show to the Queen."[39]

By the time that Marlborough had taken the resolution to draft a letter to the Queen, it was far too late for appeals to have any effect. On June 12th, when the Lord Treasurer was having his audience, her Majesty spoke of her intention to dismiss Sunderland. She knew this would cause him concern;

therefore, as a mark of her confidence she had notified him herself. Furthermore, she assured him that she was for moderation and did not intend any further changes. Yet again Godolphin represented the ill consequences that might flow from the dismissal and still more from a subsequent dissolution of parliament. Then he took his leave, perfectly convinced that he had made not the slightest impression on the Queen.

The next morning Godolphin waited on her Majesty in order to read Marlborough's letter to her. But she listened coldly: it was manifest that she was beyond the reach of arguments.[40] Nor did the letter fare better when the Treasurer showed it to Shrewsbury and Somers. It was clear that the General's stock was falling fast, and on that very day a letter arrived from the Queen formally announcing that she had already sent for the Seals from Sunderland; ". . . and I do not see why the Duke of Marlborough's letter should make me alter my resolution," she added, "unless I could agree with him that I had done him hardships, which I am not conscious to myself that I have, and I cannot think but all impartial people will be of the same opinion. It is true, indeed, that the turning a son-in-law out of his office may be a mortification to the Duke of Marlborough; but must the fate of Europe depend on that, and must he be gratified in all his desires, and I not in so reasonable a thing as parting with a man whom I took into my service with all the uneasiness imaginable, whose behaviour to me has been so* ever since and who, I must add, is, I believe obnoxious to all people, except a few. I think the Duke of Marlborough's pressing so earnestly that I should delay my intentions is using me very hardly; and I hope both he and you, when you have considered this matter more calmly and impartially, will not wonder that I do not comply with his desires."[41] The Queen offered Sunderland a pension, which he declined. "If I cannot have the honour of serving my country," he nobly declared, "I will not plunder it." High office was to be his again in another reign. Meanwhile, he retired to Althorp and his books.

To this unfeeling letter Godolphin immediately replied warning her Majesty that further mortifications might lead to the Duke's retirement, and telling her frankly that in that event he would resign also. Anne answered early the next morning; though she remained firm, she was clearly perturbed. The simultaneous resignation of Marlborough and Godolphin would be fatal. "I have no thoughts of taking the Duke of Marlborough from the head of the army," she wrote, "*nor I dare say nobody else*:" and she instructed Boyle to inform the Pensioner that the dismissal of Sunderland was not with the intention of diminishing Marlborough's credit.[42] What are we to think of a Sovereign who could write thus to a

* Word missing.

lifelong servant whom she had already determined to remove and in fact did remove some two months later? "If he and you should do so wrong a thing at any time," she continued, "as to desert my service, what confusion might happen might be at your door, and you alone would be answerable, and nobody else. But I hope you will both consider better of it."[43]

The appeal to duty was an artful move. At a great meeting of Whig leaders held at Devonshire House on the day of Sunderland's fall, it was universally held that the retirement of Marlborough would be nothing short of a disaster, and they drew up a memorial to that effect to be transmitted to the General. This was signed by Cowper, Godolphin, Somers, Newcastle, Devonshire, Orford, Halifax and Boyle.[44] It had its effect, and neither Marlborough nor Godolphin resigned. Not weakness, as has often been suggested, but a strong sense of duty impelled the two Ministers to stay at their posts. Without Marlborough, the whole Grand Alliance would crumble. Without Godolphin the General could not be sustained at home. Neither of them was under any illusions. But duty called, and must be obeyed.

The removal of Sunderland, though long expected, created the greatest scare. All the diplomatic corps was agog. On June 27th, Count Galles, the Imperial Envoy, dined with Shrewsbury in Kensington Palace, where he lodged by virtue of his office as Lord Chamberlain to the Queen. Several ambassadors were present. The guests were received by Shrewsbury's Italian Duchess, by whom they were conducted to the Queen's apartments. There they found Shrewsbury and Somerset, who had the ill taste to speak to his host in such unbridled terms of Lord Godolphin that it was clear to Galles that his fall was imminent.* As soon as the Queen entered, dinner was announced. As they moved into the banqueting room, Anne motioned Count Galles to her side. She begged him to assure the Emperor and the King of Spain that she was still determined to continue the war till an honourable peace had been secured: meanwhile, she would do nothing to embarrass the common cause. After dinner, Galles was surprised and disconcerted to find the Duke of Shrewsbury expatiating to the Portuguese Ambassador on England's need for peace. "What is this intended to show?" asked his Excellency. "Do you wish to make peace without driving the Duke of Anjou from Spain?" Shrewsbury was embarrassed by the question. "Certainly not," he replied. "We ask for a good but a rapid peace." "Such language is common here," recorded Galles, "and they talk as though they had peace in their hands—as though other persons were

* No wonder Godolphin wrote of Somerset ". . . for I know him to bee a most worthless wretch & capable of any mischief; . . ." Godolphin to Duchess of Marlborough, "Newmar. Sat. morning April 8th." (1710). Blenheim MSS. E. 20.

diligently prolonging the war. The majority of the English nation is now urgent in its demand for peace. The new party find peace very desirable owing to the turmoil they have caused in the country."[45]

But it was not only the foreign diplomats who were alarmed. The reader will recall the happy conversation that the Lord Treasurer had with the Governor of the Bank of England, Sir Gilbert Heathcote, after the victory of Malplaquet, when the Bank contracted for the circulation of £600,000 more in Exchequer Bills for the carrying on of the public service. Godolphin had then told the governor that he and Marlborough were constantly under attack from those who accused them of prolonging the war. "They are a company of rotten rogues," Sir Gilbert had replied. "I'll warrant you we'll stand by you." That was in the autumn of 1709. Now some nine months later, things were very different, and the governor and his fellow directors took alarm. The decline of the Whigs had caused a rapid fall in the funds: public credit was affected. Accordingly, on June 15, a deputation of directors of the Bank, headed by Heathcote, was introduced into the Queen's presence by the Duke of Newcastle. The directors expatiated to her Majesty on the impending financial panic caused, they told her, by the rumours of an imminent change of Ministry. Damage had been done by the dismissal of the Secretary of State: further changes might well be fatal to the whole new credit system, of which we were so justly proud. The Queen replied evasively, but in a style designed to allay alarm. "I have for some time resolved to remove the Earl of Sunderland, for particular reasons of state," she said, "I have no present intention to make any further changes, but should I alter any of my ministers, it shall be no prejudice either to the Bank or to the common cause."

This equivocal answer seems to have been taken as a promise that neither the Lord Treasurer would be dismissed nor the Parliament dissolved, and it was doubtless intended by the Queen to give just that impression. But if the bankers were deceived Godolphin was not. So long as he could be of the slightest service to his friend, no slight would make him retire. But he was losing all influence, becoming useless, and circumstances might force him out. Yet whatever might happen to him, the General must remain at his post. The Queen was entirely in the hands of Harley, Abigail, Somerset and Shrewsbury, none of whom had the slightest regard for him, the Lord Treasurer, of whom they were simply making use. This situation could not long continue. But the Queen would not listen: she seemed to look upon the whole matter "as a personal contest for power and favour, and whether the Whigs or Tories shall have the greatest sway;..." The new parliament, on the other hand, might be expected to be "entirely at the queen's disposal, and having nothing so much at heart, as to deliver her from the tyranny of the Whigs and their supporters." When this happens, Godolphin opined, he and his colleagues will be forced out.

So much for them. "Now, as to you, I think your conduct must be quite the contrary. You must still represent the mischief of this measure, and the ill consequences of it with the allies, and most particularly with the States and the Emperor etc; but at the same time, *continue to give assurances of your best and most faithful services.*"* He then discussed the prospects under the new parliament to be chosen at the next election, and warned Marlborough of what he thought was in the wind with Harley and his associates; this was ". . . to prepare the elector of Hanover for an offer from the Queen of your post in another year; and this they reckon will have two advantages; one, to deliver them from your great power, of which they give the queen all possible apprehension, in the least disputable manner; the other, to take from themselves the imputation, which is not unnatural, of their being inclined to the king of France's pupil (the Pretender). Now, if this scheme of theirs can be made practicable, which I think is extremely difficult, I think the elector or the queen will be duped in it; and, of the two, I think it is more likely to fall upon the latter. What effect advances of this kind are likely to have on the elector, I am not able to guess; but am pretty clear that the States will never be prevailed with to enter into this scheme."[46]

How right Godolphin was! For this was the true secret of the recently announced appointment of Cresset to succeed Howe at the Court of Hanover. He being well known there was especially suited to convey pledges of loyalty to the Hanoverian House from the Juntilla and to make the very offer that Godolphin mentioned in his letter to Marlborough, that his Highness should be invited to succeed Marlborough as Commander-in-Chief. But unfortunately for Harley and his plans, on July 25th Cresset suddenly died. On hearing this quite unexpected news, Harley had shown unwonted concern for the safety of certain papers that had been in Cresset's hands, and was very much relieved when it was learnt that before his death the envoy designate had been able to seal up these documents and address them to the Secretary of State. Indeed, the whole Juntilla was gravely disturbed, and on the following morning Somerset sent an agitated summons to Harley to a conference with the Queen and Shrewsbury at or before 9 o'clock that night. They had talked the situation over and were convinced that somebody in the Queen's confidence must go immediately to Hanover to discuss with the Pensioner "on the present changes of persons and of the Parliament . . ." In these circumstances, neither Shrewsbury nor the writer, Somerset, would refuse to go, if it were thought advisable.[47]

All this was perfectly well known to Godolphin. Harley and his

* Author's italics.

associates, now generally known as the Court Party, were plotting for his removal and quarrelling over who should succeed him. Somers, it seems, was deeply involved. "32 (the Queen) grows every day more and more uneasy with 37 (Godolphin) and 39 (the Duchess of Marlborough), and both of them continue to give daily more and fresh occasion of *distate* [*sic*];" Robert Harley informed the Duke of Newcastle on July 1st. And again a month later: "33 (Somers) is so full of himself and his own schemes that he would have 34 (perhaps Dartmouth) and 48 (me) assist him in serving his revenge on 37 (Godolphin). . . . However, this is plain, it is impracticable 32 (the Queen) and 37 (Godolphin) can live together. He every day grows sourer and indeed ruder to 32 (the Queen), which is unaccountable, and will hear of no accommodation, so that it is impossible he can continue many days."[48] No wonder the Lord Treasurer was "very peevish!"[49] Furtive conclaves were being held in the Queen's apartments. It was all very ignoble, and Anne herself, it seems, stooped so low as to try to deceive her faithful old servant, by suggesting in a vague sort of way that he should be reconciled to Harley. If she hoped thereby to draw the Lord Treasurer away from the Whigs, she was doomed to disappointment. Sidney Godolphin was the last man to desert his friends!

But his hour had come. At a Cabinet meeting on August 6th, Godolphin had an altercation with Shrewsbury, whom he was provoked, possibly deliberately, into upbraiding for his "French counsels". On Anne's intervention in Shrewsbury's support, Godolphin began to argue with her, probably letting fall some home truths distasteful to the royal ear. The same evening the Treasurer had a long audience of her Majesty, when he harangued her on the evils of government by secret cabals behind the Throne. He concluded by asking her pointedly, "Is it the will of your Majesty that I should go on?" The Queen did not waver in her answer. She replied unhesitatingly, "Yes." Godolphin straightway penned an account of his audience and sent it to Marlborough. "I think the safety or destruction of the parliament remains still under a good deal of uncertainty;" he told him, "and though that uncertainty occasions a great deal of mischief, yet I don't see the least inclination to relieve us from those ill consequences; though, at the same time, the queen seems to be convinced there is no safety but in the good success of the war, yet often as the necessary measures for compassing that end are proposed, *there is a lion in the way*."[50]

With Anne's ungracious "Yes" the Treasurer had to be content, but he must have left the presence chamber with grave doubts in his mind. Perhaps, therefore, he was not altogether surprised when the next morning he received a letter from her Majesty, though its cold, unfeeling tone could hardly have been anticipated. "The uneasiness which you have showed for some time has given me very much trouble, though I have born it;" the Queen wrote, "and had your behaviour continued the same it was for a few years after my coming to the crown, I could have no dispute with myself what to do. But the many unkind returns I have received since, especially what you said to me personally before the lords, makes it impossible for me to continue you any longer in my service; but I will give you a pension of four thousand a year, and I desire that, instead of bringing the staff to me, you will break it, which, I believe, will be easier to us both."[51]

There is some doubt how this message was conveyed to the Minister. According to Sarah, it was delivered by "no worthier messenger than a man in livery;"* on the other hand Lord Dartmouth tells us the messenger was Godolphin's personal friend, John Smith, the Chancellor of the Exchequer.[52] Perhaps the account which Swift gave to Archbishop King is not far from the mark, for it to some extent reconciles the two stories. "A letter was sent him by the groom of the Queen's Stables, to desire he would break his staff, which would be the easiest way, both to her Majesty and him," wrote the Dean. "Mr. Smith, Chancellor of the Exchequer, happening to come in a little after, my lord broke his staff; and flung the pieces in the chimney, desiring Mr. Smith to be witness that he had obeyed the Queen's commands; and sent him to the Queen with a letter and a message, which Mr. Smith delivered, and at the same time, surrendered up his own office."[53]

Be that as it may, Godolphin's dignified reply is in pleasing contrast to Anne's unworthy letter. "May it please your Majesty," he wrote, "I have received this morning the honour of your Majesty's Letter with your Commands in it to break my staff, which I have done with the same duty and satisfaction in what relates to my self as when I had the honour to receive it from your Majesty's hands. Since your Majesty is not pleased to allow me to wait upon you, I must humbly beg leave to take this last occasion to assure your Majesty in the most sincere as well as the most submissive manner, that I am not conscious of the least undutifull act—or of one undutiful word to your Majesty in my whole life, and in the instance which your Majesty is pleased to give I have the good fortune to have several witnesses of undoubted Credit. I should never bee able to forgive myself if I had not always served your Majesty with the most particular respect and duty, as well as with the greatest zeal and integrity. I shall only presume to add that my heart is entirely sensible of all the honours and favours your Majesty has done mee and full of the most zealous wishes for your prosperity and happyness, in this world and in that to come, which I beg leave to assure your Majesty shall always bee the hearty and constant prayer of, May it

* Presumably the royal livery. Duchess of Marlborough, *Conduct*, 260.

please your Majesty, The most humble and dutiful of all your subjects, Godolphin."[54]

Eight years of loyal service to end thus! No word of gratitude. No farewell audience. His sole reward a curt dismissal. To make matters worse, his removal was speedily followed by that of his son, Lord Rialton, from the office of Cofferer of the Household, and the pension of £4,000 a year promised by her Majesty was never paid. Thus the resentful Queen took revenge on her faithful servant.

CHAPTER X

"THE BEST MAN THAT EVER LIVED"

On the day following his fall, Godolphin wrote to Marlborough[1] begging him not to think of resigning on his account, for "What I am chiefly concerned for just now is that you should take this matter in the manner that is most advisable for yourself and all the world besides." A dignified protest to the Queen might be appropriate; but he implored him ". . . by no means think of leaving your post till you have had an answer from the queen to this letter, from which you will be best able to judge what step you are next to take."[2] And again the next day: "Though my circumstances at present are a little discouraging, yet nothing can ever make me regret doing what is best for the whole, or thinking of every thing that may be most for your honour and safety. I do, therefore, now and resolve to continue to take the same pains and care I did before, that you may be effectively supported to the end of this campaign in the post where you are, in hopes this may enable you the better to persuade the States and the Emperor not to break quite loose from the queen of England but to expect, as patiently as they can, the opening of the session, or the new parliament." Both, he is sure, will be "entirely for supporting the alliance." "This, then, I lay down as the most probable method to save the whole from destruction, with most honour and advantage to yourself. I hope, therefore, you will govern yourself accordingly; and I pray God to continue the same success to you that you have hitherto had.[3]

Though my circumstances at present are a little discouraging . . . This was indeed an understatement, for Lord Godolphin left office a poorer man than he entered it. Had not his elder brother, Sir William Godolphin, died at this time, his financial position would have been serious. As it was, he found himself unexpectedly in possession of a fortune of some three thousand pounds a year.*

* On the Queen's letter dismissing Godolphin, the Duchess of Marlborough has penned these words: "Had not his elder brother happened to die, he had been in very low circumstances after having been in several reigns more than twenty years, though he was a man that never made any great expenses, for he won at play, and mortally hated all kinds of show and grandeur, but he was very charitable and generous; and though he had lived so long, and had great employments, when he died,

(Continued on next page)

The Whigs, though taken by surprise, seem to have been still hopeful of coming to terms with the new powers: indeed, Lord Halifax hastened to write a congratulatory letter to Harley on his displacing Sidney Godolphin's old friend, John Smith, as Chancellor of the Exchequer, the office that had once been the writer's own province.[4] The Treasury was put in commission with "Swallow" Poulett at its head. That to Godolphin was ". . . a very plain indication of a new parliam[t]; but how soon the proclamation will come out I can't tell. Upon a good or an ill election off that parliament will depend, in my opinion, not only the fate of Brittain, but of all Europe."[5] Things looked black indeed for the Whigs and well might Swift write to Stella that "Every thing is turning up side down; every Whig in great office will, to a man, be infallibly put out; and we shall have such a winter as hath not been seen in England."[6] Nevertheless Sunderland, optimistic and rash as always, wrote post-haste to his father-in-law that ". . . if you, Lord Godolphin and the Whigs do act cordially and vigorously together, without suspicion of one another, which I am sure there is no reason for, it is impossible but everything must come right again; . . ."[7] How wrong he was soon became apparent.

The Whigs, who had acted so timidly, were not to find sanctuary in the new government fold. As Godolphin prognosticated to Seafield, "all the most arbitrary proceedings in the Elections are to bee expected . . ."[8] and there was nothing for them to do but to bare their heads for the slaughter. At the polls in October, the Tory party, strengthened and rejuvenated by recent events, swept their antagonists from the field.★ Nevertheless, the position of the new Ministers was not altogether happy. "There is indeed a great man fallen," wrote Godolphin's old friend, Weymouth, to Matt Prior, "but he is not buried, and whoever shall be his successors will have work enough to keep the tottering cart upon the wheels."[9] And so it was to prove; for the Tory party was united on one question only, a determination at all costs to stop the war. And with this object in view, they longed

★ In England and Wales, there were about 320 Tories, 150 Whigs, and 40 "doubtful". The 45 Scottish M.P.s showed a fair proportion of Whigs and Jacobites, for there were no Tories of the English type north of the Tweed. Trevelyan, *Queen Anne*, III, 73.

he had not in the world but about fourteen thousand pounds in tallies, of which sum seven was mine, three Mrs. Rundue's, a thousand Mrs. Curtis's, a woman that looked after my two elder children, and many other small sums that he took of helpless people, who thought themselves safe in his hands; and when all his debts were paid there could hardly be enough to bury him." Elsewhere Sarah asserts that before Sir William Godolphin's death, Godolphin's estate, exclusive of what he had settled on his son, did not exceed one thousand pounds a year.

to effect the removal of Marlborough. But for the moment they lacked courage. "It seems to mee," wrote Godolphin "as if the new ministers had the same intentions of displacing him (Marlborough) as they have don mee, but that while the peace seems still so uncertain, they have not dared to venture upon that stepp; so that I hope your lordship may still reckon that you have one firm friend in the Queen's Counsells and government."[10]

On the other great question of the hour, that of the succession, there was no agreement among the Tory party. They were divided into two factions, a Jacobite and a Hanoverian clique; and in between the two extremes a large central mass swayed uneasily from side to side. The "October Club", a body of High Tory members of Parliament, who met to quaff ale and swear damnation to the Whigs, were in revolt against what they regarded as the undue moderation of the Harley government. "We are plagued here with an October Club," wrote Swift, who, though still nominally a Whig, had been enraged at the unfriendly reception he had received from Godolphin just before his fall,[11] "that is a set of above a hundred parliament men of the country, who drink October beer at home, and meet every evening at a tavern near parliament to consult affairs, and drive things to extreme against the Whigs, to call the old Ministry to account, and get off five or six heads. The Ministry seem not to regard them, yet one of them in confidence told me, that there must be something thought on to settle things better.... The Ministry is for gentler measures and the other Tories for more violent."[12] "The Ministry is on a very narrow bottom and stand like an Isthmus between the Whigs on one side and violent Tories on the other. They are able seamen, but the tempest is too great, the ship too rotten, and the crew all against them."[13] A narrow bottom on a tempestuous ocean, the vessel rotten and the crew mutinous: thus Swift portrayed the plight of Harley, the ship's master. Yet the Captain's skill kept his craft afloat, safe from the rocks and shoals in the stormy sea.

On the question of the need for peace, however, the whole party joined in regarding themselves as the men ordained by Heaven to perform the will of the nation. The rest of the reign of Queen Anne is the story of the methods they employed in order to achieve their ends. Nor was the soil altogether infertile, for since long before Godolphin's fall, a French agent, the Abbé Gaultier, had been living in this country under various aliases and had been in close touch with the English Jacobites. It was by means of this spy that the negotiations were opened which were destined to end at Utrecht.

Yet when Parliament met on November 25th, the Queen's speech was disarmingly moderate, though the choice of the High Church Bromley as Speaker in place of Godolphin's friend Smith, showed the prevailing temper of the House. The speech made no reference to peace and demanded supplies for the vigorous prosecution of the war in all parts, and especially in Spain. Thus a reflection was cast on the late Ministry, who had shown special zeal in prosecuting the war in the Netherlands. They were further outraged by the complete silence observed on the Grand Alliance and by the pointed omission of any reference to the General's successes in the recent campaign.

Godolphin watched these events from the seclusion of Newmarket or his house in St. James's. And much that he saw distressed him. On December 17th, eight days before the meeting of Parliament, he wrote to a friend cloaked under the cipher of "No. 126" an interesting letter in which he summarized the evils of the moment on foreign affairs. He was careful to disclaim any wish to return to office and he declared that he had not "the least resentment or animosity against any one person whatsoever, whom I either know, or think to bee in her Majesty's Confidence, and trust. . . ." What worried him was the renewed confidence of France, engendered by the new Ministers' disregard of the great services of Marlborough. "Though their Armys have been beaten for 7 years together," he complained of the French, "the Warr is yett to begin afresh, and they are become so haughty and insolent as wholly to lay aside all thoughts of accommodation by a general peace. . . ." He knew, no doubt, of Harley's earnest desire to terminate hostilities, but perish appeasement; overwhelming strength alone would bring the sort of peace that he and Marlborough had devoted their lives to achieve.

The causes of the French intransigence were threefold; the blow to our public credit, the dissolution of Parliament, and the assurances sent to France that Marlborough would soon be dismissed. The first two were only significant for the effect they had on our allies, to ". . . increase their distrust and jealousy of the brittish [sic] counsells." From this all the present evils flowed. Nor did Godolphin see any prospect of steps being taken in Parliament to remove the unfortunate impression, for ". . . talking never soe big nor voting never so well, signifies very little towards carrying on the Warr with effect, if there bee not an entire conjunction and harmony betwixt her Majesty and the Allys abroad as it has been hitherto . . . particularly if the French should . . . have the further satisfaction of seeing the assurances from their friends here made good by the Duke of Marlborough's not serving any more, this must needs give the finishing stroak to the drooping Allyance, and make it fall to pieces immediately; nor when this is more certainly known, will france so much as hearken to any proposalls for a general peace, but expect the Allys shall treat separatly, as they certainly will be obliged to doe, for they always looked upon the Duke of Marlborough as the great *Cement*★ by which the whole Confederacy was held together, and

★ Godolphin's italics.

246

the States will not trust any other subject of the queens with the Command of their Army but will rather, as well as the rest of the Allys, make the best terms they can for themselves; and when the Allyance is once broken, can it enter into any bodys imagination that the Queen and the brittish [sic] Nation will have any terms from france, but what shall bee in favour of the pretender!" Furthermore, may not the country in its dilemma petition Parliament to address the Queen in favour of the Elector of Hanover being made commander of her army, and what a difficulty, he comments, "that would bring upon her Majesty either in granting or refusing, I leave you to judg."[14] Thus Godolphin in the autumn of 1710, when, as he thought, all that he and his friend had stood for was being sacrificed.

Meanwhile, Swift had thrown in his lot with the Tories. "'Tis good to see what a lamentable confession the Whigs all make me of my ill usage; but I mind them not. I am already represented to Harley as a discontented person, that was used ill for not being a Whig monger; and I hope for good usage from him. The Tories dryly tell me I may make my fortune, if I please; but I do not understand them, or rather, I do understand them."[15] Of course the witty Irish parson understood them very well, and was bent upon making his fortune. In November he opened fire in the *Examiner*,[16] taking revenge on Godolphin, Marlborough and the Whigs by stooping to revive the meanest slanders that had been circulated by Mrs. Manley in her *New Atalantis*. Once more Marlborough and his Duchess, monsters of avarice, had purloined vast sums; once more Sarah was dubbed Godolphin's mistress.* Indeed, no shred of character was allowed to any Whig. The very ferocity and meanness of the attack overreached itself. The Duchess of Marlborough drew up a dignified vindication of herself and her husband and sent it, together with the scurrilous number of the *Examiner,* for submission to the Queen. Anne showed her disgust by her dry comment. "Every one knows," she said, "that cheating is not the Duchess of Marlborough's fault." Nevertheless, her Majesty determined that her former friend must vacate her Court appointments, and Sarah's place of Mistress of the Robes was bestowed on the Duchess of Somerset and that of Keeper of the Privy Purse on Abigail Masham.

But it was not the journalistic talents of the author of the *Tale of a Tub,* great as they certainly were, that raised the popularity of Robert Harley and his Tory Ministry; it was Guiscard's murderous attack upon him that made him a national hero overnight. Now was the Queen's moment to raise her

---

* This libel from Mrs. Manley's *New Atalantis* was repeated by Swift in his *Memoirs relating to the Change in the Queen's Ministry in 1710.* Swift, *Prose Works* (ed. Scott), V, 368.

favourite to the highest pinnacle. Immediately upon his recovery, therefore, she promoted him from Chancellor of the Exchequer to Godolphin's vacant post of Lord High Treasurer; at the same time elevating him to the peerage with the proud titles of Oxford and Mortimer. Swift hastened to announce this to the two Irish ladies who were his friends. "This man has grown by persecutions, turnings out and stabbing," he added, "What waiting and crowding and bowing, will be at his levee? Yet, if human nature be capable of so much constancy, I should believe he will be the same man still, hating the necessary forms of grandeur he must keep up. 'Tis late, sirrahs, and I'll go to sleep."[17]

No sooner had the new Lord Oxford recovered from his wounds than he began to show his malice towards the late Government. In May he caused a Committee to be appointed to investigate the public accounts; and later in the month another Committee was nominated to draw up a report on certain alleged abuses to be laid before the Queen. The accusations of the Commissioners were briefly that, of the financial grants of Parliament up to Christmas 1710, no less a sum than £35,302,107 could not be accounted for, and that of this total no accounts for a great part had ever been laid before the Auditor.

So far as Godolphin was concerned, the charge was founded on the statements of the two Jacobites, Lockhart of Carnwath and Baillie of Jerviswood, which have already been considered.[18] The position was undoubtedly delicate because it was apparent from the evidence that the money had been remitted to Scotland to enable certain of the Scottish nobility who were in the confidence of the English Cabinet to fulfil promises that they had made to engage the services of various individuals to pass the Union, and that for obvious reasons these transactions had not been disclosed in the Treasury accounts. In his reply, Godolphin did not materially contradict the statement of the Commissioners, but contented himself with the reply that her Majesty had agreed not to exact the reversion of the debt. From the fact that the enquiry was pursued no further, we may conclude that the money had been disposed of as intended and in a way that could not be well revealed. At least one shrewd observer saw how things were tending. "It is now beleeved (and I think not without good ground) that the warm enquiry is dropt, and matters are compounded," wrote Thomas Bruce from London to his fellow Scot, and Lord Justice Clerk in Edinburgh. "The first symptom was that the committee of the whole House was tourned into a select committee, which was plainly to lessen the authority of the matter." Then he ventured upon some prognostications. "Hitherto it has been incertain whither the Duke of Marlbarrow [sic] was to go over or not," he continued, "and when people observed the indignities pute upon him by taking away his dutchess key and places, it was reasonable to think he was not to go. But this day it is als good as certain that he commands for the ensuing year. . . . Some are enclyned to believe that this compounding upon the old friendship betwixt Duke of Shrewsbury, Duke Mar., and Earl Godolphin, joyned with the present straits in point of public credit, and Duke Marborrow's interest in the foreign alliances, (especially considering the chief obstacle which lay in the way of uniting the Tories is now removed, viz. the Treasurer's unwillingness to joyn with the Tories least Earl Rochester should have overtoppt him), and now, I say, Godolphin having allready lost the whyt staff, he is willing with Duke Malborow [*sic*] for joyn with the Tories."[19]   There was much good sense in Bruce's views.   Furthermore, we may conclude, seeing that the matter had been brought forward by men hostile to Godolphin, that no shadow of guilt could be found against the ex-Lord Treasurer.   That he was acquitted of corruption by so malicious a witness as Dean Swift is the strongest possible evidence in his favour.[20]

But Godolphin in retirement watched events from afar.   And what he saw must have been extremely distasteful to him.   With what disgust must he have viewed the Ministers' strivings for peace and the questionable methods of Oxford's disreputable colleague, St. John: for it was he and not Harley who showed the strong ungloved hand.   It was St. John who set on Swift, now to prove himself the greatest pamphleteer of the age, to write down the Whigs and the Allies.   How brilliantly the unscrupulous Irishman performed his task in the pages of his *Examiner* and in the most effective of his political writings, *The Conduct of the Allies*!   It was St. John, too, who did not shrink from the necessity of achieving his ends by disgracing the Duke of Marlborough, regardless of all his great services to the nation, and by persuading the Queen by the creation of new peers to coerce the House of Lords.   For this he overcame whatever scruples Anne may have felt by the ingenious suggestion that the husband of her favourite Abigail might be one of the new lords.   No one could dispute her Majesty's prerogative to create peers, but many were found to question the wisdom of the action; and the town was soon filled with quips at the new lords' expense.   Wharton asked the twelve when they took their seats in the Lords, whether they voted by their foreman.   "Oh madam" declared the Italian Duchess of Shrewsbury to Oxford's wife, "I and my Lord are so weary of talking politics.   What are you and your Lord?"   To which the devout Lady Oxford replied with a sigh that "she knew no Lord but the Lord Jehovah."   "Oh dear, Madam! who is he?" cried the Duchess.   "I believe 'tis one of the new titles, for I never heard of him before."[21]   It was St. John who took the leading part in these stirring, well-known events, but it was Oxford who profited from his colleague's brilliant devices.

Godolphin eyed these events with contemptuous disapproval, for the new Ministers seemed to be throwing away all that he and his great friend had striven to achieve. When Sidney Godolphin and John Churchill had first come to Court in the days of Charles II, England had sunk to the status of a second-class power, her once proud Sovereign now no more than a henchman of the French monarch. These humiliating circumstances had been gradually overcome, first by the steadfast efforts of the redoubtable Willaim of Orange, and then by the glorious victories of Marlborough and Eugene which saved Europe from catastrophe: and in the great achievements of the two generals, the civilian Minister had played his essential part. By their united efforts England was once more making her influence felt in the councils of the nations. But not only by war had England extended her influence, for her importance was immeasurably augmented by the Union with Scotland. No longer need she fear that Scotland would ally herself with France or that Scots would set up a dynasty of their own. Henceforth, in spite of personal envy and jealousy between them, Englishmen and Scotsmen were found fighting shoulder to shoulder in their common cause in all quarters of the globe. One thing further the Ministers of Queen Anne had achieved, the Hanoverian succession. Hitherto, there had always been on the horizon the threat of a Stuart restoration, bringing in its train the menace of Catholicism and inevitable civil war. Dynastic uncertainty was now at an end. The settlement of the accession question, a triumph for the Whigs, sounded the death-knell of Jacobite hopes.

These were the things that Godolphin, the Minister without a party, and Marlborough, the moderate Tory, had attained during one of the most crucial periods of our history. How long would they last under the tender mercies of Harley and St. John? No wonder that Godolphin in retirement wrote in such pessimistic tone to his unknown correspondent, "No. 126."

But he was old, ill, and tired, and had no ambitions to return to public life. Much of his time during the summer and autumn months of 1711 were spent at his beloved Newmarket, whence he continued to carry on a correspondence with his lifelong friend. The old man was suffering much pain from the stone, a complaint that had long afflicted him, and he must by now have realized that his end was near. In the spring and summer of 1712 he spent many weeks with Sarah at Woodstock Lodge, a small house she inhabited during the building of Blenheim. Thence he went in August to visit his sister Jael's elder daughter, Dorothy, who had for some years been the wife of Sir Philip Meadows, and was living near Winchester. "... wee gott well to this place yesterday from the Lodg, by half an hour past two, through the finest road and pleasantest country that can be seen," he told Sarah, "the place it self is very agreeable, the prospect extreamly fine, and the house strong and substantiall, not quite big enough for a family where there are so many children, but they propose additions which will make it very convenient. The country is delightfull all round it, as farr as ones eye can reach. . . ."²² The next day he dined with the Bishop of Salisbury, "and his new daughter-in-law, who is a good pretty woman with a very modest look. I did not fail to make your compliments to him," he assured Sarah, "nor hee to drink your health. He seemed to bee a good deal dejected about politicks; but shewed us all the improvements he had made about his house and garden; . . ." The next day he was going to dine with his sister, "and fryday will finish all we have to doe here, so wee are in hopes of being at Woodstock very soon. . . ."²³ From Tilshead he wrote again: "I dined yesterday at my sisters who has one of the prettiest little places that ever was seen, she keeps it very neatly, and has very good choise fruit . . . she gave us the best dinner and the cleanest that I ever saw, and I am sure you would have thought soe . . . our business at this place is all dis-patched; and wee design to bee going tomorrow towards Woodstock. . . ."²⁴ Evidently Sarah was at Saint Albans, because he wrote on Sunday to inform her of their safe arrival at Woodstock to find the Marlboroughs' old friend Maynwaring, who had been seriously ill, just going to supper with Lord Sunderland and Vanbrugh, the architect engaged on Blenheim. "Wee had dined so late that we could not take any share in it," he added, "but their fish and their mutton was much commended and their desert [sic] was peaches nectarines figgs and green plums. . . ."²⁵

His stay at Woodstock was short, and in a day or two he joined his friends at Holywell. No sooner had he arrived than he was seized with a violent attack of the stone. Within a few days, the young Robert Walpole, who had recently through the malice of St. John been lodged in the Tower and had twice been visited by Godolphin, the Marlboroughs, Sunderland and other leading Whigs, came to bid his old chief a last farewell.²⁶ He found the Duke sick at heart and sick in body. But it was evident that Godolphin was dying. He rallied somewhat, however, at the welcome appearance of the visitor, and, turning to Sarah standing by his bedside, he said to her in a failing voice, "If you ever forsake that young man, and if souls are permitted to return from the grave to the earth, I will appear to you and reproach you for your conduct."²⁷ A few days later, early in the morning of September 15th, he died. "The Whigs have lost a great sup-port in the E. of Godolphin," Swift reported. "'Tis a good jest to hear the Ministers talk of him now with Humanity and Pity, because he is dead, and can do them no more hurt."²⁸

For several days the body of Lord Godolphin lay in state in the Jerusalem Chamber, until sufficient Whig Garter Knights could be assembled to uphold the Pall. These, headed by the Duke of Marlborough, privately and at night laid him to rest in the great Abbey that holds the dust of so many of the nation's most illustrious dead. No word of regret at the passing of Lord Godolphin came from the ungrateful Queen, who owed so much of her greatness to his faithful service. But Sarah, mourning the loss of her life-long friend, penned these words on the first leaf of her Bible. They are his epitaph for all time—

"The 15th of September 1712 at two in the morning the Earl of Godolphin dyed at the Duke of Marlborough's hous in St. Albans, who was the best man that ever lived."*

* The Duchess of Marlborough's Bible, the property of Earl Spencer, is still preserved at Althorp.

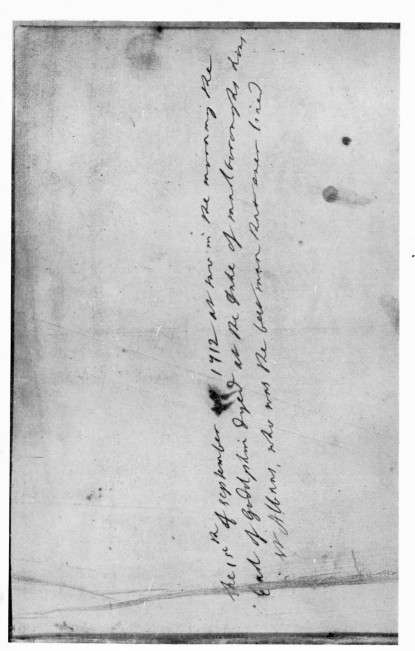

THE DUCHESS OF MARLBOROUGH'S BIBLE

at Althorp

POSTSCRIPTUM

POSTSCRIPTUM

Soon after Lord Godolphin's death the Duke of Marlborough was dismissed from all his appointments: whereupon his daughter resigned her office of Lady of the Bedchamber to Queen Anne. Sarah, much gratified at this spirited action, copied out in her own hand Lady Godolphin's letter of resignation and she appended a note signifying her approval.

In the following year, 1713, when Marlborough and his wife were roving the Continent, exiles from their native land, Lady Godolphin suggested that her daughter Henrietta might join her grandparents as soon as they were in some place where they could receive her. "She speaks french now, to bee of great use to you," Lady Godolphin wrote, "and the longer she is a broad the better it will be for her, for it will make it, So young as She is, like her natural language, which will be very prittey and useful to her. any roome in the world, for Such a child is good enough, and as well, as what she has here."[1] "She was so desirous to part with Her daughter," wrote Sarah bitterly some ten years later, "that she thank'd me for it before I had her, which was the only thanks I ever had."[2]

With Sarah in that mood, relations between mother and daughter rapidly deteriorated. The final wrench came on June 16th, 1722, the eve of the death of the Duke of Marlborough. When Henrietta and her sister Mary, now Duchess of Montagu, called, their mother sent them word that they must not stay long with their father. Whereupon Mary replied haughtily that "she did not understand Her, but if she meant that they were not to see their Mother, they were very well used to That." In spite of the injunction, however, it appears that the two sisters remained for some time with their father, and when their Mother entered, they curtsied but did not speak to her. After the Duke had been moved back to his own room, the sisters followed, and were joined by Henrietta's daughter, since 1717 the wife of the Duke of Newcastle, afterwards the despised minister of the Georges. At length the Duchess of Newcastle left, and Henrietta and Mary went into the drawing-room, where they waited until four o'clock in the morning. "When they went to London," recorded the indignant Sarah, "They and their Creatures reported to every body That I had turn'd them out of My house, and that I had order'd that no body should give them any thing to eat or to drink. That I had told the Dutchess of Newcastle That I was glad it was over, for now I should never see Her again; and that as I had put the two Sisters out, I took Mrs. Kingdom in, and that they heard us talk a great deal and laugh as they sat in the next room; That the Drs. and Surgeons all knew every thing that had pass'd, and therefore there was no keeping it a Secret, and that after such as Behaviour as I had had to their Father, they would never any more take any notice of me."³

Unfortunately, we have not either Henrietta's or Mary's version of the controversy, but we have a brief mention of these domestic troubles from their gentle sister Anne. "I am so sensible of my own misfortunes," wrote Lady Sunderland to her mother, "that I must say all I can for my sisters, which is that I never saw what you think in eather of 'em."⁴ And when Mrs. Kingdom, the family friend, tried to take the sisters' part, she risked exciting Sarah's ire. "I cannot see how it c'd be wrong to your Grace, to wish yu might yet be happy in one another, nor that, it c'd ever be disagreeable to you, to hear it said, that I beleiv'd those ladys (& perticularly Ldy Go. whom I had formerly loved extreamly and who had done a thousand obliging things to me) had a great many vertues, and that I hop'd at last they w'd see their errors, and be every thing yu c'd wish them."⁵

After Marlborough's death, when Sarah had persuaded herself that the Godolphins were aggrieved at the terms of the Duke's will, Sir John Vanbrugh strove to refute the contention. "I shew'd the young Dutchess★ what your Lordship writ, about so great a Fortune falling into such generous hands;" he told Lord Carlisle, "which she took very well. She says, Covetousness has happen'd to appear to her so very odious in some other people, that she is sometimes frightened, lest she shou'd have seeds in her blood, that may Spring up one time or other. I tell her, now is the time if ever, Since it generally go's along with Riches. This will was made, but in March last; and hurts nobody but her; I don't find however that either she or my Lord Godolphin have the least disposition to dispute it; and I hope nobody else will. Her grace has by this Will (for to be sure that was her doings) made my Lord Blandford Independent of his Father and Mother, Depriv'd her Daughter of the jewells, and Cater'd bravely for herself. . . ."⁶ That the will made Willigo independent of his parents may well have been resented by them, for indeed they were finding him a sore trial.

The relations between these three had for some time been strained. Henrietta was turbulent, vain, in some ways no doubt rather silly; but she

---

★ On Marlborough's death Henrietta succeeded to the Dukedom, becoming Duchess of Marlborough in her own right. At the same time her eldest son William assumed the title of Marquess of Blandford. Henrietta was usually known as 'the young Duchess" to distinguish her from her mother "the old Duchess."

LADY MARY GODOLPHIN
DUCHESS OF LEEDS
From the portrait after Sir Joshua Reynolds at Temple Newsam House

had beauty and charm. Francis was easy-going, rather lazy, and, like his
father, something of a valetudinarian. Doubtless he stood in some awe of
his formidable mother-in-law. "I am come to town to day My Dear
Child," he wrote on one occasion to his daughter, the Duchess of Newcastle, "but having business with Marl: House that lyes heavy on my hands,
god know how long it maybe before I may get time to see you."[7] Yet at
times he could stand up to Sarah. Though the beloved Willigo had grown
up into a selfish, lazy, drink-sodden man, a constant anxiety to his parents,
he managed to retain the affection of his grandmother, who on one
occasion sought to recover from her daughter, to whom she had given
it, the little lodge in Windsor Park, in order to bestow it upon her grandson,
and begged Lord Godolphin to use his influence with his wife to dissuade
her from disposing of the property. This was too much for even Francis's
patience, and he resolutely declined to interfere.[8]

Yet the relations of Henrietta and Francis can hardly have been cordial.
The reader will recall the friendship that had sprung up in Sidney's day
between the great Congreve and the Godolphin family. This intimacy had
increased since the first lord's death. Early in 1723 the author of *The Way of
the World* spent the whole season at fashionable Bath. There too was the
fair Henrietta, and she and Congreve seemed almost inseparable. The play-
wright had deserted all his old loves—sweet Anne Bracegirdle, the heroine
of all his plays, and not so sweet Lady Mary Wortley Montagu—and was
concentrating the whole of his attention upon this latest charmer.
Henrietta Marlborough was just forty-one. She had had four children,
Willigo, now Marquess of Blandford, Henrietta, wife of the Duke of Newcastle, and two others who had died infants. For close on twenty years she
had ceased bearing. But the waters of Bath, the traveller John Macky tells
us, "have a wonderful Influence on barren Ladies, who often prove with
Child, even in their Husbands Absence."[9] What then could be less surprising than the announcement in the fashionable newspapers that Henrietta
Duchess of Marlborough had given birth to a daughter? Francis was not
surprised, it seems. "You will, I dare say, my Dear Child, be glad to hear
that your Mama is very well," he told his other daughter, "after having
been brought to bed, about two hours ago, of a little girl, who is likewise
in a prosperous way; . . ."[10] Nor was Lady Mary Wortley Montague,
who used some very unkind language about "my poor friend"; "she is as
much embarrassed with the loss of her big belly," she told her sister, Lady
Mar, "as ever a dairy-maid was with the getting one."[11] But Lady Mary
was no impartial critic, for be it not forgotten that Henrietta had stolen her
friend Congreve, and was not above boasting of her conquest. "I am sure
you won't dislike to have Mr. Congreve tomorrow, if you can get him,"

she had told Lady Mary on one occasion, "for he is like all good things, hard to come at, and tho' I shan't add to your company, I have wit enough not to spoyle it, which you must allow is being tolerable. What hour would you have me come?"[12] "The reigning Duchess of Marlborough had entertained the town with concerts of Bonocini's composition very often:" Lady Mary told Lady Mar, "but," she added, "she and I are not in that degree of friendship to have *me* often invited: we continue to see one another like two people who are resolved to hate with civility."[13] Nor was the old Duchess Sarah an impartial critic of her eldest daughter, to whom she henceforth referred as "Congreve's Moll", or "Moll Congreve."[14]*

In these circumstances it is not perhaps surprising that before long rumours were afloat as to the child's paternity and soon it was alleged that the play-wright was the father of the infant Mary. This scandal was still rife forty years later, when young James Boswell first came to London. "Mrs. Douglas, who has a prodigious memory and knows a thousand anecdotes, especially of scandal," wrote he, "told me that Congreve the poet lived in the family of old Lord Godolphin, who is yet alive, and that Lady Godolphin was notoriously fond of him. In so much that her lord having gone abroad upon an embassy for two years, on return she presented him with a fine girl by the author of *Love for Love*, which he was so indulgent to accept of; nay, after Congreve's death, he joined with her in grief, and allowed her to have an image of him in wax daily set at table and nightly in her bed-chamber, to which she spoke, believing it through heat of fancy, or be-lieving it in appearance to be Congreve himself. The young lady was most tenderly educated, and it is a certain fact that she was never suffered to see the moon for fear she would cry for it. She is now Duchess of Leeds, and has turned out extremely well."† The story of the waxen image daily set upon Henrietta's table refers to a scurrilous story told in *The Daily Post* for

* A romantic account of Congreve's courtship of Henrietta was published shortly after her death, *The Court Parrot; a new miscellany, in Prose and Verse*, (London 1733), 13–22. It was entitled *The Secret History of Henrietta Maria Teresa*. Lynch, *A Congreve Gallery*, 62–4.

† Boswell, *London Journal*, 1762–63 (1950 ed. Pottle), 156–7. Nevertheless, Lady Mary Godolphin herself, even when Duchess of Leeds, seems to have been ignorant of the doubts raised about her birth, as would appear from the following anecdote recorded by Lady Louisa Stuart. According to this story, the Duchess of Portland once borrowed Mary's jewels to wear at a masquerade; and whilst the two Duchesses were examining them together asked the Duchess of Leeds whether she could guess why the letters W.C. were engraved upon the back of every collet? "I have often puzzled myself to divine what could be my mother's meaning in it," came the reply, "do you think it was the name of the jeweller?" "Oh yes, it must have been so," replied the Duchess of Portland, well knowing the cipher meant William Congreve, and anxious to change the subject. *The Private Letter-Books of Sir Walter Scott* (1930, Ed. Partington), 345.

Saturday, July 15, 1732 and to a no less scurrilous poem entitled *The Amorous D-h-ss; or, Her G- Grateful,* which appears soon afterwards.* This rubbish was palpably scandal: but there may have been a substratum of truth in it, for Henrietta was certainly devoted to Congreve, and when early on Sunday morning, January 19th, 1729, he died, she sat by his body throughout the night. But the rest of the story cannot be so easily dismissed; and the rumour as to the true paternity of little Lady Mary receives support from the Will of Congreve. Of this the poet made Henrietta and Francis Godolphin executors, but the document was so drawn that Francis had no check on his wife who was just as free and independent to act as if she were sole executrix. Virtually the whole of his property Congreve bequeathed to Henrietta Duchess of Marlborough, with private instructions that it was to pass to the infant Lady Mary Godolphin.[15] May not the true explanation be that the poet chose to leave the bulk of his small property, not to his family, not to Anne Bracegirdle to whom, however, he bequeathed a small legacy, but to the richest woman in England because he believed her to be the mother of his child?†

Meanwhile, the tiresome Willigo was giving his family a great deal of trouble. His drunken habits and partiality for low company put him on bad terms with his mother, which in itself was probably sufficient to commend him to his grandmother. Thus by 1725 Blandford, then mostly in Paris, was wont to write to Sarah with unworthy comments on his mother. "Sir J. Evelyn's Second Son, Who is here and at present out Wth My Mother, has giv'n Me such an account of things at home, that I've all the reason in the world to think, if it had not been for this distribution of things I shou'd have been left in a very uncertain state as to my income."[16] And again: "Lord Walgrove[17] . . . told Me ye other day that before his leaving England, he had seen My Father, but not My Mother, so that I suppose He and She are out at present."[18] From Paris he drifted to Utrecht, whence there were

---

* For various versions of this absurd tale, see Cibber, *Lives of the Poets,* IV, 92: Davies, *Dramatic Miscellanies* (ed. 1784) III, 382; *Biographia Britannica* (ed. 1789), IV, 79. Lynch, *A Congreve Gallery* (1951), 65-7.

† I am indebted to Mr. Kingsley Adams, Director of the National Portrait Gallery, for the transcript of a letter written by Henrietta, Duchess of Marlborough, in 1729 to Jacob Tonson the younger, nephew of the Secretary of the Kitcat Club. It seems reasonable to assume that the picture she refers to is Sir Godfrey Kneller's Kitcat portrait of William Congreve. The letter runs thus: "Sir, I know 'tis only the Sett off those Pictures that your Uncle Values and not that yt I would give the world for. Therefore sure except 'tis purely out of Ill-Nature and having no respect for that Picture, he would change with me for an Originall one off Sir Godfrey Knellers, just the same Size off the Kitcat ones—I wish this was in your own Power. I am, Sir Your humble Servant, Marlborough. Novem, yt 29th—1729. For Mr. Tonson." The original letter is in the Malone MSS., Yale University Library.

soon rumours of his pending marriage. His sister, the Duchess of New-castle, usually charitable, wrote bitterly that ". . . the young man has told his father and mother, that he is too farr engaged to break it of [sic]. I believe Ld. Worthless is not yet come to town," she adds. "I doubt he deserves that name more than ever . . ."[19]

This marriage was a bitter pill for the family to swallow, for not only was the young lady some years older than Blandford, but she was a mere Dutch burgomaster's daughter.* "As I take it for granted that Ld. Blandford is unalterably bent on his marriage," wrote Francis Godolphin sadly to his mother-in-law, "I the less wonder your Grace has had no answer to the last letter you honour'd him with, because I take the arguments, contain'd in it agt. his design, to have been such as would puzzle a wiser man than himself to refute. All I can say is, his best friends have done what they could to divert him from this weak, improper, ill-judg'd step: Since that can have no effect (tis a coarse and vulgar proverb to make use of, but) as he has baked so he must brew."[20] The marriage duly took place, and Sarah wrote anxiously to beg her grandson to return to England and seek to be reconciled to his mother. Probably she will refuse an interview; in that case, adds Sarah most improperly: ". . . your father can have nothing to take ill of you, for tis not possible to believe that my lord Godolphin with his sense, and good nature can refuse to see, and live well with his only son, because he has the misfortune of having a madd woman for his wife."[21] Several letters on this unpromising theme passed between Blandford and his grandmother, to be terminated with this heartless statement: "Madam, I fear I did not sufficiently explain my self in my last wth regard to the Circumstance of seeing my Mother; which I have so determind a Resolution *not to do* that as My Father persists that I should see Her, as the condition of my living well with him, I should (notwithstanding the Honour I ever had for Him), think my self acquitted from the Obligation of seeing either of them."[22]

Meanwhile, the Blandfords had returned to England—not very much to the comfort of the family. In January they dined with the Newcastles at Claremont, and displayed the strangest manners. "Papa was so good as to dine with us last Sunday at Claremont from Windsor," wrote the Duchess to her aunt, wife of the Provost of Eton,† ". . . my B(rother) and Lady Blandford din'd with me last Fryday, Sr. John & Lady Evelyn was so good to meet them here. You may be sure I satt in a good deal of pain till t'was over, nothing extraordinary happned, but a few of his agreeable Laughs,

---

* Maria Catherina, daughter of Peter de Jong of Utrecht.

† Henry Godolphin, Sidney's younger brother, was Provost of Eton from 1695 till 1717 when he became Dean of St. Paul's. In 1726 he returned to Eton as Provost and held the appointment until his death in 1733.

which dispos'd me much more to cry, than to join with him in his mirth. . . ."
Then she refers to a dinner at Lord Blandford's house. The guests were the
old Duchess of Marlborough, her grandchild Lady Di Spencer, the Win-
chelseas, the Denbighs, and Sir John and Lady Evelyn. ". . . they were all
there a little after three. four o'clock came, and five, but no Ld. Blandford,
and by that time my Lady thought fitt to call for dinner, and when they had
half dined he came in, so that the Ds. of M. said in all the good humour in
the world, oh my Ld, I conclude you have been in the house of commons; ★
indeed madam but I have not. then say she, I wish I was nearer to you,
that I might beat you: then I am very glad you are not. I did not think you
wd. have come before five, nor I did not think you wd. have staid for me,
says my Ld. . . ." The host went to the play at about six o'clock leaving
his guests to play Quadrille the whole evening. "When he came home
from the play," continued the Duchess of Newcastle, "he came into the
room again for a minute, went away again before the Ds. of M. went away,
and Ld. Winchelsea put her into her chair. to compleat my history, the
occasion of his being so late was, that he went and din'd at Lady Meadows's,
and so came to his company at his own house between 5 and 6 o'clock that
he knew was waiting for him all that time. sure there never was such a
creature born, I fancy t'would be entertaining to hear the Ds. of M, give an
account of it. but Lady Evelyn says she kept her good humour all day, and
was perfectly easy, and did not seem as if there was anything odd or wrong
in him, any more than what she said to him, which was quite in good
humour."[23] No wonder Willigo was not popular with his family!
"What you say is certainly very true," Henrietta Newcastle wrote to her
aunt a few weeks later, "that one ought never to expect any thing right or
reasonable from a certain person, but that is the misfortune; and I'm afraid I
shall never be able to help thinking it one. I can't learn that her Grace had
held forth about his pretty behaviour that day, nor I don't believe she will
till the parliament is up, so may be you'd have the first of it. . . ."[24]

But Willigo had not much longer to mortify his relatives. In the
summer of 1731 he died suddenly and under unfortunate circumstances at
Oxford. His father was staying at the time at Wotton with the old
family friends, the Evelyns. Thence he wrote enigmatically to his daughter
at Claremont. "I am extreamly glad," he told her, "to find your thoughts
and mine so nearly the same with relation to the melancholy event at Oxford."[25] But others, naturally enough, were less reticent. One was particularly enlightening, for Lord Hervey, the scurrilous diarist of Ickworth,
wrote thus from Hampton Court to his friend Stephen Fox: "He died

★ Blandford was M.P. for Woodstock at this time.

suddenly of a drunken fit or fever at Oxford. It is a fine accident for our lucky friend, Lord Sunderland.* He will be no longer obliged to manage that unloving, capricious, extravagant Fury of a grandmother. I could not help reflecting how particular it was, that the only remaining branch of such a family as the Lord Treasurer Godolphin, and the head of such a family as the late Duke of Marlborough, should go off so universally unregretted, especially when nobody ever pretended to say he had not sense, good-nature, and honesty. With those three qualities to want a friend is very extraordinary."[26] Indeed, even his mother, it seems, could not feel much sorrow. "I had not time in my last to answer your question concerning the Duchess of Marlborough's concern for her son, but can assure you she is neither so unaccountable as (not) to feel any affliction, nor so ridiculous as to affect it. She very truly says that his behaviour towards her must justify her being at least indifferent to his death; and that anybody who had any regard to *Papa's* memory must be glad that the Duke of Marlborough was now not in danger of being represented in the next generation by one who must have brought any name he bore into contempt. The death of her son makes a very great change in her present circumstances, and a much greater still in what must devolve upon her at her mother's death: but to do her justice, I believe that consideration of interests affects her (though daughter to the Duke and Duchess of Marlborough) as little as it would anybody I know."[27]

The reaper was busy with Churchills just now and scarcely two years were to pass before Henrietta was to follow her son into the unknown. Her husband wrote somewhat dispassionately of her illness. "My dear Child, Your poor Mama's present and chief illness may more properly I think be called dropsy in her Limbs than anything else, for it does not affect her belly in the same degree as it does them; from yesterday sennight she had made little or no water, and from that time therefore has gradually grown weaker and been in more pain; nor does any one of the Doctors who just now happen to be all here, think it is possible she can recover."[28] And again, "Things here, my Dear, continue just the same as when you left this place; your poor Mama seems not to suffer near so much as she did o' Sunday to Munday, not even at such times as she appears fully awake; at those times she makes pertinent and sensible answers to what the Doctors say to her; but when she says any thing of her own accord (which is but seldom, for she generally lyes quiet and without *constant* moaning) its rambling and out of the way, and yet ... one may suppose it a kind of dreaming rather than a downright delirium, but that, to a degree her head is that way affected, I doubt, is too sure. She takes her cordialls and her nourishment when they

*By the death of Blandford, his cousin Sunderland became heir to the Dukedom of Marlborough.

propose them to her, but has not yet ask'd for any thing her self.   Her convulsions are less strong and less frequent than yesterday, but Dickens fears
that is more owing to a decay of strength than to any good cause, and tho
nothing be grown worse yet neither will he allow me to say there is any
amendment or more hope than when you went from hence."   And he
closes his letter tenderly: "God send you a good night My Dear."[29]

Half an hour later, poor Henrietta Marlborough was released from her
sufferings.   Next morning, on Lord Godolphin's instructions, the attendant
Ambrose Dickens announced her loss to the Duchess of Newcastle.[30]
When her Will was opened, it was found that Henrietta had given instructions that she should "be buried in Westminster Abbey in the very same
place with the Right Honourable Sidney, late Earl of Godolphin," which
incidentally was very near to her beloved Congreve, and not at Blenheim.
Furthermore, she made most careful provision for her younger daughter,
now ten years old, to whom she bequeathed the larger portion of her own
fortune and also Congreve's entire personal estate.*

But if there was doubt as to the paternity of little Mary Godolphin,
there can be no doubt as to the affection in which "the poor child" and
"poor Minos" as Francis called her, was held by her putative father and her
childless sister.†   Mary's childish letters to Henrietta from November 1735
to August 1737, some in French, many in verse, and all in an excellent copper-
plate hand, though stilted and formal, yet show an open, lively nature that
is wholly charming.[31]   Within a few weeks of the mother's death, Francis
was writing anxiously to his elder daughter about "the child."   "Mary
Spencer tells me that all last winter none of the Men Servants danc'd country
dances with the Child, nor either then or since have ever play'd at Cards
with Her except Pivain," he told Henrietta.   "As this therefore is the utmost
that the Child her self will have thought of, I see no great harm in permitting it yet for some time longer; and upon her Birthday it's likely she
may have a mind to it.   She is to begin again next week to learn upon the
Harpsichord and to dance, and to write, only her French-man, which is what
she least likes, is to be respited till after her Birthday.   Her eyes Mary

---

* Will dated July 11, 1732.   Brit. Mus. Add. MSS. 28,071, ff. 34–9.

† At first Newcastle protested at the wish expressed by Henrietta that after her
death her elder daughter and her husband should make a home for little Lady Mary
at Claremont, and Newcastle wrote in unwontedly strong terms to Lord Godolphin
(Newcastle to Godolphin, "Claremont," no date.   Brit. Mus. Add. MSS. 33,064,
f. 481), to which Godolpin replied hardly less strongly next day (Godolphin to
Newcastle, no date.   Brit. Mus. Add. MSS. 33,064, f. 482).   Miss Kathleen M.
Lynch opines that Newcastle was frightened of the scandal about Mary's birth, but
who knows?   Lynch, *A Congreve Gallery*, 92–3.   In any case, he seems ultimately to
have withdrawn his objection as Mary spent much of her youth at Claremont.

tells me . . . are still a little tender, for which, if it do not soon go off of itts self, Dr. Broxholm I find is inclin'd to give her some gentle remedy."[32]

Later in the month Mary is with her sister at Claremont, and Francis writes anxiously from his house near Cambridge.* "I have seldom observ'd that purging is of much use towards the cure of any indisposition of the eyes," he tells Henrietta, "and am therefore not at all *sorry* to find that Dr. Broxholm is slow in administering any remedy of that sort, in the poor child's case; . . ."[33] A few days later he is glad that the inflammation of the eyes has subsided;[34] but this appears too optimistic for he is soon telling his, daughter ". . . if a dose or two of Rhubarb (together with the bleeding) should quite free her from any disorder in her eyes, I confess it is more than I could almost have hop'd for . . ."[35] Later there are rumours that Mary's kidneys are affected;[36] but her indisposition does not seem to have been at all serious, for towards the end of January she is in London. "From what I saw and heard of the Child this morning at Kensington, my Dear Child, all I can say is that I hope she does not grow worse, nor does appear either weak or dispirited. I got hither just at 11, and just as she was going to have her breakfast a-bed; toast and butter with a little tea, both of which she took with appetite enough. Her cough having troubled her pretty much yesterday, towards evening she took some Carduus tea, which brought a great deal of flegm off her stomach, and was, as I imagine the cause of her getting more sleep last night than had happen'd to her of late, for she wak'd to cough but 4 times, and slept to within a quarter of 11 this morning."[37] "Since I rec'd the inclos'd, my Dear Child, I have see Dr. Brox: who has been at Kenston and says the Rhubarb has done very well for that she has a Stomach to days and her countenance much better than yesterday."[38] Two days later, Francis tells his daughter that there has been "some little pull-back", but nothing sufficiently serious to force him to postpone his excursion to Newmarket with the Duke of Bridgwater on the morrow. Their absence from London can only be a short one, as "we propose to be back again so as to dine at the Jockey Club here o' wensday next."[39]

Five months later, we find the devoted father worrying himself about Henrietta's health ". . . tho the *operation* still to come is such as, I fear, is to *you* terrible," he writes, "yet when it's over, I hope in God you will find reason my dear Child, to be glad you have submitted to it."[40] But at first

* It was here that Godolphin kept the famous stallion that he had imported in 1729 at the age of five, "almost the last of the Eastern horses to be imported that had any influence in the development of the present-day racing thoroughbred." *Book of the Horse* (ed. Vesey-Fitzgerald, 1949), 535. For a reproduction of the only known painting of the horse from life, that painted by J. Wootten in 1731, see Lady Wentworth, *The Authentic Arab Horse* (ed. 1945), Colour Plate 3. The Godolphin Arabian died in 1753 and is buried in the stables: the grave can still be seen.

Henrietta was not glad. "To have submitted to such an operation my dear Child, as you have lately done, without finding any benefit or relief from it, seems to me a cruell and vexatious grievance, and such as, I'm sure, I am heartily sorry should have happen'd to you."[41] But in a couple of weeks or so the Duchess was better, and her father wrote of his delight to hear ". . . that you had been gaining ground every day since I left London. If you have not . . . any more relapses, I shall hope to find you o' Saturday morning allmost without complaint."[42]

The following winter, however, Mary's health was again causing anxiety. "We have not here, had any evacuation yet to day," he told Henrietta on December 8th.[43] Four days later, however, he was able to write more optimistically. "You have already heard, My Dear, that the poor Child pass'd the night better than we hoped for. Since she wak'd this morning she has had three of the same sort of evacuations, notwithstanding which I left her just now mighty cheerful and in spirits such as to me seem wonderfull, and her temper at the same time cool and good. . . ."[44] "The evacuations its true are of the same thin sort as yesterday," he wrote next day, "but when I came down just now she had had but two of them and was talkative and in very good spirits."[45] "You know before now, My Dear, that the poor Child slept through the whole night. The first thing she took after waking was a cup of Panada. Now just before I came down from her I saw her take a cup of nice broth. I left her playing upon her spinette in bed, and she had not then had any evacuation to day."[46]

A year later the "poor Child" has become "Dear Minos." Much of her time is spent at her sister's home at Claremont, whither a constant stream of letters flow from a tender father. He thanks "Dear Minos" for her letter which "I think was very well writt. I have presum'd to mark a few errors I find in it, which are no other than what I am sure she can correct the moment she sees them, and might possibly committ out of her affectionate concern for Papa."[47] But Mary was still subject to childish ailments. "Though I am prodigiously glad to hear that the heats in Dear Minos's face are abated, yet your finding such daily improvement in her temper and manner, and her growing still more good and agreeable than you know how to describe, is what you may be sure, My Dear, must give me infinite satisfaction and Pleasure." I rejoyce in your saying a second time that you think the heats in Dear Minos's face do rather diminish both in colour and number, and entirely agree with you that their lessening so gradually is rather a good sign than otherwise."[48]

A fortnight later, Lord Godolphin is writing to Henrietta "to give dear Minos a thousand thauks for her charming, pretty, well written letter of yesterday."[49] The following March dear Minos is reported to be suffering from the same complaint as troubled her the previous year: once again rhubarb is tried,[50] with satisfactory results.[51] A few weeks later, Mary Godolphin has gone with the Newcastles to Bath, where her father hopes that "Dr. Oliver has hit upon a proper as well as an easy method of making the Rhubarb effectuall whenever there is occasion for taking it." Then he begs Henrietta to assure Mary "of the satisfaction it is to me to hear of her present health and happyness, and *your self*, of being most tenderly yours, My Dear Child.* Who can doubt that Francis Godolphin was a most dutiful and loving father to both his daughters?

The reader will, however, be somewhat disconcerted to learn that on at least three occasions the wealthy Duke of Newcastle found it necessary to borrow money from his father-in-law. The first was in 1729, when he borrowed £5,000. This, it seems, the indulgent Francis was not unwilling to lend, ". . . yet I can not but own it would in some measure disconcert my affairs were I to be disappointed in my expectations of receiving it again," he told the Duke. "However, as I have the fullest confidence in your Honour and Justice, and do hope in God that for all manner of reasons your life will continue many and many years beyond the short time in which you design to repay me this money, I shall most willingly accommodate you with it upon the terms you your self propose . . ."[52] It was nearly eight years later that Newcastle had recourse again to his father-in-law, and then, significantly, the request came through the Duchess. Again Godolphin agreed, but less willingly than upon the previous occasion. Most people would be surprised to learn that he was considerably in debt, which he begs his daughter and her husband to believe. "This, however, I premise, only to prevent in the first place, any further Sollicitation of the same kind with That I receiv'd from you yesterday, and, in the next, to show you how materiall it is to me both that the rents should in reality be sufficient to answer the intended purpose, and likewise that the Terms and method propos'd for repayment of the money should be compunctually comply'd with, and made as certain as the nature of the security will admit; . . ." Nevertheless, since the loan ". . . will be so great an ease to Him (Newcastle) and so agreeable to You, I will (for This time) submit both to some Hazard and some inconvenience, rather than not do Him and my self the pleasure to put an end to his present distress."[53] Once again, some five years later, a further loan, this time for £2,000, was asked for: the request was readily granted. "It happens, My Dear Child," her father assured Henrietta, "to be not at all inconvenient to me at this time to lend the Duke

* At the foot is added, "I think I ought not to omitt telling you that I have been lucky enough to win to day what is called the great stakes." Godolphin to Duchess of Newcastle, "Newmarket, 23 Aprill 1737." Brit. Mus. Add. MSS. 33,079, f. 153.

of N. the £2,000 he is in want of . . ." and he is glad to do so ". . . since his occasions for it are pressing."[54] Was it, one wonders, his passion for electioneering that had driven Newcastle to these straits?

Early in 1740, that is some two years before the date of the last of the loans just mentioned, Henrietta and her husband were able in some degree to repay her father's generosity. In November 1740 Mary Godolphin became seventeen; but even before that age she had become a gay and beautiful young woman. The time had come for her to marry, and doubtless there was no lack of suitors. One of them the Duke of Leeds,* was looked upon with particular favour by Mary's family and by Mary herself. The Newcastles and the Evelyns were active in the marriage negotiations which appear to have been opened early in February. By the 20th Lord Godolphin was writing to his elder daughter of "the pleasure I have in the success of your negotiations,"[55] though they were still continuing in April,[56] and in May, Godolphin, on a visit to the Evelyns at Wotton, assigned the cause of delay where it is often assigned in our own time. "When the Lawyers will give us leave to come to a conclusion I do not *now* pretend to guess," he told Henrietta sarcastically, "for tho I cannot even *yet* see why it might not be tomorrow-fortnight, if *They* so pleas'd, I am however, easy to believe it may very probably (as you say it will) drill on to a week longer."[57] By July, however, Mary's fond father is glad ". . . to hear of her being so happy and so well pleas'd (which) you may be sure gives me great joy, especially as the case is the same in the Duke of Leeds's part . . ."[58]

So Mary became Duchess of Leeds, and before long the mother of several children. The first two died at birth, but soon two promising boys survived. "Dear Panky," wrote the elder to the younger, "I hope your Flea continues safe under lock and key; I have inclos'd a silver penny, which I desire you'd accept of, it being given me as a reward for getting Captain of my fform, I am your affectionate Brother Spanzy."[59] And again, "Dear Panky, I desire your acceptance of the inclos'd, they being what I receiv'd as an Encouragement for my Holidays Task being well done: pray my Duty to Papa and Mama, and tell them I am in great expectation of being in the first Form to-morrow. I am Dear Panky your affectionate Brother Carmarthen."[60] In the ducal household of Claremont, young Tom Carmarthen, it seems, was known as *Beast*. Here are two delightful letters that the boy wrote to his Aunt, the Duchess of Newcastle, from Westminster School. "Dear Aunt," he wrote, "I hope this will find you well in *Heaven* (i.e. Claremont) as it leaves us here in *Hell* (i.e. School), & as we are Devils I hope you will for once excuse the ill-writing of my black Claws: Saturday the

* Thomas Osborne, fourth Duke of Leeds (1713–89).

18th being a whole Holiday is very convenient for us to go to Heaven, and I hope will be convenient for you also; if it luckily is I hope you will send me word before hand; & I think if Convenient it will be the best way to send the Post-Chaise and 4 horses on the Friday Evening, because it will hold us three better than the Coach & besides that is more expeditious; it does not signifie one straw whether we lay in the same room that we did before or no because we don't care where we lay so we have but a bed, as we are never in our room but at night; Pray give my Duty to Uncle, burn this as soon as you have read it; & believe me to be Dear Aunt your affectionate *Beast*."[61] In the summer of the following year he wrote again, "Dear Aunt, I hope this will find the sweet Canary-Bird well, as it was when it went from me; Friday is a Vigil & therefore as School will be up early, the Coach or one of the Post-Chaises may be with us at 6 o Clock; Mr. Cooper thinks that will be the best time; I mean in the Evening; I wish you much Joy of the good news, that is, that there is *a Pound of Cherries* taken. If you can, pray give my Duty to Uncle who is (I dare Say) in a violent splutter for joy of the good news & believe me to be, dear Aunt, ever Your most Dutiful *Beast*. Turn over. P.S. Brother desires his Duty to the *Duke of Newcastle*."[62]

Alas! less than a month later, this gay, hopeful youth succumbed to small-pox. His mother was broken hearted; and as much as two years later we find her writing of her surviving son, now Lord Carmarthen: "Panky is, thank God, a very good Boy, in all respects, and look'd so like his poor Brother this morning, as made me burst into Tears; he was dress'd in a new Frock, and his waist was very long."[63] And when Panky is taken ill at school, he is snatched away and taken to North Mimms[64] to recuperate. "Dear Sister, we arriv'd safe & sound, yesterday, at one o'clock, or a little after," wrote his anxious mother, "Panky, quite fresh, and not the least fatigued with his journey, & has taken Physic to-day, wch has done very well. I was so much so, that I burst into Tears, after dinner, being quite spent & worn out, but am quite well to-day. I believe 'twas oweing to having cry'd so very little before; and after such a flurry is over, & one's spirits come to subside, one feels the effect of it . . ."[65]

But Mary Leeds had a natural gaiety, as we may see from her sprightly correspondence with the Newcastles. "My sister flatters me, we shall have the pleasure of your company to eat *Eels*, at least;" she writes on one occasion to her brother-in-law, "but does not *promise* any thing more now. I shall be really disapointed if you don't lye here; for your Grace knows, I'm always happy in your company; besides, that I've been at the Expence of a New Matress, for your bed, and it has been airing on purpose for you." Then she adds a postscript. "I don't expect an answer; but do let me know by my sister how the Eels are to be done but I think they were stew'd eels

FRANCIS, SECOND EARL OF GODOLPHIN
From the portrait by Jonathan Richardson in the National Portrait Gallery

that you liked so well."[66]   Let us hope that their Graces of Newcastle and Leeds enjoyed their stewed eels that August evening in 1762!   A year later Mary is expecting her sister and brother-in-law to stay at their house at North Mimms.   "he (her husband Leeds) joins me in kindest compts to you and the Duke of Newcastle."   She adds in a postscript, "he (Newcastle) shall have Eels the same way; and his bed thoroughly air'd."[67]   Newcastle, as is well known, was always anxious about his health.   It is clear that his young sister-in-law had learnt to take good care of him!

In another letter Mary concludes and signs herself exuberantly, employing all her husband's peerages, "I'm dear sister, affectionately yrs. M. Leeds, Carmarthen, Danby, Latimer, Dumblin, Osborne."[68]   At this time she was anxiously begging her sister to pay her a visit.   "I hope it won't be long before I've the *happiness*, of seeing you here: putting selfishness out of the case, I know t'will do you good"; she adds, "so pray don't let any *wise head* hinder you."[69]   "I've often heard that nothing is sure but Death;" she wrote to Henrietta a few weeks later, "and do now verily believe that 'tis the only thing certain, for I had not only depended myself upon seeing you *here* this year, but flew in a Passion wth any body that doubted it, the first passion of crying I've had, for above these two years (but upon *one* subject) was upon thinking I should *not* see you here, before I went to Town; and a very violent one it was."[70]   This exuberance appears to have upset the more level-headed Henrietta, for we find Mary writing apologetically a couple of weeks later.   "I'm vastly sorry, my dear Sister was so much griev'd at any expressions in my letter.   I was so sincerely disapointed at not seeing you, when I so fully expected it, that I could not help expressing myself as I did."[71]   Shall we be accused of indulging in flights of fancy if we detect in Mary's spritely affectionate letters to the sister who had been a mother to her some slight traces of the wit, the vivacity and the charm of no less a personage than William Congreve?

While these letters and many like them were passing between the sisters, their father was visibly ageing.   Always something of a valetudinarian, as he grew older Lord Godolphin became very fat; this made him still more careful of his health.   "This cold evening and my deafness (taken together) discourage me, my Dear Child, from attempting to visit you tonight," he wrote to Henrietta in 1749.   "I hope in God," he added, "this will not long be the case."[72]   And again a few years later: "I will hope, however, that This may find you better now;" he wrote to his elder daughter, "and if you are enough so to care to be troubled with a guest that is *at Least half* deaf, I shall gladly wait on you on wensday between One and Two; . . ."[73]   Gradually the hand-writing becomes more feeble.   In April 1753 he writes from Newmarket to complain of "a defluxion" upon one of his eyes, and to say that he is coming immediately to London.[74] The next day he writes again that it had "very much abated, so that I hope to be soon entirely free from it."[75] In May he writes of Henrietta's trials and troubles. "Were itt as much in my power to relieve you, My Dear Child, from the weakness of your nerves and the depression of your spirits, as, I thank God, it has been to set you at ease in the point of your *Finances*, I'm sure you would soon be free'd from all complaint of that kind ..."[76]

And so the letters continue until almost the close of 1762. It is clear that the old man is very frail, and for some time now the eccentric Dr. Messenger Monsey* has been looking after him.[77] But his love for Henrietta is undimmed by his great age. "Tho the state of my weighty affairs is so far, at Least, alter'd for the better as that I (now) fully propose to my self the pleasure of kissing your hands, My Dear Child, on Tuesday next about my usual hour, yet it grieves me that I can neither attend you so soon, nor (I doubt) stay quite so long as You were so good to propose: But half a Loaf, you know, is better than no bread: And so it had need be, for I have no expectation of being permitted to come without my usual companion, (that is Dr. Monsey) nor do I well know how to compass it. A revoir Ma tres Chere."[78]

A revoir Ma tres Chere: the love that shines forth from those pathetic words comes down to us through nearly two centuries.

No more letters survive. Yet a few years, and they were full of sorrow, were still to remain to Francis Godolphin. In August 1764 his "dear Minos" died suddenly at North Mimms. She was only forty. When the sad news reached Claremont the next day, Horace Walpole was walking round the garden with Newcastle in "his one-horse chair; we were passing to the other side of the house," he records, "when George Onslow met us, arrived on purpose to advertise the Duke of the sudden death of the Duchess of Leeds, who expired yesterday at dinner in a moment. . . . The Duke received the news as men do at seventy-one, but the terrible part was to break it to the Duchess who is ill . . . It is a heavy stroke too for her father, poor old Lord Godolphin, who is eighty-six."[79].

A heavy stroke indeed it must have been. Yet he lingered on awhile, lonely and tired, until at last in January 1766, his summons came. He was in his eighty-eighth year. In his Will he provided that his body should be laid "without pomp"—not with his wife and his father in Westminster Abbey, not with the mother, who had died in giving him birth, in distant Cornwall—but in Kensington Church. There sleeps the only child of Sidney Godolphin and Margaret Blagge.

* For particulars of this extraordinary character, see Lynch, *A Congreve Gallery*, 110–38, Ketton-Cremer, *Norfolk Portraits*, 85–95.

APPENDICES, NOTES, AND ABBREVIATIONS

	1702	1703.	1704	1705
Lord Treasurer.	Sidney, Lord Godolphin.	—	—	—
Lord President of the Council.	Thomas Herbert, Earl of Pembroke.	—	—	—
Lord Privy Seal.	John Sheffield, Duke of Buckinghamshire.	—	—	Succeeded by *Jol* Holles, *Duke* Newcastle.
Chancellor of the Exchequer.	Hon. Henry Boyle.	—	—	Boyle may be sa to have become Whig about nov
Lord Keeper of the Great Seal (no Ld. Chancellor these years).	Sir Nathan Wright.	—	—	Succeeded by S William Cowpe
Secretary of State (Northern Depart.).	Sir Charles Hedges.	—	Succeeded by Robert Harley, May, 1704.	—
Secretary of State (Southern Depart.).	Daniel Finch, Earl of Nottingham.	—	Succeeded by Sir Charles Hedges, May, 1704.	—
Secretary of State (Scottish Affairs)	—	—	—	—
Lord Lieutenant of Ireland.	Lawrence Hyde, Earl of Rochester.	Succeeded by James Butler, Duke of Ormonde, February, 1703.	—	—
Lord High Admiral.	Prince George of Denmark, Prince Consort.	—	—	—
Secretary of War.	William Blathwayt.	—	Succeeded by Henry St. John, May, 1704.	—
Master-General of The Ordnance.	John Churchill, Duke of Marlborough.	—	—	—
Lord Chamberlain.	Edward Villiers, Earl of Jersey.	—	Succeeded by Henry Grey, Earl of Kent.	Created *Marqu* of *Kent.*

THE GODOLPHIN MINISTRY

talics.)

1706	1707	1708	1709	1710
eated Earl of odolphin (Dec.).	—	—	—	Dismissed Aug, 1710. No Lord Treasurer till May 1711
—	—	—	Lord Somers.	Laurence Hyde, Earl of Rochester, September, 1710.
—	—	—	—	On death of *Newcastle* John Robinson, Bishop of Bristol.
—	—	*John Smith,* April, 1708.	—	Robert Harley, August, 1710.
eated *Lord* '*owper* December 706.	*Lord Cowper* becomes Lord Chancellor.	—	—	Sir Simon Harcourt (Ld. Keeper only).
—	—	*Hon. Henry Boyle,* February, 1708.	—	Henry St. John
arles *Spencer, arl of Sunder-nd,* Dec., 1706.	—	—	—	William Legge, Lord Dartmouth.
—	—	—	*James Douglas, Duke of Queensbury,* Feb., 1709.	—
—	Thomas Herbert, Earl of Pembroke.	*Thomas, Earl of Wharton,* November, 1708.	—	James Butler, Duke of Ormonde.
—	—	Thomas Herbert, Earl of Pembroke on death of Prince George, November, 1708.	*Edward Russell, Earl of Orford,* November, 1709.	Sir John Leake (First Lord of Admiralty).
—	—	*Robert Walpole,* February, 1708.	—	—.
—	—	—	—	—
—	—	—	—	*Charles Talbot, Duke of Shrewsbury,* April, 1710.

GODOLPHIN AND THE ART OF POETRY

THERE is one question for which the evidence is so uncertain that it is better dealt with on its own, the question whether Sidney Godolphin had any appreciation of poetry and any standing as a poet. There is a tradition that in his youth he was regarded as a poet of some ability and that he was the friend and companion of the famous Court wits of the Restoration. On the other hand, Mr. Hugh Elliot, in his short sketch of Godolphin published in 1888, considered that he never wrote a line of verse and that the view to the contrary was the result of confusion with his uncle and namesake, Suckling's "Little Sid". But the poet Sidney Godolphin was fatally wounded in the skirmish at Chagford in 1643, two years before his nephew was born; so it seems doubtful if there can have been confusion with him.

To take first the question whether Godolphin was or was not a good judge of poetry, all views on the point derive their origin from the accounts of the inception and publication of Addison's famous panegyric on Marlborough's victory at Blenheim entitled *The Campaign. A Poem, To His Grace the Duke of Marlborough.* The first of these is the statement by Thomas Tickell (1686–1740) in the biographical preface to his edition of Addison's *Works*. This was published by Jacob Tonson in 1721. The second is the longer and more elaborate account given by Eustace Budgell (1686–1737) in his *Memoirs of the Boyles* published in 1732. Tickell's brief Statement is as follows:

> "He (Addison) remained for some time, after his return to *England*, without any public employment, which he did not obtain 'till the year 1704, when the Duke of *Marlborough* arrived at the highest pitch of glory, by delivering all Europe from slavery, and furnished Mr. Addison with a subject worthy of that genius which appears in the Poem called *The Campaign*. The Lord-Treasurer *Godolphin*, who was a fine judge of Poetry, had a sight of this work, when it was only carried on as far as the applauded simile of the Angel; and approved the Poem, by bestowing on the Author, in a few days after, the place of Commissioner of Appeals, vacant by the removal of the famous Mr. Locke to the council of Trade."

(Addison, *Works,* ed. Tickell, Vol. I, x, xi.)

From this we gather that Godolphin was a "fine judge of Poetry", that he read Addison's poem when it had proceeded as far as the well-known simile which is well beyond the mid-point, that he approved the poem, and that he rewarded the poet a few days later.

Budgell's account is far longer and is in complete contrast. For comparison it must be quoted in full.

"Soon after the Battle of *Blenheim*, Mr. *Boyle*, then Chancellor of the Exchequer, was entreated by the Lord Godolphin to go to Mr. *Addison*, and desire him to write something that might transmit the memory of that glorious Victory to Posterity.

As I believe this Story is not commonly known, and as I think it does Honour to the late Lord *Halifax* (whose memory I must ever love and respect) I shall lay it before my Readers.

Upon the arrival of the news of the Victory of *Blenheim*, the Lord Treasurer *Godolphin*, in the Fullness of his Joy, meeting with the late Lord *Halifax*, told him, *It was a pity the memory of such a victory should be ever forgot. He added that he was pretty sure his Lordship, who was so distinguished a patron* of men of Letters, *must know some Person, whose* Pen *was capable of doing* Justice *to the Action.* My Lord Halifax replied, That *he did indeed* know such a Person; *but would not desire him to write upon the Subject his Lordship had mentioned.* Then Lord Treasurer entreated to know the Reason of so unkind a Resolution, Lord Halifax briskly told him, That *he had long with Indignation observed that while too many* Fools *and* Blockheads *were maintained in their* Pride *and* Luxury, *at the Expence of the* Publick, *such Men as were really an Honour to their* Country, *and to the age they lived in, were shamefully suffered to languish in* obscurity: that, *for his own Part, he would never desire any Gentleman of Parts and Learning to imploy his Time in celebrating a Ministry, who had neither the* justice *or generosity to make it worth his while.* The Lord Treasurer calmly replied, That *he would seriously consider of what his Lordship had said, and endeavour to give no Occasion for such Reproaches for the future: but that in the present Case he took upon* himself *to promise, That any gentleman whom his Lordship should name to him as a Person capable of celebrating the late Action, should find it worth his while to exert his genius on that Subject.* The Lord *Halifax* upon this encouragement, named Mr. *Addison*; but insisted that the Lord Treasurer himself should send to him. Mr. *Addison*, who was at that Time but indifferently Lodged, was surprized the next Morning with a visit from the Chancellor of the *Exchequer*; who after having acquainted him with his Business, added, *That the Lord Treasurer, to encourage him to* enter upon his Subject, *had already made him one of the* Commissioners of Appeals; *but entreated him to look upon* that post *only as an ernest of something more considerable*. In short, the Chancellor said so many obliging Things, and in so graceful a Manner, as gave Mr. *Addison* the utmost *spirit* and *Encouragement* to begin that *Poem*, which he afterwards published, and entitled *The Campaign* : A Poem equal to the action it celebrates; and in which that *Presence of Mind* for which the late *Duke of Marlborough* was so remarkable in a *Day of Battle*, is illustrated by a nobler *Simile* than any to be found in *Homer* or *Virgil*. The Lord Treasurer kept the promise he had made by Mr. *Boyle*; and Mr. *Addison*, soon after the Publication of his Poem was preferred to a considerable Post."

(Budgell, *Memoirs of the Life and Character of the late Earl of Orrery, and of the Family of the Boyles, 150–3.*)

Here then we get quite a different version. According to Budgell, Godolphin not only had no appreciation of poetry, but was head of a Government which was grievously neglectful of poets. Which account is nearer to the truth?

In the first place, it is interesting to note the ingenious way in which Macaulay in his essay on *The Life and Writings of Addison*, combined both versions. It appears that Macaulay drew his narrative, which neatly combined Budgell and Tickell, from the article on Addison in the *Biographia Britannica* (1747) Vol. I, 33–4 and from Theophilus Cibber's *Lives of the Poets* (1753) Vol. III, 309. In this essay Macaulay quotes three lines to demonstrate the "exquisite absurdity" of poems on the victory of Blenheim:

"Think of two thousand gentleman at least,
        And each man mounted on his capering beast;
Into the Danube they were pushed by shoals."

which have now been shown by Professor Robert D. Horn of the University of Oregon to be a misquotation from an absurd effusion entitled "Le Feu de Joye: or, a Brief Description of Two most Glorious Victories obtain'd by *Her Majesty's Forces and those of Her Allies* over The *French* and *Bavarians*; In July and August, 1704, at *Schellenbergh* and *Blainhaim* near *Hocksted*. Under the magnanimous and Heroick Conduct of His Grace the Duke of *Marlborough* A POEM. By a *British* Muse . . . LONDON: Printed by *Freeman Collins* for W. Henchman, at the *Kings Head, Westminster Hall*, 1705."

(Brit. Mus. 11631, bb 12). No wonder that the British muse of this trash remains anonymous!

Several considerations, however, incline us to favour the Tickell version to that of Budgell. In the first place it was written in 1721, only nine years after Godolphin's death, and by a man who would be likely to know the facts about his friend Addison's advancement. Budgell, on the other hand, was writing in 1732, twenty years after Godolphin's death: moreover, his reputation for veracity is certainly not of the best. Furthermore, according to Professor Horn's most interesting article on *Addison's Campaign and Macaulay* (Publications of the *Modern Language Association of America*, Vol. LXIII, No. 3. September 1948), there is a letter extant, the postscript of which also goes to show that Tickell's story is the more reliable. The letter, dated "November 6" (1704), is quoted by Professor Horn thus:

Sir,

I should have waited on you to have return'd my most Humble thanks for your late generous and unexpected favour had not I fear'd to have bin troublesome by my acknowledgements. I must desire you will be pleas'd to think me very justly sensible to your just kindnesse in this particular, and to believe that I am not a little proud of having it known whom I am Obliged to. I have had a letter from Mr. Tilson (of the Treasury), to whom I shall apply my-self this after-noon for the taking out of a Patent which he mentions to me. Be pleased Sr. to pardon this trouble and to believe me with all possible gratitude and respect

Yo^r most Dutifull and
most Obedient servant
J. Addison.

I am told that I ought to return my thank, to the Treasurer and should be glad of having the honour of waiting on you and him if you think it proper."

From this it would seem as if Godolphin was neither so unsympathetic to poets and poetry as Budgell makes out. Perhaps Tickell is not so far out in saying that he was "a fine judge of Poetry."

But was Godolphin something of a poet himself? The evidence is confusing. When early in the nineteenth century the late Archdeacon Coxe was working in the muniment room at Blenheim Palace, he found amongst the papers of Sarah, Duchess of Marlborough three fables in verse imitated from la Fontaine, the manuscript of which was in Godolphin's hand. These he published in 1818. Of the published volumes, only ten copies were printed on imperial paper and twelve on demy paper. A copy of the former is in the Grenville Library at the British Museum. The three fables are as follows:

APPENDIX II

I

The Lion in Love

This fable was addressed to Lady Anne Churchill, the Marlboroughs' second daughter, who early in 1701 married Charles, Lord Spencer, son of the 2nd Earl of Sunderland. It was probably written in the previous year.

II

The Rats in Council

This fable was dedicated to the Earl of Marlborough and was written in 1702, when Marlborough's conduct of the war was being so disastrously hampered by the restraining influence of the Dutch Field Deputies.

III

The Fable of the Woodward and the Forest

This fable was written in 1712, soon after the dismissal of the Duke of Marlborough, and alludes to the ingratitude of the Queen and the country for forgetting the Duke of Marlborough's great services to the State.

In fact, there are in the Blenheim muniment room some fourteen fables and verses in all, in the hand of Godolphin, not every one of which appears to be in imitation of la Fontaine. Here is a selection from the titles: "Of a Hern", "A fable of a Mayd", "A Fable of love and folly", "To a young Lady that kept a flea chayned in a box", "Some rules to be observed by writers for the stage", "The Prince of Condé's retirement to Ghantilly", "A letter in verse to M. Mazarin", "Leander to Hero, and Hero to Leander." The fact that these verses are indubitably in Godolphin's handwriting is, of course, no conclusive evidence that he composed the lines, but there is, I suggest, a strong presumption that he did.

Furthermore there is in the British Museum a sheet headed:

> The E – l of G – d – n to D ct – r.
> G – – th, upon the loss of Miss Dingle:
> In return to the D – ct – r's Consolatory Verses
> to Him, upon the loss of his Rod.

The date is interesting, 1711. The verses that follow read as under:

Thou, who the Pangs of my embitter'd Rage
Coud'st, with thy never-dying Verse asswage;
Immortal Verse, secure to live as long
As that curs'd Prose, whose rouble-gifted Pen,
Alike can Cure an aking Corn, or Spleen;
Whose lucky Hand administers Repose
As well to breaking Heart, as broken Nose;
Accept this tribute: Think it all I had,
In Recompense of Thine, when I was sad.

What tho' it comes from an unpractis'd Muse,
Bad at the best, grown Worse by long disuse;
In Silence lost, since once I did complain
Of Wiv – l's cold Neglect in humble Strain;
When check'd by slavish Conscience, she deny'd
To throw aside the Viell, and act the Bride:
Yet sure I may be thought among the Throng
If not to Sing, to Whistle out a Song:
Then take the kind Remembrance of my Verse
While Dingle's Loss with sorrow I rehearse.

Dingle is lost, the hollow Caves rebound,
Dingle is lost, and multiply the Sound;
'Till Eccho chaunting it by just Degree,
Shortens to *Ding*, then softens it to *D*.
Dingle is lost; where's now the Parents Care,
The boasted Force of Piety and Prayer?
No more shall She, within thy speacious Hall
Lead up the Dance, and Animate the Ball;
Deserted Thus, no more shalt thou Engage
Under thy Roof, to *Whartonize* the Age.

Train'd by their Care, by thy Example led,
Early she learnt to scorn the Nuptial Bed;
And Vow'd, like Thee, to multiply Her kind:
For *Dingle* Thou did'st bless the neather Skies;
In hopes a mingl'd Race might once arise
To sooth thy Hoary Age, and close thy dying Eyes.

T

Learn ye Indulging Parents, learn from hence:
Think not Compliance e'er will influence.
The *Fifth* Command alone you did enjoin,
And Frankly gave her up the other *Nine*:
Yet She, tho That, and That alone was press'd,
Regardless of your Will, the *Fifth* transgressed.

But oh! my Friend, consider, tho she's gone,
She left no Coffers empty but her own;
Her Mind that did direct *the great Machine*
Mov'd *like the Universe, by Springs unseen;*
And tho' from thy Instructions she *retreats,*
Her Globe of Light grows larger as she sets:
For nought could brighter make her Lustre shine,
Than to withdraw, and single it from Thine.
Then think of this: and Pardon when ye see
Those Virtues, you so late admir'd in Me.

(Brit. Mus. 1876, f. 1. p. 57.)

All this goes to show, perhaps, that in middle and old age it was in Godolphin's power to produce a few heroic couplets and leaves him still a long way from being, as some have represented him as having been, the boon companion of Rochester, Sedley, Buckhurst, Etherege, Buckingham and the rest! On what evidence does this supposition rest?

In the winter of 1662/3 a group of young men of fashion on friendly terms with the distinguished poet, Waller, formed the habit of meeting in his pleasant new house in what is now St. James's Street. The conversation at their gatherings would naturally turn to poetry and the theatre, and, as all things French were at the Restoration very much in the vogue, especially to the classical drama of France, then in the meridian of its triumph. Not unnaturally, therefore, the company conceived the idea of attempting some translations into English rhyming verse of the works of the great Corneille, and the first to be selected was his "La Mort de Pompée", which had been played in France nearly twenty years before. Each of the five acts was to be translated by a different hand. The secret of the project was soon out, and the news evoked some slightly anxious enquiries from a rival poetess of some distinction, Katherine Philips, better known as "The Matchless Orinda", who by chance had recently produced a translation of Pompey herself. "I long to hear what becomes of the other Translation of Pompey and what Opinion the Town and Court have of it," she wrote to her friend, Sir Charles Cotterell, known in her strange cousinhood as Poliarchus. "I have laid out several ways to get a Copy, but cannot yet procure one except only of the first act that was done by Waller. Sir Edward Filmer did one, Sir Charles Sidley another, and my Lord Buckhurst another; but the fifth I cannot learn" (January 10th, 1662/3; *Letters of Orinda to Poliarchus*, 1705, 112). The only copy of the translation that I have seen, the volume in the British Museum (London 1664), gives no clue to the translators, but tradition has it that Sidney Godolphin was responsible for the last act. "*Biographia Dramatica*" (ed. 1782, Vol. II, 288) states, "Mr. Waller, who translated only one act, was assisted in it by the Earl of Dorset and Middlesex"; but the 1812 edition (Vol. II, 172) gives, apart from Dorset, "Sir Charles Sidley and Mr. Godolphin" as the translators. But if this be correct, "Mr. Godolphin" probably does not refer to Sidney at all, but to the future Sir William Godolphin, (1634?–1696), the Ambassador to Spain. From 1651 till the Restoration, he was at Christ Church, Oxford, where in 1654 he composed a poem in compliment to Cromwell and an answer to Waller's "Upon the late Storm and of the Death of his Highnesse Oliver Lord Protector, Sept ye 3d, 1658" (All Souls MSS., 174). Slightly differing versions of this are printed in Dryden's *Miscellaneous Poems* (1716), Vol. I, 191–2; "*Poems on Affairs of State*" (1703), 246–6; and "*Select Collection of Poems*" (1780), Vol. I. 116–19. In the last it is incorrectly attributed to Sidney Godolphin. (See also Professor Souers, *The Matchless Orinda*, 1931.)

From the foregoing I think it is reasonably safe to assume that the future Lord Treasurer had nothing to do with the translation of Pompey; though as late as 1679 he was, it seems, still associating with Waller and his circle, for in that year the two of them published jointly a translation of *The Passion of Dido for Aeneas* (Brit. Mus. 11355 b).

There remain to be considered Rochester's famous lines, which in the Antwerpen (?1680) edition of his *Imitation of the Tenth Satire of the First Book of Horace* (*Poems on Several Occasions, by the Rt. Hon. the E. of R. Antwerpen*) appear in the following form:

> "I loathe the Rabble, 'tis enough for me
> If S . . . , S . . . , W . . . ,
> G . . . , B . . . , B . . . , B . . . ,
> And some few more whom I omit to name,
> Approve my Sense, I count their Censure Fame."

In the later edition of Rochester's works, under the title *The Works of the Right Honourable the Earl of Rochester and Roscommon . . .*" etc., (1709), p. 22, the blanks are filled with the names of Sedley, Shadwell, Sheppard, Wicherley, Godolphin, Butler, Buckhurst, and Buckingham. This version is followed by John Hayward in his *Collected Works of John Wilmot, Earl of Rochester* (1926), 58, where in his note he gives Godolphin as Sidney Godolphin (p. 361).

But Hayward, who was very young and inexperienced when he edited Rochester's works, is an unreliable guide. Thus in the poem *Rochester's Farewell* (1630), 149, the Godolphin of the lines:

> "Their names shall equal or exceed in story
> Chit Sund(erlan)d, Chit Godo(lphin), and Chit L(or)y."

he states to be William, the future Ambassador, which is obviously incorrect; and of William, too, he quoted the remark that he was never in the way and never out of the way (p. 385), though everybody knows that this famous remark of Charles II was made of Sidney Godolphin. Hayward also ascribed to William the Godolphin of the lines in "*A Ballad*":

> "G(odolph)in to tempt him, fell off from her Horse,
> To perfect the Conquest of Face by her—
> A pleasanter sight than a Newmarket Farce
>   Which no Body can deny." (pp. 307, 402).

though a woman is obviously intended. The connection of Sidney Godolphin with Newmarket suggests the horrid thought that Margaret Godolphin may here be referred to, even though she had left the Court before her marriage and only returned for the performance of Crowne's masque *Calisto* in 1675; for, be it remembered, the production of the masque was supervised by Rochester, so Margaret would certainly have come much under his notice at this time.

On the other hand there is a further probable reference to Sidney Godolphin in Rochester's works:

> "R(ichmond) had a Thousand T . . . rfes,
>   *Mazarine* as many more,
> Sometimes her . . . sometimes her . . . is
>   . . . and . . . o'er and o'er.
> Let Mistress Buckley not be troubled
>   Whilst her G(odolphin) will be bubbled." (p. 312).

The "Mistress Buckley" of this poem was the lovely Sophia Stuart, a younger sister of the better known Frances, "la belle Stuart" of King Charles II's Court, who had married Henry Bulkeley, son of the first Viscount Bulkeley. This Henry Bulkeley has made a brief but not unimportant appearance in my life of Godolphin. With Sophia Bulkeley's name that of Sidney Godolphin had long been coupled: it may well be, therefore, that Hayward is correct in ascribing this reference to him (p. 413). But enough has been said to show that John Hayward is not an altogether reliable guide.

To sum up. The evidence, though admittedly unreliable, seems on the whole to show that Godolphin had some poetic feeling and was not unsympathetic towards poets. On the other hand, it does not seem as if he had any very marked poetic gifts beyond what were required to compose a few heroic couplets—an ability that would have been within the range of most cultured men of his day. It must not be forgotten that he was concerned in at least one translation with his friend Waller, but I can only think that his part must have been very much of a secondary nature. But, as I have said, the whole subject is not free from doubt, and it would be unwise to be dogmatic.

APPENDIX III

SARAH, DUCHESS OF MARLBOROUGH'S CHARACTER STUDY OF LORD GODOLPHIN.

(Printed in Sarah, Duchess of Marlborough, *Private Correspondence*, II, 125–6).

"LORD GODOLPHIN had conducted the Queen, with the care and tenderness of a father, or a guardian, through a state of helpless ignorance, and had faithfully served her in all her difficulties before she was Queen, as well as greatly contributed to the glories she had to boast of after she was so. But there was no sense left now of such matters, nor any memory of those past services which she had need to think invaluable, a long series of services perhaps the most disinterested that were ever performed by any prime minister to any prince upon earth.

"He was a man of few words, but of a remarkable thoughtfulness and sedateness of temper; of great application to business, and of such dispatch in it, as to give pleasure to those who attended him upon any affair; of wonderful frugality in the public concerns, but of no great carefulness about his own. He affected being useful without popularity; and the inconsiderable sum of money, above his personal estate, which he left at his death, shewed that he had been indeed the nation's treasurer, and not his own, and effectually confuted the vile calumnies of his enemies and successors."

NOTES

(Numbers in brackets at head of each page indicate the pages to which the notes thereon refer).

BOOK I

CHAPTER I (3-6)

[1] Ogg, *England in the Reign of Charles* II, I, 34.

[2] Pepys, *Diary*, September 19th, 1664, IV, 246. January 1st, 1662-3, III, 1.

[3] Evelyn. *Diary*. February 6th, 1685, IV, 413-4.

[4] September 29th, 1662, and the salary was £120 a year. *Cal. Treas. Books, 1660-7*, 719-20.

[5] Godolphin to Cromwell, "at my house, 25 March," (1539). *Letters and Papers ... Henry VIII*. XIV, pt. i, No. 589.

[6] Godolphin to Essex. "Godolphin, being upon special occasion newly returned from Scilly, 10 July 1595." H.M.C. *Salisbury*, V. 274.

[7] Clifford to Essex, "July 26th" (1595) signed "Your poor kinsman and servant." H.M.C. *Salisbury*, V. 290.

[8] Richard Carew, *Survey of Cornwall*, (ed. 1811), 371-2, 381-4.

[9] Godolphin to Cecil, "Hanworth, 18 March 1596." H.M.C. *Salisbury*, VII, 118.

[10] Godolphin to Raleigh, "Godolphin, 3rd. November, 1597." Endorsed by Raleigh,—"a letter of Sir Francis Godolphin declaring the weakness of Pendennis Castle and the importance of the place," and by Cecil—"3 November, 1597. Sir W. Godolphin [sic] to Sir W. Raleigh." ibid., VII, 466.

[11] Godolphin to Cecil, "From her Majesty's little fort in Scilly 17 May, 1599." H.M.C. *Salisbury*, IX, 171.

[12] Godolphin to Cecil. "From her Majesty's Fort in the Silley, 6 August 1599." ibid., IX, 273-4.

[13] Godolphin to Cecil, "from her Majesty's little fort in Sylley, 13 August, 1599." ibid., IX, 292-3.

[14] Godolphin to Cecil, "from Tavistock, the 8th of October, 1601." ibid., XI, 412.

[15] Penwarn to Godolphin. "From her Majesty's fort in St. Mary's Isle in Scilly, the 10th of October 1601." Godolphin's covering letter to Cecil is dated October 14th. ibid., II, 428.

[16] Godolphin to Cecil, "From Tavistock, the 6 of October, 1602." ibid., XII, 423.

[17] Somers' *Tracts*, VI, 574.

[18] Clarendon, *History*, II, Pt. I, 201.

[19] Wood, *Athenae Oxonienses*, III, 46. See also Hobbes, *English Works* (ed. Molesworth, III, 703.

[20] Not Sir Charles Berkeley, as stated by Hugh Elliot. Elliot, *Godolphin*, p. 28.

[21] H. of C. *Journal*, January 5th, 1646.

[22] Nicholas to Godolphin, December 5th, 1661. *Cal. S.P. Dom. 1661-2*, 169.

[23] In November, 1668, when Lady Godolphin made her will, thirteen children—six sons and seven daughters—were surviving. Brit. Mus. Add. MSS. 28,071, f. 3.

[24] Godolphin to——, no date. Brit. Mus. Add. MSS. 28,052, f. 7.

[25] *Cal. S.P. Dom. 1660-1*, 445.

[26] See letter from Thomas Blagge to Prince Rupert, dated from Wallingford Monday (1643). *Morrison Catalogue*.

[27] Whitelock's *Memorials*, 215-17.

[28] The letter, dated "New Castle, Augt. 8th. 1646", warmly commends Colonel Blagge as "one that hath served me with courage and fidelity, for which thou knowest that I have given him a place in my son's bedchamber. . . ." *Charles I. in 1646* (Camden Society), 58.

[29] Stafford was Izaak Walton's birthplace; he was born there in 1593.

[30] Ross to Holles, "Antwerp, August 14-24, 1659." H.M.C. *Bath*, II, 136-7.

[31] *Cal. S.P. Dom. 1651*, 454. Whitelock's *Memorials*, 510. *Cal. S.P. Dom. 1651*, 430.

[32] Brit. Mus. Add. MSS. 5,832, f. 220. Ashmole, *Order of the Garter*, 228.

[33] *Clarendon S.P.*, IV, 269, 271, 291, 312. *Cal. S.P. Dom. 1651*, 492

[34] *Cal. S.P. Dom. 1660-1*, 445. *Mercurius Politicus*, July 5-12, 1660, 463: *Parliamentary Intelligence*, July 9-16, 1660, 468.

[35] Mary Blagge to Williamson, "the sixt of November" (1662). *Cal. S.P. Dom. 1662*, 548.

[36] *Cal. S.P. Dom. 1662*, 549.

[37] ibid. 1663-4, 577, 600.

[38] H.M.C., *5th Report*, (4), 145, 184.

[39] Hamilton, *Grammont*, 95 *et seq.*

[40] H.M.C. *Heathcote*, 144. We can safely ignore the spiteful and absurd remarks about Yarborough in the Grammont memoirs.

[41] £213. 10. 0. *Cal. S.P. Dom.*, 1663-4, 548.

CHAPTER II

[1] Godolphin to Sir William Godolphin, "March 27th," (1667). Brit. Mus. Add. MSS. 28,052, f. 61.

[2] Lady Godolphin to Lady Fitzhardinge, no date, Brit. Mus. Add. MSS. 28,052, f. 4.

[3] Godolphin to Sir William Godolphin, "April ye 8th." (1667). Brit. Mus. Add. MSS. 28,052, f. 49.

[4] ibid., "Sat. June ye 15th" (1667). Brit. Mus. Add. MSS. 28,052, f. 59.

[5] Godolphin to Sir William Godolphin, "July ye 2nd." (1667.) Brit. Mus. Add. MSS. 28,052, f. 57.

[6] ibid., "July ye 6th." (1667). Brit. Mus. Add. MSS. 28,052, f. 53.

[7] ibid., "Sat, Au: 24th." (1667). The original is incomplete. Brit. Mus. Add. MSS. 28,052, f. 51.

[8] Lady Godolphin to ?, no date. Brit. Mus. Add. MSS. 28,052, f. 11.

[9] Henry Godolphin, to Lady Godolphin "qber ye 12th." (1668). Endorsed, "For my Lady Godolphin at Godolphin in Cornwall. Leave this with Mr. Hall, Goldsmith at the Angell in Cheapside London." Brit. Mus. Add. MSS, 28,052, f. 17.

[10] Godolphin to Lady Godolphin, "Dec: the 3d." Endorsed "My brother Sids." Brit. Mus. Add. MSS. 28,052, f. 31.

[11] Godolphin to Sir William Godolphin, "Aug. ye 8th" (1668). Brit. Mus. Add. MSS. 28,052, f. 47.

[12] ibid., "Althorpe, Wednesday Aug. ye 20th" (1668), Brit. Mus. Add. MSS 28,052, f. 39.

[13] ibid., "London, Sept. 1st." (1668). Endorsed, "For Sir Wm. Godolphin at Godolphin in Cornwall." Brit. Mus. Add. MSS. 28,052, f. 71.

[14] ibid., "Mich: Day." (1668). Brit. Mus. Add. MSS. 28,052, f. 65.

[15] ibid., "Audley, Oct. 20th." (1668). Brit. Mus. Add. MSS. 28,052, f. 65.

[16] ibid., "Dec. 3rd." (1668). Brit. Mus. Add. MSS. 28,052, f. 35.

[17] Godolphin to ? Arlington, "Paris, July 16th." (1669). *Cal. S.P. Dom. 1668–9*, 412.

[18] Montagu to Arlington, "Aug, 3. Paris, 69." H.M.C. *Buccleuch & Queensberry*, I, 433.

[19] H.M.C. *Hodgkin*, (39). 12. *Cal. Treas. Books, 1669–72*, 600.

[20] *Cal. Treas. Books, 1669–72*, 934.

[21] Evelyn, *Diary*, June 28th, 1669 and July 31st, 1672, III, 529, 622.

[22] ibid., July 31st, 1672, III, 622.

[23] ibid., August, 1672, III, 623.

[24] *Cal. S.P. Treas. Book, 1669–72*, 445.

[25] Evelyn, *Mrs. Godolphin*, 12.

[26] ibid., 12.

[27] ibid., 14–17. Hiscock, *John Evelyn and Mrs. Godolphin*, 21–2.

[28] ibid., 23.

[29] Godolphin to Jael Boscawen, "Newmarkett, ye 6th of Oct. 72" Evelyn MSS., Christ Church Oxford.

[30] *Cal. S.P. Dom. 1671–2*, 234.

[31] Godolphin to Arlington, Easter Day, 1672. *Cal. S.P. Dom. 1671–2*, 290.

[32] Acland to Hickes, "Truro, April 18th" (1672). *Cal. S.P. Dom. 1671–2*, 340.

[33] As early as April 2nd the Ambassador was urging the despatch of Godolphin to Paris. Montagu to Arlington "March 26 Paris 72." H.M.C. *Buccleuch & Queensberry*, I, 5 and 8.

[34] Godolphin to Arlington, "Paris, Aprill 23rd." P.R.O. *S.P. France, 1672*, 133, f. 165, 168.

[35] ibid., "Paris, May ye 2d N.S." P.R.O. *S.P. France, 1672, 133*, f. 189.

[36] ibid., "Paris May ye 11th." P.R.O. *S.P. France, 1672, 134*, f. 6.

37 Perwick to Arlington, P.R.O. *S.P. France*, 134, f. 10.

38 Godolphin to Arlington, P.R.O. *S.P. France*, 134, ff. 15, 18.

39 ibid., "From Wesell, June 13th." (1672), P.R.O. *S.P. France, 1672*, 134, f. 55.

40 ibid., "Wessell, June 14" (1672), P.R.O. *S.P. France, 1672*, 134, f. 58.

41 ibid., "From ye Camp near Arnheim, June ye 17th" (1672). P.R.O. *S.P. France, 1672*, 134, f. 65.

42 ibid., "From ye Camp before Doesburgh, 21 of June 1'o a'clock in ye morning." (1672). P.R.O. *S.P. France, 1672*, 134, f. 71.

43 ibid., "From ye Camp before Doesburgh. Sunday ye 22nd of June" (1672) P.R.O. *S.P. France, 1672*, 134, f. 70. Godolphin has misdated this letter, as June 22nd N.S. in 1672 was a Wednesday.

44 ibid., "From ye Camp neare Doesburg, June ye 23rd." P.R.O. *S.P. France, 1672*, 134, f. 75.

45 ibid., "at ye Camp a day's march from Doesburgh, 28," (June 1672), P.R.O. *S.P. France, 1672*, 134, f. 94.

46 ibid., "From ye Camp w^thin 2 days march of Utrecht, June ye 28th" (1672). P.R.O. *S.P. France, 1672*, 134, f. 107.

47 ibid., "From ye Camp near Utrech ye first of July in ye morning 9 n." P.R.O. *S.P. France, 1672*, 134, f. 111.

48 ibid., "From ye Camp at 7 (?) o'clock in ye morning." P.R.O. *S.P. France, 1672*, 134, f. 127.

49 Godolphin to Arlington, "From ye Camp neare Bois le duc. July ye 22nd, 1672." P.R.O. *S.P. France, 78/134*, f. 155. See also Godolphin's letter to an unknown correspondent, "from ye Camp neare Boisleduc friday ye 22nd of July att midnight." P.R.O. *S.P. France, 1672*, 134, f. 153. There are two copies of this letter at Longleat; Coventry Papers, XLI, f. 57, and Thynne Papers, Book 181, f. 18.

50 Coventry to Godolphin, "Whitehall, July 15th, 1672." Coventry Papers at Longleat, LXXXII, f. 13.

51 Godolphin to Arlington, "From ye Camp at Boutell near Bois leduc, July ye 24." (1672). P.R.O. *S.P. France, 1672*, 134, f. 158.

52 Sunderland to Arlington, "Paris, August 5, 72." P.R.O. *S.P. France, 1672*, 134, f. 167.

53 Godolphin to Coventry, "Paris, August ye 10th, 1672." Coventry Papers at Longleat, II, f. 31.

54 Godolphin to Arlington, "Paris—Aug ye 12th 1672." P.R.O. *S.P. France, 1672*, 134, f. 181.

55 ibid., "Paris, August ye 16th 1672." P.R.O. *S.P. France, 1672*, 134, f. 190.

56 ibid., "Paris, Sept. ye 17 72." P.R.O. *S.P. France, 1672*, 135, f. 11–12.

57 ibid., "Paris, Sept. ye 24th 72." P.R.O. *S.P. France, 1672*, 135, f. 207.

58 Sunderland to Arlington, "Paris, October 15/25 72." P.R.O. *S.P. France, 1672*, 135, f. 82.

59 P.R.O. *S.P. France, 1672*, 135, f. 66.

60 ibid., 135, ff. 74–5.

61 For Evelyn's description of the mansion, see *Diary*, September 25th, 1672, III, 624–5.

[62] Evelyn, *Diary*, January 7th, 1673, IV, 1.

[63] Evelyn, *Mrs. Godolphin*, 40.

[64] ibid., 41.

[65] ibid., 41.

[66] For details of the production of *Calisto*, see Eleanore Boswell, *The Restoration Court Stage* (1660-1702), 177-227.

[67] Evelyn, *Diary*, December 15th, 1674, IV, 49-50, 50-1.

[68] Evelyn's dates have been disputed. See Eleanore Boswell, *The Restoration Court Stage* (1660-1702). 181-2, and Evelyn, *Mrs. Godolphin*, appendix C, 231-6.

[69] "This day was my deare friend Mrs. *Blagg* married to Mr. *Sidney Godolphin* groome of the Bed-Chamber to his Majestie at the Temple Church by Mr. *Leake* chap: to the Duke." Evelyn, *Diary*, May 16th, 1675, IV, 63. As Evelyn was not informed of the marriage at the time, this entry must have been interpolated at a later date. The marriage entry reads thus:

| Sidney Godolphin & Mrs. Blayne | Sidney Godolphin, Esqr and Margarett Blayne were married in The Temple Church May: 16th 1675 By Dr. Lake. |

This entry is on the left-hand page of the register and stands alone. On the right are many entries, the second of which reads thus:

| Mr. Lake married | May: 16th, 1675 Mr. Lake married a Cupple in the Temple Church on a Sunday morning their names I doe not knowe 1675. |

On a separate slip there are the following words:

on the front:	Sidney Godolphin Esq. one of the Grooms of ye Bed-chamber to his Ma^ty
	Mrs. Margarett Blague one of ye Maids of Hono^r to ye Queen
on the back:	this is the persons names that Mr. Lake did marrie May: 16: 75.

The slip was formerly pinned to the left-hand page but has recently got misplaced and now appears on a different page of the Register. It will be observed that the bride's name in the entry is written Blayne. No doubt someone wrote down Blague and the clerk misread the g for a y and the u for an n: both are letters that can easily be confused.

CHAPTER III

[1] Evelyn, *Diary*, May 18th, 1675, IV, 63-4.

[2] ibid., May 20th, 1675, IV, 64.

[3] *Morrison Collection*, Bulstrode Papers, I, 302.

[4] Evelyn to Mrs. Evelyn, " 7th July—75." Evelyn MSS. Christ Church, Oxford.

[5] Evelyn, *Diary*, Octobe r 27th, 1675, IV, 77. See also Evelyn, *Mrs. Godolphin*, 60.

[6] ibid., October 27th, 1675, IV, 77.

[7] ibid., November 9th, 1675, IV, 78-9.

[8] ibid., November 9th, 1675, IV, 79. In a few months, alas, she was to be widowed. Three years later Lady Hamilton married Richard Talbot, afterwards Duke of Tyrconnel.

⁹ Evelyn, *Diary*, November 13th, 1675, IV, 79–80.

¹⁰ Berkeley of Stratton to Coventry, "Paris, December 7–75." Endorsed, "Lord Berkeley Paris Decm^{re} 7, S.N. Answered at Decr 6 S.V": Paris 1ober 27. S.N. (75): "Paris 1ober 31 s.n. (75)." Coventry Papers at Longleat, XXXIII, 189–90, 210–4.

¹¹ Charles Godolphin to William Godolphin, undated. Brit. Mus. Add. MSS. 28,052, f. 75.

¹² Margaret Godolphin to Evelyn. Evelyn MSS., Christ Church, Oxford. Hiscock, *John Evelyn and Mrs. Godolphin*, 145–9.

¹³ Berkeley of Stratton to Coventry, "Paris, Jan: 15 (75)." S.N. Endorsed "Paris Lrd Berkeley Jan 5/15 75/6 Rd. Jan. 9." See also "Paris, Jan 25 S.N. (75)." Endorsed "Lrd. Berkley Jan 23 Paris." Coventry Papers at Longleat, XXXIII, 207–8, 211–12.

¹⁴ Evelyn to Browne undated. Endorsed in Evelyn's hand, "My son John from Paris 1676." Brit. Mus. Add. MSS. 15,948, f. 149. Mr. Hiscock quotes from two rather similiar letters from young Evelyn about Margaret Godolphin. One is addressed to his father, the other to one of his sisters. They are in the Evelyn Papers at Christ Church, Oxford. Hiscock, *John Evelyn and Mrs. Godolphin*, 155.

¹⁵ Evelyn, *Diary*, April 6th, 10th and 14th, 1676, IV, 88.

¹⁶ ibid., April 26th, 1676, IV, 89.

¹⁷ ibid., May 3rd, 1676, IV, 90.

¹⁸ ibid., May 12th, 1676, IV, 91.

¹⁹ Jael Boscawen to Frances Godolphin, "April ye 25th." Endorsed "For Mrs. Frances Godolphin at Godolphin, Cornwall." Brit. Mus. Add. MSS. 28,052, f. 13.

²⁰ Hooke, *Diary*, 243, 244, 253.

²¹ For John and Mary Evelyn's advice to Mrs. Godolphin, see (i), "Fragment of paper on regulation of time written for 'Electra' by John Evelyn." Brit. Mus. Add. MSS. 15,950, ff. 106–7 and (ii) "Mrs. Evelyn's Instructions to Mrs. Blague for setting-up and keeping house, upon her marriage with my Lrd. Godolphin." The Carl H. Pforzheimer Library. Evelyn, *Mrs. Godolphin*, 218–30.

²² Evelyn, *Mrs. Godolphin*, 68.

²³ ibid., 70.

²⁴ Godolphin to Henry Sidney, "Windsor Aug: ye 18th, 1677." Brit. Mus. Add. MSS. 32,680, f. 83.

²⁵ For Godolphin's instructions see Brit. Mus. Add. MSS. 25,119, ff. 21–27, and Coventry Papers at Longleat, III, ff. 89–94, 104. There are also among the Coventry Papers at Longleat copies of the instructions to Godolphin in the British Museum. XCIII, ff. 12–16.

²⁶ Godolphin to Coventry, "from Bruges, Sund: ye 13/23." (January 167 7/8). Endorsed by Coventry, "Mr. Godolphin 13/23 Jan '7 7/8." Coventry Papers at Longleat, XLI, f. 295.

²⁷ H.M.C. *Beaufort* (27), 67. For Danby's version of his instructions to Godolphin from a copy or draft in Danby's hand see Leeds MSS. Packet 10. Danby, *Copies and Extracts*, 346–50. Browning, *Danby*, I, 264–5, II, 598–601.

²⁸ For Godolphin's instructions see Bodl., Firth MSS. b. 1/1. (Summary catalogue 28, 25375), 195. Southwell to Ormond, March 5th, 1677–8, H.M.C. *Ormonde*, N.S. IV, 412. Browning, *Danby*, I, 271–2.

[29] Godolphin to Williamson, "Harwich, ye 6 March, 1677." Bodl., Firth MSS. b. 1/1, 202.

[30] Williamson to Godolphin, "Whitehall ye 12th March 7 7/8." Bodl., Firth MSS. b. 1/1, 205. Hyde to Thynne, "Hague March ye 12th, 167 7/8. Coventry Papers at Longleat, XLI, f. 327.

[31] Godolphin to Williamson, "From on board a yacht going betwize Zealand and Rotterdam March ye 10th 20 1677/8." Bodl., Firth MSS. b 1/1, 203. There is a copy at Longleat. Coventry Papers, LXI, f. 325.

[32] ibrid., "From ye Hague ye 12/22 March 167 7/8." Bodl., Firth MSS. b. 1/1, 207. See also Godolphin to Danby, "Hague 12/22 March 1677/8." Danby, *Copies & Extracts*, 351–4. Browning, *Danby*, II, 601–3.

[33] Williamson to Godolphin, "Whitehall, ye 17th March, 1678." Bodl., Firth MSS. b. 1/1, p. 209. There is a copy of this letter in Leeds MSS. Packet 10 endorsed by Danby "The Prince of Orange opened this letter and sent it to mee, Mr. Godolphin being come away from the Hague." Danby, *Copies and Extracts*, 9. 355. Browning, *Danby*, II, 603–5.

[34] Godolphin to Thynne, "Hague ye 12/22 of March, 1677/8." Coventry Papers at Longleat, XLI, f. 329.

[35] Godolphin to Williamson, "Antwerp ye 16/24 Mar. 1677/8." Bodl., Firth MSS. b. 1/1, p. 225.

[36] Mr. Godolphin's Narrative: "A Narrative of ye Discourse y^t passed betw. His High: ye P. of O, and me in ye Quarter at Boom the 17/27 March 1677/8." Bodl., Firth MSS. b. 1/1, p. 266. "A Narrative of ye Discourst y^t passed between his Highnesse ye prince of Orange and me in his quarters at Boome, ye 17/27 of March, 1677/8." Coventry Papers at Longleat, XLI, ff. 333–4. See also Godolphin to Danby, "Hague, May 12 /22, 1678." and "Hague, May 24 /14, 1678." Leeds MSS. Packet 10. Danby, *Copies & Extracts*, 358–62. Browning, *Danby*, II, 695–8.

[37] Godolphin to Thynne, "Antwerp, May ye 9th/Aprill ye 29th 1678." Coventry Papers at Longleat, XLI, f. 388.

[38] Hyde and Godolphin to Williamson and/or Thynne, "Hague May 14/24 1678." "Hague May the 17/27 1678." "Hague May the 21th [sic] /31 1678." "Hague, May 24th/June 3d 1678." "Hague May the 28th/June the 7th 1678." "Hague May the 21th [sic]/31, 1678." "Hague May the 31th [sic] /June the 10th, 1678." "Hague 7th/17th June, 1678." Coventry Papers at Longleat, XLI, ff. 420–3, 428–34, 440–3, 444–5, 450–1, 460–1, 468–9, 482–3.

[39] Hyde to Thynne, "Ap: ye 2d/12th 1678." Coventry Papers at Longleat, XLI, f. 341.

[40] Godolphin to Thynne, "Hague ye 9/19th of May, 1678." But he reversed this decision a few days later. "I am very sorry to heare Mr. Secy (Coventry) continues ill but it ought to bee no small comfort to him that he escapes the house of Commons by it, for ought I see one is better any where than there and I begin to recant my last Letter to you upon this subject." "Hague ye 24/14th of May, 1678." Coventry Papers at Longleat, XLI, ff. 404, 424.

[41] ibid., "Hague, ye 17/27 of May, 1678." Coventry Papers at Longleat, XLI, f. 436.

[42] ibid., "Hague, ye 31/21th [sic] of May, 1678." Coventry Papers at Longleat, XLI, f. 446.

[43] ibid., "Hague, ye 3d of June/24th May, 1678. 12 a clock at night." Coventry Papers at Longleat, XLI, f. 456.

44 Godolphin to Thynne, "Hague ye 3d of June/22d of May [*sic*] 1678." Coventry Papers at Longleat, XLI, f. 454.

45 ibid., "Hague ye 4th/14 of June 78." Coventry Papers at Longleat, XLI, f. 476. With this he sends Thynne a copy of his letter of the same date to Williamson. The copy can be seen in the Coventry Papers at Longleat, XLI, ff. 478-9.

46 ibid., "Hague, ye 7/17th of June 1678." Coventry Papers at Longleat, XLI, f. 484.

47 ibid., "Hague ye 11th/21 of June, 1678." Coventry Papers at Longleat, XLI, ff. 485-7.

48 ibid., "Hague, June ye 12th/22, 1678." Coventry Papers at Longleat, XLI, f. 491.

49 ibid., "Honslaerdyke, July ye 1st/June ye 21, 1678." Coventry Papers at Longleat, XLI, ff. 501-2.

50 ibid., "Hague, ye 8/18 of July 3 in ye morning, 1678." Coventry Papers at Longleat, XLI, ff. 503-4. "July" must be Godolphin's mistake for "June."

51 ibid., "Hague ye 7th June/28 of May 1678." Coventry Papers at Longleat, XLI, f. 464. To another letter he appends a postscript "pray doe me the favour to send the inclosed to my lodging," the enclosure presumably being a letter for his wife. "Hague ye 11th/21 of June 1678." Coventry Papers at Longleat, XLI, f. 487. It is significant, I think, that he left his wife in charge of Thynne and not of Evelyn.

52 Godolphin to Anne Godolphin, "The Hague, 5/15 May." (1678). *Morrison Collection*, 1st Ser. II, p. 186.

53 ibid., "Hague, ye 21/31 of May, and your birthday, 1678." (?) *Morrison Collection*, 1st Ser. II, 186.

54 Godolphin to Jael Boscawen, "Hague, ye 30/20 of May, 1678." Evelyn MSS., Christ Church, Oxford.

55 ibid., "Hague, ye 11/21 of June, 1678." Evelyn MSS., Christ Church, Oxford.

56 Evelyn, *Diary*, November 11th, 1677, IV, 123.

57 Evelyn, *Mrs. Godolphin*, 73.

58 Evelyn, *Diary*, May 16th, 1678, IV, 134-5.

59 ibid., July 23rd, 1678, IV, 138-9.

60 ibid., September 3rd, 1678, IV, 147.

61 Evelyn Papers, Christ Church, Oxford. Evelyn, *Mrs. Godolphin*, 76. Evelyn, *Diary*, September 8th, 1678. Hiscock, *John Evelyn and Mrs. Godolphin*, 185.

62 Evelyn, *Diary*, September 16th, 1678, IV, 151-2.

63 Hiscock, *John Evelyn and Mrs. Godolphin*, 123-4, 193-4.

64 Evelyn, *Diary*, September 16th, 1678, IV, 151-2. Margaret Godolphin was buried in the Godolphin Chapel in the south-east corner of Breage Church. When the church was renovated about 1890, two large slabs covering the entrance to the Godolphin tomb were removed, and a lead coffin about six feet in length was exposed to view. It lay scarcely a foot below the surface. No traces of an outer coffin of oak were to be seen, and the only inscription was on the coffin lid. A tracing of this was taken, and the Latin inscription composed by Evelyn showed it to contain Margaret Godolphin's remains. (For reproduction of this inscription, see Evelyn's *Mrs. Godolphin*, 114). As soon as this had been done the coffin was again covered and concrete laid over the entrance to the tomb. A reproduction of the plate on the coffin lid has been placed in front of the Godolphin chapel altar in the south aisle, and a larger brass has been placed immediately above where her body lies. It bears these words: "Beneath this brass repose the mortal remains of Margaret Godolphin, daughter of Colonel Blagge of Horningsheath, Groom of the Bedchamber to King Charles I; the wife of Sidney Godolphin; and the friend of John Evelyn, who has told the story of her noble life. She wished to rest at Breage, the cradle of her husband's race. Born 2nd August, 1652. She died in London 9th September, 1678. This brass was placed to her memory by George Godolphin Osborne, 10th Duke of Leeds." It is curious that the ancient burying place of the family contains no monuments of any kind to preserve the memory of departed Godolphins. The helmets of three early members of the family do still hang in the Godolphin Chapel of Breage Church, but the silken banners that once accompanied them have long since mouldered to dust.

⁶⁵ Evelyn, *Mrs. Godolphin*, 79-81.

CHAPTER IV

¹ Godolphin to Evelyn, "London, Sept: ye 22nd, 1678." Evelyn MSS., Christ Church, Oxford. On many future occasions, as we shall see, was Evelyn to remind Godolphin of this letter, and as each anniversary of Margaret's death came round he would write to him in her memory.

² Anne, Lady Sunderland to Sidney, "Dec. 16." (1679). Brit. Mus. Add. MSS. 32,680, f. 164. Sidney, *Diary & Correspondence*, 209.

³ Godolphin to Jael Boscawen, "Godolphin October ye 5th, 1678." Evelyn MSS., Christ Church, Oxford.

⁴ Godolphin to Boscawen, "Godolphin, October ye 6th, 1678." Evelyn MSS., Christ Church, Oxford.

⁵ ibid., "Godolphin, Oct, ye 2nd, 1678." Evelyn MSS., Christ Church, Oxford.

⁶ Godolphin to Thynne, "Godolphin, Oct: ye 6th, 1678." Coventry Papers at Longleat, II, ff. 109-10.

⁷ Evelyn, *Diary*, January 14th, 1679, IV, 161.

⁸ *London Gazette*, Whitehall, March 26th, 1679. Evelyn states that Godolphin was at the same time sworn of the Privy Council—Evelyn, *Diary*, March 30th, 1679, IV, 166—but this appears to be incorrect. He was actually sworn in February of the following year, 1680. Luttrell, *Diary*, I, 33.

⁹ For the Committee's notes of instructions to the Envoy, see Brit. Mus. Add. MSS. 15,643. See also Secret Dutch Dispatches, June 10/20, Brit. Mus. Add. MSS. 17,677, Vol. SSS, ff. 257-61.

¹⁰ Godolphin to Sidney, "Windsor, Aug: ye 23th, 1679." Brit. Mus. Add. MSS. 32,680, f. 104.

¹¹ Sidney, *Diary & Correspondence*, I, 121.

¹² ibid., September 29th, 1679, I, 155-6.

¹³ ibid., September 9th, 1679, I, 130.

¹⁴ ibid., September 19th, 1679, I, 143.

¹⁵ Evelyn, *Diary*, January 15th, August 25th, September 14th, November 6th and 18th, 1679, I, 161, 180, 181, 184.

¹⁶ Evelyn to Godolphin, "Says Court, 19 Decr. 81." Evelyn Letter Book, (1678-97), Christ Church, Oxford, p. 11.

17 Barrillon to Louis XIV, October 31st, 1680. Dalrymple, *Memoirs*, I, app. to Chap., IV, 351.

18 Dorothy, Lady Sunderland to Sidney, "January 6th," (1680). Sidney, *Diary & Correspondence*, I, 237.

19 Barrillon to Louis XIV, January 29th, 1680. P.R.O. 31/3/144.

20 Godolphin to Coventry, "Newmarket Mar ye 16 1680/79." Coventry Papers at Longleat, II, f. 178.

21 Coventry to Godolphin, "Whitehall ye 18th of March 1679/80." Coventry Papers at Longleat, II, f. 178.

22 Godolphin to Coventry, "Newmarkett, March ye 21th [*sic*] 1679." Coventry Papers at Longleat, II, f. 187.

23 ibid., "Newmarkett, March ye 28th, 1680." Coventry Papers at Longleat, III, f. 454.

24 Godolphin to Sidney, "Febr: ye 27th, 1680/79." Brit. Mus. Add. MSS. 32,680, f. 286.

25 Godolphin to Bulstrode, "Whitehall ye 4th of February, 1680/81." Coventry Papers at Longleat, II, Appendix.

26 Godolphin, House of Commons, Wednesday, November 17th, 1680. Grey's *Debates* (ed, 1769). VIII, 29.

27 Clarke, *James II*, I, 615.

28 York to Hyde, "December 14th." (1680.) *Clarendon Correspondence*, I, 48.

29 Godolphin to Orange, "London, June 28th, 1681." S.P. Dom. *King William's Chest*, S.P. 8/1, No. 24.

30 ibid., "Whitehall, April 18, 1684." Dalrymple, *Memoirs*, I, App. to Part I, Book I, p. 126.

31 Evelyn, *Diary*, June 27th, 29th, 1684, IV, 383.

32 Evelyn to Jael Boscawen, "Says Court, 14 July—84." Evelyn, *Letter Book* (1678–1697), Christ Church, Oxford, p. 52.

33 John Evelyn, *Diary*, July 23rd, 1684, IV, 384.

34 Godolphin to Rochester, "Hampton Court Tuesday 5 o'clock:" added in pencil, "August 1684." Brit. Mus. Add. MSS. 15,892, f. 169.

35 Cal. S.P. Treas. Books, 1685/9, III, 1148.

36 Evelyn to Godolphin, "Says Court 9 Sept –84." Evelyn Letter Book (1678–1697), Christ Church, Oxford, p. 53. He also wrote to Sidney's sister in the same vein. Evelyn to Jael Boscawen, "Says-Court, 31 Aug –84." Evelyn Letter Book (1678–1697), Christ Church, Oxford, p. 53. Also see Evelyn to Godolphin, "Says, Court, 22 Apll –84." Evelyn Letter Book (1678–1697), Christ Church, Oxford, p. 49.

37 Evelyn to Godolphin, "Says Court, 11 ffeb -8 4/5." Endorsed in margin "upon the Death of K. Char: the Second." Evelyn Letter Book (1678–1697). Christ Church, Oxford, pp. 57–8.

CHAPTER V

1 Barrillon to Louis XIV, 22 Fev. Lingard, *History*, I, 121.

2 Mazure, *Histoire*, I, 393-4.

[3] Louis XIV to Barrillon, "25 May, 1685, à Versailles." Fox, *James II*, Appendix, LXXXVI.

[4] Barrillon to Louis XIV, "26 Fevrier, 1685." Fox, *James II*, Appendix, XXXII.

[5] ibid., "Mars 1, 1685." Fox, *James II*, Appendix, XXXVII, Terriesi to Grand Duke of Tuscany, "Londres, 25 Avril, 1685," Medicis Archives, Florence, 4214; and Barrillon to Louis XIV, "Londres 26 & 30 Avril, 1685." Campana de Cavelli, *Derniers Stuarts*, II, 37-39.

[6] ibid., "30 Avril, 1685." Fox, *James II*, Appendix, LXVI.

[7] Macaulay, *History*, I, 465.

[8] Barrillon to Louis XIV, "19 Fevrier, 1685." Fox, *James II*, Appendix, XVIII.

[9] ibid., "19 Fevrier, 1685." Fox, *James II*, Appendix, XXI.

[10] ibid., "26 Fevrier, 1685." Fox, *James II*, Appendix, XXIX, XXX.

[11] Louis XIV to Barrillon, "24 Avril 1685." Fox, *James II*, Appendix, LXIII.

[12] Barrillon to Louis XIV, "30 Avril, 1685." Fox, *James II*, Appendix, CXVIII.

[13] ibid., March, 1685. Dalrymple, *Memoirs*, II, 32.

[14] ibid., "16 Avril, 1685." Fox, *James II*, Appendix, LX.

[15] Feiling, *Tory Party*, 209.

[16] For this document printed in full, see Dalrymple, *Memoirs*, II, App. I, p. 288. See also Mackintosh, *History of Revolution*, App. p. 692; Ranke, *History*, IV, 399-400.

[17] Godolphin to Jael Boscawen, "Whitehall, Tuesday," (1688). Evelyn MSS., Christ Church, Oxford.

[18] Feiling, *Tory Party*, 252.

[19] The King attributed the defection of George of Denmark and of many of his officers to the work of Churchill. d'Adda to Cardinal Secretary of State, "Londres, 6 Decembre, 1688." Brit. Mus. Add, MSS. 15,397, f. 472. Campana de Cavelli, *Derniers Stuarts*, II, 361.

[20] Mazure, *Histoire*, III, 221-2.

[21] Burnet to Herbert, "Hungerford the 9th of December." Endorsed "Hungerford, Dec. 9th, 1688, Dr. Gilbt. Burnet to Admll. Herbert." Brit. Mus. Egerton MSS. 2,621, f. 69. Foxcroft, *Supplement to Burnet*, 553.

[22] Nottingham to Hatton, (undated but presumably December 1st). *Hatton Correspondence*, II, 117. Brit. Mus. Add. MSS. 29,595, f. 283. Langueville to Hatton, "1st of December, 1688." *Hatton Correspondence*, II, 118. See also unknown correspondent to John Ellis, Dec. 1st, 1688. *Ellis Correspondence*, II, 343.

[23] Evelyn, *Diary*, December 2nd, 1688, IV, 608.

[24] Mazure, *Histoire*, III, 220.

[25] H.M.C. *Rep. V*, App., 198.

[26] Berkeley to Dartmouth, December 3rd, 1688. H.M.C. *Rep. XI*, pt. 5, 223. Foxcroft, *Halifax*, II, 23.

[27] King James to Orange. "A Whitehall ce I Dec. 1688." It was countersigned by Lord Middleton and addressed "a mon fils et neveu Le Prince d'Orange." All Souls MSS., 273.

[28] "Hungerford ye 8th Decemb: 1688." From the copy in the Codrington Library. All Souls MSS., 273. This paper was probably drawn up by Halifax. Foxcroft, *Halifax*, II, 23.

29 Bodl., Rawlinson MSS. A. 139, B. p. 278. The body of the letter seems to be in Godolphin's hand, the postscript in Halifax's. The signatures are autograph. There is a copy in the Codrington Library. All Souls MSS. 273. Foxcroft, *Halifax*, II, 24-6.

30 Burnet, *Own Times*, III, 342. Macaulay, *History*, III, 1191.

31 In his contemporary account of these events, Burnet varied his account slightly. Burnet to Herbert, "Hungerford the 9th of December." Endorsed, "Hungerford, Dec. 9th, 1688, Dr. Gilbt. Burnet to Herbert." Brit. Mus. Egerton MSS. 2,621, f. 70. Foxcroft, *Supplement to Burnet*, 534.

32 "Given at Litlecote, the 9th of Decemb., 1688." All Souls MSS. 273.

33 "Littlecott, ye 10th of Decr. 1688." Brit. Mus. Add. MSS. 28,103, f. 72. There is a copy in the Codrington Library. All Souls MSS. 273.

34 Mazure, *Histoire*, III, 231.

35 H.M.C. *Stuart Papers*, I, 77.

36 "Given at Windsor the 17th day of December, 1688." Spencer MSS. 31 (1), H.M.C. *Rep. II*, 14.

37 Mazure, *Histoire*, III, 220.

38 Ailesbury, *Memoirs*, 195-7.

39 Burnet, *Own Times*, III, 345, *et seq*.

40 Mazure, *Historie*, III, 254-5.

41 Foxcroft, *Halifax*, II, 28. f.n. Feiling, *Tory Party*, 1640-1714, 236-8, 244.

42 Macaulay, *History*, III, 132.

CHAPTER VI

1 Evelyn, *Diary*, October 23rd, 1686, IV, 527-8.

2 T. 5/49, p. 439. S.P. Cal. of Treas. Books, 1685/9, p. 1107, 1689/92, p. 736.

3 Pepys, *Diary*, August 19th, 1665 and September 23rd, 1667, V. 49, VII, 115-15.

4 Godolphin to Jael Boscawen, "Thursday night". Evelyn MSS., Christ Church, Oxford.

5 ibid., "Tuesday July 2nd, 95." Evelyn MSS., Christ Church, Oxford.

6 ibid., "June 14, 90." Evelyn MSS., Christ Church, Oxford.

7 Halifax's "note book", Devonshire House. Foxcroft, *Halifax*, II, 143.

8 H.M.C. *Rep. XIV*, pt. 2, 452. We can, I think, safely ignore Edward Harley's spiteful comment, "It is said privately that Lord Godolphin comes in by Mrs. Villiers's interest." Edward Harley to Sir Edward Harley, "November 22, '90." H.M.C. *Portland*, III, 452.

9 H. of C. Journal, X, 36.

10 Grey's *Debates*, IX, 113, *et seq*.

11 H. of C. Journal, X, 37-8.

12 ibid., X, 46. Grey's *Debates*, IX, 148, *et seq*.

13 ibid., X, 56.

14 ibid., X, 104.

15 ibid., X, 357, 358-9.

[16] See *Cal. Treas. Books.* Introduction to Vol. IX, 1689–92, pt. I, and introduction to Vols. XI–XVII, 1695–1702, by William A. Shaw.

[17] Carmarthen to King William, "10th February 1690/1." P.R.O. S.P. Dom, King William's Chest, S.P. 8, No. 85. Browning, *Danby,* II, 191.

[18] Marlborough to King William, "Jan. 27th, 1690." P.R.O. S.P. Dom. 1690, p. 430.

[19] Sidney to King William, "Feb. 2, 1690/1." Ten days later, Godolphin himself makes his "present circumstances at this time" an excuse for his retirement. Godolphin to King William, February 13, 1690/1. Dalrymple, *Memoirs,* app. pt. II, bk. VII, 249–50. Curiously enough, a false rumour of Godolphin's marriage had some four months previously come to Evelyn's ears. "My Ld: I ever valued the profession of a *Man of Honor,* tho but in verbal promise, above all securities. But when it comes confirm'd under his *hand* and seale; then to be *legally obliging.* . . . Yet how would my *Lord Absolve* the person who (in a certain *Lettr* to me among so many expressions of the most intimate Indearments and *Friendships,* can be establish'd adds *this* passage: *Remember that from henceforth) looke upon you as the Depositarie of all my Concernes to be wholy guided and directed by you &c*: is, I heare (and that from good hands) *concluding* on the *greatest* and most *Important concerne* of his whole Life, and in which his *Friend* is so much concern'd who has ever *Lov'd* him, above all Man-kind, and never ceas'd to pray for his happiness, without so much as once mentioning of it to him—well, be it so—*Res Integra.* All is *still well,* and you have no neede to *Consull* a Ghostly *Father* upon the *scruple*: For whilst I understand you have made Choice of a Lady so *Transendently like her predecessor*; Accomplished in all the *vertues* and *ornaments* she was possess'd of, not only my *Consent* must be *Included* in it, but my *highest approbation*: There's *one thing yet* to render your *happy* Lady not only the *Resemblance,* but the very *prototye* of that *Incompatrable Saint*; but her *very selfe,* remaining; That she accept of my *humble service*; and *Regard* me with some *distinguishing grace* for the *sincere Honour* and *Affection* I have ever born to him on whom she had placed hers so worthily—which is all the *merite* I pleade; And so God *Almighty* give you both Joy." Evelyn to Godolphin, "Says Court, 20 Sept. 1690." Endorsed "upon report of his having married ye Lady wh. did not prove true." John Evelyn Letter Book, (1678–1797), pp. 140–1. Christ Church, Oxford.

[20] Swift, *Four Last Years* in *Works,* (ed. Scott), V, 175.

[21] Burnet, *Own Time,* III, 9 (note).

[22] Godolphin to King William, "Feb. 2d. 90/1." P.R.O. S.P. 8/8, No. 84.

[23] ibid., "Febr. 6th, 90/1." P.R.O. S.P. 8/8, No. 86.

[24] King William to Godolphin, "La Haye, le 6/16 de Feb. 1691." Brit. Mus. Add. MSS. 24,905, f. 1.

[25] ibid., "A la Haye le 17/27 de Feb. 1691." Brit. Mus. Add. MSS. 24,905, f. 2.

[26] Godolphin to King William, "Febr. 13, 90/1." P.R.O. S.P. 8/8, No. 96.

[27] ibid., "Febr. 20 91/0." P.R.O. S.P. 8/8, No. 90, f. 179.

[28] Marlborough to King William, "Feb: 24th 91." P.R.O. S.P. 8/8, No. 99.

[29] Godolphin to King William, "Feb: 24. 90/1." P.R.O. S.P. 8/8, No. 100.

[30] ibid., "Feb: 27, 90/1." P.R.O. S.P. 8/8, No. 102.

[31] ibid., "March ye 3d, 90/1." P.R.O. S.P. 8/8, No, 109.

[32] ibid., "10th March, 90/1." P.R.O. S.P. 8/8, No. 115.

[33] Sidney to King William, "Feb. 27, 1690/1." P.R.O. S.P. 8/8, No. 103.

[34] ibid., no date. P.R.O. S.P. 8/8, No. 117.

³⁵ Danby's pension of £3,000 for life had been altered because of his age to one for a fixed period of twenty-one years. There had been much criticism of this, and Godolphin and other members of the Treasury Commission had been induced to sign the warrant only by the Queen's express command. *Cal. S.P. Dom.* 1895, 168–9. Browning, *Danby,* I, 487.

³⁶ Godolphin to King William, "March 13th, 90/1." P.R.O. S.P. 8/8, No. 117.

³⁷ ibid., "March 20th, 90/1." P.R.O. S.P. 8/8, No. 121.

³⁸ ibid., "April 3d 91." P.R.O. S.P. 8/9, No. 49. See also March 23rd, 1691. Brit. Mus. Add. MSS. 24,905, f. 9.

³⁹ ibid., "May 18," (1691), P.R.O. S.P. 8/9, No. 89.

⁴⁰ ibid., "Tunbridge, August 10th, 91." P.R.O. S.P. 8/9, No. 149.

⁴¹ Blathwayt to Godolphin, "The Hague, ye 25 March, S.N. 1692." And "Hague, ye 28 1692." Brit. Mus. Add. MSS. 9,735, ff, 46, 48.

⁴² Godolphin to Blathwayt, "June 28th, 1692." Brit. Mus. Add. MSS. 9,735, f. 57.

⁴³ Godolphin to King William, September 22, 1691, Brit. Mus. Add. MSS. 24,905, f. 12. June 16, 1692. Brit. Mus. Add. MSS. 24,905, f. 15.

⁴⁴ Godolphin to Portland, "Aug, 15, 1695." Brit. Mus. Add. MSS, 28,103, f. 74.

⁴⁵ Godolphin to Blathwayt, "July 5th 92." Brit. Mus. Add. MSS. 9,735, f. 59.

⁴⁶ King William to Godolphin, "Au Camp de Grame ce 28 d'Aoust, 1692." Brit. Mus. Add. MSS. 24, 905, f. 21.

⁴⁷ ibid., "Au Camp de Lembeec ce 27 d'Aoust, 1693." Brit. Mus. Add. MSS. 24,905, f. 9.

⁴⁸Pepys, *Diary,* "Aug. 30th (Lord's Day), 1688". VIII, 94.

⁴⁹ Thus ran one stanza of "The Rabble," a satire against Charles II, written 1680:

> Not for the nation, but the fair,
> Our treasury provides;
> Bulkeley's G . . . n's only care,
> as Middleton is Hyde's.

Steinman, *Mrs. Middleton,* 45. An anonymous letter to Ormonde dated 25 Jan. 1679/80 contained the words "Godly Godolphin being enamoured and intoxicated with Mrs. Buckly" [*sic*]. H.M.C. *Ormonde* (36), New Series, V, 561. According to an entry in the Treasury Order Book at the Customs, D. 352, f. 303, when some payment was made to her under the name of "Buckley", she was living in France in 1680, when this satire was written. For a probable reference in Rochester's *Works,* see Appendix II.

⁵⁰ H.M.C. *8th Rep.* App. pt. III, p. 12a. Granger, *Biographical History of England* (ed. 1804), IV, 184. *Notes and Queries,* third series, I, 69, Dalrymple, *Memorials,* Part II, 189, where she is incorrectly styled "Lady Sophia Buckley." I know of no evidence to support the rumour of her imprisonment in the Bastille, nor have I found any correspondence between her and Godolphin. That she had Jacobite sympathies is doubtless true, and it appears certain that she was one of the Court ladies who were present at Mary of Modena's confinement in October 1688. Newsletter, "Whitehall, October 23, 1688." H.M.C. *Portland,* III, 419. This was satirized in *The Diplomats. Poems on affairs of State,* (ed. 1704), III, 260–1.

⁵¹ Clarke, *James II,* II, 444–5.

52 Clarke, *James II,* II, 446.

53 ibid., 444–50.

54 Macaulay, *History,* IV, 2019, f. n.

55 Churchill, *Marlborough,* I, 310–20.

56 Ailesbury, *Memoirs,* II, 3910.

57 Foxcroft, *Halifax,* II, 144.

58 ibid., 143, f. n. 10.

CHAPTER VII

1 For discussions of James Macpherson and the Nairne Papers, see *English Historical Review,* IX, 130–32, XII, 254–84, and XXXV, 367–76. Churchill, *Marlborough,* I. 310 *et seq.*

2 Bodl., MS. Carte, ff. 101–2.

3 ibid., 181, ff, 539–40.

4 Macaulay, *History,* V, 2376, f. n. 1.

5 Bodl., MS. *Carte,* 209, ff. 44–51. The document is dated " 5 Sep 1692." in Melfort's hand, and is headed, "To be writt by D. Ff to Russ" (i.e. David Floyd to Russell). It is also endorsed "Letter sent to Engld, ye 5 9br 1692 by D. fl." (i.e. David Floyd) and the words "concerning Russel" are added in another hand. James Macpherson gives the date as "the 1st of May 1694" but this is incorrect. Macpherson, *Original Papers,* I, 480–3.

6 ibid., 181, ff. 568–71.

7 Godolphin to King William, "Aprill 18. 93." P.R.O. S.P. 8/14, No. 7.

8 ibid., "April 25, 93." P.R.O. S.P. 8/14, No. 9.

9 ibid., "May 16, 93." P.R.O. S.P. 8/14, No. 12.

10 ibid., "Aug. 18, 93." P.R.O. S.P. 8/16, No. 15. In truth Godolphin placed little reliance on the fleet. "Your Majesty's speedy direction how our great uselesse fleet should act, would bee very reasonable; I have ventured to give my opinion that the main body of it should goe immediately and lie before Brest, as if their design was there while 2 small squadrons with the bombships might at the same time bombard the Townes on the coast of Normandy, and in the bay." Godolphin to King William, "June 12, 96." P.R.O. S.P. Dom. 8/16, No. 11.

11 Bodl., MSS. Carte, 181, f. 572.

12 "Relation du Capⁿ Floyd poste à Versailles de 11 May 1694." In Nairne's handwriting. Bodl., MSS. Carte, 181, ff. 568.

13 Clarke, *James II,* II, 521, gives the date as May 4th. But the original document in the Bodleian Library is clearly dated May 3rd.

14 Louis XIV to Vauban. "A Versailles ce 1er Mars, 1694." *Journal d l'Institut Historique,* V, 223. "Mars" is presumably a misprint for "Mai".

15 Godolphin to Jael Boscawen, "Christmas day, 1694." Evelyn MSS., Christ Church, Oxford.

16 Thorold Rogers, *Bank of England.*

17 Godolphin to King William, "May 29–96." P.R.O. S.P. Dom. 8/16, No. 11.

18 ibid., "June 5th, 96." P.R.O. S.P. Dom, 8/16, No. 13.

19 Ranke, *History*, V, 101.

20 *H. of C. Journal*, XI, 358.

21 Godolphin to King William, "June 12, 96." P.R.O. S.P. 8/16, No. 15.

22 ibid., "June 23." (1696). P.R.O. S.P. 8/16, No. 16.

23 ibid., "June 30th." (1616). P.R.O. S.P. 8/16, No. 18.

24 Thorold Rogers. *Bank of England*, 50–88.

25 Shrewsbury to King William, P.R.O. S.P. 8/16, No. 22. *Shrewsbury Correspondence*, 131.

26 King William's italics.

27 King William to Shrewsbury, "Loo., Sept. 10, 1696." (Presumably N.S.) *Shrewsbury Correspondence*, 145–6.

28 Shrewsbury to Portland, "London, Sept. 8. 96." (Presumably O.S.) H.M.C. *Buccleuch at Queensberry*, II, Part I, 400.

29 Lady Middleton and Lady Shrewsbury, Shrewsbury's mother, were sisters.

30 Nicholson and Turberville, *Shrewsbury*, 112.

31 King William to Shrewsbury, September 10/20, 1696. *Shrewsbury Correspondence*, 147–8, 151.

32 Nicholson and Turberville, *Shrewsbury*, 108–42.

33 Somers to Shrewsbury, "Octo 27–Nov. 6, 1696." *Shrewsbury Correspondence*, p. 415.

34 ibid., "Oct. 31–Nov. 10, 1696." *Shrewsbury Correspondence*, p. 420.

35 Wharton to Shrewsbury, "Whitehall, Nov. 10–20, 1606. *Shrewsbury Correspondence*, p. 428.

36 ibid., "Whitehall, Dec. 1–11, 1696. *Shrewsbury Correspondence*, p. 437.

37 Macaulay, *History*, IV, 2679.

CHAPTER VIII

1 Godolphin to Lady Marlborough, "att Southborough neare Tunbridge Wells, in Kent, Munday night Sept. 7th." (1691). Blenheim MSS. E.17.

2 ibid., "att St. Albans, Hertfordshire, Thursday night 17 Septr." (1691). Blenheim MSS. E.17.

3 ibid., "att the Cockpit Whitehall London, Septr. 9th." Blenheim MSS. E.17.

4 ibid., "Thursday night." Blenheim MSS. E.17.

5 ibid., "att St. Albans, fryday 7 at night." Blenheim MSS. E.17.

6 ibid., "att her lodgings in Bathe, London, Tuesday morning Septr. 13th." (1692). Blenheim MSS. E.17.

7 ibid., "thursday night, 15th Octr." (1702). Blenheim MSS. E.20. Lady Mary was the Marlboroughs' youngest daughter, afterwards Duchess of Montagu.

8 ibid., "at her lodgings in Windsor Castle, thursday morning." Blenheim MSS. E.20.

9 ibid., "Windsor munday morne." Blenheim MSS. E.17.

[10] Marlborough to Godolphin, "Helchteren, Aug 16–17, 1702." Blenheim MSS. A.1. 14.

[11] Henry Godolphin, Sidney's younger brother, the Provost of Eton.

[12] Evelyn to Godolphin, "White-hall, 8 Decr, 1689." Evelyn Letter Book (1679–97), p. 55, Christ Church, Oxford.

[13] Evelyn to Francis Godolphin, "Lond: 4 Apl.–90." Evelyn Letter Book (1679–97), pp. 131–2. Christ Church, Oxford.

[14] Ulissi Aldrovandi (1522–1605), Italian Naturalist.

[15] Evelyn to Francis Godolphin, "Deptford, 2 Aug –90." Evelyn Letter Book (1679–97), pp. 139–40. Christ Church, Oxford.

[16] Godolphin to Jael Boscawen, "St. Albans, 8 Novt." (1697). Evelyn MSS., Christ Church, Oxford.

[17] ibid., "St. Albans, Munday" (1697). Evelyn MSS., Christ Church, Oxford.

[18] ibid., "St. Albans, 25 Nov." (1697). Evelyn MSS., Christ Church, Oxford.

[19] Lady Henrietta Churchill to Lady Marlborough, "Sunday," Blenheim MSS. E.6.

[20] ibid., "Sunday." Blenheim MSS. E. 6.

[21] ibid., n.d. Blenheim MSS. E.6.

[22] ibid., "att her lodgings in St. James's house, London, August ye 6th." Blenheim MSS. E.6.

[23] ibid., "August ye 4th," Blenheim MSS. E.6.

[24] Godolphin to Lady Marlborough, "Wednesday at two." Blenheim MSS. E.20.

[25] Godolphin to Jael Boscawen, "Sat: morning." (1698). Evelyn MSS., Christ Church, Oxford.

[26] P.R.O. S.P. Dom. 44/347, 207.

[27] Godolphin to Jael Boscawen, "7 Febr: 1698/9." Brit. Mus. Add. MSS. 15949, f 31.

[28] ibid., "Sat. morning" (1698). Evelyn MSS. Christ Church, Oxford.

[29] Godolphin and his sister were, it seems, active in promoting the match. Coxe, *Marlborough,* I, 53. Wolseley, *Marlborough,* II, 356.

[30] Harley to Godolphin, September 10, 1707. H.M.C. *Bath,* I, 181.

[31] West to Harley, Tonbridge Wells, August 29th, 1704. H.M.C. *Portland,* IV, 118–19.

[32] Harley to——?, October 16, 1700. H.M.C. *Portland,* IV, 7.

[33] Guy to Harley, "September 24" (1700). H.M.C. *Portland,* III, 629.

[34] ibid., "January 14 (1700–1). H.M.C. *Portland,* IV, 12.

[35] ibid., "January 18 (1700–1). H.M.C. *Portland,* IV, 13.

[36] ibid., "January 23" (1700–1). H.M.C. *Portland,* IV, 14.

[37] Godolphin to Harley, December 4, 1701. H.M.C. *Portland,* IV, 28.

[38] ibid., December 9th, 1701. H.M.C. *Portland,* IV, 14.

[39] ibid., "January 25th," (1702). H.M.C. *Portland,* IV, 33.

[40] Trevelyan, *England under the Stuarts,* 460.

[41] ibid., 467.

BOOK II

CHAPTER I

[1] Queen Anne to Lady Marlborough, "St. James teusday ye 19th of May," (1702). Blenheim MSS. E.19.

[2] Chamberlayne, *Angliæ Notitia,* 523.

[3] Godolphin to Harley, "1701-2 March 8." H.M.C. *Portland,* IV, 34.

[4] ibid, "1701-2 March 9." H.M.C. *Portland,* II, 84.

[5] Feiling, *Tory Party,* 364.

[6] Churchill, *Marlborough,* Book I, 503.

[7] Brit. Mus. Add. MSS. 28,070, ff. 2-3b. Anne on frequent occasions called her brother-in-law "Mr. Caliban".

[8] Edward Harley to Sir Edward Harley, January 3, 1698 (9). H.M.C. *Portland,* III, 600.

[9] Burnet, *Own Time,* V, 8, f.n.

[10] ibid., V, 8.

[11] Queen Anne to Godolphin, "August 30 -Sept. 10." (1706). Coxe, *Marlborough,* II, 3.

[12] Lord Godolphin to Harley, May 28th, 1702. H.M.C. *Portland,* IV, 39.

[13] Cowper, *Diary,* 15.

[14] Walsh, *Golden Ages Restored.*

[15] Godolphin to Harley, August 18th, 1702, and Guy to Harley, August 22nd, 1702. H.M.C. *Portland,* IV, 44-5.

[16] Among the Nottingham papers we find letters addressed to him under the following dates: "Bath, 30 Aug." "Bath Septr. ye 3d. 1702." "Bath, 4th Sept. 1702." "Bath, Sept. 6, 1702." "Bathe, 15 Septr. 1702." "Bath 18 Septr. 1702." "Bath 23 Septr. 1702." "Bath 27 Septr. 1702." Brit. Mus. Add. MSS. 29,588, ff. 155-7, 173-4, 175, 183-4, 233-5, 242-5, 265, 271.

[17] Godolphin to Lowndes, "Bathe, 18 Sepr. 1702." P.R.O. T. 48/23, Bundle 11.

[18] ibid., "19th Septr. 1702." P.R.O. T. 48/23, f.

[19] Godolphin to Nottingham, "Eton 19 Sept. 1703." Brit. Mus. Add. MSS. 29,588, f. 279.

[20] Godolphin to Lowndes, "Eton 29 Septr. 1702." P.R.O. T. 48/23, f.

[21] Godolphin to Nottingham, "Newmarkett, 3d Octr. 1702." Brit. Mus. Add. MSS. 29,588, f. 298.

[22] Godolphin to Harley, "14 Friday" (August, 1702). H.M.C. *Portland,* IV, 43.

[23] Marlborough to Godolphin, "Duckenburg, July 13th." (1702). Blenheim MSS. A.1. 14.

[24] Godolphin to Harley, "Bath, September 27th, 1702." H.M.C. *Portland,* IV, 48.

[25] Godolphin to Harley, "Friday" (October 23, 1702). H.M.C. *Portland*, IV, 49.

[26] Godolphin to Nottingham, "Newmarkett, 5 Octr. 1702." Brit. Mus. Add. MSS. 29,588, f. 304.

[27] ibid., "Newmarkett, 8 Octr, 1702." Brit. Mus. Add. MSS. 29,588, f. 318.

[28] ibid., "Newmarkett, Sunday noon 11 Octr." (1702). Brit. Mus. Add. MSS. 29,588, f. 324.

[29] Godolphin to Harley, "December 9, 1702." H.M.C. *Portland*, IV, 53.

[30] ibid., "December 12, 1702." H.M.C. *Portland*, IV, 53.

[31] ibid., "December 14, 1702." H.M.C. *Portland*, IV, 54.

[32] Queen Anne to Duchess of Marlborough, "Wednesday, Dec. 16." (1702). Blenheim MSS. B.II, 32.

[33] Godolphin "to her Grace the Duchess of Marlborough at her lodg in Windsor great park, Berks, Aug. 5 Tuesday." (1701). Blenheim MSS. E.20.

[34] ibid., "August 5th." (1702). Blenheim MSS. E.19. The young man was already Blandford at this time, but Godolphin from force of habit seems to have retained the old style.

[35] ibid., "Newmarkett, 5 October." (1702). Blenheim MSS. 20.

[36] ibid., "Newmarkett, 6 Octr." (1702). Blenheim MSS. E.20.

[37] ibid., "Newmarkett, 8 Oct:" (1702). Blenheim MSS. E.20.

[38] ibid., "St. James's, tuesday 13." (October, 1702). Blenheim MSS. E.20.

[39] Blandford to Marlborough, "Cambridge Fe ye 2d 1702/3," and Blandford to Duchess of Marlborough, "Cambridge Feb ye 9th 1702/2." Blenheim MSS. E.6.

[40] Godolphin to Duchess of Marlborough. "Thursday 10 in ye morning" (1703). Blenheim MSS. E.20.

[41] Queen Anne to Duchess of Marlborough, "St. James's, Tuesday night." (1703). Blenheim MSS. B.11, 32.

CHAPTER II

[1] Marlborough to Duchess of Marlborough, "Camp at Hannef June 3d 1703." Blenheim MSS. E.2.

[2] Marlborough to Harley, "Alderbeeston, October 11 N.S. 1703." H.M.C. *Bath*, I, 56.

[3] Godolphin to Harley, "18 Friday" (December 1702). H.M.C. *Portland*, IV, 54.

[4] ibid., "December 24" (1702)." H.M.C. *Portland*, IV, 54.

[5] Marlborough to Duchess of Marlborough, no date but probably written early in 1703, and before Rochester's resignation on February 4th. Coxe, *Marlborough*, I, 145; Churchill, *Marlborough*, Book I, 625–6.

[6] Godolphin to Harley, January 14th, 1702–3. H.M.C. *Portland*, IV, 57.

[7] ibid., March 28th, 1703. H.M.C. *Portland*, IV, 59.

[8] Churchill, *Marlborough*, Book I, 627.

[9] *Cal. S.P. Dom.* (1702–3), 251.

[10] Godolphin to Nottingham, "Wednesday 21th [*sic*] July 1703, at four" and no date. Brit. Mus. Add. MSS. 29,589, ff. 45, 400.

[11] Nottingham to Godolphin, no date. Brit. Mus. Add. MSS. 29,595, f. 239.

[12] Godolphin to Nottingham, "Windsor, July 17, 1703." Brit. Mus. Add. MSS. 29,589, f. 28.

[13] ibid., "Windsor, Thursday 22 July 1703, nine at night and at 6 in ye morning 23." Brit. Mus. Add. MSS. 29,589, f. 46.

[14] Nottingham to Godolphin, "Whitehall July 23, 1703." Brit. Mus. Add. MSS. 29,595, f. 241.

[15] Harley to Godolphin, "Brampton, Aug. 9; 1702." Brit. Mus. Add. MSS. 28,055, f. 3.

[16] Defoe to Paterson, "April, 1703." Endorsed in Harley's hand: "Received from Mr. Wm. Paterson Friday May 28, 1703, at one o'clock." H.M.C. *Portland*, IV, 61–2. One wonders why there was so long a delay before Paterson sent the letter to Harley.

[17] Harley to Godolphin, "Sept. 20; 1703." H.M.C. *Marlborough*, 43.

[18] Godolphin to Harley, "Bath September 26th, 1703." H.M.C. *Portland*, IV, 68. It is quite clear that in this letter Godolphin is referring to Harley's letter to him of September 20th, the original of which I found in the muniment room at Blenheim Palace.

[19] Guy to Harley, "September 27," (1703: Bath). H.M.C. *Portland*, IV, 69.

[20] Godolphin to Harley, "Newmarket, October 12th, 1703." H.M.C. *Portland*, IV, 72.

[21] ibid., November 4th, 1703. H.M.C. *Portland*, IV, 75.

[22] Defoe to Harley, November 9th, 1703. H.M.C. *Portland*, IV, 75–6.

[23] Godolphin to Harley, "July 31, half-an-hour past 5, Windsor, 1704." H.M.C. *Bath*, I, 61. I assume "D" stands for Defoe.

[24] Defoe to Harley, no date (? May 1704). H.M.C. *Portland*, IV, 88.

[25] ibid., no date (? May 1704). H.M.C. *Portland*, IV, 89.

[26] ibid., "Bury (St. Edmunds.) September 28th 1704." H.M.C. *Portland*, IV, 136–8.

[27] ibid., "November 2, 1704." H.M.C. *Portland*, IV, 146–9.

[28] ibid., "Crediton, July 30, 1705." H.M.C. *Portland*, IV, 213–14.

[29] ibid., "Tiverton, August 14th, 1705." H.M.C. *Portland*, IV, 221–3.

[30] Alexander Goldsmith alias Defoe to Harley, "Kidderminster, September 10th, 1705." H.M.C. *Portland*, IV, p. 218.

[31] Defoe to Harley, "An Abstract of my journey with casual observations on Public Affairs, July 16 to November 6, 1705." H.M.C. *Portland*, IV, 269–72.

[32] Godolphin to Harley, no date. H.M.C. *Portland*, IV, 155, 156.

[33] Bateson, *The Relations of De Foe and Harley*, E.H.R. XV, 238–50.

[34] Marlborough to Duchess of Marlborough, "Camp at Hannef June 3d." (1703). Blenheim MSS. E.2.

[35] ibid., "Camp at Hanef, June 10th" (1703). Blenheim MSS. E.2.

[36] Godolphin to Harley, "Tuesday at 10." Brit. Mus. Portland Papers, Bundle 3, K. 37.

[37] ibid., "Fryday at 12." Brit. Mus. Portland Papers, Bundle 3, K. 49, 50.

[38] Queen Anne to Duchess of Marlborough, "Windsor, Saturday," (1703.) Blenheim MSS. E.18.

[39] Godolphin to Harley, "Bath, September 16, 1702." H.M.C. *Portland*, IV, 47. In the above volume Godolphin's rough draft of the speech is said to be missing. Recently, however, I acquired Godolphin's draft of this speech, as well as of several other of Queen Anne's speeches to Parliament. These I have given to the Duke of Portland who has deposited them with his other papers on loan to the British Museum.

[40] ibid., "November 4, 1703." H.M.C. *Portland*, IV, 75.

[41] ibid., "Wednesday night at 10." Brit. Mus. Portland Papers, Bundle 4, K.29.

[42] Queen Anne to Duchess of Marlborough, "Kensington, Thursday morning." (1703). Blenheim MSS. E.17.

[43] Marlborough to Godolphin, "Vorst, May 7, 1704." Blenheim MSS. A. I, 14.

[44] Godolphin to Harley, "Sunday at two, May 21, 1704." H.M.C. *Bath*, I, 57.

[45] Dowell, *Taxation*, II, 453, 1 s.c. Hardwicke Papers, Brit. Mus. Add. MSS. 35,902 and 35,903. For all these matters see, Leadam, *Finance of Lord Treasurer Godolphin, Transactions of the Royal Historical Society*, Third Series, IV, 20–32, from which I have largely drawn.

[46] Hardwicke Papers, Brit. Mus. Add. MSS. 35,902.

[47] 1 Anne, St. I, C.13. 1 Anne, St. 2, C.5. 3 Anne C.5.

[48] 1 Anne, St. 2, C.1.

[49] 3 and 4 Anne, C.4.

[50] 3 and 4 Anne, C.2.

[51] 4 Anne, C.6.

[52] 5 Anne, CC, 19, 27.

[53] 5 Anne, C.13.

[54] Marlborough to Godolphin, "The Hague, May 7." (1704). Blenheim MSS. A. I, 14.

CHAPTER III

[1] Godolphin to Harley, "September 14, Windsor." H.M.C. *Bath*, I, 62. The original MS. bears the date "1705" written apparently some years later, probably by the second Earl of Oxford, Harley's son. It is obvious, however, that the letter was written in September, 1704.

[2] Marlborough to Duchess of Marlborough, "October 20th, 1704." Blenheim MSS. E.2.

[3] Godolphin to Harley, "Windsor, September 1, 1704." H.M.C. *Bath*, I, 62.

[4] ibid., "Windsor, September 15, 1704." H.M.C. *Bath*, I, 63.

[5] ibid., 19? (September, 1705). H.M.C. *Bath*, I, 176.

[6] ibid., "November 16, 1704." H.M.C. *Bath*, I, 64–5.

[7] Godolphin to Lady Marlborough, no date. Blenheim MSS. E.2.

[8] Godolphin to Harley, no date. H.M.C. *Portland*, IV, 154.

[9] ibid., "Good Friday night." (March 22nd, 1705–6). H.M.C. *Portland*, IV, 291.

[10] Queen Anne to Godolphin, July 11th, 1705. Brit. Mus. Add. MSS. 28,070, ff. 12–13.

[11] Lady Henrietta Godolphin to Lady Marlborough, no date. Blenheim MSS. E.6.

[12] ibid., "att her Ladyships in St. Jameses House, London, June the 25th." Blenheim MSS. E.6.

[13] ibid., "London, October the 21st." Blenheim MSS. E.6.

[14] ibid., "Oct the 14th." Blenheim MSS. E.6.

[15] ibid., "London, October the 24th." Blenheim MSS. E.6.

[16] Godolphin "To the Rt. Honble the Countess of Marlborough att Windsor Castle, 16 Octr. in ye morning." Blenheim MSS. E.20.

[17] "An account of the Dutches of marl. & montagus behaviour before and after their father's death." Blenheim MSS. F. I, 35.

[18] Blenheim MSS. E.6.

[19] Godolphin "To the Rt. Honble. the Countesse of Marlborough at Windsor Castle, fryday 6 of Febr." Blenheim MSS. E.20.

[20] Lady Henrietta Godolphin to Lady Marlborough, n.d. Blenheim MSS. E.6.

[21] ibid., "att her lodgings in St. James's House, London," no date. Blenheim MSS. E.6.

[22] "An account of the Dutches of Marl. & Montagus behaviour before & after their father's death." Blenheim MSS. F. I, 35.

[23] Godolphin to Duchess of Marlborough, "Windsor 12 June, 1703." Blenheim MSS. E.20.

[24] Marlborough to Duchess of Marlborough, "Windsor 12 June 1703." Blenheim MSS. E.20.

[25] Lady Henrietta Godolphin to Duchess of Marlborough, "Munday", Blenheim MSS. E.6.

[26] Queen Anne to Godolphin, July 11th, 1705. Brit. Mus. Add. MSS. 28,070, ff. 12–13.

[27] Harley to Godolphin, September 4, 1705. H.M.C. *Bath,* I, 74–5.

[28] Godolphin to Harley, "Good Friday night," (March 22nd, 1705–6). H.M.C. *Portland,* IV, 291.

[29] Harley to Godolphin, "July 21, Saturday, 1705." H.M.C. *Bath,* I, 72–3.

[30] Somers, however, was not present, having gone to his house in the country.

[31] Cowper, *Diary,* 33.

[32] Marlborough to Godolphin, "Corbois Augt. 24th 1705." Blenheim MSS. A. I. 37. Godolphin to Harley, "Sept. 2nd 1705." H.M.C. *Bath,* I, 73.

CHAPTER IV

[1] Godolphin to Harley, "January 11, 1704–5," and ? October 10 and 25, 1704–5. H.M.C. *Bath,* I, 65.

[2] Burnet, *Own Time,* V, 242. *Parliamentary History of England* (ed. Cobbet & Wright, 1810), VI, 479–509.

[3] Duchess of Marlborough, *Conduct,* 1710.

[4] Churchill, *Marlborough,* Book II, 37.

[5] Marlborough to Duchess of Marlborough, "Helchin, August 9." (1706). Blenheim MSS. E.3.

[6] Queen Anne to Godolphin, "August 30" (1706). From a copy in the Duchess's hand. Blenheim MSS. G. I. 4.

[7] Godolphin to Queen Anne, "Saturday morning at nine." (August 31st, 1706). Blenheim MSS. E.20. From a draft in Godolphin's hand.

[8] Sunderland to Duchess of Marlborough, "London Sept. 17–28" (1706). Blenheim MSS. E.15.

[9] Marlborough to Godolphin, "Vilaine, Sept. 9th 1706." Blenheim MSS. A. I, 37.

[10] ibid., "Grametz, Sept. 16." (1706). Blenheim MSS. A. I, 37.

[11] Godolphin to Marlborough, "Windsor, Sept. 10–21" (1706). Blenheim MSS. A.I, 37.

[12] Godolphin to Duchess of Marlborough, "Windsor, Sept. 14, 1706." Blenheim MSS. A. I, 37.

[13] Godolphin to Marlborough, "Windsor, Sept. 18–29" (1706). Blenheim MSS. A. I, 37.

[14] Marlborough to Queen Anne, 'Oct. 7, 1706." Blenheim MSS. E.3. A rough copy only.

[15] Marlborough to Duchess of Marlborough, October 11th, 1706. Blenheim MSS. E.3.

[16] Marlborough to Godolphin, October 11th, 1706. Blenheim MSS. E.3.

[17] Queen Anne to Godolphin, "Sep: the 21st" (1706). Blenheim MSS. G. I, 4.

[18] Godolphin to Queen Anne, "Woodstock, Sept. 25" (1706). Blenheim MSS. G. I, 4.

[19] Queen Anne to Godolphin, "Kensington, Sept. 28." (1706). Blenheim MSS. B. II, 32. From a copy in the Duchess's hand.

[20] Duchess of Marlborough to Queen Anne, no date. Blenheim MSS. E.20.

[21] ibid., "August 30" (1706). Blenheim MSS. E.20.

[22] Godolphin to Duchess of Marlborough, "Windsor, Sunday." September 1st, 1706. Blenheim MSS. E.20.

[23] Queen Anne to Duchess of Marlborough, "Friday morning." (September 13th, 1706). Blenheim MSS. E.20.

[24] Trevelyan, *Queen Anne*, II, 170.

[25] Marlborough to Queen Anne, "Cambron, Oct. 24" (1706). Blenheim MSS. E.18.

[26] Godolphin to Duchess of Marlborough, no date. Blenheim MSS. E.20.

[27] Harley to Godolphin, "Brampton, October 15, 1706." H.M.C. *Bath*, I, 108–9.

[28] ibid., "Nov. 16: 1706." Blenheim MSS. B.2. 33.

CHAPTER V

[1] Pryde, *Treaty of Union*, 5.

[2] Godolphin to Seafield, "March 13, 1702/3." H.M.C. *Seafield*, 198.

[3] ibid., "Windsor, July 24th, 1703." H.M.C. *Seafield*, 199.

[4] March 27 (O.S.), 1702.

5 Harley to Godolphin, "Brampton, Aug. 9, 1702." Brit. Mus. Add. MSS. 28,055, f. 3.

6 *Lockhart Papers*, I, 48.

7 ibid., I, 77.

8 Godolphin to Atholl, June 19, 1703. H.M.C. *Atholl*, 601.

9 Godolphin to Seafield, "Windsor, July 17, 1703." H.M.C. *Seafield*, 198–9.

10 Godolphin to Nottingham, "Windsor 20: Aug: 1703." and "Bath ye 23d of August 1703." Brit. Mus. Add. MSS. 29,589, ff. 97, 107.

11 Fraser to Annandale, "Lovat, 19 March, 1702." H.M.C. *Hope Johnstone o Annandale*, 120.

12 *Lockhart Papers*, I, 10.

13 Godolphin to Seafield, "May 17th, 1704," H.M.C. *Seafield*, 200.

14 ibid., "24th May, 1704," H.M.C. *Seafield*, 200–1.

15 ibid., "25 May, 1704," H.M.C. *Seafield*, 201.

16 ibid., "Windsor, June 3rd, 1704." H.M.C. *Seafield*, 201.

17 ibid., Windsor June 20th, 1704." "H.M.C. *Seafield*, 202.

18 ibid., "July 13th, 1704." H.M.C. *Seafield*, 203.

19 ibid., "Windsor, July 18, 1704," "St. James's, July 25, 1704." "London Aug. 10th, 1704," H.M.C. *Seafield*, 203.

20 Trevelyan, *Queen Anne*, II, 242–3.

21 Johnstone to Baillie of Jerviswood, "London, December 2d, 1704." *Jerviswood Correspondence*, 14.

22 Roxburgh to Baillie of Jerviswood, "London, 30 November, 1704," endorsed "To my Lord Treasurer-Deput." *Jerviswood Correspondence*, 13.

23 Seafield to Godolphin, "Edinburgh, March 24, 1705." Brit. Mus. Add. MSS. 28,055, f. 374. *Letters relating to Scotland*, 17.

24 Johnstone to Baillie of Jerviswood, "London, April 9th, 1705." *Jerviswood Correspondence*, 70.

25 Seafield to Godolphin, "April 1705." Brit. Mus. Add. MSS. 28,055, f. 350. Godolphin to Seafield, "April 7, 1705," endorsed in Seafield's hand, "The Thesaurers letter about Green." H.M.C. *Seafield*, 205. Baillie of Jerviswood to Johnstone, "28th March 1705." and "3d April, 1705." *Jerviswood Correspondence*, 64–5, 68.

26 ibid., "Edinburgh, Apryle 11th, 1705." Brit. Mus. Add. MSS. 28,055, f. 154. *Jerviswood Correspondence*, 75.

27 Godolphin to Seafield, "10 of May 1705." H.M.C. *Seafield*, 205.

28 Seafield to Godolphin, "Edr. May the 29th 1705." Brit. Mus. Add. MSS. 28,055, f. 204. *Letters relating to Scotland*, 46. See especially Seafield to Godolphin, "Edinburgh, July 6th, 1704." "Edr. August 1st, 1704." and "Edr. August the 20, 1704." Brit. Mus. Add. MSS. 31,180, ff. 56, 68, 74.

29 Godolphin to Seafield, "May 19 1705." Endorsed in Seafield's hand, "The Thesaurers letter upon Argyle offering to lay down his Commission." H.M.C. *Seafield*, 205–6. That Argyll had an awkward temper and no love for Godolphin is clearly shown in this letter. "My Lord, it is surprising to me that my Lord Treasurer, who is a man of sense, should think of sending me up and down like a footman from one country to another without ever offering me any reward. Their is indeed a sairtin service due from every subject to his Prince, and that I shall pay the Queen as faithfully as any body can doe; but if her ministers thinks [*sic*] it for her service to imploy me any forder I doe think the proposall should be attended with an offer of a reward. But I am so fare from beeing treated in this manner that I cannot obtain justice even in the army, where I doe flatter my selfe I have dun the Queen as much service to say no more, as any body in my station. My Lord, when I have justice dun me here and am told what to expect for going to Scotland, I shall be reddy to obey my Lord Treasurer's commands. Till then I hope my friends will think it fitt I stay here, unless I have sum body put over my head; and in that cais I shall lett my Lord Marlboro give my post to somebody who chances to be more to his mind, which will be a very noble reward for my services. . . ." Argyll to Mar, "Camp at St. Luis le Tere, July 18, 1706." H.M.C. *Mar & Kellie*, 270.

[30] Godolphin to Seafield, "Aug: 11, 1705." H.M.C. *Seafield*, 207.

[31] ibid., "July 23d, 1705." H.M.C. *Seafield*, 206.

[32] ibid., "August 9, 1705." H.M.C. *Seafield*, 207.

[33] ibid., "St. James's, 18 of Aug: 1705." H.M.C. *Seafield*, 207.

[34] Hume Brown, *History of Scotland*, III, 126.

[35] *Lockhart Papers*, 262–72.

[36] Johnstone to Jerviswood, "September 21st." (1706). *Jerviswood Correspondence*, 160. Hume Brown states that Johnstone alleges that £10,000 was paid to Godolphin, but this is clearly incorrect. Hume Brown, *History of Scotland*, III, 126.

[37] For general summary see Burton, *History of Scotland*, VIII, 178–85.

[38] Godolphin to Seafield, "St. James's, June 5, 1704." H.M.C. *Seafield*, 202.

[39] Murray to Mar, "Edinburgh, November 20th, 1705." H.M.C. *Mar & Kellie*, 239.

[40] Cromartie to Mar, "November 17th, 1705." H.M.C. *Mar & Kellie*, 238.

[41] Baillie of Jerviswood to Roxburgh, "January 3d, 1706." *Jerviswood Correspondence*, 145.

[42] Pryde, *The Treaty of Union*, 33.

[43] Thus Lockhart of Carnwath: "It would appear odd that England should be thus catch'd napping, when as I told you before, they knew what temper Scotland was in, and that there had been trafficking with France was no secret: for besides that the design was too much divulged at home, the Duke of Hamilton was assured by a certain general officer, that during the last campaign, the Duke of Marlborough had information of the whole project, from a person belonging to the Earl of Melfort. Whether the English did not believe that the French King would have prosecuted the measure, or as sone thing that the Duke of Marlborough and the Earl of Godolphin were privy, and had consented to it, or were content it should go on, resolving e'er it ended to provide for their own security; or what other reason to assign for England's being so unprovided is what I can't determine: but certain it is, that England was in no ways in a readiness to oppose such a storm, and it's more than probable, if the King had but once set his foot in the Scots shore, all his subjects would have soon submitted, the fatal Union been dissolv'd and himself restor'd to his Crowns." And again: "The Whigs threaten'd to joyn with the Torys and call the Ministry to account for severall things in which they thought them culpable, particularly that the nations was in such a defenceless state at the Time of the invasion tho they could prove that the design, many months before the execution thereof was imparted to the Lord Godolphin, for which his head ought and should pay." *Lockhart Papers*, I. 238, 296. See also Ker of Kersland, *Memoirs*, Part I, pp. 51, 54, 71, 72–3, *passim*.

[44] Godolphin to Byng, "March 5, 1708/9." *Byng Papers*, II, 59, 69–70, 124, 125.

CHAPTER VI

[1] Marlborough to Duchess of Marlborough, Meldert, June 9, 1707. Blenheim MSS. E.3.

[2] Marlborough to Godolphin, "Meldert, June 27." (1707). Blenheim MSS. A. I, 37.

[3] Marlborough to Duchess of Marlborough, "Meldert, July 4" (1707). Blenheim MSS. E.3.

[4] Godolphin to Marlborough, "Windsor, June 24" (1707). Blenheim MSS. A. II, 23.

[5] Marlborough to Godolphin, "Meldert, July 11," (1707). Blenheim MSS. E.3.

[6] Marlborough to Duchess of Marlborough, "Meldert July 11," (1707). Blenheim MSS. E.3.

[7] Godolphin to Marlborough, "Windsor 27 June 1707," Blenheim MSS. A. II, 23.

[8] ibid., "Windsor, June 30th" (1707). Blenheim MSS. A. II, 23.

[9] Marlborough to Godolphin, "Meldert, July 18th" (1707). Blenheim MSS. A. I, 37.

[10] Marlborough to Duchess of Marlborough, "Meldert July 21." (1707). Blenheim MSS. E.3.

[11] ibid., "Meldert, July 11-22" (1707). Blenheim MSS. E.3.

[12] Godolphin to Marlborough, "Windsor, 13th July" (1707). Blenheim MSS. A. II, 23.

[13] Marlborough to Duchess of Marlborough, "Soignies, Aug. 22" (1707). Blenheim MSS. E.3.

[14] ibid., "soignies, Aug. 29" (1707). Blenheim MSS. E.3.

[15] Godolphin to Marlborough, "Windsor, 16 Aug. 1707." Blenheim MSS. A. II, 23.

[16] Marlborough to Godolphin, "Helchin, Sept. 8." (1707). Blenheim MSS. A. I, 37.

[17] ibid., "Soignies, Aug. 29." (1707). Blenheim MSS. A. I, 37.

[18] Godolphin to Marlborough, "Windsor, Aug. 25, 1707." Blenheim MSS. A. II, 23. The letter is so worded to conceal the cipher.

[19] Queen Anne to Marlborough, "Windsor, Aug 25, 1707". H.M.C. *Marlborough,* 41.

[20] Godolphin to Queen Anne, September 11, 1707. H.M.C. *Marlborough,* 41.

[21] Marlborough to Queen Anne, "Sept. 15" (1707). Blenheim MSS. E.19.

[22] Marlborough to Godolphin, "Sept. 14," (1707). Blenheim MSS. A. I, 37.

[23] Marlborough to Duchess of Marlborough, "Helchin, Sept. 15." (1707). Blenheim MSS. E.3.

[24] Godolphin to Marlborough, "Windsor, Sept. 12-21" (1707). Blenheim MSS. A. II, 23.

[25] ibid., "St. Albans Septr. 29, 1707" Blenheim MSS. A. II. 23. "St. James's fryday 17 Octr. 1707." Blenheim MSS. A. II, 23.

[26] Marlborough to Duchess of Marlborough, "Helchin, Sept. 29." (1707). Blenheim MSS. A. I, 37.

[27] Marlborough to Godolphin, "Helchin, Sept. 29." (1707). Blenheim MSS. A. I, 37.

[28] ibid., "Helchin, Sept. 29." (1707). Blenheim MSS. A. I, 37.

[29] ibid., "Helchin, Oct. 3" (1707). Blenheim MSS. A. I, 37.

[30] Marlborough to Sunderland, "Hague, Oct. 7." (1707). Blenheim MSS. A. II, 23.

[31] Sunderland to Marlborough, "Newmarket, Oct.8-19," (1707). Blenheim. MSS. A. II, 24.

[32] Marlborough to Godolphin, "Antwerp, Oct. 8." (1707). Blenheim MSS. A. I, 37.

[33] Harley to Godolphin, September 2, 1707. H.M.C. *Bath,* I, 179.

[34] Godolphin to Harley, September 10, 1707. H.M.C. *Bath,* I, 180.

[35] Harley to Godolphin, September 10, 1707. M.H.C. *Bath,* I, 180-1.

[36] ibid. September 17, 1707. H.M.C. *Bath,* I, 182.

[37] Godolphin to Marlborough, "Newmarket, 7 Octr. 1707." Blenheim MSS. A. II, 23.

[38] ibid., "24 Octr. 1707." Blenheim MSS. A. II, 23.

[39] Marlborough to Godolphin, "Hague, Nov. 8." (1707). Blenheim MSS. A. I, 37.

[40] Marlborough to Duchess of Marlborough, "Hague, Novr. 8th, 1707." Blenheim MSS. E.3.

[41] Godolphin to Harley, "Friday evening, December 5, 1707." H.M.C. *Bath,* I, 188. At the foot of the letter Harley has penned a copy of what he says he had written to Godolphin.

[42] e.g. Leadam, *History of England,* (ed. 1900), 130, and Churchill, *Marlborough,* Book II, 315-29; both following von Noorden, *Europäische Geschichte,* (ed. 1882), II, 219-20.

[43] Feiling, *Tory Party,* 399.

[44] For the whole question discussed, see Davies, *The Fall of Harley in* 1708. E.H.R. (April 1951), LXVI, No. 259, 246-53.

[45] Harley to Godolphin. Friday January 30, 1707-8. H.M.C. *Bath,* I, 189-90.

[46] Godolphin to Harley. No date, but endorsed by Harley: "Delivered to me at the Cockpit by the Lord Treasurer, Jan 30, 1707-8." H.M.C. *Bath,* I, 190.

CHAPTER VII

[1] Duchess of Marlborough to Mallet, Sept. 24, 1744. Althorp MSS.

[2] Godolphin to Marlborough, "Newmarket 8 of Apr: 1708." Blenheim MSS. A. II, 38.

[3] ibid., "Sunday night Apr: 11" (1708). Blenheim MSS. A. II, 38.

[4] ibid., "13th of Aprill 1708." Blenheim MSS. A. II, 38.

[5] ibid., "April 19, 1708." Blenheim MSS. A. II, 38.

[6] ibid., "April 22th [sic]." Blenheim MSS. A. II, 38. The letter is so worded to conceal the cipher.

[7] Queen Anne to Marlborough, "Kensington, April 22-May 3" (1708). Blenheim MSS. B. II, 32.

[8] Marlborough to Godolphin, "May 8" (1708).   Blenheim MSS. A. II, 39.

[9] Marlborough to Queen Anne, "Ghent, May 9th," (1708).   Blenheim MSS. B. I, 121.

[10] Godolphin to Marlborough, "April 23d 1708."   Blenheim MSS. A. II, 38.

[11] ibid., "April 29, 1708."   Blenheim MSS. A. II, 38.

[12] ibid., "May 4th 1708."   Blenheim MSS. A. II, 38.

[13] ibid., "Thursday night, May 6" (1708).   Blenheim MSS. A. II, 38.

[14] ibid., "May 11, 1708,"   Blenheim MSS. A. II, 38.

[15] Sunderland to Newcastle, "Whitehall May 27, 1708."   Brit. Mus. Lansdowne MSS. 1,236, f. 242.   This and other letters from Sunderland to Newcastle at this time were first printed by Dr. G. M. Trevelyan.   Trevelyan, *Queen Anne,* II, 412–16.

[16] Godolphin to Marlborough, "May 31 1708."   Blenheim MSS. A. II, 38.

[17] Queen Anne to Godolphin.   "June 22, 1708."   H.M.C. *Marlborough,* 42.

[18] Queen Anne to Marlborough, "June 18, 1708."   H.M.C. *Marlborough,* 42. On the cover is written in the Duchess's hand: "A letter of the Queen about Lord S. and the Scots business, and Lord Marlborough's answer.   I understood that Lord S. was misrepresented by the Jacobites, and if he gave any occasion for the Queen's displeasure, it was really for her true interest and the good of England; but at that time she was persuaded that nobody should be chosen in Scotland or anywhere, but such as would blindly obey her direction."

[19] Godolphin to Marlborough, "13 June 1708."   Blenheim MSS. A. II, 38.

[20] Queen Anne to Marlborough, "Windsor, July 3/14, 1708."   H.M.C. *Marlborough,* 42.   On the back the Duchess has written: "a letter of the queen's to the Duke of Marlborough, very kind and she desires to be kept out of the hands of either party; but then was advised by those that turned out the Duke of Marlborough and Lord Godolphin.   I hope when she wrote this letter she was not trusted with her own affairs."

[21] Marlborough to Duchess of Marlborough, "Camp at Oudenarde, July 12, 1708."   Blenheim MSS. B. II, 32.   Author's italics.

[22] Queen Anne to Marlborough, "July 23" (1708).   Duchess of Marlborough, *Conduct,* 258.

[23] Marlborough to Queen Anne, "Aug. 2" (1708).   Blenheim MSS. B. I, 13.

[24] Queen Anne to Marlborough, no date.   Blenheim MSS. B. II, 32.

[25] Marlborough to Duchess of Marlborough, "Aug 9" (1708).   Blenheim MSS. E.4.

[26] Sunderland to Marlborough, "Althorp, May 2, 1708."   H.M.C. *Marlborough,* 33.

[27] Sunderland to Newcastle, "Althorp, Aug. 9th, 1708."   Brit. Mus. Lansdowne MSS, 1,236, f. 244.

[28] Queen Anne to Marlborough, "July 22nd O.S." (1708).   Duchess of Marlborough, *Conduct,* 164.

[29] Marlborough to Duchess of Marlborough, no date.   Blenheim MSS. E.4.

[30] ibid., "Helchin, Aug, 16." (1708).   Blenheim MSS. E. 4.

[31] Queen Anne to Marlborough, no date, but endorsed by the Duchess, "August 27, 1708."   Taken from a copy in the Duchess's hand.   Blenheim MSS. B. II, 32.

[32] Blenheim MSS. B. I, 13.

[33] Duchess of Marlborough to Queen Anne, no date.   Duchess of Marlborough, *Conduct,* 219–20.

NOTES

34 Prof. W. T. Morgan states definitely that Anne was "acting upon Abigail's suggestion," but he cites no authority in support of the assertion. Morgan, *English Political Parties & Leaders in the reign of Queen Anne*, 361.

35 Queen Anne to Duchess of Marlborough, "Sunday" (August 22/September 2, 1708). Duchess of Marlborough, *Conduct*, 220.

36 Duchess of Marlborough to Queen Anne, no date. Duchess of Marlborough, *Conduct*, 220–2.

37 Queen Anne to Duchess of Marlborough, no date. H.M.C. *Marlborough*, 52.

38 Churchill, *Marlborough*, Book II, 417–20.

39 Sunderland to Newcastle, "London, Oct. 19th, 1708." Brit. Mus. Lansdowne MSS. 1,236, ff. 246–9. Trevelyan, *Queen Anne*, II, 414–18.

40 Godolphin to Marlborough, "Windsor, 6 July 1708." Blenheim MSS. A. II, 38.

41 ibid., "St. James's 22 Octr. 1708." Blenheim MSS. A. II, 38.

42 ibid., "29 Octr. 1708." Blenheim MSS. A. II, 38.

43 Sunderland to Newcastle, "London Oct. 26th 1708." Brit. Mus. Lansdowne MSS. 1,236, f. 253. Trevelyan, *Queen Anne*, II, 415–16.

44 ibid., "London Nov. 4th, 1708." Brit. Mus. Lansdowne MSS. 1, 236, f. 252. Trevelyan, *Queen Anne*, II, 416.

45 Trevelyan, *Queen Anne*, II, 390.

CHAPTER VIII

1 Queen Anne to Duchess of Marlborough, no date (October 28, 1708). Blenheim MSS. E.17.

2 Duchess of Marlborough, *Conduct*, 222–3.

3 Abigail Masham to Harley, November 6, 1708. H.M.C. *Portland*, IV, 511.

4 Godolphin to Marlborough, "Jan 10" (1709). Blenheim MSS. B. I, 22 (b).

5 Trevelyan, *Queen Anne*, III, 19.

6 Godolphin to Marlborough, "May 16th 1709." Blenheim MSS. B. I, 22 (b).

7 ibid., "Wednesday June 1st" (1709). Blenheim MSS. B. I, 22 (b).

8 Marlborough to Godolphin, "Tilsett 6th of June 1709." Blenheim MSS. B. I, 22 (b).

9 Godolphin to Marborough, "July 20th, 1709." Blenheim MSS. B. I, 22 (b).

10 ibid., "Sunday night, 5th of June" (1709). Blenheim MSS. B. I, 22 (b).

11 ibid., "St. James's 26th of July 1709." Blenheim MSS. B. I, 22 (b).

12 ibid., "St. James's July 29th 1709." Blenheim MSS. B. I, 22 (b).

13 ibid., "Febr: 11th 1708/9." Blenheim MSS. B. I, 22 (b).

14 ibid., "Febr. 22: 1708/9." Blenheim MSS. B. I, 22 (b).

15 ibid., "Windsor 9th Septr. 1709," Blenheim MSS. B. I, 22 (b).

16 ibid., "Fryday 16th" (September 1709). Blenheim MSS. B. I, 22 (b).

17 Queen Anne to Duchess of Marlborough, October 26, 1709. Duchess of Marlborough, *Conduct*, 225.

18 Duchess of Marlborough, *Conduct*, 225–7.

[19] Somerset to Harley, "Kensington, May 24, 1710." "Kensington June 18, 1710." "July 5, 1710." H.M.C. *Portland*, IV, 543, 545, 548.

[20] Turberville, *Shrewsbury* (ed. 1930), 167–9.

[21] Trevelyan, *Queen Anne*, III, 41.

[22] Somers to Marlborough, "Jan 16. Monday at night." (1710). H.M.C. *Marlborough*, 39.

[23] Godolphin to Marlborough, "January 16, 1710." Blenheim MSS. B. II, 8.

[24] Brit. Mus. Lansdowne MSS. 885, ff. 65, 75—two copies of the same document. *Archæologica*, XXXVIII, 1–18.

[25] Duchess of Marlborough, *Conduct*, 232–3.

CHAPTER IX

[1] Sunderland to Marlborough, "Monday, Feb. 21," (1710). Blenheim MSS. B. II. 1. Sunderland seems to have made an error in the dating of this letter, as February 21st 1709/10 was a Tuesday.

[2] Godolphin to Marlborough, "Thursday 23d of Febr:" (1709/10). Blenheim MSS. B. II, 8.

[3] 6 Anne C.5.

[4] 6 Anne C.11.

[5] 6 Anne, C.19.

[6] 6 Anne, C.17.

[7] 7 Anne, C.8.

[8] 5 W. & M., C.20.

[9] 5 Anne, C.13.

[10] 8 Anne, C.13.

[11] Leadam, *The Finance of Lord Treasurer Godolphin.* R.H.S. 3rd Series, IV, 20–32.

[12] Memoir of the Harley Family, particularly Robert Harley, first Earl of Oxford, by Auditor Harley. H.M.C. *Portland*, V, 650.

[13] This was said to be one of the publications that had inspired Defoe's *Shortest Way with Dissenters.*

[14] 2 Corinthians, XI, 26.

[15] Swift, *Memoirs relating to that change in the Queen's Ministry in 1710. Works,* (ed. Temple Scott, 1901), V, 373–4.

[16] *Moderation Display'd, a Poem,* 1705. By the Author of *Faction Display'd. Poems of Affairs of State,* IV, 98–109.

[17] Leadam, *Political History of England, 1702–1760.* (Vol. IX of Series), 165. Abigail Harley to her Aunt Abigail Harley, at Eywood, "London, March, 1709." H.M.C. *Portland,* IV, 522.

[18] Burke, *An Appeal from the New to the Old Whigs. Works & Correspondence* (ed. 1852), IV, 431.

[19] Godolphin to Marlborough, "Fryday 3d of March" (1709–10). Blenheim MSS. B. II, 8.

[20] ibid., "Sunday 5 March 1709/10". Blenheim MSS. B. II, 8.

21 Godolphin to Marlborough "March 17, 1709/10." Blenheim MSS. B. II, 8.

22 ibid., "March 20, 1709/10." Blenheim MSS. B. II, 8.

23 ibid., "March 21, 1709/10." Blenheim MSS. B. II, 8.

24 ibid., "March 21, 1709/10." Blenheim MSS. B. II, 8.

25 Godolphin to Queen Anne, "Newmarket, April 15, 1710." Duchess of Marlborough, *Conduct*, 248–53.

26 Godolphin to Marlborough, "St. James's 17 April 1710." Blenheim MSS. B. II, 8.

27 Coxe, *Marlborough*, III, 63. Churchill, *Marlborough*, Book II, 678.

28 Godolphin to Marlborough, "April 20, 1710." Blenheim MSS. B. II, 8.

29 ibid., "Aprill 25th, 1710." Blenheim MSS. B. II, 8.

30 ibid., June 2, 1710. Blenheim MSS. B. II, 8.

31 ibid., "May ye 5th 1710." Blenheim MSS. B. II, 8.

32 Argyll to Harley, July (6–) 17, N.S., 1710.; Orrery to Harley, "Camp before Bethune, July 31, 1710." H.M.C. *Portland*, IV, 548, 553.

33 Godolphin to Marlborough, "May 27th, 1710." Blenheim MSS. B. II, 8.

34 ibid., "June 2d 1710." Blenheim MSS. B. II. 8. B. II, 5.

35 Marlborough to Shrewsbury, "June 19, 1710." Blenheim MSS. B. II, 5.

36 Galles's dispatch, June 13, 1710. Klopp, *Der Fall des Hauses Stuart*, XIII, 437.

37 Hoffman's dispatch, June 24, 1710. Klopp, *Der Fall des Hauses Stuart*, XIII, 437–8.

38 Godolphin to Marlborough, "June 6th, 1710." Blenheim MSS. B. II, 8.

39 ibid., "June 8th, 1710." Blenheim MSS. B. II, 8.

40 ibid., "Tuesday 13th of June, 1710." Blenheim MSS. B. II, 8.

41 Queen Anne to Godolphin, "Tuesday, June 13." (1710). H.M.C. *Marlborough*, 43. According to Godolphin, the Queen had informed Somers of her intention the previous day. Godolphin to Marlborough, "Tuesday 13th of June, 1710." Blenheim MSS. B. II, 8.

42 Godolphin to Marlborough, "June 16th, 1710." Blenheim MSS. B. II, 8.

43 Queen Anne to Godolphin, "Wednesday morning, nine o'clock." (June 14, 1710.) H.M.C. *Marlborough*, 43.

44 Godolphin to Marlborough, "June 14th 1710." Blenheim MSS. B. II, 8.

45 Klopp, *Der Fall des Hauses Stuart*, XIII, 443–4.

46 Godolphin to Marlborough, "July 31" (1710.) Blenheim MSS. B. II, 8.

47 Harley to Newcastle, "July 1, 1710." H.M.C. *Portland*, II, 211.

48 ibid,, "August 5, 1710." H.M.C. *Portland*, II, 213.

49 ibid., "August 26, 1710." H.M.C. *Portland*, IV, 218.

50 Godolphin to Marlborough, August 7th, 1710. Blenheim MSS. B. II, 8.

51 Queen Anne to Godolphin, "Kensington, Aug, 7" (1710). Blenheim MSS. B. II, 32.

52 Burnet, *Own Times*, VI, 9, note.

53 Swift to King, "London, September 9, 1710." Swift, *Correspondence* (ed. Elvington Ball), I, 194.

54 Godolphin to Queen Anne, "Tuesday the 8th of July, 1710." (*July* an error for *August*). Brit. Mus. Add. MSS. 28,055, f. 432.

CHAPTER X

[1] Queen Anne also wrote the same day, closing her letter with the significant words, ". . . and, I do assure you, I will take care that the army shall want for nothing." Queen Anne to Marlborough, "Kensington, Aug. 8." (1710). Blenheim MSS. B. II, 32.

[2] Godolphin to Marlborough, "Tuesday, Aug. 8." (1710). Blenheim MSS. B. II, 8.

[3] ibid., "Aug. 9." (1710). Blenheim MSS. B. II, 8.

[4] Halifax to Harley, "August 10th, 1710." H.M.C. *Portland,* IV, 560.

[5] Godolphin to Seafield, "August 10th, 1710." H.M.C. *Seafield,* 209. Harley was not made Lord Treasurer until May, 1711, when he was raised to the peerage as Earl of Oxford and Earl Mortimer.

[6] Swift, *Journal to Stella* (ed. Williams), I. 7. Letter II, London, September 9, 1710.

[7] Sunderland to Marlborough, "August 24." (1710). Blenheim MSS. B. II, 1.

[8] Godolphin to Seafield, "Newmarkett, 12th Octr. 1710." H.M.C. *Seafield,* 211. See also letters "June 22th [*sic*] 1710" and "June 27, 1710." H.M.C. *Seafield,* 208–9, 209.

[9] Weymouth to Prior, August 11 (–22) 1710. H.M.C. *Bath,* III, 439.

[10] Godolphin to Seafield, "Septr. 13, 1710." H.M.C. *Seafield,* 210.

[11] "Upon my arrival here, I found myself equally caressed by both parties, by one as a sort of bough for drowning men to lay hold of; and by the other as one discontented with the late men in power, for not being thorough in their designs, & therefore ready to approve present things. I was to visit my Lord Godolphin who gave me a reception very unexpected, and altogether different from what I ever received from any great man in my life; altogether, short, dry, and morose, not worth repeating to your grace, until I have the honour to see you. I complained of it to some of his friends, as having, as I thought, for some reasons deserved much to contrary from his Lordship: they said to excuse him, that he was overrun with spleen and peevishness upon the present posture of affairs and used nobody better." Swift to King, "London, September 9, 1710." Swift, *Correspondence* (ed. Elrington Hall), I, 193–4. "The Whigs were ravished to see me, and would lay hold on me as a twig while they are drowning, and the great men making me their clumsy apologies &c. But my lord treasurer received me with a great deal of coldness, which has enraged me so I am almost vowing revenge." Swift, *Journal to Stella,* (ed. Williams), I, 5–6. Letter II. September 9, 1710. Swift's "revenge" on Godolphin was not long in coming, for his famous lampoon, "*The Virtues of Sid Hamet the Magician's Rod,* had taken shape in his mind within a few days. (Swift, Prose Works II, 5–7–15 and was ready for the printer early in October. Swift frequently mentions it to Stella. *Journal to Stella,* (ed. Williams), I, 30, 32, 59–60, 65, 86, 90, 110, 127.

[12] Swift, *Journal to Stella* (ed. Williams), I, 194–5. Letter XVI, February 18, 1,711.

[13] ibid., I, 206. Letter XVII, March 4, 1711,

[14] Godolphin to "No. 126" "December 17th, 1710." Endorsed: "this letter was shewn to 42 (the Queen) by 126 upon the 21st of December 1710." Brit. Mus. Add. MSS. 28,055, f. 434. Trevelyan, *Queen Anne,* III, 328–30.

[15] Swift, *Journal to Stella* (ed. Williams), I, 35–6. Letter V. London, September 30, 1710.

[16] *Examiner,* November 23rd, 1710. No. 17 (in reprint 16).

[17] Swift, *Journal to Stella* (ed. Williams), I, 274–5. Letter XXII, May 22, 1711.

[18] See pages 179–82.

[19] Bruce to Justice Clerk, "London, January 23, 1711." H.M.C. *Mar & Kellie,* 487–8.

[20] Swift, *History of the Last Four Years of the Reign of Queen Anne,* 177.

[21] Trevelyan, *Queen Anne,* III, 197–8.

[22] Godolphin to Duchess of Marlborough, "from my Lady Medow's house, Monday the 18th" (August 1712). Blenheim MSS. E.20.

[23] ibid., "Tilshead Wednesday night." (August 20, 1712). Blenheim MSS. E.20.

[24] ibid., "Tilshead Fryday 22th [*sic*]" (August 1712). Blenheim MSS. E.20.

[25] ibid., "Woodstock Lodg Sunday morning" (August 24, 1712). Endorsed by the Duchess, "The end of August 1712 from poor Lord Godolphin." Blenheim MSS. E.20.

[26] Coxe, *Walpole,* I, 67.

[27] ibid., I, 74–5.

[28] Swift, *Journal to Stella* (ed. Williams). II, 55, Letter LII, Windsor, Septbr. 15th 1712.

POSTSCRIPTUM

[1] Lady Godolphin to Duchess of Marlborough. No date, Blenheim. MSS. E.6.

[2] "An account of the Dutches of marl, & montagus behaviour before & after their fathers death." Blenheim MSS. F. I, 35.

[3] ibid., Blenheim MSS. F. I. 35, f. 90.

[4] Lady Sunderland to Duchess of Marlborough, no date. Blenheim MSS. E.6.

[5] Mrs. Kingdom to Duchess of Marlborough, November 7th, 1722. Blenheim MSS. G. I, 17.

[6] Vanbrugh to Carlisle, "London July ye 19th, 1722." Vanbrugh, *Complete Works* (1928 ed. Dobree & Webb), IV, 148–9.

[7] Godolphin to Duchess of Newcastle, "St. James's, 6 May, 1735." Brit. Mus. Add. MSS. 33,079, f. 71.

[8] Godolphin to Sarah, Duchess of Marlborough, November 8, 1724. Blenheim MSS. E.21.

[9] Macky, *A Journey through England* (ed. 1732), II, 143.

[10] Godolphin to Duchess of Newcastle, "23 Novr. 1723. 11 at night." Brit. Mus. Add. MSS. 33,079, f. 1.

[11] Lady Mary Wortley Montagu to Lady Mar, "Twickenham, Oct. 20, 1723." Lady Mary Wortley Montagu, *Letters & Works* (1837 ed. Wharncliffe), II, 184.

[12] Paston, *Lady Mary Wortley Montagu and her Times* (ed. 1907), 310.

[13] Lady Mary Wortley Montagu to Lady Mar, "Twickenham, 1721." Lady Mary Wortley Montagu, *Letters & Works* (1837 ed. Wharncliffe), II, 162.

[14] Taylor, *Records of My Life* (ed. 1837), I, 76.

[15] Hodges, *William Congreve, the Man,* 119–20.

[16] Blandford to Sarah, Duchess of Marlborough, August 18th, 1725. Blenheim MSS. E.8.

[17] James, 1st Earl Waldegrave, Ambassador Extraordinary.

[18] Blandford to Sarah, Duchess of Marlborough, October 5th, 1725. Blenheim MSS. E.8.

[19] Duchess of Newcastle to her Aunt, Mrs. Henry Godolphin, "Newcastle House, Jan ye 7th, 1730." Brit. Mus. Add. MSS. 28,052, f. 293.

[20] Godolphin to Sarah, Duchess of Marlborough. No date. Blenheim MSS. E.22.

[21] Sarah Duchess of Marlborough to Blandford, March 27th, 1730. Blenheim MSS. E.8.

[22] Blandford to Sarah, Duchess of Marlborough, April 4th, 1730. Blenheim MSS. E.8.

[23] Duchess of Newcastle to Mrs. Henry Godolphin, "Feb. ye 2nd, 1730." Brit. Mus. Add. MSS. 28,052, ff. 295–6.

[24] ibid., "Feb. ye 19th, 1730." Brit. Mus. Add. MSS. 28,052, ff. 297–8.

[25] Godolphin to Duchess of Newcastle, "Wotton 30 Augt, 1731, near 8 in the evening." Brit. Mus. Add. MSS. 33,179, f. 15.

[26] Hervey to Fox, "Hampton Court, August 26th, 1731," Ickworth MSS. *Lord Hervey and his Friends,* (1950 ed. Ilchester), 80.

[27] ibid., "Hampton Court, September 4th, 1731." Ickworth MSS. *Lord Hervey and his Friends,* (1950 ed. Ilchester), 83.

[28] Godolphin to Duchess of Newcastle, "Harrow, 22 Octr. 1733. 3 o'clock." Brit. Mus. Add. MSS. 33,079, f. 17.

[29] ibid., "Harrow 24 Octr. 1733. 7 in the evening." Brit. Mus. Add. MSS. 33,079, f. 19.

[30] Dickens to Duchess of Newcastle, "Thursday morning." The letter is endorsed by Godolphin, "I rejoyce My Dear, in the midst of my affliction, that you went from this dismal place at the time you did ... the whole family continue here as long as your poor Mama does, except some few that are going to town now with the poor Child [Mary Godolphin] who (as matters have been manag'd) had not hitherto the least suspicion, poor creature, of the cruel loss that has befall'n her.... Harrow 25 Octr. 1733 between 12 and 1." Brit. Mus. Add. MSS. 33,079, f. 20.

[31] Brit. Mus. Add. MSS. 33,081.

[32] Godolphin to Duchess of Newcastle, "St. James's, 8 Novr. 1733." Brit. Mus. Add. MSS. 33,079, f. 28. Mary's birthday was November 23rd.

[33] ibid., "Hogmagog, 15 Novr. 1733." Brit. Mus. Add. MSS. 33,079, f. 29

[34] ibid., "Hogmagog, 20 Novr. 1733." Brit. Mus. Add. MSS. 33,079, f. 30.

[35] Godolphin to Duchess of Newcastle, "Hogmagog, 29 Novr. 1733." Brit. Mus. Add. MSS. 33,079, f. 31.

[36] ibid., "Hogmagog, 6 Decr. 1733." "Hogmagog 13 Decr. 1733." Brit. Mus. Add. MSS. 33,079, ff. 32,33.

[37] ibid., "31 Jan: 173 4/5." Brit. Mus. Add. MSS. 33,079, f. 54.

[38] ibid., "12 Feb: 173 4/5." Brit. Mus. Add. MSS. 33,079, f. 58.

[39] ibid., "St. James's, 14 Feb: 173/4/5 late at night." Brit. Mus. Add. MSS. 33,079, f. 59.

[40] ibid., "Hogmagog, 22 July 1735." Brit. Mus. Add. MSS. 33,079, f. 75.

[41] ibid., "Hogmagog, 24 July 1735." Brit. Mus. Add. MSS. 33,079. f. 76.

[42] ibid., "Eastleach Grove," 11 Augt. 1735." Brit. Mus. Add. MSS. 33,079, f. 77.

[43] ibid., "St. James's 8 Decr. near 3 o'clock." (1735). Brit. Mus. Add. MSS. 33,079, f. 79.

[44] ibid., "fryday morning at eleven." (December 8, 1735). Brit. Mus. Add. MSS. 33,079, f. 84.

[45] ibid., "Saturday morning 11." (December 9, 1735). Brit. Mus. Add. MSS. 33,079, f. 92.

[46] ibid., "Sunday morning half an hour after ten." (December 10, 1735). Brit. Mus. Add. MSS. 33,079, f. 90.

[47] ibid., "Newmarket, 29 Novr. 1736. Monday night." Brit. Mus. Add. MSS. 33.079, f. 121.

[48] ibid., "Hogmagog, wensday night 15 Decr. 1736." Brit. Mus. Add. MSS. 33,079, f. 127.

[49] ibid., "Hogmagog 29 Decr. 1736." Brit. Mus. Add. MSS. 33,079, f. 132.

[50] ibid., "Hogmagog, 16 March 173/6/6 at night." Brit. Mus. Add. MSS. 33,079, f. 142.

[51] ibid., "Newmarket, 19 March 173 5/7." Brit. Mus. Add. MSS. 33,079, f. 143, 149.

[52] Godolphin to Newcastle, "17 Septr. 1729." Brit. Mus. Add. MSS. 30,064, f. 351.

[53] Godolphin to Duchess of Newcastle, "Newmarket, 22 Aprill, 1737." Brit. Mus. Add. MSS. 33,079, f. 148.

[54] ibid., "St. James's, 24 June, 1742." Brit. Mus. Add. MSS. 33,080, f. 82.

[55] ibid., "20 feb: 17 39/40 soon after 9 morning." Brit. Mus. Add. MSS. 33,080, f. 17.

[56] ibid., "St. James's, 2 Aprill 1740." Brit. Mus. Add. MSS. 33,080, f. 19.

[57] ibid., "Wotton 26 May, 1740." Brit. Mus. Add. MSS. 33,080, f. 24.

[58] ibid., "Hogmagog, 24 July, 1940." Brit. Mus. Add. MSS. 33,080, f. 35.

[59] Carmarthen to Godolphin Osborne, "31 July 1756." Endorsed "Brothers 31 July, 1756." Brit. Mus. Add. MSS. 28,050, f. 226.

[60] ibid, "Westminster Octr 5, 1756." Endorsed "From his Brother Oct. 1756." Brit. Mus. Add. MSS. 28,050, f. 228.

[61] Carmarthen to Duchess of Newcastle, "West^r 9th Oct 1760." Brit. Mus. Add. MSS. 33,067, f. 232.

[62] ibid., "West^r 21st July 1761." Brit. Mus. Add. MSS. 33,067, f. 293.

[63] Duchess of Leeds to Duchess of Newcastle, "St. James's Square, May ye 6th, 1763." Brit. Mus. Add. MSS. 32,948, f. 244.

[64] North Mimms Place (now North Mymms Park), a property in possession of the Leeds family until 1800.

[65] Duchess of Leeds to Duchess of Newcastle, "N.M. (North Mimms) July ye 26th, 1763." Brit. Mus. Add. MSS. 33,067, f. 368.

[66] Duchess of Leeds to Newcastle "N.M. Aug: ye 5, 1762." Brit. Mus. Add. MSS. 33,067, ff. 339–40.

[67] Duchess of Leeds to Duchess of Newcastle "N.M. Aug. ye 17th, 1763." Brit. Mus. Add .MSS. 33,067, f. 372.

[68] ibid., "N.M. Septr, ye 4th, 1763." Brit. Mus. Add. MSS. 33,067, f. 378.

[69] ibid., "N.M. Septbr. ye 25th, 1763." Brit. Mus. Add. MSS. 33,067, f. 380.

[70] ibid., "N.M. Novbr. ye 9th, 1763." Brit. Mus Add. MSS. 33,067, f. 384.

[71] ibid., "N.M. Novbr. ye 24th, 1763." Brit. Mus. Add. MSS. 33,067, f. 387.

[72] Godolphin to Duchess of Newcastle, "St. James's 7 Aprill, 1749." Brit. Mus. Add. MSS. 33,067, f. 172.

[73] ibid., "St. James's. 16 July, 1753." Brit. Mus. Add. MSS. 33,067, f. 250.

[74] ibid., "Newmarket 23d Aprill, 1755." Brit. Mus. Add. MSS. 33,067, f. 266.

[75] ibid., "Newmarket 24 April, 1755." Brit. Mus. Add. MSS. 33,067, f. 267.

[76] ibid., "St. James's 10 May, 1755." Brit. Mus. Add. MSS. 33,067, f. 268.

[77] Taylor, *Records of my Life* (ed. 1832), I, 876.

[78] Godolphin to Duchess of Newcastle, "St. James's. 11 Dec. 1762." Brit. Mus. Add. MSS. 33,080, f. 282.

[79] Walpole to Hertford, "August 4th" (1764.) Walpole, *Letters,* (1904, ed. Toynbee), VI, 99–100.

SOME ABBREVIATIONS USED IN THE NOTES

Ailesbury, *Memoirs* = Thomas Bruce, second Earl of Ailesbury, *Memoirs* (1890, ed. Buckley).

Bodl. = Bodleian Library, Oxford.

Brit. Mus. = British Museum, London.

Browning, *Danby* = Professor Andrew Browning, *Thomas Osborne, Earl of Danby and Duke of Leeds*. Vol. I, Life. Vol. II, Letters. Vol. III, Appendices.

Burnet, *Own Time* = Bishop Burnet, *History of My Own Time* (ed. 1833).

Cal. S.P. Dom. = *Calendar of State Papers, Domestic Series.*

Cal. S.P. France = *Calendar of State Papers. French Series.*

Cal. Treas. Books = *Calendar of Treasury Books.*

Campana de Cavelli, *Derniers Stuarts* = La Marquise Campana de Cavelli, *Les Derniers Stuarts à Saint-Germain en Laye* (1871).

Chamberlayne, *Angliae Notitia* = Edward Chamberlayne, *Angliae Notitia, or the Present State of England* (ed. 1704).

Churchill, *Marlborough* = Rt. Hon. Winston S. Churchill, O.M., C.H., *Marlborough, his Life and Times* (ed. 1947).

Clarendon, *History* = Edward Hyde, Earl of Clarendon, *The History of the Rebellion and Civil Wars in England* (ed. 1807).

Clarke, *James II* = J. S. Clarke ed. *Life of James II—collected out of memoirs writ of his own hand* (1816).

Coxe, *Marlborough* = Archdeacon Coxe, *Memoirs of the Duke of Marlborough* (ed. 1847).

Dalrymple, *Memoirs* = Sir John Dalrymple, *Memoirs of Great Britain and Ireland* (1681–92).

Danby, *Copies and Extracts* = *Copies and Extracts of some letters written to and from the Earl of Danby . . . with particular remarks upon some of them* (ed. by Thomas Osborne, Earl of Danby and Duke of Leeds, 1710).

d'Avaux, *Negotiations* = *The Negotiations of the Count d'Avaux.*

Dowell, *Taxation* = Stephen Dowell, *A History of Taxation and Taxes in England from the earliest Times to the Present Day* (ed. 1888).

Duchess of Marlborough, *Conduct* = Sarah, Duchess of Marlborough, *An Account of the Conduct of the Dowager Duchess of Marlborough from her first coming to Court to the year 1710* (ed. 1742).

E.H.R. = *English Historical Review.*

ABBREVIATIONS

Elliot, *Godolphin* = Hugh Elliot, *Life of Sidney, Earl of Godolphin, Lord High Treasurer of England*, 1702–10 (ed. 1888).

Ellis Correspondence = *The Ellis Correspondence: Letters written during the years 1686–88 and addressed to John Ellis, Secretary of the Commissioners of H.M. revenue in Ireland* (1851, ed. Dover).

Evelyn, *Diary* = John Evelyn, *Diary* (ed. Esmond S. de Beer).

Evelyn, *Mrs. Godolphin* = John Evelyn, *The Life of Mrs. Godolphin* (ed. Harriet Sampson, 1939).

Feiling, *Tory Party* = Professor Keith Feiling, *History of the Tory Party* (ed. 1924).

Fox, *James II* = Charles James Fox, *A History of the early part of the reign of James II* (1808, ed. Holland).

Foxcroft, *Halifax* = H. C. Foxcroft, *Life of Sir George Savile, first Marquess of Halifax* (ed. 1898).

Foxcroft, *Supplement to Burnet* = H. C. Foxcroft, *Supplement to Burnet's History of my own Time*.

Grey's *Debates* = *Debates of the House of Commons from 1667 to 1694, collected by Anchitel Grey*, (ed. 1769).

Hamilton, *Grammont* = A. Hamilton, *Memoirs of the life of Count de Grammont, containing in particular the amorous intrigues of the Court of England in the reign of Charles II* (ed. Walpole, 1772).

Hatton Correspondence = *Correspondence of the family of Hatton being chiefly letters addressed to Christopher, first Viscount Hatton*, 1601–1704, (1878, ed. Thompson).

H.M.C. = *Historical Manuscripts Commission*.

H. of C. *Journal* = *Journal of the House of Commons*.

Hume Brown, *History of Scotland* = P. Hume Brown, *History of Scotland till the Present time* (ed. 1911).

Jerviswood, *Correspondence* = *Correspondence of George Baillie of Jerviswood*, 1702–8 (ed. Minto, Bannatyne Club, Edinburgh, 1842).

Klopp, *Der Fall des Hauses Stuart* = Otto Klopp, *Der Fall des Hauses Stuart und die Succession des Hauses Hannover*, (1660–1714).

Letters and Papers . . . Henry VIII = *Letters and Papers Foreign and Domestic of the Reign of Henry VIII*.

Letters relating to Scotland = *Letters relating to Scotland in the Reign of Queen Anne by the Earl of Seafield and others* (ed. Hume Brown).

Lingard, *History* = John Lingard, *History of England* (ed. 1849).

Lockhart Papers = Lockhart of Carnwath, *The Lockhart Papers*, 1702–15 (ed. 1817).

Lodge, *History* = Richard Lodge, *Political History of England from the Restoration to the Death of William III* (ed. 1910).

Luttrell, *Diary* = Narcissus Luttrell, *A Brief Historical Relation of State Affairs from September 1678 to April 1714*.

Macaulay, *History* = Lord Macaulay, *The History of England from the Accession of James II* (ed. Firth).

ABBREVIATIONS

Mackintosh, *History of Revolution* = Sir James Mackintosh, *History of the Revolution in 1688, comprising a view of the reign of James II, from his accession to the enterprise of the Prince of Orange.*

Macpherson, *Original Papers* = James Macpherson, *Original Papers containing the Secret History of Great Britain from the Restoration to the Accession of the House of Hanover* (ed. 1775).

Mazure, *History* = F. A. J. Mazure, *Histoire de la revolution de 1688 en Angleterre,* (ed. 1825).

Morrison Catalogue = *Catalogue of the collection of autograph letters and historical documents formed . . . by Alfred Morrison,* (ed. Thibaudeau).

Pepys, *Diary* = Samuel Pepys, *Diary* (ed. Wheatley, 1895).

P.R.O. = Public Record Office, London.

Ranke, *History* = Leopold von Ranke, *A History of England principally in the Seventeenth Century* (ed. 1875).

Sidney, *Diary and Correspondence* = Henry Sidney, *Diary and Correspondence of the Times of Charles II* (ed. Blencowe 1843).

Somers, *Tracts* = *Collection of scarce and valuable tracts . . . selected from . . . public as well as private libraries, particularly that of the late Lord Somers* (ed. Scott).

Stanhope, *Queen Anne* = Earl Stanhope, *History of England in the Reign of Queen Anne* (ed. 1870).

Thorold Rogers, *Bank of England* = J. E. Thorold Rogers, *The First Five years of the Bank of England* (ed 1887).

Trevelyan, *Queen Anne* = G. M. Trevelyan, *England under Queen Anne.* Vol. I, *Blenheim.* Vol. II, *Ramillies and the Union with Scotland.* Vol. III, *Peace and the Protestant Succession.*

Whitelock, *Memorials* = B. Whitelock, *Memorials of the English Affairs . . . from the beginning of the reign of Charles I to Charles II his happy restoration* (ed. 1853.)

INDEX

INDEX

INDEX

INDEX

Eglinton, Alexander Montgomerie, 9th Earl of, 181*n*.

Enquiry into Occasional Conformity, 134.

Essex, Algernon Capel, 2nd Earl of, 220.

Essex, Arthur Capel, 1st Earl of, 47–9, 53–4.

Eton, 109, 129.

Eugene, Prince, 143, 250.

Evelyn, John, 3, 25, 37, 47, 71; and Margaret Godolphin (Blagge), 17–19, 24, 27–9, 31, 41, 77; writes *Life of Mrs. Godolphin*, 24*n*., 45; describes illness and death of Margaret, 38–41; and Godolphin, 44, 50, 56, 58; and Francis Godolphin, 108–10.

Evelyn, John, (junior), 28–30.

Evelyn, Mrs. John, 27–8, 38.

Evelyn, Sir John and Lady, 8, 259–61, 266.

Examiner, The, 247, 249.

Exclusion Bill, 53–4.

Fagel, Pensionary, 33.

Fenwick, Sir John, 102–5.

Finch, Sir Heneage, Lord Chancellor (later 1st Earl of Nottingham), 47.

Fitzgerald, Katherine, of Dromana, 25.

Fitzhardinge, Charles Berkeley, 2nd Viscount, 7.

Fitzhardinge, Lady, 150–1.

Fitzhardinge, Penelope, Viscountess (*née* Godolphin), 7, 11–12.

Fitzroy, Lady Anne, (*see* Sussex, Countess of).

Flanders, 32–7, 89, 115.

Floyd, Captain David, 92, 94–9.

Fraizer, Sir Alexander, 3, 13, 25.

France, 9, 12–13, 16, 19–23, 27, 33–5, 37, 52, 74, 115, 120, 156, 172, 210, 215–16, 235, 246.

Galles, Count, 235, 237.

Gay, John, 149*n*.

Gaultier, Abbé, 245.

George, Elector of Hanover, 198, 206, 239.

George, Prince, of Denmark, 69, 132, 134, 185, 198, 200–2, 209–12.

Glasgow, David Boyle, 1st Earl of, 179–80.

Godolphin, Anne, 7, 37, 45, 48*n*.

Godolphin, Charles, 29, 37, 80.

Godolphin, Dorothy, Lady (*née* Berkeley, 7–8, 11, 13–16.

Godolphin, Francis Godolphin, 2nd Earl of (Lord Rialton), 38, 42–3, 48*n*., 7,7 86, 109–10, 130–1, 146*n*., 150–1, 242, 256, 263*n*.,; marriage of, 108, 112, 148, 257; family of, 112–13, 141, 257–60; letters to daughters, 257, 262–9; death of, 269.

Godolphin, Henry, (Provost of Eton and Dean of St. Paul's), 7 13–14, 109, 126.

Godolphin, Katherine, 45–6.

Godolphin, Lady Henrietta (*née* Churchill), *see* Marlborough, Henrietta, Duchess of.

Godolphin, Margaret, (*née* Blagge), 3–4, 9–10, 16–19, 23–31, 37–42, 50, 281.

Godolphin, Penelope, 7, 42, 48*n*.

Godolphin, Sidney ("Little Sid"), 6–7, 274.

Godolphin, Sidney, Godolphin, 1st Earl of, at Court of Charles II, 3–4, 7, 10–13, 16, 37; enters politics, 12, 14–15; missions of, to France and Netherlands, 16, 19–23, 32–7; betrothal and marriage of, 18–19, 25–6, 27, 29–30; ill-health of, 20–1, 23, 55–6, 79, 86, 106, 231, 250; personal letters of, 31, 36–7, 44–7, 58, 68, 78–9, 106–8, 110, 112–13, 129–30; illness and death of wife, 38–43; his friendship with Evelyn, 44, 50, 56, 58; rumours of second attachment of, 45, 82–3, 87, 281–2; Commissioner to Treasurer, 47, 56–7, 78–87, 100–1, 113–14; and succession question, 48, 51, 157, 172*n*.; his association with Sunderlands, 49–57; and William, 54–5, 70, 78–9, 83–7, 97–8, 100–1; honours for, 57–8, 167–8; Chamberlain to Queen, 60–2; his loyalty to James, 60, 69, 76, 90–1; and loans from Louis, 63–5; sent to William as Commissioner, 70–3; and flight of James, 74–6; home of, 77–8; seeks to retire, 79, 82–6, 125, 139, 159–162, 164, 186, 190–1, 193, 202–3, 206–7, 231, 234, 236–7; Jacobite "conspiracies" of, 87–91, 92–4, 96–9, 103–4, 182, 214; resignation of, 104, 115; his friendship with Marlboroughs, 106–8, 119, 128, 144, 148, 230; and Harley, 113–14, 153–5, 165, 167, 184, 192–6, 216–17; Anne's dependence on,

329